Mathematics Teachers at Work

Mathematics Teachers at Work is the first collection to compile and synthesize research on teachers' use of mathematics curriculum materials and the impact of curriculum materials on teaching. In response to this rapidly growing field of research, the book places a particular emphasis on – but is not restricted to – those curriculum materials developed in response to NCTM's *Standards*.

Each chapter offers a valuable understanding of teachers' behaviors, practices, and learning in relation to mathematics curriculum materials. Commentaries from both a researcher and a practitioner follow each of the book's four parts, highlighting insights, questions, and challenges that speak to the significance of the chapters for research and practice. Taken together, the chapters in this important new volume not only report empirical research findings, but also offer frameworks and perspectives on the teacher–curriculum relationship that can guide future research.

Janine T. Remillard is Associate Professor of Education and Chair, Foundations and Practices of Education Division, Graduate School of Education, University of Pennsylvania.

Beth A. Herbel-Eisenmann is Assistant Professor of Teacher Education, Michigan State University.

Gwendolyn M. Lloyd is Professor, Department of Mathematics, Virginia Tech.

Studies in Mathematical Thinking and Learning
Alan H. Schoenfeld, Series Editor

Wood/Nelson/Warfield (Eds.) *Beyond Classical Pedagogy: Teaching Elementary School Mathematics*

Zaskis/Campbell (Eds.) *Number Theory in Mathematics Education: Perspectives and Prospects*

Mathematics Teachers at Work
Connecting Curriculum Materials and
Classroom Instruction

Edited by
Janine T. Remillard
University of Pennsylvania

Beth A. Herbel-Eisenmann
Michigan State University

Gwendolyn M. Lloyd
Virginia Tech

Routledge
Taylor & Francis Group

NEW YORK AND LONDON

First published 2009
by Routledge
270 Madison Ave, New York, NY 10016

Simultaneously published in the UK
by Routledge
2 Park Square, Milton Park, Abingdon, Oxon OX14 4RN

Routledge is an imprint of the Taylor & Francis Group, an informa business

© 2009 Routledge, Taylor and Francis

Typeset in Minion by Wearset Ltd, Boldon, Tyne and Wear
Printed and bound in the United States of America on acid-free paper by Edwards
Brothers, Inc.

Library of Congress Cataloging-in-Publication Data
Mathematics teachers at work: connecting curriculum materials and classroom
instruction/editors, Janine T. Remillard, Beth A. Herbel-Eisenmann, Gwendolyn M. Lloyd.
p. cm. – (Studies in mathematical thinking and learning)
Includes bibliographical references and index.
1. Mathematics–Study and teaching–United States. 2. Mathematics teachers–Training
of–United States. 3. Curriculum planning–United States. I. Remillard, Janine. II. Herbel-
Eisenmann, Beth A. III. Lloyd, Gwendolyn M.
QA13 .M1648
510.71–dc22   2008027762

ISBN10: 0-415-99010-6 (hbk)
ISBN10: 0-203-88464-7 (ebk)

ISBN13: 978-0-415-99010-3 (hbk)
ISBN13: 978-0-203-88464-5 (ebk)

For our sons
Alexander, Kaleb, and Owen

Contents

Figures

Tables

Preface

The study of teachers and mathematics curriculum materials is a fledging, yet rapidly growing, field of research. Much of the growth, particularly in the United States, has been prompted by the explosion of curriculum development projects in response to the publication of the *Standards* (National Council of Teachers of Mathematics [NCTM], 1989). This book compiles and synthesizes research on teachers' use of mathematics curriculum materials and the impact of curriculum materials on teaching and teachers, with a particular emphasis on – but not restricted to – those materials developed in response to the *Standards*. Several books and published reports address questions about the influence of curriculum materials on student learning (e.g., National Research Council [NRC], 2004; Senk & Thompson, 2002). Despite the substantial amount of curriculum development activity over the last 15 years and growing scholarly interest in their use, this book represents the first compilation of research on *teachers* and mathematics curriculum materials, and the first volume with this focus in any content area since 1990.

In educational research, more broadly, some work has focused on teachers' use of texts. As early as 1978, Stake and Easley's report on the state of science education brought attention to the role that teachers play in enacting curriculum. These case studies provided examples of teachers struggling to use new curriculum programs and making adaptations to the written teacher's guides that fit conventional notions about teaching and the nature of the subject matter. In the decade that followed, however, few researchers took up these questions. It was not until *Standards*-based mathematics curriculum programs became available in the mid-1990s that interest in teachers and curriculum materials took hold among researchers. Apple's (1986) analysis of teachers and texts focused on the textbook industry and critiqued the ways that the politics of the textbook position teachers. Many of the criticisms leveled by Apple still apply; however, since the publication of the *Standards* (NCTM, 1989) the K-12 mathematics textbook market has been complicated by non-commercially-developed materials sold in the commercial market.

At least two publications have addressed questions related to teachers and curriculum materials. Ben-Peretz (1990) took the position that there is a distinction between the curriculum proposed in the materials and the curriculum enacted by the teacher. Her focus was on teachers' interpretation process, its different forms, and the knowledge needed to engage in curriculum interpretation. More recently, Heaton's (2000) book included a discussion of the potential role of curriculum materials in the kind of teaching she was learning to enact. The present volume adds to the conversation begun by Heaton and Ben-Peretz and offers a wealth of empirical studies of teachers and mathematics curriculum materials.

In the international arena, a book based on the TIMSS study examined the role mathematics and science textbooks play in translating national policy into practice. Valverde, Bianchi, Wolfe, Schmidt, and Houang (2002) offered a comparative analysis of a number of features of textbooks in 36 countries. They concluded by asserting that: "It is the primary professional responsibility of teachers to be concerned with their [curricular goals of a school system] implementation. Understanding teachers' instructional behaviors is necessary to characterize educational opportunities" (p. 167). Understanding teachers' behaviors, practices, and learning in relation to mathematics curriculum materials is a primary focus of the chapters of our book.

The process for the development of this book was extensive and rigorous. A wide solicitation of chapter proposals was distributed in May 2005. Through a blind, peer-review process, we selected 15 chapters from 45 chapter proposals that represented relevant themes and approaches emerging in the field. Authors from each accepted chapter participated in a writers' conference[1] in February 2006. A team of Practitioner and Research Advisors and some *Commentary* writers also attended the conference and provided critical feedback to authors. The conversations at this meeting contributed to the development of individual chapters and themes for the different parts of the book, and allowed the authors and editors to generate a shared vision for the focus and purpose of the book.

The book is divided into an introduction and four main parts, each of the latter containing a set of chapters followed by two invited *Commentary* chapters, one written by a researcher and one written by a practitioner.[2] Taken together, the chapters in the volume not only report empirical research findings, but also offer frameworks and perspectives on the teacher–curriculum relationship that can guide future research. The reactive commentaries offer insights, questions, and challenges that speak to the significance of the chapters for research and practice.

Part I consists of an introduction to the book in which we describe some of the central ideas that frame the book and the field as a whole. The chapters in *Part II: Conceptual and Analytical Frameworks for Studying Teachers' Use of Curriculum Materials* frame the terrain of the book, discuss theoretical and conceptual frameworks, and offer research and practice-based questions. *Part III: Understanding the Relationships Among Teachers, Mathematics Curriculum Materials, and the Enacted Curriculum* puts the classroom context at the center of understanding the relationship between teachers and curriculum materials. As a set, the chapters in *Part III* establish a distinction between the written and enacted forms of curriculum, and illustrate multiple ways that curriculum materials are used and interpreted by teachers. The chapters in *Part IV: Teachers' Use of Curriculum Materials at Different Stages of Implementation and at Different Points on the Professional Continuum* consider patterns and issues in curriculum material use that emerge at different stages of teachers' careers. Together, these chapters suggest that teachers' interactions with curriculum materials are likely to change as teachers gain experience. Finally, *Part V: Teacher Learning Through and in Relation to the Use of Curriculum Materials* examines how forms of professional learning shape teachers' interactions with curriculum materials, and how curriculum material use can contribute to teacher learning.

Throughout the book, authors use specific terms to describe curriculum materials and the contexts in which curriculum materials are developed and used. We asked authors to refer to curriculum materials developed in response to the *Standards* (NCTM, 1989) as *Standards*-based curriculum materials or NSF-funded curriculum materials (rather than *reform-oriented, reform-based,* or *reform curriculum materials*). In fact, we asked the authors to avoid using the term *reform* in a general way and instead to describe specific efforts to initiate change.

Because there is a substantial body of literature about *curriculum* in general, the authors of the chapters in this volume do not use *curriculum* and *curriculum materials* interchangeably. Instead, authors use the term *curriculum materials* to refer to the specific print materials with which teachers and students have physical contact. The term *curriculum program* refers to the larger program to which the physical materials belong (e.g., *Everyday Mathematics* is a *curriculum program* rather than a *curriculum*). We asked authors to use *curriculum programs,* rather than *curricula,* to refer to multiple textbook series (e.g., *Standards*-based curriculum programs rather than *Standards*-based curricula).

The intended audience for this book is *consumers of research*. This audience includes researchers, curriculum decision-makers, teachers, and teacher educators – particularly those who seek to understand the complex interaction between teachers and curriculum. We use the term *curriculum decision-maker* to refer to practitioners in school systems responsible for decisions related to curriculum material adoption and implementation. Although curriculum designers are not a primary audience, the research findings and perspectives discussed in several chapters have important implications for the design of curriculum materials for teachers. The book has particular relevance to those working in the area of mathematics; however, the issues explored in the chapters related to teachers' authority in the curriculum design process and the relationships they develop with curriculum resources are pertinent to all school subjects.

Notes

1. The authors' meeting was funded by the National Science Foundation, Grant Number 0600171.
2. Although we differentiate *researcher* from *practitioner* based on the author's primary position and responsibility, we also recognize that these roles are not necessarily distinct.

References

Apple, M. W. (1986). *Teachers and texts: A political economy of class and gender relations in education.* Boston, MA: Routledge & Kegan Paul.

Ben-Peretz, M. (1990). *The teacher–curriculum encounter: Freeing teachers from the tyranny of texts.* Albany, NY: State University of New York Press.

Heaton, R. (2000). *Teaching mathematics to the new standards: Relearning the dance.* New York, NY: Teachers College.

National Council of Teachers of Mathematics. (1989). *Curriculum and evaluation standards for school mathematics.* Reston, VA: Author.

National Research Council. (2004). *On evaluating curricular effectiveness: Judging the quality of K-12 mathematics evaluations.* Washington, DC: National Academies Press.

Senk, S. L., & Thompson, D. R. (Eds.). (2002). *Standards-based school mathematics curricula: What are they? What do students learn?* Hillsdale, NJ: Erlbaum.

Stake, R. E., & Easley, J. (1978). *Case studies in science education.* Urbana, IL: University of Illinois.

Valverde, G. A., Bianchi, L. J., Wolfe, R. G., Schmidt, W. H., & Houang, R. T. (2002). *According to the book: Using TIMSS to investigate the translation of policy into practice through the world of textbooks.* Dordrecht: Kluwer.

Acknowledgments

Editing this book has been a collaborative process. We have each contributed in equal yet differing ways, bringing our own perspectives and commitments to the process. We appreciate the opportunity this work has provided us to cultivate a productive collegial relationship and genuine friendship. We believe the final product has been enhanced by both. Still, bringing this book to completion would not have been possible without the generous contributions of many people.

We wish to acknowledge and thank Alan Schoenfeld and the anonymous reviewers of the book proposal for their feedback and encouragement to publish this volume. We thank Naomi Silverman for her guidance and support throughout the publication process. We extend special thanks to the reviewers of the chapter proposals: Fran Arbaugh, Stephanie Behm, Óscar Chávez, Jeffrey Choppin, Kathryn B. Chval, Michelle Cirillo, Shea Culpepper, Jon Davis, Corey Drake, Caroline Ebby, Ruhama Even, Jeff Frykholm, Theresa Grant, Douglas Grouws, Jean Hallagan, Joanna Higgins, Mary Ann Huntley, Kara Jackson, Amanda Jansen, Debra Johanning, Signe Kastberg, Valerie Klein, Kate Kline, Eric Knuth, Diana Lambdin, Glenda Lappan, Joy Lesnick, Amy Roth McDuffie, Rebecca McGraw, Vilma Mesa, Ralph Putnam, Barbara Reys, Robert Reys, Laurie Rubel, Jennifer Seymour, Miriam Sherin, Jeffrey Shih, Jack Smith, Laura Spielman, Jon Star, Mary Kay Stein, James Tarr, Iris Weiss, and Erna Yackel.

We are also grateful to the Advisory Board Members (Ellen Clay, Thomas Cooney, Chris Cox, Linda Davenport, June Mark, William McCallum, David Pimm, Susan Jo Russell, Mellisa Smith, and Iris Weiss) for their critical feedback at the 2006 authors' meeting. We owe special thanks to the graduate students who were involved in the evaluation process of the authors' meeting as well as those who helped with editing and formatting book chapters: Stephanie Behm, Nesrin Cengiz, Michelle Cirillo, Jackie Flicker, Jill Newton, Elizabeth Radday, and Troy Regis.

The development of this book was supported by Grant Number 0600171 from the National Science Foundation and by the Center for the Studies of Mathematics Curricula (NSF Grant Number 0333879). The opinions and findings expressed herein are those of the chapter authors and do not necessarily express the position or support of the Foundation or CSMC.

Beth A. Herbel-Eisenmann
Gwendolyn M. Lloyd
Janine T. Remillard

I
Introduction

1
Teachers' Use of Curriculum Materials
An Emerging Field
Gwendolyn M. Lloyd, Janine T. Remillard, and Beth A. Herbel-Eisenmann

The chapters in this book represent a growing body of scholarship in mathematics education and research on teaching that places teachers at the center of questions about the effects of curriculum materials on classroom instruction and student learning. Authors seek to understand what happens (for the teacher and the students) when teachers use curriculum programs, and why. An underlying assumption of this work is that teachers are central players in the process of transforming curriculum ideals, captured in the form of mathematical tasks, lesson plans and pedagogical recommendations, into real classroom events. What they do with curriculum resources matters. As a result, understanding what teachers do with mathematics curriculum materials and why, as well as how their choices influence classroom activity, is critical for informing ongoing work surrounding the development of new programs, their adoption in the world of practice, and what students learn as a result.

Although this field of research on teachers' use of curriculum materials is growing, it is still underdeveloped. Studies of teachers using textbooks in mathematics, reading, and history (e.g., Durkin, 1983; FitzGerald, 1979; Komoski, 1977) and the influence of textbooks on the curriculum taught (Kuhs & Freeman, 1979) began to emerge in the mid- to late 1970s. Still, interest in the questions underlying this research has waxed and waned over the years. Over time, researchers have gradually added to a collection of studies that offer insights into the teacher–curriculum relationship. Nevertheless, prior to the mid-1990s, this field never gathered momentum or cohered around a particular set of questions. Over the last decade, however, the field has grown tremendously, signaling increased interest in questions about how teachers use curriculum materials and whether and how newly designed materials can influence classroom practices and teaching more broadly.

Several converging phenomena have contributed to the growth of this field. The publication of the *Standards* (National Council of Teachers of Mathematics [NCTM], 1989) and the nationwide interest generated by this document led to revisions of existing mathematics textbooks by commercial publishers and the development of many new curriculum programs. Most prominent among these development projects were those funded by the National Science Foundation [NSF]. These programs, commonly referred to as *Standards*-based or NSF-funded curriculum programs, were developed by mathematics educators and mathematicians and were designed to support the *Standards*.[1] These curriculum materials contain mathematical emphases (e.g., mathematical thinking and reasoning, conceptual understanding, and problem-solving in realistic contexts) and pedagogical approaches that were previously uncommon in textbooks published in the United States. Around the world, many countries took up comparable curriculum reform efforts at the same time.[2] Early use of *Standards*-based curriculum programs in the mid-1990s prompted considerable interest in how teachers used them. Between 1995 and 2006, over 25 articles on the topic appeared in major research journals, in addition to countless dissertations and conference presentations. (For reviews of these studies, see Remillard, 2005; Stein, Remillard, & Smith, 2007.)

Scholarship that focuses on mathematics teachers' practices laid the groundwork for questions generated by these new materials. Since the mid-1980s, research on teacher cognition and teachers' thought processes (e.g., Clark & Peterson, 1986; Thompson, 1984) has made a compelling case for viewing teachers as decision-makers, and teaching behaviors as rooted in teachers' beliefs and knowledge. Since that time, a good deal of research has examined mathematics teachers' classroom practices with an eye toward characterizing the complex work of teaching. Scholars naturally applied these frameworks to studies of teachers using and navigating novel curriculum materials.

Activity in the policy and practice arenas has also generated substantial interest in the potential impact of curriculum materials on teachers and teaching. In the current era of accountability and increased pressure brought about by the No Child Left Behind Act (NCLB, 2002), school districts and schools are under intense pressure to raise students' achievement scores. As a result, many districts have begun to regulate mathematics teaching practices through mandating the use of a single curriculum program at each level or content area (Archer, 2005). As a result, there is considerable emphasis on the widespread adoption of new curriculum programs as the primary strategy for improving mathematics education. In many cases, the curriculum materials being adopted are *Standards*-based and are unfamiliar in form and content to most teachers.

As *Standards*-based and other new curriculum programs were being rolled out for their initial debuts in schools, researchers faced strong pressure to provide evidence of their impact on student learning (Schoenfeld, 2002). Although there was general interest in assessing the impact of the new programs, the pressure to produce results on student outcomes at this particular moment in history was intensified by both substantial skepticism about the value of *Standards*-based materials and the contemporary interest in using scientific evidence of effectiveness to guide curriculum program adoption decisions. In 2004, a National Research Council [NRC] panel charged with reviewing existing research on the success of existing curriculum programs found insufficient evidence of the effectiveness of any of the programs studied, "due to the restricted number of studies for any particular curriculum, limitations in the array of methods used, and the uneven quality of the studies" (p. 3). Among its recommendations for improving the research on programs' effects was a call for consideration of the quality of teachers' implementation. By making this assertion, the NRC panel acknowledged the distinction between the curriculum as written and the curriculum as enacted.

An Overview of the Book

Taking this distinction between the written and enacted curriculum as a starting place for this volume, we distributed a call for chapter proposals that would make both theoretical and empirical contributions to understanding the teacher as a critical link between the written and enacted curriculum. The majority of chapter proposals we received investigated elementary or middle school settings and materials, involved experienced classroom teachers (as opposed to prospective or beginning teachers), took place in classrooms in which *Standards*-based curriculum materials were being used, and drew on qualitative research methods. Indeed, these trends, represented in the set of final chapters selected for the book, reflect much of the research currently available in the field. Through the peer-review process, we were able to compile a set of high-quality chapters that, despite uneven representation across some of the categories listed above, address a range of theoretical and empirical issues, making valuable contributions to the field. The chapters are grouped into four parts, which we outline in the remainder of this section. In the following section, we describe what we see as the primary contributions that these chapters make to the field of research on teachers' use of mathematics curriculum materials.

Part II begins by considering theoretical and conceptual frameworks and perspectives intended to guide research in the field. In Chapter 2, Brown draws on sociocultural perspectives to conceptualize the relationship between teachers and curriculum resources as akin to that of agent and tool. He uses this framing to examine different ways that teachers might draw on a curriculum resource. In Chapter 3, Stein and Kim identify and analyze two elementary curriculum programs' features that are salient to their use across a large school system. They consider how levels of social and human capital are likely to influence teachers' use of these features. The authors of Chapter 4, McClain, Zhao, Visnovska, and Bowen, draw on empirical data to articulate a framework that captures the interplay between teachers and texts in the context of school and districts. In Chapter 5, Chval, Chávez, Reys, and Tarr discuss conceptual and methodological considerations and challenges of studying textbook integrity. Remillard's commentary (Chapter 6) synthesizes the constructs offered in these four chapters into a single framework, capturing the complex nature of the factors that influence the teacher–text relationship. In Chapter 7, Larson considers how these conceptual frameworks might influence the work of a curriculum decision-maker in a school district.

The chapters in Part III put the classroom context at the center of understanding the relationship between teachers and curriculum materials. In Chapter 8, Grant, Kline, Crumbaugh, Kim, and Cengiz examine how teachers elicit and extend student thinking in mathematically productive ways during whole-group discussions, and how different types of guidance provided by a teacher's guide support teachers in doing so. With the aim of emphasizing the important role that teachers play in the curriculum development process, the El Barrio-Hunter College PDS Partnership Writing Collective (El Barrio Collective) (Chapter 9) describes their adaptations of a *Standards*-based curriculum program and makes recommendations for how curriculum developers might use teacher research (and teacher researchers) to inform their work. In Chapter 10, Herbel-Eisenmann uses classroom examples to theorize about the teacher–textbook–student relationship by examining teachers' language choices that mediate this relationship. In Chapter 11, Eisenmann and Even compare the tasks used by a single teacher enacting the same curriculum materials in two different schools. The authors of Chapter 12, Ziebarth, Hart, Marcus, Ritsema, Schoen, and Walker, describe the negotiation processes between developers of curriculum materials and the teachers who pilot the materials during the revision of a *Standards*-based curriculum program. In his response to these chapters, Pimm (Chapter 13) points out that pedagogical intention is a central theme in each of these chapters and that making pedagogical intention explicit might shed light on the authority relationships described in the chapters. Schnepp's response (Chapter 14) connects the issues raised by chapter authors to his experiences as a high school mathematics teacher, pointing out the limited opportunities most teachers have to reflect on these issues.

The chapters in Part IV examine critical issues related to curriculum material use that emerge for teachers at different stages of their careers. In Chapter 15, Behm and Lloyd analyze three student teachers' interactions with mathematics curriculum materials and consider a number of factors that may play into the different approaches they take. In Chapter 16, Christou, Menon, and Philippou report on an investigation of the types of concerns that novice teachers communicate after using a new curriculum program. Silver, Ghousseini, Charalambous, and Mills (Chapter 17) consider teachers' experience with curriculum materials later in their careers. They discuss a phenomenon, called the curriculum implementation plateau, observed in the work of mathematics teachers who are experienced users of *Standards*-based curriculum materials. In response to these chapters, Cooney (Chapter 18) discusses how teachers, when using *Standards*-based curriculum materials, are challenged to take advantage of "critical moments" in the classroom and explore multiple solutions to mathematics problems. From her perspective as a principal and teacher, Phillips (Chapter 19) draws attention to key issues from the chapters in Part IV: the potential for learning from student-teaching placements, preparation of teachers for curriculum material adoption, and support for sustainable change.

The chapters in Part V examine the relationship between teacher learning and development and curriculum material use. Chapters 20 and 21 provide accounts of small groups of middle school teachers collaborating to use *Standards*-based curriculum materials, with the support of university faculty. Doerr and Chandler-Olcott (Chapter 20) examine teachers' experiences with the literacy demands of the materials, showing how, over time, they shifted from seeing the curriculum materials as barriers to students' learning to seeing them as supporting language and mathematical learning. Roth McDuffie and Mather (Chapter 21) identify and discuss the "curricular reasoning" in which teachers engaged as they used curriculum materials for instruction: analyzing materials from learners' perspectives, doing tasks together as learners, mapping learning trajectories, and revising plans based on instructional experiences with students. In Chapter 22, Drake and Sherin offer a method – namely their "curriculum strategies framework" – for characterizing changes in teachers' use of curriculum materials over time. Jaworski's commentary (Chapter 23) identifies compelling issues in the chapters related to the social settings of the classrooms studied, the research as a factor in what is studied, and assumptions made in curriculum resources. In Chapter 24, Davenport draws on the accounts in the chapters of Part V to offer her views about how school districts might support the learning of large numbers of teachers as they use *Standards*-based curriculum materials for mathematics instruction.

The Contribution to the Field

Because this book is the first compilation of research on teachers and curriculum materials, it provides us with the opportunity to highlight important themes that cut across the chapters and to identify issues that are central to the field. In this way, the book allows us to begin to frame a set of issues that are representative of the field in its current state. Here we offer five themes that are salient to contemporary research on teachers' use of curriculum materials and briefly discuss the ways they are addressed in various chapters in the volume. Because each chapter touches on a number of these themes, our references to the chapters are representative rather than exhaustive.

What Do We Mean By "Use"?

At the center of this book is the question of how teachers use mathematics curriculum materials and the factors that influence this use. Across the chapters, *use* means a variety of interrelated pedagogical activities. It includes how teachers engage or interact with these resources as well as how and the extent to which they rely on them in planning and enacting instruction, and the role resources play in teachers' practice.

It is common, in practice and a good deal of research, to use the term "implement" to refer to what happens when curriculum programs are put in teachers' hands. Because *implement* means "to put into practice," we find it does not always measure up to the kind of work that takes place when teachers *use* curriculum materials. In fact, we find the notion that curriculum materials are implemented by teachers to be problematic in two ways. First, it assumes that embedded in these resources is everything a teacher would need to enact the curriculum precisely as envisioned by the designers. Second, this view of implementation suggests that the process of putting the ideas captured in previously designed curriculum materials into practice is a straightforward one and does not involve substantial engagement, interpretation, and decision-making on the part of the teacher. We have found that discussions of curriculum material implementation can diminish the importance of considering the activity of the teacher and the influence of the classroom in this process. In Chapter 5, on measuring textbook integrity, Chval, Chávez, Reys, and Tarr suggest that measures of textbook fidelity are problematic for this reason. Their construct, *textbook integrity*, focuses on the extent to which the teacher relies on the textbook to guide curricular and pedagogical decisions.

Our initial view that the work of using a curriculum program is a complex intellectual activity has been reconfirmed as we have worked on this book. Many of the chapters uncover the kind of work teachers engage in when they use mathematics curriculum materials. They also begin to uncover factors that influence this work. Below, we point to a few of the factors that have emerged in this volume as particularly salient for understanding teachers as users of curriculum materials.

Teachers, Professional Identities, and Curriculum Resources

It is well established in the literature that personal factors, including beliefs and commitments, experience, and understanding of mathematics, influence teachers' pedagogical decisions. Previous studies of teachers using mathematics curriculum materials have confirmed the significance of these factors in teachers' decisions with respect to curriculum materials use (e.g., Lloyd, 1999; Manouchehri & Goodman, 2000). A number of chapters in this volume continue in this vein, highlighting the complex interaction between teachers' beliefs, mathematical knowledge, and their use of curriculum materials (e.g., Chapters 11, 15, and 21).

Several chapters in this volume offer insights into a component of teachers' individual characteristics that plays a substantial role in influencing their engagement with and decisions about curriculum materials. We think of it as a component of professional identity,[3] which includes how individual teachers understand and position themselves, and are positioned, in relation to curriculum materials. McClain et al., for instance, argue in Chapter 4 that how teachers use curriculum materials is influenced by how they view the institutional context in which they teach. An important aspect of this context is the extent to which the text or the teachers are given authority over instructional decision-making, which in turn influences their sense of agency as users of curriculum materials. Their analysis was based on research in districts in which high value was placed on fidelity to the adopted curriculum program and teachers tended to treat it as an authority on how and what they should teach. At the opposite end of the spectrum, in Chapter 9 the El Barrio Collective provides a glimpse of teachers whose professional identities include trust in themselves and their knowledge of students. In their chapter, they describe how systematic teacher research provided them with specific expertise that contributes to the mathematical expertise embedded in the curriculum program they were using.

The relationship between professional identity and how individual teachers position themselves in relation to curriculum resources is also a theme that runs throughout the chapters in Part IV. As a set, these chapters explore how teachers understand and interact with curriculum materials at various phases in their careers, from preservice, to beginning teachers, to experienced teachers. Specifically, these chapters suggest that a teacher's stance on the role of curriculum materials in the work of teaching is an important dimension of his or her professional identity that influences how the materials are used in his or her teaching. In their comparative exploration of three student teachers' uses of mathematics curriculum materials, Behm and Lloyd (Chapter 15) consider the role that mathematical and pedagogical comfort played in the participants' decisions. The two student teachers who demonstrated strong mathematics knowledge and voiced comfort with teaching tended to make adaptations to the written materials in order to meet their goals for students. In contrast, the student teacher who expressed concern about teaching mathematics tended to follow the curriculum guide rigidly. Working with teachers at the opposite end of the professional spectrum, Silver et al. (Chapter 17) found that very experienced users of *Standards*-based curriculum materials had "conceptions of their role as active mediators of the interaction between students and content through the tasks found in the mathematics curriculum materials" that influenced how they used these resources.

Curriculum Use as Relational

When we understand identity as a critical factor in shaping teachers' curriculum decisions, factors that were previously considered as "personal" or "individual" can be understood as social. Identity is a social construct that develops in relation to others and in particular contexts (Boaler & Greeno, 2000; Holland & Lave, 2001). A number of chapters in this volume shed light on the ways that curriculum material use is indeed relational. Brown (Chapter 2) initiates this particular view by framing use as an interaction between the teacher and the text to which both contribute. Drawing on sociocultural theory, Brown describes curriculum resources as artifacts of curriculum design that embody the ideas of the designer. When using teacher's guides, teachers enter into a relationship with the material's designers.

In Chapters 10 and 12, Herbel-Eisenmann and Ziebarth et al., respectively, provide two different examples of ways that teachers enter into the kind of relationship with curriculum materials and their developers described by Brown. Ziebarth et al. describe the complex, yet often invisible, process through which field-testing teachers and program developers negotiate the meaning of the intended curriculum captured in written materials. From this perspective, the written curriculum materials represent a relational process between developers and teachers. Herbel-Eisenmann focuses on another step in the relational process of curriculum material development and use; one that begins after the text, in its finished form, is in the hands of teachers. She demonstrates how teachers' language choices in the classroom shape the teacher–student–textbook relationship that emerges. Of particular concern to Herbel-Eisenmann is how these language choices give the text authority over the mathematical knowledge and position students as consumers of it.

A second aspect of the relational nature of curriculum material use that is evident in this volume is the critical nature of the social and collaborative context within which teachers use curriculum materials. In at least five of the chapters (i.e., Chapters 9, 12, 17, 20, and 21), the presence of a collegial network of teachers co-participating in the process of making sense of and using curriculum materials is a fundamental component of the story. Chapter 21, by Roth McDuffie and Mather, provides a particularly striking example of two teachers and a researcher/teacher educator engaged in a collaborative, iterative process of planning, teaching and reflecting on their lessons. Through this process, which situates teachers' learning in their own teaching practices, the teachers learn together about both the mathematics in the unit and the process of reasoning about and with curriculum resources. As Roth McDuffie and Mather point out, collegial and practice-based approaches to structuring teachers' professional development are not new; they are at the heart of practices like lesson study and video clubs as well as teacher inquiry group work described by Wilson and Berne (1999) and others. The chapters in this volume add the development of the teacher–text relationship to the list of teaching activities that can be enhanced by teacher collaboration.

How Context and Curriculum Materials Matter

Many studies on teaching and mathematics curriculum use have identified aspects of the teaching context as influential factors in teachers' decisions. Indeed, most studies highlight the ways in which particular features of the context constrain teachers from using curriculum materials as intended by authors or by the teachers. Some contextual features that figure prominently in this body of research are: (a) time (e.g., Keiser & Lambdin, 1996), (b) aspects of the local cultures, including departmental, district, school, or community culture (e.g., Manoucheri & Goodman, 2000), and (c) the extent and nature of support provided for the teacher (e.g., Van Zoest & Bohl, 2002). Other studies have considered the way that students' expectations and responses to the curriculum materials are influential factors in teachers' curricular decisions (Stein, Grover, & Henningsen, 1996). In these studies, the context is often seen as a constraining factor, used to explain why the enactment of the curriculum program did not happen as intended.

Many of the studies in this volume confirm the influential role that context plays in teachers' curriculum material use. Looking across the chapters at the diverse collection of instructional contexts, we see the context as an integral component of what must be considered in order to understand teachers' work. This view is informed by Herbel-Eisenmann, Lubienski, and Id Deen's (2006) argument that the particular impact of the curricular context – the complex and layered context in which curriculum material use occurs – is often de-emphasized in attempts to uncover patterns that hold true across settings. Herbel-Eisenmann and her colleagues suggest that the relevance of the context *is* one essential cross-cutting pattern. Further, they illustrate the complexity of the curricular context by showing its many sociocultural dimensions, including local political histories that have evolved over time. An important aspect of the curricular context, illustrated in by Eisenmann and Even in Chapter 11 of this volume, is the expectations and actions of the students. They studied a teacher using the same curriculum program in two different schools. They found that in response to differences in student behavior, the tasks the teacher posed and the way she engaged students in exploring them differed in the two schools to the extent that they could argue that students were learning different mathematics.

The particular curriculum program in use is also a critical piece of the curricular context to be understood. This assertion seems obvious. Interest in how teachers use curriculum materials that embody mathematical and pedagogical visions that differ from the status quo can be traced back to studies of teachers using curriculum materials in the 1970s and 1980s (e.g., Donovan, 1983; Stake & Easley, 1978; Stephens, 1982), and has continued with the publication of the *Standards*-based curriculum programs in the 1990s. Still, we continue to know very little about how the variety of design features of curriculum resources influence teachers' decisions. A number of the designers of *Standards*-based programs, for instance, experimented with different ways of communicating with teachers about such things as pedagogical approaches, likely student responses, or rationales behind particular tasks. How do these features influence how teachers use them? In the chapters by Grant et al. and Stein and Kim, the authors undertake analyses of specific features of teacher's guides in order to consider the types of support they provide for teachers. Stein and Kim (Chapter 3) offer a comparative analysis of two *Standards*-based programs, focusing on, among others, the differing ways that these materials make their rationales transparent to teachers and help them anticipate students' responses. Grant et al. (Chapter 8) examine how curricular features such as these actually support and fall short of their goals of guiding teachers in the work of leading whole-class discussions.

In keeping with our claim that context matters, Stein and Kim embed their analysis of the features of two elementary programs in an analysis of the local context in which the program is being used. Using human and social capital theory, they consider the likelihood that certain curricular design features will be supported or constrained by particular social arrangements in a school or district. In short, they offer a frame for analyzing the structure of the school system and the features of the curriculum program to consider potential areas of match and mismatch.

Curriculum Use and Teacher Learning

The themes discussed above relate to the variety of contextual and social factors that influence the ways that teachers engage with and use curriculum materials in their teaching. The focal outcome of these interactions is the enacted curriculum. A good deal of research on teachers and curriculum materials has uncovered another critical outcome of the teacher–curriculum material relationship – its impact on teachers. Many researchers and educators have argued that the types of pedagogical change called for in the NCTM (1989) *Standards* (and subsequently designed curriculum materials) require substantial learning on the part of teachers. Indeed, research on teacher learning and change has received a good deal of attention in the last decade, including studies of teacher learning (e.g., Collopy, 2003; Remillard, 2000) and preservice teacher learning (Lloyd, 2006) as an outcome of curriculum material use.

All three of the chapters in Part V of this volume offer accounts of teacher learning through extended use of *Standards*-based materials. The chapters by Doerr and Chandler-Olcott and Drake and Sherin capture a slice of an iterative process in which initial use results in certain kinds of classroom activities, often not previously imagined by the teacher, which in turn lead to shifts in perspective and changes in use. For the teachers described by Drake and Sherin (Chapter 22), grappling with the ideas and recommendations in the materials and navigating their use in the classroom over two years allowed them to consider the "big ideas" that guided the design of the program. The teachers described by Doerr and Chandler-Olcott (Chapter 20) expressed initial skepticism about the high demands on literacy skills embedded in the program they were using. Through designing activities that supported their students' literacy *and* mathematical development, they shifted in their thinking about the role of literacy in mathematics instruction, particularly for students whose literacy skills are assessed as below grade-level. In both cases, the teachers developed what Drake and Sherin refer to as a "curriculum vision" or "an understanding of what the curriculum materials are intended to help students accomplish and how the various pieces (activities, lessons, materials, etc.) fit together to accomplish these goals." And in both cases, this vision influenced subsequent use of the materials. These findings serve as reminders that curriculum material use is not static and needs to be studied as dynamic and evolving.

With these themes in mind, we present the collection of chapters in this volume as insights into the dynamic and evolving process of teachers' curriculum material use and as a representation of the field in its current evolution.

Notes

1. See Senk and Thompson (2003) for details on the development of these materials and initial studies of their impact on students.
2. See, for example, Australian Education Council, 1990; Ministry of Education (New Zealand), 1992; Office for Standards in Education (England), 1994.
3. Spillane (2000) refers to teachers' identity as "who they are, their sense of self, and their habits of mind ... an individual's way of understanding and being in the world" (p. 308).

References

Archer, J. (2005). Guiding hand. *Education Week, 25*(3), S5–S10.

Australian Education Council (1990). *A national statement on mathematics for Australian schools.* Canberra: Curriculum Corporation.

Boaler, J., & Greeno, J. (2000). Identity, agency, and knowing in mathematics worlds. In J. Boaler (Ed.), *Multiple perspectives on mathematics teaching and learning* (pp. 171–200). Westport, CT: Ablex.

Clark, C. M., & Peterson, P. (1986). Teachers' thought processes. In M. C. Wittrock (Ed.), *Handbook of research on teaching* (3rd Edition) (pp. 255–296). New York, NY: Macmillan.

Collopy, R. (2003). Curriculum materials as a professional development tool: How a mathematics textbook affected two teachers' learning. *Elementary School Journal, 103*(3), 287–311.

Donovan, B. F. (1983). *Power and curriculum in implementation: A case study of an innovative mathematics program.* Unpublished doctoral dissertation, University of Wisconsin, Madison.

Durkin, D. (1983). *Is there a match between what elementary teachers do and what basal manuals recommend?* (Tech. Rep. No. 44). Urbana, IL: Center for the Study of Reading.

FitzGerald, F. (1979). *America revised.* Boston, MA: Little, Brown.

Herbel-Eisenmann, B. A., Lubienski, S. T., & Id-Deen, L. (2006). Reconsidering the study of mathematics instructional practices: The importance of curricular context in understanding local and global teacher change. *Journal of Mathematics Teacher Education, 9,* 313–345.

Holland, D., & Lave, J. (Eds.). (2001). *History in person: Enduring struggles, contentious practice, intimate identities.* Santa Fe, NM: School of American Research Press.

Keiser, J. M., & Lambdin, D. V. (1996). The clock is ticking: Time constraint issues in mathematics teaching reform. *Journal of Educational Research, 90*(1), 23–30.

Komoski, P. K. (1977). Instructional materials will not improve until we change the system. *Educational Leadership, 42,* 31–37.

Kuhs, T. M., & Freeman, D. J. (1979). *The potential influence of textbooks on teachers' selection of content for elementary school mathematics* (Research Series No. 48). East Lansing, MI: Institute for Research on Teaching.

Lloyd, G. M. (1999). Two teachers' conceptions of a reform-oriented curriculum: Implications for mathematics teacher development. *Journal of Mathematics Teacher Education, 2*(3), 227–252.

Lloyd, G. M. (2006). Using K-12 mathematics curriculum materials in preservice teacher education: Rationale, strategies, and teachers' experiences. In K. Lynch-Davis, & R. L. Rider (Eds.), *The work of mathematics teacher educators: Continuing the conversation* (vol. 3, AMTE monograph series, pp. 11–27). San Diego, CA: Association of Mathematics Teacher Educators.

Manouchehri, A., & Goodman, T. (2000). Implementing mathematics reform: The challenge within. *Educational Studies in Mathematics, 42,* 1–34.

Ministry of Education. (1992). *Mathematics in the New Zealand curriculum.* Wellington: Learning Media.

National Council of Teachers of Mathematics. (1989). *Curriculum and evaluation standards for school mathematics.* Reston, VA: Author.

National Research Council. (2004). *On evaluating curricular effectiveness: Judging the quality of K-12 mathematics evaluations.* Committee for a Review of the Evaluation Data on the Effectiveness of NSF-Supported and Commercially Generated Mathematics Curriculum Materials. J. Confrey & V. Stohl (Eds.). Washington, DC: The National Academies Press.

No Child Left Behind Act of 2001, Pub. L. No. 107–110, 115 Stat. 1425 (2002).

Office for Standards in Education. (1994). *Science and mathematics in schools: A review.* London: Her Majesty's Stationery Office.

Remillard, J. T. (2000). Can curriculum materials support teachers' learning? Two fourth-grade teachers' use of a new mathematics text. *Elementary School Journal, 100*(4), 331–350.

Remillard, J. T. (2005). Examining key concepts in research on teachers' use of mathematics curricula. *Review of Educational Research, 75*(2), 211–246.

Schoenfeld, A. H. (2002). Making mathematics work for all children: Issues of standards, testing, and equity. *Educational Researcher, 31*(1), 13–25.

Senk, S. L., & Thompson, D. R. (2003). *Standards-based school mathematics curricula: What are they? What do students learn?* Mahwah, NJ: Lawrence Erlbaum.

Spillane, J. P. (2000). A fifth-grade teacher's reconstruction of mathematics and literacy teaching: Exploring interactions among identity, learning, and subject matter. *Elementary School Journal, 100*(4), 307–330.

Stake, R. E., & Easley, J. (1978). *Case studies in science education.* Urbana, IL: University of Illinois.

Stein, M. K., Grover, B. W., & Henningsen, M. (1996). Building student capacity for mathematical thinking and reasoning: An analysis of mathematical tasks used in reform classroom. *American Educational Research Journal, 33*(2), 455–488.

Stein, M. K., Remillard, J. T., & Smith, M. S. (2007). How curriculum influences student learning. In F. K. Lester Jr. (Ed.), *Second handbook of research on mathematics teaching and learning* (pp. 319–369). Charlotte, NC: Information Age.

Stephens, W. M. (1982). *Mathematical knowledge and school work: A case study of the teaching of developing mathematical processes.* Unpublished doctoral dissertation, University of Wisconsin, Madison.

Thompson, A. (1984). The relationship of teachers' conceptions of mathematics and mathematics teaching to instructional practice. *Educational Studies in Mathematics, 15*(2), 105–127.

Van Zoest, L. R., & Bohl, J. V. (2002). The role of reform curricular materials in an internship: The case of Alice and Gregory. *Journal of Mathematics Teacher Education, 5*(3), 265–288.

Wilson, S. M., & Berne, J. (1999). Teacher learning and the acquisition of professional knowledge: An examination of research on contemporary professional development. In A. Iran-Nejad & P. D. Pearson (Eds.), *Review of research in education* (pp.173–210). Washington, DC: American Educational Research Association.

II

Conceptual and Analytical Frameworks for Studying Teachers' Use of Curriculum Materials

2

The Teacher–Tool Relationship

Theorizing the Design and Use of Curriculum Materials

Matthew W. Brown

To understand the complex relationship between curriculum materials and the practices they facilitate, consider an example from jazz. The song *Take the A Train*, written by Billy Strayhorn, was the signature tune of the Duke Ellington Orchestra, and was performed by countless others. If we compare Duke's rendition to one by Ella Fitzgerald, we have little difficulty identifying each rendition as being the same song. Yet, despite their essential similarities, the songs sound distinctly different. (The same can often be said for two renditions by the same artist.) We can examine some of the sources of this variation – ranging from obvious differences such as instruments used to less obvious ones such as cultural influences, contextual factors, and stylistic preferences. But it is also the case that, although performers use pre-rendered scores as foundations to support their practice, a great deal of the creative work takes place during the performance.

This relationship is similar with curriculum materials and teacher practices. In both cases, practitioners bring to life the composer's initial concept through a process of interpretation and adaptation, with results that may vary significantly while bearing certain core similarities. Just as modern music has come to rely on sheet music as a representational medium for conveying musical concepts, forms, and practices (see Goodman, 1976), classroom instruction has come to rely on curriculum materials as tools to convey and reproduce curricular concepts, forms, and practices. Musicians interpret musical notations in order to bring the intended song to life; similarly, teachers interpret the various words and representations in curriculum materials to enact curriculum. In both cases, no two renditions of practice are exactly alike.

Understanding the ways that teachers transform the core ideas of curriculum materials into practice is important, given how frequently curriculum materials are used by reformers and policy-makers as tools to influence instruction. Indeed, curriculum materials have long played a central role in educational reform, with mixed results (Ball & Cohen, 1996; Cohen, 1988a; Cuban, 1992, 1993; Snyder, Bolin, & Zumwalt, 1992). Explanations for the continual disappointments from curriculum-based reform efforts have focused on practitioners (Cohen, 1990; Spillane, 1999), policies (Spillane, 1998), and professional development (Putnam & Borko, 2000; Wilson & Berne, 1999). Recently, researchers have devoted increased attention to the ways teachers interpret and use innovative curriculum resources (Ben-Peretz, 1990; Brown, 2002; Brown & Edelson, 2003; Lloyd, 1999; Remillard, 2000, 2005; Wiley, 2001), as well as how designers might create resources that better accommodate instruction (Brown, 2002; Brown & Edelson, 2003; Davis & Krajcik, 2005; Davis & Varma, accepted; Schneider & Krajcik, 2002).

In this chapter, I contribute to these latter approaches by presenting a theoretical framework for considering the relationship between curriculum materials and teacher practice. This perspective is rooted in the notion that all teaching involves a process of design in which teachers use curriculum materials in unique ways as they craft instructional episodes. Understanding how teachers use curriculum resources to craft instruction requires being explicit about the representations curriculum materials use to communicate concepts and actions, being attentive to the ways in which teachers perceive and interpret these representations, and understanding how these representations can constrain and afford teacher practice. The ultimate goal of this endeavor is to inform the way researchers examine teachers' use of curriculum materials and the way designers create materials that are intended to influence practice.

I begin by framing teachers' use of curriculum artifacts as a design activity and exploring this perspective in light of cognitive theory on the role of artifacts in shaping human activity. Then, I introduce three theoretical constructs that help interpret the teacher–tool relationship and apply them in a study that revealed the different ways that teachers interact with curriculum artifacts. I conclude the chapter by exploring the implications of this perspective for the design of materials and professional development that support a design-oriented stance toward instruction.

There is good reason to be skeptical about the influence curriculum materials can have over teacher practice, particularly as vehicles for instructional reform. The use of curriculum materials provides no guarantee of instructional change. If, however, developers appreciate that teaching involves a process of design and view materials as resources to support such a process, then the errand of such materials shifts from simply transmitting instructional ideas to transforming practice by serving as a catalyst for local customization (see Jackson, 1986; Pea, 1994). More than mere conduits for a particular reform effort, materials that support teacher design stand a better chance of engaging practitioners with the curricular ideas the reform intends to foster and thus have a greater potential to transform teacher practice.

Teaching as Design

Teaching is commonly viewed as a craft (e.g., Eisner, 1983). In this chapter, I expand this viewpoint by arguing that teaching is, in many ways, a design activity. Teachers must perceive and interpret existing resources, evaluate the constraints of the classroom setting, balance tradeoffs, and devise strategies – all in the pursuit of their instructional goals.

The interpretation of teaching as design is relatively new. Yet the notion of teachers as designers is compatible with a range of established cognitive theories that emphasize the vital partnership that exists between individuals and the tools they use to accomplish their goals – what Wertsch (1998) characterizes as the "irreducible tension" that exists between agent and tool (Hutchins, 1996; Norman, 1988, 1991; Pea, 1993; Wertsch, 1991, 1998). The accomplishments of individuals, according to this tradition, are inextricably bound up in their use of cultural and physical tools. And it is not just the capacities of individuals that dictate human accomplishment, but also the affordances (Gibson, 1977) of the artifacts they use. This theory base brings to light three key points for understanding the interaction between teachers and curriculum artifacts: (a) curriculum materials play an important role in affording and constraining teachers' actions; (b) teachers notice and use such artifacts differently given their experience, intentions, and abilities; and (c) "teaching by design" is not so much a conscious choice as an inevitable reality.

Theoretical Background

According to Wartofsky (1973), artifacts are tools created by humans in order to produce and reproduce the means of existence. Artifacts, he claimed, are created through a deliberate transformation of part of the environment for the purposes of survival and include the physical tools we use, as well as the language, social organizations, and divisions of labor that help us to accomplish the needs of existence.

Given their function in species survival, a crucial element of artifacts is that they can be transmitted, and thus preserved, across time and place. To do this, humans require a means of symbolically communicating – or representing – these artifacts and the skills involved in their use. Such representations become artifacts themselves. Artifacts, therefore, include not only tools used to accomplish modes of action, but also those used to represent and transmit such modes of action through social and cultural arrangements.

Artifacts can Extend Human Capacities

A key feature of artifacts is that they assist people in achieving goals they could not accomplish on their own. In many instances of accomplishment, humans and artifacts are inseparable. Wertsch (1998) illustrated the inseparable nature of this relationship through a discussion of the history of pole-vaulting, demonstrating how improvements in pole technology enabled athletes to vault to new heights. It is ridiculous, he claimed, to attempt to consider the task by isolating either the pole or the agent, for neither can engage in the activity without each other. Rather, the two elements must be considered in terms of a dynamic interaction. A similar situation exists with "cognitive" tools such as calculators. As Pea (1985) observed, an individual's ability to accomplish complex mathematical calculations using tools such as calculators cannot be understood as mental capacity alone, since such partnerships are characterized by the "sharing" of functional capacity across people and tools.

Artifacts Mediate Action

Another important property of artifacts is that they *mediate* activity in very specific ways. Given the fundamental role of artifacts in human activity, it follows that the nature and composition of a specific tool will have a significant influence on the nature of the tasks that can be accomplished with it. This notion of *mediated action*, derived from Vygotsky (1978) and advanced by Wertsch (1991, 1998), emphasizes *affordances* and *constraints* that artifacts place on activity. These two terms – affordances and constraints – serve to describe the range of possibilities and limitations that artifacts may present for human activity. They essentially represent two sides of the same coin. Wertsch (1998) explained the role of affordances and constraints in terms of the "half-empty" and "half-full" views. The "half-full" outlook emphasizes the enabling potential of mediating artifacts. Gibson (1977) used the term affordances to describe the functional properties that determine how an item may be used. Norman (1988) expanded on this notion at great length by describing the ways in which everyday objects signal intended uses through perceptual cues. For example, pliers send a strong perceptual message that they are *for* grabbing hold of an object.

On the other hand, the "half-empty" outlook points out that the tools we use not only open doors to new experiences but also place important restrictions on activity. According to this view, our ability to act on reality is inherently limited, or constrained, by the tools we use. Burke (1966) and Wertsch (1998) referred to these constraining properties of artifacts as "terministic screens." Consider, for example, a travel guide. This tool – namely, a book containing maps, descriptions of attractions, and suggested itineraries – serves to define a set of possibilities for visiting a new place: where to go, how to get there, how much time to allow, and how to interpret what one sees. In so doing, the travel guide helps to provide meaning and coherence to an otherwise unbounded set of possibilities, providing meaningful constraints. Rather than being framed as hindrances (as the term often implies), these constraints can be interpreted in terms of how they define the nature of the task and how they provide clear boundaries that define activity.

Curriculum Materials as Artifacts

The faith in artifacts to afford and constrain human activity is at the core of many curriculum-based reforms. According to Norman (1988), humans commonly design artifacts with the capability to cue activity through constraints and affordances, and curriculum materials are no different. According to this view, it is possible to craft curriculum materials (e.g., lesson plans, domain representations, lab tools) that, through their constraints and affordances, can trigger or cue the instructional activities of individual teachers. Like all tools, curriculum materials assist people (in this case, teachers) in achieving goals that they presumably could not or would not accomplish on their own. As with the pole vaulter and the pole, a teacher's ability to enact a curriculum unit cannot be understood solely in terms of individual instructional capacity, since the activity is characterized by the sharing of functional capacity across both the teacher and the curriculum materials.

Following Wartofsky (1973), this characterization of curriculum materials as artifacts calls attention not only to the physical tools used to accomplish class-room activity – rulers, calculators, and pencils – but also to culturally rooted tools that represent and transmit modes of action, such as lesson plans, teacher guides, and texts. Curriculum materials are a means of communicating – typi-cally via text and diagrammatic representations – ideas and practices that make up classroom activity. Their designs can signal intended uses – their affordances – in a number of ways. Lesson plans, for instance, commonly contain annota-tions that describe objectives, intended audience, duration, and key skills – all of which signal to a teacher specific ways to structure a lesson. Other features, such as diagrams of subject matter or elaborations of common student errors, contain subtle affordances that signal to users different possibilities for how the materials might be used. These cues may be direct or subtle, explicit or implicit, and may draw upon a host of professional norms and understandings (see Chapter 3 of this volume).

Curriculum designs can also provide important constraints for instruction. Consider, for example, a teacher's activity guide that describes how to prepare a classroom for an activity. In such cases, the artifact – namely, a document con-taining words and diagrams – serves to define a set of parameters for the activity space: how to arrange the desks, what sorts of participant structures to use, how much time to allow, and which instructional techniques to employ. In so doing, the activity guide helps to provide meaning and coherence within an otherwise enormous range of instructional possibilities. Similarly, a curriculum program designer's choice to include certain descriptions of the subject matter over others can productively constrain a teacher's interaction with the curriculum, thus serving to influence classroom instruction in deliberate ways. These sorts of con-straints help to define an instructional space.

How Curriculum Artifacts Influence Instruction

The above consideration of curriculum materials as artifacts highlights their potential for representing ideas, conveying practices, reinforcing cultural norms, and influencing teachers. Practitioners attend to and utilize various features of curriculum materials when crafting classroom instruction, so understanding how these features can represent curricular ideas and instructional activities, and in turn afford and constrain teachers' decisions, is critical to understanding teaching as design. Again, the analogy to music helps to reify these qualities. Curriculum materials, like sheet music, possess the following characteristics:

1. They are static representations of abstract concepts and dynamic activities – a means for transmitting and producing activity, not the activity itself.
2. They are intended to convey rich ideas and dynamic practices, yet they do so through succinct shorthand that relies heavily on interpretation.

3. They observe a number of culturally shared notational rules, norms, and conventions in their representations – although fewer consistently used conventions exist for curriculum materials than for sheet music.
4. They may reflect common or existing practices and at the same time aim to shape innovative or new practices.
5. They represent an interface between the knowledge, goals, and values of the author and the user.
6. They require craft in their use; they are inert objects that come alive only through interpretation and use by a practitioner.

Though the music and education communities differ greatly in terms of shared beliefs about practices and outcomes, both rely on static artifacts to document and convey intended practices, and both involve dynamic practices that involve a combination of planning, interpretation, and improvisation. In both cases, practitioners practice and plan according to instructions embodied in the artifacts, but they also adapt and improvise in response to local factors and creative ability. Understanding the specific ways in which curriculum artifacts can afford and constrain instructional activity is important to helping curriculum program designers create resources that both communicate instructional ideas and support creative modes of enacting them.

How Teachers Interpret and Use Curriculum Artifacts

Despite the many ways that curriculum artifacts can influence teacher practice, they represent only half the story. Understanding how teachers' skills, knowledge, and beliefs influence their interpretation and use of curriculum materials is critical to understanding the teacher–tool relationship. Research has shown that when teachers interact with curriculum artifacts, they do so in dynamic and constructive ways (Barab & Luehmann, 2003; Brown, 2002; Davis & Krajcik, 2005; Matese, 2005; Remillard, 2005), revealing the importance of understanding how teachers perceive, interpret, and utilize curriculum artifacts.

Researchers have revealed a number of ways that teachers interact with curriculum artifacts. First, they *select* materials. Although the selection of a curriculum program is often decided by others, teachers make day-to-day decisions about which of the program's available resources to use. These decisions are dictated by their knowledge, beliefs, skills, and goals (Freeman & Porter, 1989; Tarr, Reys, Reys, Chavez, Shih, & Osterlind, 2008). Conversely, in situations in which teachers are using mandated or "scripted" curriculum materials, researchers often find that teachers resist adoption (Cohen, 1990; Remillard, 1992; Wilson, 1990) and this resistance is rooted in their goals, beliefs, and capacities (Cohen, 1988b, 1990; Lloyd, 1999; Lloyd & Wilson, 1998; Wilson & Goldenberg, 1998). Second, they *interpret* these materials, both in planning and during instruction. How they perceive and understand different features of the materials is determined by both the quality of the designs and their own capacities, as well as features of the context (Ben-Peretz, 1990; Stein, Remillard, & Smith, 2007). (Factors that influence teachers' meaning-making of curriculum materials are discussed in the other sections of this volume.) Third, they *reconcile* their perceptions of the intended goals with their own goals and capacities, as well as with the constraints of the setting. In some cases, this process may be deliberate; in others it is unconscious (Ben-Peretz, 1990; Remillard, 2005). Fourth, they *accommodate* the talents, interests, experiences, and limitations of their students. They must provide constant feedback and adjust their own practices based on the performance of both individuals and the group as a whole (Stein, 1996; Wilson & Lloyd, 2000). Finally, they often depart from the intended plan to *add* their own embellishments, *modify* existing structures, or *omit* parts that do not interest them or are beyond their own capacities or the capabilities of their students (Remillard, 1992; Tarr et al., 2008).

How a teacher engages in these processes is influenced both by the design of the materials (as discussed in the previous section) and by the teacher's own knowledge, skills, beliefs and goals, and context. Moreover, each of these steps – selection, interpretation, reconciliation, accommodation, and modification – is the sort of thing people typically do when they engage in design. Ultimately, the teacher–tool relationship involves bi-directional influences: how curriculum artifacts, through their affordances and constraints, influence teachers, and how teachers, through their perceptions and decisions, mobilize curriculum artifacts.

How Teaching is Design

Design is more than the process of creating something; it is about crafting something in order to solve a human problem, to change the state of a particular situation from a current condition to a desired one, and to accomplish a goal. I use the term "craft" because it implies a certain quality – some designs are more elegant than others. Moreover, design, like all goal-directed human activity, involves the use of tools, be they physical or cultural.

Teaching involves a particular brand of design. When teachers use curriculum materials to craft instructional episodes in order to achieve goals, when they use materials as tools to transform a classroom episode from an existing state to a desired one, they are engaging in design – whether or not they intend to do so. Whether teachers modify an existing set of materials or integrate them in a literal manner, they are engaging in the sort of goal-directed activity I am calling design.

Applying the design metaphor to teaching is useful because it calls attention to the constructive interplay that takes place during instruction between agent (teachers) and tools (curriculum materials), and the manner in which the characteristics of each shape the outcome. Understanding teaching as design is important to understanding the dynamic interplay that unfolds when teachers use curriculum materials.

Analyzing Teacher Use of Curriculum Artifacts

Framing teaching as design helps to illustrate the dynamics that influence the outcomes of teachers' use of curriculum materials. In this section, I provide three analytical constructs to help understand teachers' use of curriculum materials in light of this perspective.

First, I argue that teachers' interactions with instructional materials can be understood in terms of different degrees of artifact appropriation: *offloading*, *adapting*, and *improvising*. In the first part of this section, I illustrate each kind of use and present a taxonomy for understanding these different characterizations of the teacher–tool relationship. Next, to illustrate the factors influencing these degrees of use, I present a framework for analyzing the interactions that occur between features of curriculum materials and teachers' own capacities. This framework examines the resources that teachers and the curriculum materials bring to the exchange. Finally, these different types of curriculum use also suggest the importance of understanding what I call teachers' *pedagogical design capacity* – that is, their ability to perceive and mobilize existing resources in order to craft instructional contexts.

Types of Curriculum Use: Offloading, Adapting, and Improvising

To understand the different ways teachers use curriculum materials, it is useful to examine the dynamic interplay between teachers and the curriculum artifacts they use. Consider, for example, the following three ways a teacher might inter-act with curriculum materials. These scenarios are adapted from an extensive study of how three middle school teachers used the curriculum materials of a ten-week inquiry-based science unit (Brown, 2002).[1]

Rather than giving students explicit instructions for setting up a classroom experiment provided in the curriculum guide, a teacher decided to have students design their own set-ups. She used the lesson plan to inform how she coached the students, ensuring that their results matched the essential structure and format of the lesson. In the process, she exhibited a deep enough understanding of the experiment's overall rationale to guide students in creative substitutions of materials without compromising the experiment's accuracy.

To teach students how to perform a complex calculation of the experiment's results, the same teacher relied on the scripted instructions in a lesson plan to lead students through each step of the calculation. During this segment of instruction, the teacher consulted the curriculum guide at each step of the process, often reading the lesson plan's directions aloud as she showed students how to do the calculation.

To conclude the activity, the teacher initiated a discussion using discussion questions provided by the materials. In the course of the discussion, the teacher seized upon a disagreement between two students in order to initiate a multi-day debate on competing interpretations of the model – a complete departure from the original design that nonetheless achieved compatible goals.

Examples such as these suggest a scale that characterizes the different extents to which the teacher *offloaded*, *adapted*, or *improvised with* the materials as she taught. When calculating the results, the teacher used the curriculum materials in a literal manner, following the materials as closely as possible. In these cases, she offloaded a large degree of agency for guiding instructional activity onto the materials. When fostering the debate, she improvised her own strategies for instruction with minimal reliance on the materials. Here the agency shifted in large part to the teacher. When guiding the lab's set-up, she adapted the curriculum resources in ways that reflected contributions of both the materials and her personal resources.

These three types of use characterize different ways in which teachers appropriate curriculum resources within their designs, resulting in differential distributions of agency for guiding instruction across the teacher and the available instructional resource. Drawing upon personal and material resources, teachers may craft an instructional episode in which they rely on tasks, worksheets, and pedagogical steps from the materials (offloading), or may craft an episode in which they devise a spontaneous strategy for sparking student discussion of a lab (improvising). Each possibility represents a specific case of design-based decision-making (Edelson, 2002), in which teachers determine how to use instructional materials to accomplish their goals.

These decisions may involve a range of considerations at multiple levels – from organizing and structuring a classroom, to supporting student activity, to teaching specific concepts. Each decision involves its own consideration of instructional goals and student needs and how best to use available resources to achieve desired outcomes, and each decision may result in a different type of use of instructional materials. As the above example illustrates, a single class period, therefore, might involve various instances of offloading, adapting, or improvising. Such decisions may be nested, so high-level decisions about classroom structure may precede and encompass later decisions that arise in the course of teaching.

This scale for characterizing curriculum materials does not necessarily correlate to teacher expertise. Each type of use is intended to describe the distribution of resources contributed by the curriculum artifact and by the teacher; one type of use is not considered superior to the others. The notion of offloading, for instance, derives from the view that intelligence can be distributed across people and artifacts, and that people may rely on artifacts to achieve their goals (Pea, 1993). Such a case can represent a strategic decision by the teacher as to where instructional agency rests (see Chapter 4 of this volume) and is not necessarily an indication of deficiency. Just as a novice teacher might offload instructional responsibility to a scripted lesson due to limited understanding of the subject matter, so might an expert teacher offload instructional responsibility to a worksheet that supports her goals, freeing her to roam the room and respond to student needs as they arise.

Moreover, the scale is not intended to measure fidelity to designer intent. Offloading means using the materials in a literal fashion, but this may or may not result in outcomes intended by the designers of those materials. Similarly, a teacher may improvise in a manner that is perfectly compatible with the goals of the designer or in a way that mutates the original intent. The scale characterizes the nature of a teacher's interaction with a given resource, but it does not evaluate the outcomes of this interaction.

The distinction between teacher decisions that involve offloads, adaptations, and improvisations reveals the different ways in which materials may contribute to the craft of instruction. Understanding how teachers appropriate curriculum artifacts within their daily craft can help curriculum and professional development designers create materials that are more useful to teachers and professional learning experiences that support them in using these materials to meet their goals. This understanding can also contribute to research on teaching by clarifying particular aspects of teacher practice.

Facets of the Teacher–Tool Relationship: The Design Capacity for Enactment Framework

Understanding why teachers interact with curriculum materials in these different ways requires examining how the features of the materials interact with the capacities that teachers bring to the interaction. To do this, I analyzed the resources that the teachers and the curriculum materials in the above-referenced study brought to the teacher–tool exchange using the *Design Capacity for Enactment* (DCE) framework (Brown, 2002). I developed this framework (see Figure 2.1) to represent the teacher–tool exchange and the factors that influence it.

The DCE framework captures the different elements of the teacher–tool dynamic and represents the different types of interactions that occur between teacher resources and curriculum resources as teachers adapt, adopt or improvise with curriculum resources. On one hand, the framework encompasses teachers' knowledge, skills, goals, and beliefs and how they influence the ways teachers perceive and appropriate different aspects of curriculum designs. On the other hand, the framework encompasses the design features and embedded knowledge that comprise curriculum materials – including representations of action, representations of content, and representations of physical objects. These aspects reflect the implicit and explicit intentions of curriculum designers.

In the DCE framework, I focus on three basic aspects of curriculum materials: (a) physical objects and representations of physical objects, (b) representations of tasks (procedures), and (c) representations of concepts (domain representations). Physical objects denote the material nature of the curriculum materials

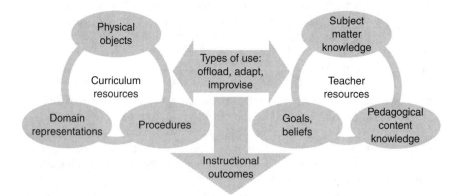

Figure 2.1 The Design Capacity for Enactment framework.

themselves, including accompanying supplies. Representations of physical objects account for materials that are recommended by, but not included within, the curriculum materials. They also include blueprints for assembling or arranging other objects. Representations of tasks include instructions, procedures, and scripts that are intended for enactment by teachers and students. These may include recommendations for how to structure a lesson (for teachers) or problems to solve (for students). Curriculum materials may also represent tasks in other more indirect ways. For example, the deliberate sequencing of activities may implicitly represent high-level domain practices that the designers intend to convey. Finally, representations of concepts refer to the depiction and organization of domain concepts and their relationships through means such as diagrams, models, explanations, descriptions, and analogies. Larger structures, such as topic sequences, may also represent domain concepts. This is frequently the case in textbooks, which are often sequenced according to the ways that experts think about the domain. Together, these three facets encompass the most fundamental aspects of a curriculum's content and structure: its core ideas, the activities undertaken in their exploration, and the objects that support such activity.

On the other side of the analysis, teachers bring at least three different types of resources to their use of curriculum materials: (a) subject matter knowledge, (b) pedagogical content knowledge (Shulman, 1986), and (c) goals and beliefs. Subject matter knowledge denotes knowledge of the facts and concepts in the domain (Ball, 1991; Stodolsky & Grossman, 1995). Pedagogical content knowledge combines general pedagogical knowledge with domain knowledge to describe knowledge of how to teach a particular domain. It includes the aims and purposes of teaching the subject matter, knowledge of how learners relate to the subject matter, knowledge of available resources and representations for teaching the subject matter, and knowledge of the instructional strategies and methods for teaching the particular subject matter (Shulman, 1986). Goals and beliefs – what Ball & Cohen (1999) term "commitments" – refer to teachers' orientations toward the material they teach. This goes beyond their ability to teach something to focus on their motivations for teaching it. Researchers have documented what happens when curriculum reforms fail to accommodate – or in some cases challenge – teachers' own goals and beliefs. For instance, Spillane (1999) and Wilson (1990) document how teachers' beliefs about the nature of learning and student capabilities can impede their adoption of new instructional approaches. Similarly, Cohen (1988a, 1988b) observes how conflicting goals – both individual and social – can result in significant barriers to the implementation of instructional reforms. Thus, the nature of teachers' goals and beliefs is highly relevant to understanding how teachers perceive and appropriate curriculum materials.

The Design Capacity for Enactment framework provides a starting point for identifying and situating the factors that can influence how a teacher adapts, offloads, or improvises with curriculum resources. Yet the teacher resources and curriculum resources I have selected are by no means exhaustive, and reflect the particular goals and limitations of my own research context – what I could observe within classroom interactions. Other research has examined additional characteristics of curriculum materials, such as the narrative "voice" of the text (Herbel-Eisenmann, 2007) and the transparency of the materials (Stein and Kim, see Chapter 3 of this volume). Some important teacher resources lie outside the scope of this analysis. For instance, the DCE does not encompass teachers' knowledge of context (Grossman, 1990), cultural norms of teaching (Stigler & Hiebert, 1998), issues of professional identity (Chapter 4 of this volume; Smith, 1996), and teachers' orientation toward curriculum materials (Remillard & Bryans, 2004). And I broadly include within the category of goals and beliefs such factors as ideology, cultural norms, values, and habits, each of which could warrant its own separate treatment. Further research is needed to understand how these and other factors fit within frameworks such as the DCE. My goal is to highlight an approach to tracing observable interactions between qualities of teachers and curriculum materials that occur in the flow of everyday instruction.

Applying the Design Capacity Enactment Framework

Each instance cited in the earlier classroom case is explainable in terms of this interaction between teacher resources and curriculum resources. Detailed examples of how this framework can be tied to teachers' use of curriculum materials are available in previous studies (see Brown, 2002). Here, I briefly highlight a few key observations. First, the teacher's transformation of the classroom science experiment from guided set-up to student-directed experimental design was influenced, among other things, by her extensive experience with student-directed learning and her desire to nurture authentic practices. Her reliance on the script for calculating the results stemmed from her stated discomfort with the mathematical operations involved. Further, her goal of nurturing classroom discourse influenced her transformation of the recommended discussion into a spontaneous, student-driven classroom debate on competing interpretations of the experiment.

These examples represent select paths through the DCE framework. Other cases reveal very different factors leading to teachers' decisions to offload, adapt, or improvise with the curriculum materials. For instance, another teacher's decision to rely extensively on worksheets to guide student activity stemmed from his conscious decision to create a multi-tasking classroom environment in which two groups of students worked on different activities – one group on a computer activity and the other group on a traditional lab. This offload is not traced to his discomfort with the subject matter (as in the case above), but rather to his ability to recognize a pedagogical benefit to teaching two conceptually related activities simultaneously, and his reliance on the materials to accomplish this goal (Brown & Edelson, 1999). In other words, the outcomes do not necessarily correlate with teacher expertise or the quality of educational designs, but rather they are a reflection of how a complex interaction of factors and conditions influence a particular distribution of resources between agent and tool. Judgment-laden determinations related to expertise and fidelity require other forms of analysis.

Pedagogical Design Capacity

Although the DCE framework accounts for the resources contributed by the teacher and the curriculum materials – the nouns of the interaction, as it were – it does not fully account for the actions involved in their mobilization – the verbs of the interaction. The capacity of the first teacher described above to mobilize the curriculum resources in productive ways involves more than just knowledge, skills, and commitments. She possesses a skill in perceiving the affordances of the materials and making decisions about how to use them to craft instructional episodes that achieve her goals. I call this competence *pedagogical design capacity*, defined as a teacher's capacity to perceive and mobilize existing resources in order to craft instructional episodes (Brown, 2002; Brown & Edelson, 2003).

Pedagogical design capacity (PDC) goes beyond the resources that are present in an instructional episode to describe the skill by which the various pieces are put into play. This theoretical construct emanates from a vision of instructional capacity as not just a function of what teachers know, but as their ability to accomplish new things with that knowledge (Ball & Cohen, 1999) – a distinction akin to what Ryle (1984) referred to as knowledge *that* versus knowledge *how*. Similar to Wertsch's (1998) discussion of agents' "skills in using mediational means," and Pea's (1993) "situated invention of uses," I mean to highlight the creative and constructive dimensions of teachers' instructional capacities. This skill represents yet another characteristic that teachers bring to their interactions with curriculum materials. Thus, PDC itself ultimately warrants inclusion within the DCE framework.

PDC represents a teacher's skill in perceiving affordances, making decisions, and following through on plans. Whether such design decisions manifest as offloads, adaptations, or improvisations is a separate matter. It is the skill in weaving various modes of use together and in arranging the various pieces of the classroom setting that is the mark of a teacher with high PDC, not whether they happen to be offloading, adapting, or improvising at any given moment. Rather, PDC describes the manner and degree to which teachers create deliberate, productive designs that help accomplish their instructional goals.

By focusing attention on how teachers perceive and mobilize curricular resources, PDC can help explain how two teachers who have very different knowledge, skills, and commitments – and who therefore produce very different enacted curricula – might nonetheless share important similarities in how they craft instruction. By the same token, PDC can also help explain why two teachers who have seemingly similar knowledge, skills, and commitments can produce very different enacted curricula because they possess very different capacities to create deliberate, productive designs (exhibiting different degrees of PDC). Again, consider the following scenarios, adapted from an earlier study of PDC (Brown, 2002).

The first teacher, Janet (described earlier in this chapter), was experienced at managing student-centered classrooms. She possessed a strong grasp of the scientific process and believed that students need to drive the flow of classroom activity. A second teacher, Bill, was expert at creating analogies and representations to clarify complex ideas and relied extensively on supplemental classroom tools to augment his teaching. He too possessed a strong grasp of the scientific process, though he believed that students require structure and conceptual clarity.

In light of their different skill sets and beliefs about students, it should not be surprising that Janet and Bill produced very different versions of the same laboratory activity. Janet adapted the activity to foster student-directed experimental design. Bill adapted the activity to make the recommended lab set-up more accurately model the real-world phenomenon. Janet improvised a debate to expose her students to the contested nature of scientific knowledge. Bill improvised with supplemental illustrations of key concepts in order to provide greater clarity.

Both, however, demonstrated a keen ability to anticipate and respond productively to student needs – Bill in a structured teacher-centered fashion, Janet in an open-ended student-centered fashion. Their different approaches stemmed from their differing views about how students should learn, yet both teachers demonstrated a strong capacity – pedagogical design capacity – to interpret key affordances within the materials and utilize those features to craft instructional episodes in order to meet perceived student needs and achieve their instructional objectives.

PDC can also help illuminate important differences among teachers who might otherwise appear to have similar knowledge, skills, and commitments, and therefore can help to explain differences in their enacted curricula. Take Brenda, who (like Bill) favored a teacher-centered classroom in order to provide students with the structure she felt they needed. Like Bill, she possessed the necessary pedagogical content knowledge to craft useful representations aimed at providing conceptual clarity for her students. Like Bill, she introduced the lab with a clever analogy to clarify the connections between the experimental model and the real-world phenomenon; however, unlike Bill, Brenda's adaptation was isolated to a five-minute introduction and failed to resurface throughout the activity. Further, she did not mobilize additional resources to help illustrate the analogy. In other words, even when demonstrating her own pedagogical content knowledge, Brenda lacked the PDC necessary to weave it into a larger fabric of classroom instruction. She perceived a key affordance in the underlying lab model, but she did not mobilize it in a productive way.

Brenda's case also helps illustrate an important point about the development of PDC. Following her enactments, she continually noted that, by following the curriculum guide, she was able to "notice" instructional opportunities which, although she failed to act on them initially, she hoped to take advantage of during subsequent enactments. She seemed to be feeling her way through the curriculum materials as she learned what they offered and how students responded to them. Whereas Janet and Bill displayed greater abilities to notice and utilize the materials' affordances, and therefore were able to reinvent the activity to make it their own, Brenda seemed to be figuring it out. This observation – that Brenda's increasing familiarity with the resources might help her envision creative ways to use them in the future – suggests that pedagogical design capacity may emerge over time, as familiarity with the pedagogical affordances of available resources and ability to use them increases. Further research is needed to learn about how teachers develop pedagogical design capacity, the relationship between perception and mobilization of pedagogical affordances, and the degree to which other personal resources influence the emergence of PDC.

Although the scale of offload–adapt–improvise and the DCE framework are both judgment-neutral tools for describing teachers' use of curriculum materials, the notion of pedagogical design capacity is evaluative. This fact is inevitable since design involves craft, and craft often has a certain ineffable quality. To a certain extent, the elegance of a teacher's design is a subjective determination. Yet the fact remains that not all designs are equally effective at helping teachers reach their goals, not all designs reflect the same responsiveness to the needs of a particular setting, not all designs are purposeful, and not all designs embody the same degree of utility. PDC is not simply an indicator of whether a teacher will be likely to design something for the classroom; it is an indicator of whether the teacher's designs are pedagogically beneficial.

The challenge, then, is finding ways to measure PDC. Doing so would require identifying criteria for judging it, such as degree of purposefulness, effectiveness in achieving desired outcomes, and degree of alignment with overarching goals. Despite the subjective nature of this enterprise, it is theoretically possible to measure the quality of teachers' designs. Further research is needed to sort out the key dimensions of PDC and find precise ways to measure these and foster their development in teachers.

Design Implications

If teachers' use of curriculum materials can be understood as a design process, then it follows that some teachers may be more adept than others at designing instructional contexts. Therefore, understanding pedagogical design capacity holds important implications for how teachers are prepared, how materials are designed, and how researchers and school officials evaluate instructional practice.

The concept of pedagogical design capacity suggests that it may be possible to design materials and professional development in ways that facilitate different types of productive curriculum use by teachers. Teachers who possess high pedagogical design capacities are able to deconstruct curriculum materials, recognize their essential elements, and reconstruct them in order to suit their needs. But teachers with less PDC need additional support in ascertaining the different ways that a curriculum design may be used to accomplish instructional goals.

One way to realize the potential of teaching as design is to rethink traditional modes of curriculum material design, dissemination, and use. Rather than designing curriculum materials as one-size-fits-all documents, designers could endeavor to support different modes of use by teachers. Dissemination and professional development, in turn, should occur in a context that supports teachers as they learn to craft customized solutions that meet their own instructional goals and their students' needs.

The Design of Materials

The challenge in designing a system to support multiple goals and users with varying levels of instructional design and content expertise is finding the appropriate balance between being sufficiently open-ended to accommodate flexible use, yet sufficiently constrained to provide coherence and meaning with respect to its intended uses. In an initial attempt to realize the principles of teaching by design, my colleagues and I developed an online system to support the dissemination and local adaptation of instructional resources by teachers (Brown et al., 2004). The system, dubbed *AIM* (Adaptive Instructional Materials) integrates an indexed and annotated database of electronic resources with the ability to compose and adapt such resources into personalized lesson and course plans. AIM is designed to accomplish two primary objectives: (a) to support teacher engagement with the concepts and issues of a given subject area, and (b) to support teachers with resources and activity ideas that they can use to create or adapt instructional materials of their own.

Much work has been done on the development of flexible instructional materials at the levels of both system design and curriculum development. For instance, research on "learning objects" (Wiley, 2001) has attempted to explore the use of "modular" and "reusable" learning resources that can be pieced together in various forms depending on the particular needs of their users. At the other extreme, researchers have studied the stifling impact that "scripted" curriculum resources can have on teachers' agency in addressing the plethora of unique issues and needs that arise in their classrooms during instruction (e.g., Ben-Peretz, 1990). Our approach to program design attempts to deal with these tradeoffs by working from three main principles discussed below.

Multiple Points of Access

The first principle is to support a range of instructional and content expertise by providing multiple points of access to the instructional resources. Teachers with high pedagogical design capacity can browse or search the database, assembling collections of instructional resources, as well as pre-authored lessons, that they can later import into a course authoring tool. Teachers with low pedagogical design capacity, perhaps due to inexperience with the resources or the particular content, can use pre-authored materials that have been annotated by designers with pedagogical affordances describing how they might be used to teach in different ways. The system supports users in adapting existing courses or lessons by adding or subtracting resources, altering the enactment plan, or modifying the learning objectives.

Resource-Centric Material Design

The second principle is to adopt a resource-centric approach to the design of curriculum materials that allows for their re-use and adaptation in multiple instructional contexts. The resource-centric approach emphasizes the key building blocks of a lesson over its procedural steps. Resources that are applied to a specific lesson are accompanied by annotations that describe the designers' intent as well as the pedagogical affordances of the resource, a design strategy referred to as transparency by Davis and Krajcik (2005) and one intended to facilitate growth in teachers' pedagogical design capacity. By highlighting multiple ways in which resources may be used and organized within lessons, this approach seeks to avoid the highly contextualized qualities of procedure-centric approaches and promote mindful engagement on the part of teachers. It does not eschew procedures (indeed, they are one among many available representations of the units), but it avoids the conventional practice of relying on them as the core organizing element.

Creating Reusable Resources and Supporting Customization

One of the major challenges in designing flexible curriculum resources is defining the grain size of the modular units. The risk is that units are either too context-specific to be usable by others or so flexible that they amount to little more than a generic set of resources. For an instructional unit to be both adaptable and meaningful, it needs to organize instructional resources and activities according to a clear rationale, but not be so structured as to require any single mode of use. The AIM system attempts to highlight each unit's design rationale through annotations that address the pedagogical affordances for each resource (e.g., "How did I use this resource?" and "What does this resource help students do or understand?"). In addition to seeing a resource's affordances for a given unit, users can follow links to other situated uses of the resource (and therefore see additional ways to use the same resource) in order to gain a richer understanding of its potential instructional uses.

The Design of Professional Development

The concept of pedagogical design capacity suggests the potential benefits of professional development that is situated in customization tasks. In addition to receiving support in learning subject matter and ways of teaching the content, which many have long advocated, teachers also require support in exploring which resources to use and how to use them.

This latter aspect of professional development should help teachers link their instructional goals to the specific features and affordances of curriculum materials and support teachers in making the necessary design modifications required to achieve this alignment. Thus, teacher preparation and professional development might explicitly target the design skills required for effective use of instructional materials. Professional development of this kind would serve not only to enhance teachers' grasp of the utility of such resources and develop their skills in crafting instruction, but also to provide a context for deepening professional dialogue about instruction and student learning.

Acknowledgments

Portions of the work presented in this chapter were supported by the Center for Learning Technologies in Urban Schools (LeTUS) under National Science Foundation Grant REC-9720383 and the WorldWatcher Curriculum Project under National Science Foundation Grant ESI-9720687. Additional work was supported by Center for the Study of Learning, Instruction, and Teacher Development under the K-12 Learning Consortium project (Atlanta Philanthropic Foundation). The views represented herein are those of the author and do not represent the views of the funding agencies. I wish to acknowledge the contributions and guidance of Daniel C. Edelson, James Pellegrino, and Susan Goldman, as well as the dedicated teachers who participated in the research.

Note

1. Although this study examined science instruction, the analysis is relevant to mathematics.

References

Ball, D. L. (1991). Research on teaching mathematics: Making subject-matter knowledge part of the equation. *Advances in Research on Teaching, 2*, 1–48.

Ball, D. L., & Cohen, D. K. (1996). Reform by the book: What is – or might be – the role of curriculum materials in teacher learning and instructional reform? *Educational Researcher, 25(9)*, 6–8, 14.

Ball, D. L., & Cohen, D. K. (1999). *Instruction, capacity, and improvement.* Philadelphia, PA: Consortium for Policy Research in Education, University of Pennsylvania (CPRE RR-43).

Barab, S. A., & Luehmann, A. L. (2003). Building sustainable science curriculum: Acknowledging and accommodating local adaptation. *Science Education, 87(4)*, 454–467.

Ben-Peretz, M. (1990). *The teacher–curriculum encounter: Freeing teachers from the tyranny of texts.* Albany, NY: State University of New York Press.

Brown, M. W. (2002). *Teaching by design: Understanding the intersection between teacher practice and the design of curricular innovations.* Unpublished doctoral dissertation, Northwestern University, Evanston, IL.

Brown, M. W., & Edelson, D. C. (1999). *A lab by any other name: Integrating traditional labs and computer-supported collaborative investigations in science classrooms.* Paper presented at the Computer Supported Collaborative Learning Meeting, Palo Alto, CA, December 12–15.

Brown, M. W., & Edelson, D. C. (2003). Teaching as design: Can we better understand the ways in which teachers use materials so we can better design materials to support changes in practice? Evanston, IL: Center for Learning Technologies in Urban Schools, Northwestern University (Available at: http://letus.org/PDF/teaching_as_design.pdf).

Brown, M. W., Pellegrino, J., Goldman, S., Nacu, D. C., Julian, K., Tarnoff, A., et al. (2004). *Adaptive instructional materials: Making the knowledge base on learning, instruction, and assessment usable for educational practice.* Paper presented at the Annual Meeting of the American Educational Research Association, San Diego, CA.

Burke, K. (1966). *Language as symbolic action: Essays on life, literature, and method.* Berkeley, CA: University of California Press.

Cohen, D. K. (1988a). Educational technology and school organization. In R. S. Nickerson & P. P. Zodhiates (Eds.), *Technology in education: Looking toward 2020* (pp. 231–264). Hillsdale, NJ: Erlbaum.

Cohen, D. K. (1988b). Teaching practice: Plus ca change ... In P. W. Jackson (Ed.), *Contributing to educational change: Perspectives on research and practice* (pp. 27–84). Berkeley, CA: McCutchan.

Cohen, D. K. (1990). A revolution in one classroom: The case of Mrs. Oublier. *Educational Evaluation and Policy Analysis, 12*, 327–345.

Cuban, L. (1992). Curriculum stability and change. In P. W. Jackson (Ed.), *Handbook of research on curriculum: A project of the American Educational Research Association* (pp. 216–247). New York, NY: Macmillan.

Cuban, L. (1993). The lure of curricular reform and its pitiful history. *Phi Delta Kappan, 75*(2), 182–185.

Davis, E. A., & Krajcik, J. S. (2005). Designing educative curriculum materials to promote teacher learning. *Educational Researcher, 34*(3), 3–14.

Davis, E. A., & Varma, K. (accepted). Supporting teachers in productive adaptation. In Y. Kali, M. C. Linn & J. E. Roseman (Eds.), *Designing coherent science education.* New York, NY: Teachers College Press.

Edelson, D. C. (2002). Design research: What we learn when we engage in design. *Journal of the Learning Sciences, 11*(1), 105–121.

Eisner, E. W. (1983). The art and craft of teaching. *Educational Leadership, 40*(4), 4–13.

Freeman, D. J., & Porter, A. C. (1989). Do textbooks dictate the content of mathematics instruction in elementary schools? *American Educational Research Journal, 26*(3), 403–421.

Gibson, J. J. (1977). The theory of affordances. In R. E. S. J. Bransford (Ed.), *Perceiving, acting, and knowing.* Hillsdale, NJ: Erlbaum Associates.

Goodman, N. (1976). *Languages of art: An approach to a theory of symbols* (2nd Edition). Indianapolis, IA: Hackett.

Grossman, P. (1990). *The making of a teacher: Teacher knowledge and teacher education.* New York, NY: Teachers College Press.

Herbel-Eisenmann, B. A. (2007). From intended curriculum to written curriculum: Examining the "voice" of a mathematics textbook. *Journal for Research in Mathematics Education, 38*(4), 344–369.

Hutchins, E. (1996). The social organization of distributed cognition. In L. Resnick, J. M. Levine & S. D. Teasley (Eds.), *Perspectives on socially shared cognition.* Washington, DC: American Psychological Association.

Jackson, P. (1986). *The practice of teaching.* New York, NY: Teachers College Press.

Lloyd, G. M. (1999). Two teachers' conceptions of a reform-oriented curriculum: Implications for mathematics teacher development. *Journal of Mathematics Teacher Education, 2*(3), 227–252.

Lloyd, G. M., & Wilson, M. (1998). Supporting innovation: The impact of a teacher's conceptions of functions on his implementation of a reform curriculum. *Journal for Research in Mathematics Education, 29*(3), 248–274.

Matese, G. (2005). *A cognitive framework to inform the design of professional development supporting teachers' classroom assessment of inquiry-based science.* Unpublished doctoral dissertation, Northwestern University, Evanston, IL.

Norman, D. A. (1988). *The design of everyday things.* New York, NY: Basic Books.

Norman, D. A. (1991). Cognitive artifacts. In J. Carroll (Ed.), *Designing interaction: Psychology at the human–computer interface.* Cambridge: Cambridge University Press.

Pea, R. D. (1985). Beyond amplification: Using the computer to reorganize mental functioning. *Educational Psychologist, 20,* 167–182.

Pea, R. D. (1993). Practices of distributed intelligence and designs for education. In G. Salomon (Ed.), *Distributed cognition* (pp. 47–87). New York, NY: Cambridge University Press.

Pea, R. D. (1994). Seeing what we build together: Distributed multimedia learning environments for transformative communications. *Journal of the Learning Sciences, 3*(3), 285–299.

Putnam, R. T., & Borko, H. (2000). What do new views of knowledge and thinking have to say about research on teacher learning? *Educational Researcher, 29*(1), 4–15.

Remillard, J. T. (1992). Teaching mathematics for understanding: A fifth-grade teacher's interpretation of policy. *Elementary School Journal, 93*(2), 179–193.

Remillard, J. T. (2000). Can curriculum materials support teachers' learning? Two fourth-grade teachers' use of a new mathematics text. *The Elementary School Journal, 100*(4), 331–350.

Remillard, J. T. (2005). Examining key concepts in research on teachers' use of mathematics curricula. *Review of Educational Research, 75*(2), 211–216.

Remillard, J. T., & Bryans, M. B. (2004). Teachers' orientations toward mathematics curriculum materials: Implications for teacher learning. *Journal of Research in Mathematics Education, 35*(5), 352–388.

Ryle, G. (1984). *The concept of mind* (Reprint [1st Edition, 1949]). Chicago, IL: University of Chicago Press.

Schneider, R., & Krajcik, J. (2002). Supporting science teacher learning: The role of educative curriculum materials. *Journal of Science Teacher Education, 13*(3), 221–245.

Shulman, L. S. (1986). Those who understand: Knowledge growth in teaching. *Educational Researcher, 15*(2), 4–14.

Smith, J. P. I. (1996). Efficacy and teaching mathematics by telling: A challenge for reform. *Journal of Research in Mathematics Education, 27*(4), 387–402.

Snyder, J., Bolin, F., & Zumwalt, K. (1992). Curriculum implementation. In P. W. Jackson (Ed.), *Handbook of research on curriculum: A project of the American Educational Research Association.* New York, NY: Macmillan Publishing Co.

Spillane, J. P. (1998). *Challenging instruction for "all students": Policy, practitioners, and practice* (No. WP-85–5). Evanston, IL: Institute for Policy Research, Northwestern University.

Spillane, J. P. (1999). External reform initiatives and teachers' efforts to reconstruct their practice: The mediating role of teachers' zones of enactment. *Journal of Curriculum Studies, 31*, 143–175.

Stein, M. K. (1996). Instructional tasks and the development of student capacity to think and reason: An analysis of the relationship between teaching and learning in a reform mathematics project. *Educational Research and Evaluation, 2*, 50–80.

Stein, M. K., Remillard, J. T., & Smith, M. S. (2007). How curriculum influences student learning. In J. F. K. Lester (Ed.), *Second handbook of research on mathematics teaching and learning* (pp. 319–370). Greenwich, CT: Information Age Publishing.

Stigler, J. W., & Hiebert, J. (1998). Teaching is a cultural activity. *American Educator, 22*(4), 4–11.

Stodolsky, S. S., & Grossman, P. L. (1995). The impact of subject matter on curricular activity: An analysis of five academic subjects. *American Educational Research Journal, 32*, 227–249.

Tarr, J. E., Reys, R. E., Reys, B. J., Chavez, O., Shih, J., & Osterlind, S. J. (2008). The impact of middle grades mathematics curricula on student achievement and the classroom learning environment. *Journal for Research in Mathematics Education*, in press.

Vygotsky, L. S. (1978). *Mind in society: The development of the higher psychological processes* (A. Kozulin, Trans.). Cambridge, MA: Harvard University Press.

Wartofsky, M. (1973). *Models.* Dordrecht: D. Reidel.

Wertsch, J. V. (1991). *Voices of the mind: A sociocultural approach to mediated action.* Cambridge, MA: Harvard University Press.

Wertsch, J. V. (1998). *Mind as action.* New York, NY: Oxford University Press.

Wiley, D. A. (2001). Connecting learning objects to instructional design theory: A definition a metaphor, and a taxonomy. In D. A. Wiley (Ed.), *The instructional use of learning objects* (pp. 3–24). Bloomington, IN: Association for Educational Communications and Technology.

Wilson, M., & Goldenberg, M. P. (1998). Some conceptions are difficult to change: One middle school mathematics teacher's struggle. *Journal of Mathematics Teacher Education, 1*(3), 269–293.

Wilson, M., & Lloyd, G. M. (2000). The challenge to share mathematical authority with students: High school teachers' experiences reforming classroom roles and activities through curriculum implementation. *Journal of Curriculum and Supervision, 15*, 146–169.

Wilson, S. M. (1990). A conflict of interests: The case of Mark Black. *Educational Evaluation and Policy Analysis, 12*(3), 293–310.

Wilson, S. M., & Berne, J. (1999). Teacher learning and the acquisition of professional knowledge: An examination of research on professional development. In A. Iran-Nejad & P. D. Pearson (Eds.), *Review of Research in Education* (Vol. 24, pp. 173–209). Washington, DC: American Educational Research Association.

3

The Role of Mathematics Curriculum Materials in Large-Scale Urban Reform

An Analysis of Demands and Opportunities for Teacher Learning

Mary Kay Stein and Gooyeon Kim

Mathematics curriculum materials have historically been viewed as a key vehicle for infusing new ideas about teaching and learning into practice in order to affect large-scale, instructional reform. Theoretically, curriculum materials are well-positioned to influence large numbers of teachers and classrooms. Educational institutions are set up to purchase and disseminate materials, and teachers are accustomed to using textbooks to guide instruction. Yet there is also evidence that curriculum program adoptions have had limited influence on teachers' beliefs and approaches to instruction (Ball & Cohen, 1996, 2002; Coburn, 2001; Collopy, 2003; Fullan & Pomfret, 1977; Stein, Grover, & Henningsen, 1996). Although it may be relatively easy to get curriculum materials to large numbers of teachers, it is much more difficult to assure that those materials are used and used well.

The challenge of getting curriculum materials implemented well is greatest when those materials are expected to take on the role of change agent – that is, when they are expected to facilitate a fundamental transformation of practice. Such is the case with the *Standards*-based materials[1] introduced in the mid- to late 1990s. Proponents of student-centered, active, and conceptually-based approaches to mathematics instruction hope that these materials will help teachers move beyond the algorithmically-based approaches shown to dominate current instructional practice in the United States (Stigler & Hiebert, 2004). Unfortunately, research has also illustrated the steep hurdles that teachers face as they attempt to use curriculum materials that are based on an approach to teaching and learning that differs from their experiences as teachers or learners (Ball, 1988; Stein, Grover, & Henningsen, 1996).

Despite these obstacles, many large and mid-sized urban districts have adopted *Standards*-based materials with the expectation that teachers' use of these materials will engender large-scale change in practice (and increased levels of student achievement). This wide-scale program adoption has led to the need to educate large numbers of teachers simultaneously, a central challenge of scaling up any ambitious instructional reform. Given the current climate of accountability and the impatience of governing entities, the challenge is not only to educate a large number of teachers, but also to do so quickly, showing results on high-stakes achievement tests within a year or two (Hightower et al., 2002; Hubbard et al., 2006).

Districts have taken on this challenge primarily by providing unprecedented levels of professional development in the forms of workshops and coaching. Less commonly acknowledged is the role that the curriculum materials themselves might play in the mediation of large-scale teacher learning. Although districts cannot guarantee the quality of coaches (especially when large numbers must be hired and trained in a short amount of time) or the content of the professional development (much of which occurs locally in schools or regions), they can control the type of curriculum materials that are placed into the hands of teachers.

Assuming that *Standards*-based curriculum programs are desired, what features should leaders attend to when selecting them? *Standards*-based curriculum programs usually are viewed as more alike than different (Remillard, 2005), with adoption decisions typically framed as a choice between *Standards*-based versus conventional curricula. We seek to identify how *Standards*-based curriculum programs might differ from one another in ways that matter for large-scale teacher change. We note the fact that schools and districts differ along a variety of dimensions, including (a) the kinds of students and teachers who comprise them, (b) the extent to which professional communities among teachers flourish within them, and (c) the amount and kind of professional development they offer. For example, certain schools serve disproportionately large numbers of low-income students with inexperienced, transient faculty; others have stable, experienced teaching faculty (Darling-Hammond, 2004). Some schools have reputations as being collegial while others are characterized by distrust (Bryk & Schneider, 2002). Some districts are known for their investment in professional development while others leave teachers to fend for themselves (McLaughlin & Oberman, 1996).

The purpose of this chapter is to identify and illustrate a framework for analyzing curriculum materials that takes into account these varying organizational characteristics – characteristics that, we argue, create different starting points and different conditions for both teacher and student learning from curriculum materials. Analyses of teacher–curriculum material relationships typically assume that teachers interact with curriculum materials as individuals, independent of the school or district contexts in which they work. We view the primary contribution of this chapter as the identification of an analytical framework for understanding the relationship between teachers *as situated in their schools and districts* and curriculum materials. Unpacking and illustrating this relationship, in turn, allows us to draw out implications for curriculum design that provide opportunities for teacher learning as shaped by organizational conditions. (McClain et al., in Chapter 4 of this volume, also examine the role the local context plays in teachers' interactions with curriculum resources.)

We begin with an overview of how we conceptualize curriculum materials as tools for teacher learning, and the organizational conditions within which teacher learning unfolds. Next we identify a framework for analyzing how curriculum programs vary – a framework that comprises a set of dimensions that we propose matter for large-scale teacher learning. We then illustrate the framework with an analysis of two *Standards*-based curriculum programs: *Everyday Mathematics* (University of Chicago School Mathematics Project, 2004) and *Investigations in Number, Data, and Space* ("*Investigations*"; TERC, 1998). In the final section, we outline a set of conjectures for how and under what organizational conditions these two programs might be expected to support large-scale change in teachers' practice.[2]

Curriculum Materials as Supports for Large-Scale Teacher Learning

Our analysis of how curriculum materials might mediate large-scale teacher change draws on particular conceptualizations with respect to (a) how teachers interact with curriculum materials, and (b) how various organizational conditions shape these interactions.

Teacher–Curriculum Material Interactions

Researchers have conceptualized the manner in which teachers use curriculum materials in a variety of ways (Remillard, 2005). Some researchers assume that the overall objective is to implement curriculum materials with fidelity, and thus conceptualize curriculum material use as following them (e.g., Freeman & Porter, 1989). Others view curriculum materials as subject to interpretation, and hence examine different teachers' styles of interpretation (e.g., Ben-Peretz, 1990). We view the teacher–text relationship in yet a third way, as one that includes active participation by *both* teacher and text, referred to by Remillard as teachers "participating with" text. This view attends to particular features of the text as well as teachers' interpretation of those features. Building on the concept of "mediated action," developed by Wertsch (1998) and applied to teachers' use of curriculum materials by Brown (see Chapter 2 of this volume), we assume that teachers and curriculum materials are engaged in a dynamic interrelationship in which each participant (teacher and text) shapes the other; together they shape instruction.

Central to the notion of mediated action is the assumption that artifacts afford and constrain activity in particular ways (Gibson, 1979). They enable or afford activity by providing capacities not readily available to the user; they constrain activity by constricting or narrowing one's frame of perception, thereby reducing what is attended to. When considered as artifacts that shape activity, the influence of curriculum materials on *both* students and teachers must be examined. Curriculum materials cue certain ways of thinking for students (e.g., solving a problem using a particular strategy); students' ways of thinking, in turn, influence teachers (e.g., teachers react to the student's solution strategy). Central to our analyses is the examination of the materials' constraints and affordances on *both* students and teachers and the relationships between them.

Organizational Conditions that Shape Teacher–Curriculum Material Interactions

The ways in which teachers interact with various curriculum features are shaped by a range of organizational characteristics. We focus on two characteristics that have played a prominent role in analyses of innovation in the private sector (as well as in education, although under different labels): human and social capital.

In the economics of education, *human capital* is defined as the expertise, experience, and preparedness of individuals for the roles they are expected to perform (Becker, 1964). A human-capital approach to understanding teacher change mediated by curriculum materials focuses on the capacity of teachers to learn from and implement given curriculum programs. We know from prior research that the ways in which teachers interact with curriculum materials are shaped by characteristics of teachers themselves, such as their knowledge, beliefs, and experiences (Collopy, 2003; Lloyd, 1999; Remillard, 1999; Schneider & Krajcik, 2002). Teachers who have deep knowledge of mathematics or who have experience with a particular set of curriculum materials (see Chapter 22 of this volume) will react to materials differently than will less knowledgeable or experienced teachers.

Although mathematics educators are accustomed to thinking about human capital as an individual attribute, it also can be viewed as an attribute of an organization (Coleman, 1988). In a given organizational unit (grade-level, school), teacher human capital can be characterized as limited (most teachers have a low degree of experience or capability), high (most teachers have a high degree of experience or capability), or variable. At the organizational level, human capital is shaped by the teacher training institutions that supply teachers to schools, professional development offerings available to teachers, and the relative stability or transience of the faculty.

Social capital refers to "the aggregate of the actual and potential resources which are linked to possession of a durable network of more or less institutionalized relationships of mutual acquaintance or recognition" (Bourdieu, 1985, p. 248). These resources are generally viewed as having positive consequences for individuals and for the community (Portes, 1998). From the perspective of social capital theory, teachers are members of social networks; features of these networks can create a normative environment that enables instructional improvement. In most education research, the influence of social factors on teacher change has been subsumed under the constructs of teacher professional community (Elmore, Peterson, & McCarthy, 1996; Louis & Marks, 1998; Louis, Marks, & Kruse, 1996; McLaughlin & Talbert, 2001) and communities of practice (Franke & Kazemi, 2001; Gallucci, 2003; Stein, Silver, & Smith, 1998). Recently some scholars have begun to apply the concept of social capital as a lens through which to view how social factors shape instructional innovation (Frank, Zhao, & Borman, 2004; Smylie & Evans, 2006; Smylie & Hart, 1999).

Prior research suggests three features of social relationships that influence implementation of innovations: structure (the quality and configuration of ties within a network), social trust (the extent to which members of networks have faith in and depend on one another), and the presence of expertise in the network (Adler & Kwon, 2002). The quality and configuration of ties are important because they create opportunities for social capital transactions (Burt, 1992). Social trust is important because it motivates teachers to share information (Adler & Kwon) and enables the meaningful coordination of action (Bryk & Schneider, 2002). Studies of where expertise is located within particular networks of teachers are important because the strategic lodging of expertise can be used as a mechanism to employ the human capital of some members of a social group in the development of the human capital of others (Smylie & Hart, 1999). Networks comprised entirely of struggling first-year teachers have less potential for productive relationships than networks in which at least one competent, experienced teacher resides (Frank, Zhao, & Borman, 2004).

Our approach to studying the role of curriculum programs in large-scale teacher learning involves examining the interactions between (a) the affordances and constraints of features of the materials, and (b) the levels and kinds of human and social capital present or to-be-developed in schools or districts.

General Approach to Analysis of Curriculum Materials

Our study also builds on the work of researchers who have investigated the role of curriculum materials in teacher learning and instructional reform. Davis and Krajcik (2005) use the term "educative" to refer to K-12 curriculum materials that are intended to promote teacher learning in addition to student learning. In order to stimulate a theoretical discussion about the educative role for curriculum materials, they produced a set of design heuristics for what educative curriculum materials might look like. As described below, we have extended their work to include an explicit focus on the role of curriculum materials in teacher learning under conditions of large-scale reform.

Following Davis and Krajcik (2005), we distinguish the base curriculum materials from those designed for direct consumption by teachers. We use the term "base programs" to refer to that portion of the materials that is directly pitched to students and their learning, primarily the tasks with which students are asked to engage – be they sets of exercises or open-ended investigations. The term "teacher materials," on the other hand, refers to the parts intended to guide teachers as they use the materials.

Analyses of curriculum materials typically focus on the base programs, primarily attending to the nature of student activities and the potential for student learning. Only recently have researchers begun to focus on the teacher portion of these programs in an attempt to theorize the role that curriculum materials might play in fostering *teacher* learning (Davis & Krajcik, 2005).

Our analyses focus on both the base program and the teacher materials. We examined the base program because the nature of the tasks with which students engage afford and constrain the nature of student thinking (Doyle, 1983); in turn, the level and kind of student thinking expected influence the demands placed on teacher learning. We examined the teacher materials because they comprise the opportunities for teacher learning. Specifically, teacher materials can treat the teacher as an instrument for the unaltered delivery of the curriculum (speaking through the teacher) or can speak directly to the teacher as a professional user of the materials who necessarily influences what, how, and when curricular ideas are presented (Remillard, 1999).

Base Program

Base programs are comprised primarily of instructional tasks for students. We examined these materials for the characteristics of instructional tasks found in individual lessons and for how those tasks were organized and sequenced across the grade levels. These tasks typically differ with respect to the level of cognitive demand they place on students (Stein et al., 1996). Many tasks in conventional textbooks ask students to demonstrate procedures in a routinized way, and hence place low-level, mostly proceduralized demands on student learning. Other tasks, including the majority of those found in *Standards*-based programs, ask students to make conceptual connections and to think and reason in sustained and thoughtful ways.

Previous research has shown that instructional tasks that place high-level cognitive demands on students are also the most challenging for teachers to implement well (Stein et al., 1996). First, these tasks tend to be conceptually demanding for teachers, many of whom have had limited opportunities to learn mathematics in non-procedural ways. Second, classroom lessons in which students engage with high-level tasks are difficult to orchestrate. In contrast to conventional mathematics lessons, during which teachers typically demonstrate a procedure and then observe students as they practice the same procedure on a set of similar problems, lessons comprised of high-level tasks tend to make demands on students to solve problems and offer approaches or solutions. Lessons like these place demands on a teacher's capacity to reference the conceptual territory in which the problem is located, listen to and understand students' ways of solving the problem, and help them align their thinking with formal knowledge of the discipline.

Standards-based curriculum materials are challenging for teachers because they include many high-level tasks. Further, our previous work also demonstrates that high-level tasks differ from one another. Some high-level tasks consist of open-ended problems with limited guidance for students on how to solve them. We categorize these tasks as *doing mathematics* (hereafter referred to as DM tasks). DM tasks require complex, non-routine thinking and reasoning such as making and testing conjectures, framing problems, representing relationships, and looking for patterns. In practice, DM tasks often prompt some level of student anxiety and uncertainty due to the unpredictable nature of the solution process that is required.

Other high-level tasks focus students' attention on the use of procedures for the purpose of deepening students' understanding of mathematical concepts and ideas. We categorize these tasks as *procedures with connections*, because the procedural work is designed to illuminate connections to underlying concepts, meaning, or understanding (hereafter referred to as PWC tasks). These tasks offer more structure than DM tasks by suggesting pathways or procedures to follow (either explicitly or implicitly), but not mindlessly. PWC tasks are designed to encourage students to bump into and grapple with important conceptual ideas.[3]

Starting with our assumption that artifacts shape human activity, we argue that these two kinds of instructional tasks afford and constrain students' actions and thinking in different ways, placing different demands on teachers. We have found that DM tasks tend to open up the classroom discourse space in ways that can be difficult for teachers to manage (Ball, 2001; Leinhardt & Steele, 2005; Schoenfeld, 1998; Sherin, 2002). Because a solution pathway is not specified, students approach these tasks in unique and sometimes unanticipated ways. Teachers must not only strive to understand how students are making sense of the problem, but also begin to align students' disparate ideas and approaches with canonical understandings in mathematics.

PWC tasks, on the other hand, tend to channel the route of student thinking along a finite number of pathways. Because the solution route is constrained, the possible space of the classroom discourse is expected to be more bounded and predictable than with DM tasks. Hence, we expect the learning demands placed on teachers by PWC tasks to be lower than DM tasks.

A second feature of the base program that we propose influences demands on teacher learning is how the to-be-learned material is organized and sequenced. In *integral* curriculum programs, knowledge and skills to be learned by students are tightly woven into the fabric of the curriculum, are not easily separated out, and must be taught in a specified sequence over the years. In contrast, *modular* approaches to structuring curriculum materials generally have identifiable and easily articulated student outcomes for each segment that are independent of other segments. Modular programs can be taught in variable sequences (within a given grade level or sometimes across two consecutive grades). (See Schilling, 2000, and Sanchez, 1995, for discussion of modularity and integrality in the business sector.)

Integral curriculum materials are often referred to as spiral in structure. In spiral curriculum materials, the emphasis is placed on the manner in which concepts and skills are introduced, developed, and mastered over a sequence of units and years, rather than in one unit or grade level. Anecdotally, we know that a spiral approach to curriculum structure produces dissonance in teachers who are accustomed to teaching for mastery and are reluctant to move on, even when assured the concept will be revisited at a later point. A teacher's decision to move on or re-teach a concept may depend on her assessment of the students' next teacher. If she respects that teacher's competence and trusts his allegiance to the curriculum program, and if she is confident that she will not be judged harshly if her students have not mastered a given concept, she will be more willing to embrace the spiral approach than if she does not. Thus, we propose that successful implementation of spiral or integral curriculum designs demands social trust among colleagues centered on commitment to use of the curriculum program – important elements of social capital discussed earlier.

In summary, *Standards*-based curriculum programs place significant learning demands on teachers. DM and PWC tasks, however, differ in their demands. PWC tasks constrain the space of interactive discourse enough to make instruction significantly less complex than with DM tasks. Further, we propose that integral curriculum materials will place greater demands on social trust than will modular materials.

Teacher Materials

The demands that curriculum materials place on teacher learning need to be examined with the opportunities for teacher learning that the materials provide. Survey research conducted alongside this curriculum material analysis confirmed that in two large urban districts using them, the vast majority of teachers did not consult materials that appeared in books separate from their daily guides. Thus, we considered only the information designed for teachers that appears in the guide books and in close proximity to daily lessons for students.

Ball and Cohen (1996) have identified – and Davis and Krajcik (2005) have elaborated – ways in which curriculum materials can be designed to be educative for teachers. Here we take up the design heuristics of (a) making visible developers' rationales for including particular tasks in terms of the mathematical understandings to be gained, and (b) helping teachers learn how to anticipate what learners may think about or do in response to instructional activities. We conjecture that materials that arm teachers with an understanding of the mathematical significance of the tasks that appear within them, as well as ideas about how students might respond to those tasks, are more likely to lead to successful enactments in the classroom than materials that do not provide these supports.

MAKING VISIBLE DEVELOPERS' RATIONALES

Curriculum developers purposefully design tasks that direct students into particular situations that they believe will help them learn a skill or achieve insight into some aspect of mathematics. The rationales that underlie their designs are often implicit. Remillard (2000) notes that teachers' manuals typically offer "steps to follow, problems to give, actual questions to ask, and answers to expect" (p. 347), without engaging teachers in the rationales, assumptions, or agendas that undergird these actions. In doing so, they leave the teacher hostage to a set of actions without the knowledge needed to select and adapt tasks. When the developers talk directly to teachers about the mathematical and pedagogical ideas underlying these tasks – thereby making their agendas and perspectives accessible – we refer to the curriculum materials as *transparent*.

Davis and Krajcik (2005) have noted yet another reason for explicating what they call "design rationales" for teachers. Such rationales help teachers to see connections among suggested activities in the program, their own understanding of mathematics, and what they believe is important to learn, thereby moving them away from teaching a list of unconnected, isolated topics and toward teaching mathematical concepts and ideas.

Based on years of cognitive science research, mathematics educators are keenly aware that mathematical understanding rests upon students' capacities to connect new information to their existing cognitive networks (Hiebert & Carpenter, 1992). A hallmark of the reform efforts inspired by the *Standards* (NCTM, 1989) is instructional approaches that seek to build on student thinking and ways of understanding their unguided efforts to solve novel problems. Research has documented challenges that many teachers face when they try to conduct lessons that productively build on student-designed solution strategies (e.g., Ball, 2001; Leinhardt & Steele, 2005; Schoenfeld, 1998; Sherin, 2002). For example, teachers must make rapid online assessments of students' understandings, compare them with the desired response, and then fashion a response that will simultaneously help move both the responding student and the rest of the class towards an increased understanding of the mathematics in question.

Research suggests that effective teachers prepare for lessons by actively envisioning how students might approach the selected tasks mathematically (e.g., Fernandez & Yoshida, 2004; Schoenfeld, 1998; Smith, 1996; Stigler & Hiebert, 1999). This preparation involves much more than simply evaluating whether a task will be at the right level of difficulty or of sufficient interest to students, and goes beyond considering whether students are likely to get the "right answer." Anticipating students' responses involves developing considered expectations about how students might interpret a problem, the array of strategies – both correct and incorrect – they might use to tackle it, and how those strategies and interpretations might relate to the mathematical concepts, procedures, and practices that the teacher would like her students to learn (Schoenfeld, 1998; Yoshida, as cited in Stigler & Hiebert, 1999). Curriculum materials can support teachers' capacity to anticipate student responses by including details on how students typically respond to such problems, sometimes with actual examples of student work, as is done in many Japanese programs (Fernandez & Yoshida, 2004; Schoenfeld, 1998; Stigler & Hiebert, 1999).

Comparative Analysis of Curriculum Materials

Selection of Curriculum Programs

We selected two widely-used elementary programs, *Everyday Mathematics* (EM) and *Investigations in Number, Data, and Space* (INV), for analysis. These two programs were selected because they possess strategic similarities and differences. They are both *Standards*-based and have been adopted as the district-sanctioned curriculum programs by urban districts in the past decade. Both are designed to broaden the scope of topics beyond arithmetic and contain instructional tasks that aim to develop students' conceptual understanding. Further, both place emphasis on the strategies that students use to find answers (not just the correctness of the answer) and the benefits to be gained by the use of multiple representations.

Despite these similarities, the two programs differ in a number of ways that matter for large-scale teacher change. In EM, the central concepts of elementary mathematics are organized into a continually rising spiral; students are sequentially exposed to extensions and greater depth of each concept as they revisit them time and time again throughout the elementary grades. Facets of to-be-learned ideas are tightly woven into the fabric of the program. Developers recommend that adopters use the materials in a comprehensive and controlled sequence to assure that students will be exposed to all of the requisite components. Thus we consider it an example of an integral curriculum program. In INV, on the other hand, the central ideas are organized into conceptual themes or mathematical topics that are packaged as individual booklets or modules. Each module contains units that house individual lessons. Unlike the spirals of *Everyday Mathematics*, the modules of *Investigations* are less susceptible to difference in ordering or coverage. Developers of INV have touted its modularity as supportive to an implementation style preferred by many districts: slow and gradual. Thus, we classified it as a modular program.

Selection of Lessons

We randomly selected lessons/sessions[4] from each grade level (one through five) in each program for the study. There were 10–12 units in each grade level of EM; each unit consists of 7–15 lessons. We analyzed one randomly selected lesson in each unit at each grade level for a total of 57 lessons. There were 6–11 separate unit books for each grade level in INV. We randomly selected one session from each unit book, leading to a sample of 44 sessions from this curriculum program. For each selected lesson, we assembled the materials that most closely represented what teachers are likely to consult when preparing to teach the lesson – the Teachers' Lesson Guide for EM and the unit books for INV.

Coding

First, the main instructional task in each lesson[5] was assigned a code based on the level of cognitive demand it represented for student learning. Drawing on prior research (Stein et al., 1996), we coded each task, as written, as focusing on (a) *memorization* and reproducing previously learned facts, rules, or definitions (M), (b) the use of *procedures without connection* to concepts, meaning or understanding (PNC), (c) the use of *procedures with connection* to concepts, meaning or understanding (PWC), or (d) *doing mathematics* by engaging in thinking, reasoning, problem solving, justifying, and communicating about mathematics (DM). The codes of M and PNC represent low-level tasks; DM and the PCW represent high-level tasks.

Second, we examined the teacher materials for transparency. We defined transparency as the visibility of the curriculum developers' rationales for specific instructional tasks or particular learning pathways found in the base curriculum materials. Transparent materials contain explanations for why a particular task or route through a teaching-and-learning territory was selected, including how that task or route might lead to students' understanding of worthwhile mathematical processes and ideas. When the materials provided the developers' reasons for the tasks or an explanation of the mathematical ideas related to the task, the lesson was identified as transparent. When such reasons were not included, we identified the lesson as not transparent.

Finally, the material specifically written for teachers in each lesson was also examined to determine whether it prompted the teacher to anticipate how students might approach tasks. Such prompting included examples of actual student work, such as students' drawings, invented strategies, or representations. It could also include information about ways in which students might interpret or approach tasks, the difficulties or confusions they might encounter, or students' possible reactions to particular mathematical tasks. Entries that were not counted as prompting teachers to anticipate student thinking included the provision of "correct answers" or hypothetical student responses with no elaboration of the significance of those responses in the context of the overall goal of the lesson.

Of the above lessons, 21 percent were coded independently by the two authors. The coders agreed on the cognitive demand of 76 percent of the instructional tasks, 81 percent of the codes on transparency, and 92 percent of the codes on support for the anticipation of student thinking. Disagreements were discussed and a consensus code was reached.

Findings of Analysis

Here we provide an overview of the findings about the cognitive demand of the tasks. As shown in Table 3.1, the vast majority of the sampled tasks from both programs were high-level: 91 percent of the EM tasks were high-level whereas virtually 100 percent of the INV tasks were high-level. Within the category of high-level, however, there were distinct differences between the two programs. The majority of tasks in INV (89 percent) were DM tasks, whereas the majority of tasks in EM (79 percent) were PWC tasks.

There were differences between the two programs in terms of the extent to which the curriculum developers explicated the purpose or rationale for each

Table 3.1 Cognitive Demand of Instructional Tasks in *Everyday Mathematics* and *Investigations*

	Everyday Mathematics (%)	Investigations (%)
Memorization	7 (4/57)	0
Use of procedures *without* connection	2 (1/57)	0
Use of procedures *without* connection	79 (45/57)	11 (5/44)
Doing mathematics	12 (7/57)	89 (39/44)

lesson. INV lessons were judged to be 80 percent transparent (35 out of 44) with respect to why a particular instructional activity was designed and how it represented important and worthwhile mathematics. Throughout the descriptions of the activities, the authors provided explanations for various design decisions, making reference to important mathematical ideas and particular needs of students. In contrast, 21 percent of EM lessons (12 out of 57) were judged to be transparent. The typical EM lesson tended to tell teachers *what* to do, but not *why* they were doing it.

Finally, there were differences between the two programs in the extent to which they provided teachers with support in anticipating students' thinking. Of the INV lessons, 91 percent (40 out of 44) incorporated student responses, student work, examples of possible students' difficulties or confusions, students' strategies for solving problems, or explanations of how students might make sense of mathematical ideas and interpret problems. In contrast, 30 percent (17 out of 57) EM lessons included examples of student work or thinking. Typically, student responses were very general and did not include illustrations of actual student work or explanations of the kind of thinking students might engage in.

Discussion

In this section, we interpret the above findings in terms of their implications for teacher learning in general and large-scale teacher learning in particular. We begin with a synthesis of differences between features of EM and INV and how these differences shape opportunities for teachers to learn. Then, we offer conjectures about how each curriculum program might interact with different levels of human and social capital.

The Curriculum Materials

These two *Standards*-based programs were very different along two primary dimensions: demands on teacher learning, and opportunities for teacher learning. The PWC tasks, which dominate EM, tend to be less demanding than DM tasks for teachers to implement. At the same time, EM provided fewer opportunities for teachers to learn about expected student responses or the mathematical importance of these tasks. Although more demanding of teachers, the DM tasks in INV were accompanied by greater support for teachers to anticipate student responses and to situate the tasks within important and worthwhile mathematics. In essence, EM and INV exhibit consistency within themselves in that their base programs and teacher materials can be viewed as aligned. For example, if the PWC tasks in EM constrain the pathway of student learning, the teacher materials may not need to provide examples of student responses; PWC tasks are designed to place the engaged students into a bounded cognitive space within which they will confront the to-be-learned concepts. If, on the other hand, the DM tasks of INV lead students into less well-marked territory, teachers will need to be equipped with a map of the terrain and typical routes students might take through that territory.

With this difference in mind, Figure 3.1 illustrates the assumed location of student learning within the teacher–curriculum materials relationships in these

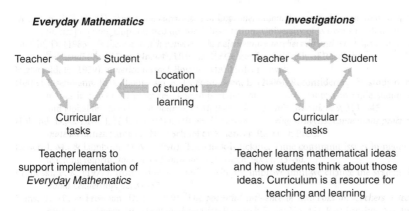

Figure 3.1 Role of curriculum materials in student learning.

two programs. As shown on the left side of the figure, the design of EM locates student learning primarily in the interaction between curricular tasks and students. In this view, the role of the teacher is to engage students with the tasks and keep them on track. The teacher materials, rather than providing information on how students might think about the task or what important mathematics is contained in the task, focus primarily on guiding teachers' actions (what Remillard [1999] called talking *through* the teacher). Although the teacher materials may offer specific guidance, the details are procedural in nature, focusing on how to make activities easier or harder, how to find or create manipulatives, and how to assure that students use them properly. The implicit message is that a relatively complete image of practice is captured in the curriculum materials, and that the closer students stay to the prescribed actions, the more successful the lesson will be.

As illustrated on the right side of Figure 3.1, the design of INV locates student learning primarily in the interaction between teachers and students. The role of the teacher is to listen to and observe students closely and to provoke advances in their thinking by asking good questions and exposing them to just-right tasks. In addition to outlining what teachers should do, the materials suggest how they might think about the mathematics contained in the tasks and how they might observe students as they work on them, including what to look for and how to interpret what they observe. This approach to guiding teachers suggests that the curriculum materials do not contain a complete image of classroom practice but rather are a resource for teaching and learning. (Remillard [1999] referred to this approach to curriculum design as talking *to* the teacher.)

In EM, most of the opportunities for teacher learning involve learning to implement the contents of the curriculum guide. Although not trivial, this is the kind of learning to which teachers are accustomed. It provides less challenge to teachers' views of mathematical knowledge, how students come to understand mathematics, or their roles as teachers in that process. In INV, the opportunities for teacher learning consist of learning how students think about mathematics and how various tasks tap into and represent important mathematical ideas. Most teachers are not accustomed to this type of learning; nor are they accustomed to their new classroom role. Rather than viewing teaching as transmitting the content in the text, teachers are asked to view teaching as assisting student learning, with curriculum materials as a tool for – not the determinant of – this process.

Brown (see Chapter 2 of this volume) uses the terms *resource-* and *procedure-centric* to describe the core organizing principles of curriculum materials. A resource-centric approach to the design of teacher materials (INV) emphasizes the key building blocks of a lesson and tries to make visible the pedagogical affordances of such building blocks. A procedure-centric approach focuses on the actions involved in carrying out the lesson (EM).

Interactions Between Curriculum Materials and Organizational Features

The above analyses point to the role of curriculum materials in student and teacher learning absent the organizational conditions under which they study and work. This is the manner in which most analyses of instructional reform have been carried out. We now consider the implications of our analyses for the levels of human and social capital that either exist or can be developed in organizations.

Our earlier review suggests that the challenges of large-scale teacher change vary depending on the aggregate levels of teacher human and social capital represented in schools and districts. Given the above analysis, it is tempting to propose that organizations characterized by low or variable human capital in their teaching force would be better served by adopting procedure-centric curriculum programs. First, the instructional tasks are less complex to learn to implement well because of the manner in which they constrain student activity. Second, if much of the architecture needed to spur student learning is indeed embedded in the design of the tasks (and therefore can occur between students and the curriculum materials), the need for in-depth teacher training would be lessened, and perhaps the effects of teacher transience would be less problematic. If the teacher materials are sufficiently robust to assist teachers in keeping student learning on track, then it would appear that the adoption of a procedure-centric program would be an effective way to achieve large-scale change in practice.

One might be particularly predisposed to argue for the adoption of procedure-centric curriculum programs in organizations that are experiencing the need for rapid gains in student achievement or that are plagued by high teacher turnover, low expectations for students, and a disproportionate number of inexperienced teachers. Procedure-centric curriculum materials (like EM) might provide a way to maintain the goal of conceptual learning for students. Instead of accomplishing this goal through the long-term development of teachers, it invests in the immediate learning of today's students. Although foregoing an investment in teacher development, this approach acknowledges the conditions on the ground in many urban schools and seeks to provide educative experiences for students.

Despite the logic of the above argument, we offer several caveats. The lack of opportunities in the teacher materials for teachers to learn how students might respond or the mathematical importance of the tasks may have ramifications for how capably teachers can guide students' engagement with the tasks in the curriculum materials. Just as students need connection to meaning in order to perform well under situations of uncertainty, so do teachers. A teacher who follows a set of activities for which the rationale or purpose is not apparent can be viewed as acting just as mechanically as a student who follows an algorithmic procedure without connecting it to underlying concepts. When students experience procedures in this way they become prisoners of them, not understanding when and how to apply them in novel situations or how to respond when they fail them (Carpenter, Hiebert, & Moser, 1983; Schoenfeld, 1985).

Similarly, teachers who follow activities without understanding their underlying purpose may have difficulty when those activities do not go according to plan. Regardless of how well designed the activities are and how clearly the learning pathways have been illuminated, curriculum developers cannot anticipate every student interpretation or response to an instructional task. A well-marked route through the mathematical territory is of little help if students are unable to follow it and if the teacher does not understand why that particular route was blazed or to what destination it is leading. When curriculum materials are not transparent, teachers can have difficulty redirecting students who fall off the expected learning route; in such cases, teachers' on-the-spot decisions about how to guide them back to the path can be hampered by limited understanding of the underlying purpose of the lesson. Indeed, preliminary analyses of the implementation of a procedure-centric, low-transparency curriculum program as part of an urban elementary mathematics reform suggests that teachers often enacted the program in ways that departed from the intentions of the designers (Stein, Kim, & Seeley, 2006).

A second caveat concerns the level of social capital needed to support effective implementation of integral curriculum programs (such as EM). As noted earlier, the spiral of the EM program places more demands on social trust and shared norms than do modular programs (such as INV). In schools characterized by teacher transience, however, trust among teachers may be in short supply, thereby leading individual teachers to take an entrepreneurial approach to what and how they teach as opposed to committing their allegiance to a common curriculum. When teachers pick and choose what they teach from a spiral, integral program, students are exposed to a patchwork view of the mathematical terrain rather than an integrated one.

Resource-centric curriculum materials (such as INV) might be a better fit for situations in which teacher human capital or teacher stability is high, and some teachers are capable and others have the motivation and opportunity to learn. Although DM tasks are difficult to implement, the curriculum materials can help teachers prepare to work with students around them. The adoption of resource-centric curriculum materials would represent a long-term investment in teachers, an investment that makes the most sense in schools characterized by low teacher transience. Appropriate opportunities for teacher learning would involve more than familiarization with the materials. Rather, they would need to include the development of increased understanding of the mathematical ideas that lie at the heart of the tasks, how students might think about those ideas, and how to bring the two into closer contact with one another.

Nevertheless, leaders who disregard the need for social capital among teachers who are implementing challenging curriculum programs, such as INV, do so at a risk. The depth of learning required of teachers is intense; research suggests that complex learning is best facilitated over time, within group situations characterized by asymmetries of expertise and opportunities to learn from more capable others (Grossman, Weinberg, & Woolworth, 2001; Stein & Brown, 1997). In social capital terms, the requirements are for strategic embedding of expertise into networks of teachers such that each teacher has someone that he or she can go to for help with lessons. The need for strategically embedded expertise does not diminish the need for opportunities provided by network ties and social trust – the other two features of social capital. Without the opportunity to interact, or motivation on the part of the experts to share their knowledge, teacher learning will not occur.

Implications

Our aim in this chapter has been to offer a new approach to analysis of curriculum materials. Rather than asking which program is better, we ask: which program is best suited to which conditions? Alternatively, what human and social capital needs must be attended to if a leader adopts a particular curriculum program? Although research on mathematics teaching has always had notions of teacher human capital front and center, the strategic arrangement of human capital in organizations and the levels of social trust needed to coordinate teacher learning have not been foregrounded. By surfacing these human- and social-capital related characteristics of organizations and proposing ways in which they interact with features of *Standards*-based curriculum materials, we provide not only a new framework for analyzing curriculum materials but also an alternative logic for describing districts and schools with respect to their capacity to support curriculum-embedded learning of teachers as well as students.

Acknowledgments

The work herein was supported from a grant from the National Science Foundation (IERI Grant REC-0228343). The content or opinions expressed herein do not necessarily reflect the views of the National Science Foundation or any other agency of the United States Government. An earlier version of this chapter was presented at the Annual Meeting of the American Educational Research Association, April 2006, San Francisco.

Notes

1. We use "*Standards*-based" curriculum materials to refer to materials that were designed to align with the *Standards* (National Council of Teachers of Mathematics [NCTM], 1989).
2. This study is one of a set of studies being conducted under the auspices of the Scaling Up Mathematics project. Forthcoming papers will present empirical findings regarding the extent to which our predictions hold up across teachers and schools in two urban districts.
3. See Stein, Smith, Henningsen, & Silver (2000) for examples and hallmarks of DM and PWC tasks.
4. In *Investigations*, lessons are called "sessions."
5. In EM, the main instructional task was identified as Part 1 of a three-part lesson. In INV, the main instructional task was identified as Session 1; when several activities comprised Session 1, coders combined those activities that were mathematically connected into one task and coded the task(s) that comprised the major share of the lesson.

References

Adler, P. S., & Kwon, S. (2002). Social capital: Prospects for a new concept. *Academy of Management Review, 27*(1), 17–40.

Ball, D. L. (1988). Unlearning to teach mathematics. *For the Learning of Mathematics, 8*(1), 40–48.

Ball, D. L. (2001). Teaching with respect to mathematics and students. In T. Wood, B. S. Nelson, & J. Warfield (Eds.), *Beyond classical pedagogy: Teaching elementary school mathematics* (pp. 11–22). Mahwah, NJ: Erlbaum.

Ball, D. L., & Cohen, D. K. (1996). Reform by the book: What is – or might be – the role of curriculum materials in teacher learning and instructional reform? *Educational Researcher, 25*(9), 6–8.

Ball, D. L., & Cohen, D. K. (2002). *Instructional improvement and the problem of scale.* Unpublished manuscript, University of Michigan.

Becker, G. S. (1964). *Human capital.* National Bureau of Economic Research. New York, NY: Columbia University Press.

Ben-Peretz, M. (1990). *The teacher–curriculum encounter: Freeing teachers from the tyranny of texts.* Albany, NY: SUNY Press.

Bourdieu, P. (1985). The forms of capital. In J. G. Richardson (Ed.), *Handbook of theory and research for the sociology of education* (pp. 241–258). New York, NY: Greenwood.

Bryk, A. S., & Schneider, B. L. (2002). *Trust in schools: A core resource for improvement.* New York, NY: Russell Sage Foundation.

Burt, R. S. (1992). *Structural holes: The social structure of competition.* Cambridge, MA: Harvard Press.

Carpenter, T., Hiebert, J., & Moser, J. (1983). The effect of instruction on children's solutions of addition and subtraction work problems. *Educational Studies in Mathematics, 14*, 55–72.

Coburn, C. E. (2001). *Making sense of reading: Logics of reading in the institutional environment and the classroom.* Ann Arbor, MI: University Microfilms.

Coleman, J. S. (1988). Social capital in the creation of human capital. *American Journal of Sociology, 94*, Supplement: Organizations and Institutions: Sociological and Economic Approaches to the Analysis of Social Structure, S95–S120.

Collopy, R. (2003). Curriculum material as a professional development tool: How a mathematics textbook affected two teachers' learning. *Elementary School Journal, 103*, 287–311.

Darling-Hammond, L. (2004). Inequality and the right to learn: Access to qualified teachers in California's public schools. *Teachers College Record, 106*(10), 1936–1966.

Davis, E. A., & Krajcik, J. S. (2005). Designing educative curriculum materials to promote teacher learning. *Educational Researcher, 34*(3), 3–14.

Doyle, W. (1983). Academic work. *Review of Educational Research, 53*, 159–199.

Elmore, R., Peterson, P., & McCarthey, S. (1996). *Restructuring in the classroom: Teaching, learning, and school organization.* San Francisco, CA: Jossey-Bass.

Fernandez, C., & Yoshida, M. (2004). *Lesson study: A Japanese approach to improving mathematics teaching and learning.* Mahwah, NJ: Erlbaum.

Frank, K., Zhao, Y., & Borman, K. (2004). Social capital and the diffusion of innovations within organizations: The case of computer technology in schools. *Sociology of Education, 77*, 148–171.

Franke, M., & Kazemi, E. (2001). Teaching as learning within a community of practice: Characterizing generative growth. In T. Wood, B. Nelson, & J. Warfield (Eds.), *Beyond classical pedagogy in teaching elementary mathematics: The nature of facilitative teaching* (pp. 47–74). Mahwah, NJ: Erlbaum.

Freeman, D. J., & Porter, A. (1989). Do textbooks dictate the content of mathematics instruction in elementary schools? *American Educational Research Journal, 26*(3), 403–421.

Fullan, M., & Pomfret, A. (1977). Research on curriculum and instruction implementation. *Review of Educational Research, 47*(2), 335–397.

Gallucci, C. (2003). Communities of practice and the mediation of teachers' responses to standards-based reform. *Education Policy Analysis Archives, 11*(35). Retrieved January 8, 2008 from http://epaa.asu.edu/epaa/v11n35.

Gibson, J. J. (1979). *The ecological approach to visual perception.* Boston, MA: Houghton Mifflin.

Grossman, P. A., Weinberg, S., & Woolworth, S. (2001). Toward a theory of teacher community. *Teachers College Record, 103*(6), 942–1,012.

Hiebert, J., & Carpenter, T. (1992). Learning and teaching with understanding. In D. Grouws (Ed.), *Handbook of research on mathematics teaching and learning* (pp. 65–101). New York, NY: Macmillan.

Hightower, A. M., Knapp, M., Marsh, J. A., & McLaughlin, M. (Eds.). (2002). *School districts and instructional renewal.* New York, NY: Teachers College Press.

Hubbard, L., & Mehan, H, & Stein, M. K. (2006). *Reform as learning. School reform, organizational culture, and community politics in San Diego.* New York, NY: Routledge.

Leinhardt, G., & Steele, M. D. (2005). Seeing the complexity of standing to the side: Instructional dialogues. *Cognition and Instruction, 23*(1), 87–163.

Lloyd, G. M. (1999). Two teachers' conceptions of a reform curriculum: Implications for mathematics teacher development. *Journal of Mathematics Teacher Education, 2,* 227–252.

Louis, K. S., & Marks, H. M. (1998). Does professional community affect the classroom? Teachers' work and student experiences in restructuring schools. *American Journal of Education, 106,* 532–575.

Louis, K. S., Marks, H. M., & Kruse, S. (1996). Teachers' professional community in restructuring school. *American Education Research Journal, 33*(4), 757–798.

McLaughlin, M., & Oberman, I. (Eds.). (1996). *Teacher learning: New policies, new practices.* New York, NY: Teachers College Press.

McLaughlin, M. W., & Talbert, J. E. (2001). *Professional communities and the work of high school teaching.* Chicago, IL: University of Chicago Press.

National Council of Teachers of Mathematics. (1989). *Curriculum and evaluation standards for school mathematics.* Reston, VA: Author.

Portes, A. (1998). Social capital: Its origins and applications in modern sociology. *Annual Review of Sociology, 24,* 1–24.

Remillard, J. T. (1999). Curriculum materials in mathematics education reform: A framework for examining teachers' curriculum development. *Curriculum Inquiry, 29,* 315–342.

Remillard, J. T. (2000). Can curriculum materials support teachers' learning? Two fourth-grade teachers' use of a new mathematics text. *The Elementary School Journal, 100*(4), 331–350.

Remillard, J. T. (2005). Examining key concepts in research on teachers' use of mathematics curricula. *Review of Educational Research, 75*(2), 211–246.

Sanchez, R. (1995). Strategic flexibility in product competition. *Strategic Management Journal, 16,* 135–405.

Schilling, M. (2000). Toward a general modular systems theory and its application to interfirm product modularity. *Academy of Management Review, 25*(2), 312–334.

Schneider, R., & Krajcik, J. (2002). Supporting science teacher learning: The role of educative curriculum materials. *Journal of Science Teacher Education, 13*(3), 221–245.

Schoenfeld, A. (1985). *Mathematical problem solving.* New York, NY: Academic Press.

Schoenfeld, A. (1998). Toward a theory of teaching-in-context. *Issues in education, 4*(1), 1–95.

Sherin, M. (2002). When teaching becomes learning. *Cognition and Instruction, 20*(2), 119–150.

Smith, J. P. (1996). Efficacy and teaching mathematics by telling: A challenge for reform. *Journal for Research in Mathematics Education, 27*(4), 387–402.

Smylie, M. A., & Evans, A. E. (2006). Social capital and the problem of implementation. In M. Honig

(Ed.), *New directions in education policy implementation: Confronting complexity* (pp. 187–208). Albany, NY: SUNY Press.

Smylie, M. A., & Hart, A. W. (1999). School leadership for teacher learning and change: A human and social capital development perspective. In J. Murphy & K. S. Louis (Eds.), *Handbook of research on educational administration* (2nd Edition) (pp. 421–441). San Francisco, CA: Jossey-Bass.

Stein, M. K., & Brown, C. A. (1997). Teacher learning in a social context: Integrating collaborative and institutional processes with the study of teacher change. In E. Fenemma, & B. Nelson (Eds.), *Mathematics teachers in transition* (pp. 155–191). Hillsdale, NJ: Erlbaum.

Stein, M. K., Grover, B. W., Henningsen, M. (1996). Building student capacity for mathematical thinking and reasoning: An analysis of mathematical tasks used in reform classroom. *American Educational Research Journal, 33*(2), 455–488.

Stein, M. K., Kim, G., & Seeley, M. (2006). *The enactment of reform mathematics curricula in urban settings: A comparative analysis.* Paper presented at the Annual Meeting of the American Educational Research Association, San Francisco.

Stein, M. K., Silver, E. A., & Smith, M. S. (1998). Mathematics reform and teacher development: A community of practice perspective. In J. Greeno & S. Goldman (Eds.), *Thinking practices in mathematics and science learning* (pp. 17–52). Hillsdale, NJ: Erlbaum.

Stein, M. K., Smith, M. S., Henningsen, M., & Silver, E. A. (2000). *Implementing Standards-based mathematics instruction: A casebook for professional development.* New York, NY: Teachers College Press.

Stigler, J., & Hiebert, J. (1999). *The teaching gap.* New York, NY: The Free Press.

Stigler, J., & Hiebert, J. (2004). Improving mathematics teaching. *Educational Leadership, 61*(5), 12–16.

TERC. (1998). *Investigations in number, data, and space* (1st Edition). Palo Alto, CA: Dale Seymour.

University of Chicago School Mathematics Project. (2004). *Everyday mathematics* (2nd Edition). Chicago, IL: SRA/McGraw-Hill.

Wertsch, J. (1998). *Mind in action.* New York, NY: Oxford University Press.

4

Understanding the Role of the Institutional Context in the Relationship Between Teachers and Text

Kay McClain, Qing Zhao, Jana Visnovska, and Erik Bowen

The development of guiding theories is central to progress in the field.

(diSessa & Cobb, 2004)

Introduction

Both current and historical approaches to textbook adoption have been premised on the belief that teachers can be trained to implement instructional texts[1] with fidelity and that this *fidelity to the curriculum* will lead to increased student achievement (Fullan & Pomfret, 1977; Snyder, Bolin, & Zumwalt, 1992). Snyder et al. state that a focus on fidelity entails "(1) measuring the degree to which a particular innovation is implemented as planned and (2) identifying the factors which facilitate or hinder implementation as planned" (p. 404). In this approach, support resources are designed to ensure that the developers' intended curriculum is enacted. Teacher decision-making is relegated to following scripted procedures outlined in teacher guides. In these settings, teachers can be de-professionalized and the text can be seen as the primary tool for structuring students' opportunities for learning. Remillard's (2005) review of the research literature on teachers' use of mathematics curriculum materials addresses the issue of a fidelity approach by documenting a distinction in how "use" is conceptualized. Researchers who frame curriculum material use as either *following* or *subverting* it, for example, assume that under ideal conditions, fidelity between the written and enacted curriculum can be achieved. A fidelity approach to implementation gives authority for both the mathematics that is to be taught and the sequencing and presentation of that content to text, and places strict adherence to it as the goal of teaching. This approach stands in stark contrast to other conceptualizations of use described by Remillard, including *interpreting, drawing on,* and *participating with the text,* and other approaches to implementation that characterize the text as a tool (see McClain, 2002; Meira, 1995, 1998; van Oers, 1996) and teachers as designers (see Chapter 2 of this volume). In these latter views, teaching is seen as responsive to students' contributions, and the interplay of text resources, mathematically significant discussions, and teacher intervention creates the setting in which learning can occur.

When the emphasis of classroom instruction is on building from students' current understandings, the interactions cannot be scripted. As a result, this type of complex engagement cannot be reduced to manuals, curriculum resources, or guides. This sentiment is captured by Carpenter et al. (2004) when they claim that teaching "is complex, and complex practices cannot, in principle, be simply codified and then handed over to others with the expectation that they will be enacted or replicated as intended" (p. 10). Such a view of teaching raises questions about the role of the teacher's guide.

At the same time, teachers across the country are expected or, in many cases, required to use these resources in their mathematics instruction. Further, it is not uncommon for district decision-makers to hold a fidelity view of textbook implementation. In our ongoing work in schools, we have documented the tensions inherent in conflicting views of implementation (see Bowen & McClain, 2005; Cobb & McClain, 2001; Zhao, Visnovska, Cobb, & McClain, 2006). We have found evidence of these tensions in analyses of (a) administrators' views and beliefs, (b) teachers' perceptions of district expectations, and (c) teachers' classroom instructional practices related to the use of curriculum resources. In this chapter we argue that particular features of the institutional context, including the degree to which administrators (and teachers) view the texts as the arbiter of the mathematics that is taught and the manner and sequence in which it is taught, influence the teacher–text relationship.

Our data corpus is taken from three school districts in which National Science Foundation (NSF) funded curriculum programs were in use. Although our primary work was the ongoing professional development of communities of teachers in the three districts, we were unable to achieve our goals without understanding the role that text resources played in their instructional practice. The lack of current theories to guide analyses of the interplay between teaching and texts necessitated our development of an interpretive framework and associated analytic constructs along with a data collection method that defines the data needed for analysis. As a result, our current work focuses on the refinement of the framework and associated constructs in the course of our ongoing analysis. Our goal in this chapter is therefore to articulate by example our interpretive framework and constructs. In doing so, however, we do not make claims about a new theory; rather, we offer a first step in a process of building theory. Our next step is to connect these constructs to related literature.

In order to illustrate how the framework and constructs emerged from our work, it is necessary to situate our development efforts in the context of our commitment to a design research perspective (see Brown, 1992; Cobb, Confrey, diSessa, Lehrer, & Schauble, 2003; McClain, 2004). We employ a design perspective in our work in schools; so we naturally took a design perspective in the development of an interpretive framework. Our perspective on design research entails the development of a conjectured trajectory to guide initial activity. In the case of the development of an analytical framework, this involved conjectures about both the setting of teachers' work and their orientation to mathematics instruction. Our goal in the course of data collection was to document both of these aspects of practice. The next step involved developing constructs to use in the analysis. During the first round of analysis, we were able to operationalize the constructs. It was only in the course of iterative cycles of conjecture, data collection, and analysis, however, that we were able to refine both the framework and the constructs. As a result, we engaged in cycles of conjecture and revision. This was made possible by our work in multiple sites. A conjecture that resulted from analysis at one site was tested and refined in the course of subsequent analyses at another site. Our framework has therefore been developed and refined in the course of iterations of conjecture, data collection, and analysis at the three sites.

What we offer here is a mezzo-cycle of design in building a theory. diSessa and Cobb (2004) make a strong argument for design-based theorizing in their characterization of a genre of theorizing that they claim is "strongly synergistic with design-based research" (p. 77). They describe a central element of this type of theorizing as *ontological innovation*:

> A central element of the type of productive design-based theorizing on which we focus is "ontological innovation," hypothesizing and developing explanatory constructs, new categories of things in the world that help explain how it works ... Developing and refining an ontological innovation is challenging and requires the kind of extensive, iterative work that characterizes design experiments more generally. However, the pay-off in terms of clarity of focus and explanatory power can be great.
>
> (p. 77)

Our immediate goal was to take a design perspective toward the development of explanatory frameworks in order to make sense of the settings in which we worked. Our larger goal was to contribute to the development of a theory for understanding the relationship between teachers and texts.

In the following sections of this chapter, we begin by describing the data corpus and our theoretical perspective in the subsequent analyses. Next, we situate our work in the context of design research. We then use the design process as a background for documenting the evolution of two analytical constructs. We continue by employing a design-research perspective to articulate a third construct. We follow by taking the analytic constructs as a basis for the development of an interpretive framework or what diSessa and Cobb (2004) call an *orienting framework*. We conclude with a synthesis of the design process and an articulation of next steps.

Data and Setting

This chapter provides results of iterative cycles of analyses at three sites that were designed to provide information on teachers' instructional practice in mathematics including the role of curriculum resources in supporting or constraining teacher change. Modified teaching sets (see Simon & Tzur, 1999) were conducted with groups of teachers in each setting. Analysis of these pre-interviews, observations, and post-interviews formed the basis of the analysis reported in this chapter. In addition, the analyses were central to our work with teachers as they informed our ongoing conjectures about how to support changes in their practice.

In one setting, Iris Hill, the teachers that were the focus of analysis were the fifth-grade teachers in one of 33 middle schools in the district. These teachers, along with the other mathematics teachers in the school, were in the second year of professional development collaboration with university researchers. A product of the collaboration was the introduction of NSF-funded curriculum materials. At the time of initial data collection, teachers at Iris Hill were in their first year of implementing the new materials. In the second setting, Washington Park, the teachers taught mathematics in grades six through eight, and represented all three middle schools in the district. Although the teachers were in their fifth year of an ongoing collaboration with McClain, the district had adopted NSF-funded curriculum materials at all grades four years prior to the collaboration. In addition, the district was in the second year of a three-year NSF-funded mathematics improvement effort. The third site, Jefferson Heights, included middle-school teachers representing eight of the 11 middle schools in the district. Jefferson Heights also adopted one of the NSF-funded middle-school curriculum programs, and held an NSF-funded mathematics improvement grant. The similarities across the sites along with the differences in their approaches to implementing the new curriculum programs provided a rich data corpus through which to explore our questions related to teachers and texts.

Theoretical Perspectives that Guided Analyses of the Teaching Sets

We incorporated two theoretical perspectives into our analysis of the teaching sets in order to make sense of the complex dynamics involved in teaching and the institutional contexts through which it is enacted. First, we viewed teaching as a *social practice*. That is, we saw the relationship between *social structures* (e.g., institutional settings, including the classroom within the school and the school within the district) and local *events* (e.g., teachers' enactment of instructional decisions within the context of the classroom) as mediated by the social practice of *teaching* (Fairclough, 2003). Second, we viewed teachers' instructional practices as situated within the institutional settings of the school and school district (see Cobb, McClain, Lamberg, & Dean, 2003).

We know from both first-hand experience and from a number of formal investigations that teachers' instructional practices are profoundly influenced by the institutional constraints in their local setting, the formal and informal sources of assistance on which they draw, and the materials and resources that they use in their classroom practice (Ball, 1993; Brown, Stein, & Forman, 1996; Cobb, McClain et al., 2003; Nelson, 1999; Senger, 1999; Stein & Brown, 1997). However, our approach presents a challenge in that we must coordinate the teachers' *perceptions* of the constraints and affordances within the school and district with our analyses of the institutional setting. This coordination is necessary in order to capture the intertwined system involving teachers' perspectives and experiences as they try to accomplish their instructional goals within the institutional setting in which they work. Such experiences highlight the immediate challenges that teachers encounter, the frustrations they feel, and the valuations they hold of specific aspects of their instructional reality. We therefore situated the analysis of the teaching sets in an analysis of the institutional context by drawing on the analytic approach proposed by Cobb, McClain, Lamberg, and Dean (2003).[2]

It is important to note that we are proposing a new way of looking. In our work, we seek to build theory. For that reason, our analyses of the teaching sets are not the focus of this chapter. Nevertheless, our analyses led us to make conjectures about a possible theoretical approach for understanding teachers in the setting of their school and district. For this reason, we point to these analyses in the course of describing the evolution of our work.

Designing Theory

In the introduction to this chapter, we briefly described our work as design researchers. In this section we elaborate on this perspective as it relates to the work reported in this chapter. In particular, we describe the iterative process that resulted in the formulation of conjectures about constructs that might explain the differences in the ways the teachers within and across the three sites interacted with their instructional materials.

The first step in the process of design research is to conduct a thought experiment prior to collecting data. For us this entailed developing conjectures that might explain the dramatic differences we witnessed in how the teachers were interacting with their curriculum materials. Although there was variety at any one site, there were common routines of practice within each site. This was the level at which we sought to understand the phenomena. Our initial conjecture related to the role that high stakes accountability testing played within the school and district. Although all three districts were in high-pressure situations, the way the importance of test scores was communicated to the teachers differed across the three sites.

Our next decision involved determining what data would allow us to answer our questions. We determined that we needed to both observe the teachers in their classrooms and speak with them about their decision-making processes. In addition, we needed to ask questions about their *perceptions* of the constraints and affordances that supported or inhibited their teaching. Our first round of teaching sets was therefore designed to make sense of the differences in use of text resources by focusing on the actual use of the texts and teachers' perceptions of how they were expected to use them.

The first teaching sets were conducted at Washington Park. Our initial conjecture about the influence of testing on the use of the text seemed to hold. It was only as we tested this conjecture at other sites that we became confident about our conjecture. As a result, we proposed the first construct of *instructional reality* (explained in a later section of this chapter).

Although this construct gave us explanatory power across two sites, we still had unanswered questions at the third site. We therefore conducted another thought experiment and ultimately adopted a second construct, *agency*. We then tested the predictability and power of this second construct in subsequent data collection and analysis of teaching sets at the other two sites.

It is this iterative process of conjecture testing and refining that we describe as design research. These iterations provided the foundation for our eventual claims. We considered our conjectures valid only if they could be operationalized in the course of subsequent analysis at different sites. It was therefore the years of collecting data across the three sites that gave us confidence to propose these constructs as a potential resource for understanding the relationship between teachers and texts. Our process is similar to that of the *zig-zag* that Lampert (1990) describes as one works through proofs and refutations to arrive at a conclusion. As the following discussion reveals, our work continues to evolve. Below we present three constructs that have emerged from our analysis across the three sites. We continue to develop and refine these constructs and draw connections between them and relevant literature.

The Evolution of Constructs

Instructional Reality

As we noted earlier, our initial questions were an attempt to understand the diverse ways that the teachers in Washington Park were implementing the adopted curriculum program. Although all of the teachers were strong advocates of the text resources, the variety of ways they implemented the curriculum program raised questions for us. For example, some of the teachers simply read the teacher's guide to the students while others made modifications based on their assessments of their students' understanding. In the course of trying to make sense of the data, we became aware of the importance of the *teachers' perceptions* of the demands and supports placed on their instructional practice by their local context. The term we developed to characterize these perceptions as they impact teachers' stance toward instruction is *instructional reality* (see Zhao, Visnovska, & McClain, 2004). We find this term useful because it gives us a language for talking about the factors that influence teachers' decision-making processes, such as *perceived* institutional demands, constraints, and affordances. This construct has important similarities to Herbel-Eisenmann, Lubeinski, and Id-Deen's (2006) notion of "curricular context," which points to both local and global changes that influence teachers' pedagogical decisions. Instructional reality, however, places particular emphasis on teachers' perceptions of their context and is used to characterize the regularities in practice that emerge at a district or school level as opposed to the practices of any one teacher. In this way, our construct complements the notion of curricular context.

A central principle that guided our analysis was to assume that teacher' perspectives on teaching and learning and specific instructional practices they develop are always reasonable and coherent in the context of their instructional reality (see Simon & Tzur, 1999). For example, the observation of a seemingly insensible or ineffective instructional decision made by a teacher does not merely conclude with a negative assessment of the teacher's competence. Instead, it becomes the focal point that the researchers need to account for so that it can be seen as a reasonable and coherent component within the landscape of the teacher's instructional reality. It is this explanation of what teachers do and why they do it that can provide valuable guidance for researchers in designing to support teachers' learning. Operating with this assumption therefore enabled us to avoid taking a deficit view when examining the data and instead highlighted the necessity of generating reasonable interpretations of the teachers' instructional reality against which their practices can be understood.

The construct of instructional reality encompasses (a) the perspectives that teachers hold toward teaching and learning, (b) the instructional challenges and frustrations that they encounter and their explanations of them, (c) the obligations of being a teacher as they understand them, and (d) the valuations they hold toward specific aspects of their instructional world. In other words, this construct leads us to speculate how teaching looks from teachers' perspectives. In contrast to naturalistic studies, understanding teachers' instructional reality has a strong interventionist orientation. Such understanding constitutes the foundation for researchers to conjecture possible means of supporting teachers' learning. It also lends explanatory power for researchers to decipher teachers' sense-making in professional development activities.

The construct of instructional reality covers a broad landscape of teaching. It includes teachers' conceptualizations of mathematics teaching and learning, including what mathematics is, how students learn, and what supports their learning (Heinz, Kinzel, Simon, & Tzur, 2000), but also other aspects that significantly affect teaching from teachers' points of view – for example, how to motivate students (see Zhao et al., 2004). Additionally, the construct assumes that what teachers do and how they justify their practices are significantly influenced by the particular instructional resources they use in the classroom (e.g., textbook, state-mandated curriculum, copies of students' work). Even more broadly, the notion of instructional reality situates teaching within the institutional context in which teachers develop and refine their practices. The institutional contexts in which teachers work significantly affect how they approach teaching and learning, and therefore constitute a resource for researchers when explaining what teachers do and why they do it (Cobb, McClain et al., 2003; Elmore, 2000; Spillane, 2000).

A deep understanding of every component of instructional reality can be challenging and sometimes unfeasible, given the fact that it requires high accessibility of the research site, longitudinal efforts, and massive data collection. However, it is tremendously beneficial to have at least a rudimental overview of instructional reality in its totality. This is because different aspects of teachers' instructional reality are so intricately related that any attempt to interpret one aspect in isolation may not yield enough evidence for researchers to understand the coherence that underlies teachers' observed practices.

Given researchers' different agendas for hypothesizing about teachers' learning, it is possible that they may choose to highlight certain aspects of teachers' instructional reality while backgrounding others. Our long-term goal in working with the teachers at all three sites was to support them in placing students' reasoning at the center of instructional planning and decision-making. Therefore, we found it particularly useful to focus on teachers' classroom practices with regard to students' reasoning. Other aspects of teachers' instructional reality – the institutional context, for example – may constitute the background knowledge that provides explanatory power for us to fully understand the rationales underpinning teachers' classroom practices. It is therefore essential to understand this construct at a school or district level when planning professional development interventions.

The initial conjectures about the power of the construct of instructional reality proved useful in explaining the teachers' decision-making at Washington Park. As we continued our analyses at Iris Hill and Jefferson Heights, however, we found unexplainable similarities and differences. In particular, while conducting the analysis of the teaching sets from Iris Hill, we noticed that, although the construct of *instructional reality* was important in explaining many commonalities across the classrooms, we were unable to account for the strict adherence to the teacher guides (e.g., reading them word for word to the students). Instructional reality only explained one layer of these differences. For this reason, a second construct seemed necessary – that of *agency*.

Agency

We define agency as having authority over both the mathematics that is taught and the sequencing and presentation of that content. We tested the construct of agency as we analyzed the data from Iris Hill. Our preliminary analysis revealed that the teachers at Iris Hill gave agency to the textbook as the authority on the mathematics that was taught and the sequencing and presentation of that content (or what they considered new teaching practices) as well as on student thinking. In general, the teachers believed that the NSF-funded curriculum program was a useful resource for not only enhancing student reasoning, but also demonstrating effective instructional practices for promoting student thinking. As a result, when the teacher guide gave anticipated student responses, the teachers only responded to those ways of thinking that fit with the teacher guide. They did not demonstrate the flexibility to judge the quality of students' reasoning. This surprised us because our observations of the teachers in the professional development workshops revealed that, over time, they began to view student reasoning as an essential resource for their instruction. Focusing our analysis on understanding this discrepancy between our interpretations of the teachers' participation in the workshops and their practice led us to conclude that although the teachers perceived themselves as valuing student reasoning, they placed the text resources, not student reasoning, at the center of their practice.

This result had implications for the ways in which teachers could be supported in changing their practice, and therefore for our intervention design

(Bowen & McClain, 2005). It was this process of design research that allowed us continually to modify our tasks and interactions with the teachers to achieve our goals. As an example, many conventional approaches to professional development assume that teachers can be trained to enact instructional texts with relatively little consideration of teachers' current practice. This orientation toward professional development places *agency* with the text as the linchpin for instructional change. In contrast to this approach to professional development, the design-research approach (see Brown, 1992; Cobb, Confrey et al., 2003) emphasizes professional development that builds from teachers' understandings of the content of mathematics, their present mode of mathematics instruction, and the rationale behind their daily instructional decision-making. The work of the professional development is, then, to support the teachers' movement of agency away from curriculum materials to a local view in which they hold the agency. The shift in the location of agency then becomes a goal of the professional development. As part of that process, teachers are viewed as designers.

The construct of agency was therefore essential in teasing out the differences between Iris Hill and Jefferson Heights.[3] We further tested its predictive power in analyses of teaching sets collected at Washington Park.

Teachers' Professional Status

The next iteration of our work involved a conjecture about an additional analytic construct. Having articulated the utility of our first two constructs, *teachers' instructional reality* and *agency*, we still had phenomena that remained unexplained by these two constructs. In particular, we had questions about the relationship between teachers' professional status in their district and their district's perception of the role of text resources. To answer these questions, we propose a third analytic construct, *teachers' professional status*. In doing so, we argue that the degree to which teachers face a fidelity approach to textbook implementation is related to the extent to which they are viewed as professionals. In other words, a fidelity approach contributes to the de-professionalization of teachers. In contrast, when teachers are viewed as professionals, the textbook is more likely to be viewed as a tool that teachers use in the course of instruction. In this latter view, the teachers are viewed as professionals who design the curriculum on an ongoing basis as they interact with their students.

We have seen teachers' professional status influence textbook use in three different ways. First, in settings where the mathematics to be taught is defined by the textbooks, the task of administrators is to ensure that teachers follow the text by adopting a fidelity approach. Administrators monitor teachers to ensure that they adhere to the timelines or pacing guides articulated in the text resources. This approach de-professionalizes teachers, giving them limited official decision-making capacity in the process of implementing of texts.

Second, in settings in which teachers articulate their goals while working exclusively from documents such as textbook pacing guides, teachers have some professional flexibility and freedom to make decisions. However, it is frequently the case that ensuring student achievement is necessary for this professional status to be acknowledged. As a result, teachers often relinquish part of their professional status to ensure necessary student gains by relying heavily on texts.

Finally, there are also settings in which the teacher is seen as the instructional authority in the classroom and the text is viewed as a tool to be used in instructional decision-making. In these situations, the teacher is viewed as the designer of curriculum (see Chapter 2 of this volume). This design orientation assumes that tools have to be organized and sequenced in a manner that supports student learning. In these settings, teachers make modifications to their texts that are attentive to students' ways of reasoning, and administrators support teachers' efforts and understand the important role the teacher plays in learning. Teachers in these contexts are highly professionalized; they and their administrators view teachers as central to the instruction process.

Despite our delineation of these three levels of professional status above, we do not see the interplay between the texts and the professionalism of teachers as static and determined solely by the institutional context. Teachers play a role in how they are perceived professionally. Likewise, the agency given to texts influences the professional status of teachers. Although we do not want to characterize the professional status of teachers solely by the status of the texts in relation to teacher autonomy, we do argue that a relationship exists. As we continue to analyze data from the three school districts in which we worked, we will test and revise the utility of this proposed construct in further clarifying the relationship between teachers and texts.

In Search of Theory: An Orienting Framework

Although the constructs we have used in our analyses have proved helpful, we find that the lack of theory to guide our analysis places our work in the space between analysis and anecdote. Remillard (2005) raises this concern in her review of the literature on research on teachers' use of mathematics curriculum materials:

> A number of scholars over the last 25 years have studied how teachers use curriculum materials and the role that textbooks and curriculum materials have played in mathematics classrooms ... Findings from these studies, however, have not been consolidated to produce reliable, theoretically grounded knowledge on teachers' interactions with curriculum materials that might guide future research or the design or implementation of curricula.
>
> (p. 212)

She continues with a call for theoretical work in the field, asserting "the current body of literature rests on underdeveloped theoretical ground" (p. 212).

We concur with Remillard and use our analyses and the development of constructs to propose an interpretive framework, or what diSessa and Cobb (2004) call an *orienting framework*:

Orienting frameworks seldom provide strong constraints or detailed prescriptions. Their value instead resides in the general perspectives that they provide for conceptualizing issues. Orienting frameworks are probably best viewed as meta-theories, presumed general constraints that define general aspects of hoped for and needed specific theoretical frameworks.

(p. 8)

Orienting frameworks are therefore in service of the development of grand theory. Our goal is to engage in the development of theory by explicating constructs that build an orienting framework. We are guided by both theoretical and pragmatic concerns. From a theoretical perspective, we do not believe that the research can build or progress unless guided by theory. We therefore believe that all analysis should be based on or in service of theory development. Our current and ongoing work involves collaborations with teachers who are working with *Standards*-based curriculum materials. Unless we can understand the complexity of the interplay of the text and practice from a theoretical level, we cannot proceed in a reasoned way. From a pragmatic perspective, we want to make decisions that address teachers' day-to-day concerns. Doing so involves tailoring our work in professional development settings such that we maintain a strong relationship between our goals and the teachers' classrooms (see Zhao & Cobb, 2006).

A starting point in the proposal of an orienting framework is the development of useful constructs. These constructs must then be used in analyses so they can be extended and refined. It is through this process that the robustness of the constructs across various settings can be determined. This process of extension and refinement contributes to the constructs becoming operationalized so that other researchers can both use the construct and monitor analyses in which it has been employed (diSessa & Cobb, 2004).

Since our work is grounded in a design-research orientation, the very nature of our analysis is iterative. The construct of *instructional reality* emerged from a lack of ability to clearly articulate the results of analysis. This construct then informed the next set of analyses. Its explanatory power was sustained, and contributed to our claim that the construct is a part of our proposed orienting framework.

In Figure 4.1, we highlight the relationship between the three constructs. We use the boldness of the arrows to indicate the strength of the relationship. We begin by noting that the construct of instructional reality has a strong influence on both agency and teacher professional status. Although both of these contribute to a teacher's instructional reality, we believe the strength of the primary relationship is *from* instructional reality *to* both agency and professional status. We purport that the strength of the relationship between agency and professional status is roughly equivalent. It is therefore important to realize that these constructs are more powerful – doing more work – when the relationships between them are taken into account within the institutional context.

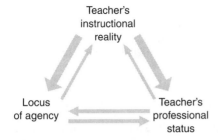

Figure 4.1 The interplay between teachers and text.

Continuing this iterative approach to analysis and theory development, we propose this orienting framework can be used as a theoretical tool for analyzing the interplay of mathematics teachers' practice and their instructional texts. The use of the framework in various settings will contribute to its restructuring and/or refinement. This mezzo-level iterative process then offers the opportunity for grounded theory to emerge.

Conclusion

We view the offer of our interpretive framework or *orienting framework* as a first step toward the development of a guiding theory. By taking a design approach to theory development, it then becomes possible for theory to "delineate classes of phenomena that are worthy of inquiry and specify how to look and what to see in order to understand them" which, in turn, "teach[es] us how to see" (diSessa & Cobb, 2004, p. 79). The development of theories to guide analyses of the relationship between teachers and texts therefore requires the field to engage in serious critique and analysis of our own and other's work. The cyclic process of analysis and critique allows the field to build logically from what is already known. This process then creates the opportunity for theory to emerge from practice in a systematic, disciplined manner.

Acknowledgments

Support for this research was provided by the National Science Foundation under Grants no. REC-0135062 and REC-9814898.

Notes

1. In this chapter, we use *textbook* or *curriculum materials* to refer to the district-adopted textbook. *Curriculum* refers to what gets constituted at the district level as what is to be taught.
2. This approach builds from Wenger's (1998) work by delineating communities of practice within a school or district and analyzing three types of interconnections between them that are based on boundary encounters, brokers, and boundary objects.
3. See Herbel-Eisenmann (Chapter 10 of this volume) for an exploration of similar authority and agency issues as they emerged in the classroom through language choices made by teachers.

References

Ball, D. L. (1993). With an eye on the mathematical horizon: Dilemmas of teaching elementary school mathematics. *Elementary School Journal*, 93(4), 373–397.

Bowen, E., & McClain, K. (2005). Accounting for agency in teaching mathematics. In G. M. Lloyd, M. R. Wilson, J. L. Wilkins, & S. L. Behm (Eds.), *Proceedings of the 27th Annual Meeting of the North American Chapter of the International Group for the Psychology of Mathematics Education*. [CD-ROM]. Eugene, OR: All Academic.

Brown, A. L. (1992). Design experiments: Theoretical and methodological challenges in creating complex interventions in classroom settings. *Journal of the Learning Sciences*, 2, 141–178.

Brown, C. A., Stein, M. K., & Forman, E. A. (1996). Assisting teachers and students to reform the mathematics classroom. *Educational Studies in Mathematics*, 31, 63–93.

Carpenter, T. P., Blanton, M. L., Cobb, P., Franke, M., Kaput, J. J., & McClain, K. (2004). *Scaling up innovative practices in mathematics and science*. NCISLA, Wisconsin Center for Education Research. Retrieved 2006, from http://www.wcer.wisc.edu/NCISLA/publications/reports/NCISLAReport1.pdf.

Cobb, P., & McClain, K. (2001). An approach for supporting teachers' learning in social context. In F. L. Lin & T. Cooney (Eds.), *Making sense of mathematics teacher education* (pp. 207–232). Dordrecht: Kluwer.

Cobb, P., Confrey, J., diSessa, A. A., Lehrer, R., & Schauble, L. (2003). Design experiments in education research. *Educational Researcher*, 32(1), 9–13.

Cobb, P., McClain, K., Lamberg, T., & Dean, C. (2003). Situating teachers' instructional practices in the institutional setting of the school and school district. *Educational Researcher*, 32(6), 13–24.

diSessa, A. A., & Cobb, P. (2004). Ontological innovation and the role of theory in design experiments. *Journal of the Learning Sciences*, 13(1), 77–103.

Elmore, R. F. (2000). *Building a new structure for school leadership*. Washington, DC: Albert Shanker Institute.

Fairclough, N. (2003). *Analysing discourse: Textual analysis for social research*. New York, NY: Routledge.

Fullan, M., & Pomfret, A. (1977). Research on curriculum and instruction implementation. *Review of Educational Research*, 47(1), 335–397.

Heinz, K., Kinzel, M., Simon, M. A., & Tzur, R. (2000). Moving students through steps of mathematical knowing: An account of the practice of an elementary mathematics teacher in transition. *Journal of Mathematical Behavior*, 19, 83–107.

Herbel-Eisenmann, B. A., Lubienski, S. T., & Id-Deen, L. (2006). Reconsidering the study of mathematics instructional practices: The importance of curricular context in understanding local and global teacher change. *Journal of Mathematics Teacher Education*, 9, 313–345.

Lampert, M. (1990). When the problem is not the question and the solution is not the answer: Mathematical knowing and teaching. *American Educational Research Journal*, 27, 29–63.

McClain, K. (2002). Teacher's and students' understanding: The role of tools and inscriptions in supporting effective communication. *Journal of the Learning Sciences*, 11(2&3), 217–249.

McClain, K. (2004). *An articulated framework for action for teacher development: In search of theory*. Paper presented at the Annual Meeting of the American Educational Research Association Conference, San Diego, CA.

Meira, L. (1995). The microevolution of mathematical representations in children's activity. *Cognition and Instruction*, 13(2), 269–313.

Meira, L. (1998). Making sense of instructional devices: The emergence of transparency in mathematical activity. *Journal for Research in Mathematics Education*, 29, 121–142.

Nelson, B. S. (1999). *Building new knowledge by thinking: How administrators can learn what they need to know about mathematics education reform*. Cambridge, MA: Educational Development Center.

Remillard, J. T. (2005). Examining key concepts in research on teachers' use of mathematics curricula. *Review of Educational Research*, 75(2), 211–246.

Senger, E. (1999). Reflective reform in mathematics: The recursive nature of teacher change. *Educational Studies in Mathematics*, 37, 199–201.

Simon, M. A., & Tzur, R. (1999). Explicating the teacher's perspective from the researchers' perspectives: Generating accounts of mathematics teachers' practice. *Journal for Research in Mathematics Education, 30*(3), 252–264.

Snyder, J., Bolin, F., & Zumwalt, K. (1992). Curriculum implementation. In P. W. Jackson (Ed.), *Handbook of research on curriculum: A project of the American Educational Research Association* (pp. 402–435). New York, NY: Macmillan.

Spillane, J. P. (2000). Cognition and policy implementation: District policy-makers and the reform of mathematics education. *Cognition and Instruction, 18,* 141–179.

Stein, M. K., & Brown, C. A. (1997). Teacher learning in a social context: Integrating collaborative and institutional processes with the study of teacher change. In E. Fennema & B. Scott Nelson (Eds.), *Mathematics teachers in transition* (pp. 155–192). Mahwah, NJ: Erlbaum.

van Oers, B. (1996). Learning mathematics as meaningful activity. In P. Nesher, L. P. Steffe, P. Cobb, G. A. Goldin, & B. Greer (Eds.), *Theories of mathematical learning* (pp. 91–114). Hillsdale, NJ: Erlbaum.

Wenger, E. (1998). *Communities of practice: Learning, meaning, and identity.* Cambridge: Cambridge University.

Zhao, Q., & Cobb, P. (2006). Articulating the relation between teachers' learning in professional development and their practice in the classroom: Implications for design research. In S. Alatorre, J. L. Cortina, M. Sáiz, & A. Méndez (Eds.), *Proceedings of the 28th Annual Meeting of the North American Chapter of the International Group for the Psychology of Mathematics Education.* [CD-ROM]. Merida, Mexico: Universidad Pedagógica Nacional.

Zhao, Q., Visnovska, J., & McClain, K. (2004). Using design research to support the learning of professional teaching community of middle-school mathematics teachers. In D. E. McDougall & J. A. Ross (Eds.), *Proceedings of the 26th Annual Meeting of the North American Chapter of the International Group for the Psychology of Mathematics Education* (Vol. 3, pp. 969–975). Toronto: OISE/UT.

Zhao, Q., Visnovska, J., Cobb, P., & McClain, K. (2006). *Supporting the mathematics learning of a professional teaching community: Focusing on teachers' instructional reality.* Paper presented at the Annual Meeting of the American Educational Research Association Conference, San Francisco, CA.

5

Considerations and Limitations Related to Conceptualizing and Measuring Textbook Integrity

Kathryn B. Chval, Óscar Chávez, Barbara J. Reys, and James Tarr

The current context of high-stakes accountability mandated by the No Child Left Behind Act of 2001 (NCLB, 2002) offers strong incentives for teachers and school administrators to seek strategies for the rapid improvement of student learning in mathematics, and schools are choosing the adoption of new curriculum materials as a primary strategy (Remillard, 2005). NCLB requires that schools receiving Title I funds "use effective methods and instructional strategies that are based on *scientifically based research.*" The resulting expectation is that schools use mathematics curriculum materials that are proven to be effective as measured by achievement tests. The resulting political context has elevated the importance of finding constructs to measure if and under what conditions mathematics curriculum materials are effective in improving student learning.

Furthermore, recent calls for scientifically based research (NCLB, 2002; National Research Council [NRC], 2002), rigorous academic standards (NCLB, 2002), criteria for evaluating curricular effectiveness (NRC, 2004), and mathematics curriculum materials that enhance student learning (Whitehurst, 2003) have elevated the importance of conceptualizing and measuring the use of mathematics curriculum materials and the resulting influence on student achievement. Thus, there is a need for economical, practical, and reliable methods of measuring the use of curriculum materials by teachers and students.

In this chapter, we discuss our approach to measuring teachers' use of district-adopted textbooks for a large-scale research study of the use of middle school mathematics curriculum materials and its relation to student achievement. We argue that such documentation is necessary in order to study the impact of particular textbooks on student learning. In the next section, we highlight problematic aspects of the construct of "fidelity of implementation," as discussed in current literature on teachers' textbook use, and introduce an alternative construct we call *textbook integrity.*

Conceptualizing Textbook Integrity

Curriculum implementation is an uneven process within and across schools (Grouws & Smith, 2000; Kilpatrick, 2003; Lambdin & Preston, 1995; NRC, 2004; Senk & Thompson, 2003; Snyder, Bolin, & Zumwalt, 1992; Spillane & Zeuli, 1999). Kilpatrick explains,

> Two classrooms in which the same curriculum is supposedly being "implemented" may look very different; the activities of teacher and students in each room may be quite dissimilar, with different learning opportunities available, different mathematical ideas under consideration, and different outcomes achieved.
>
> (p. 473)

Therefore, studies investigating the relationship between curriculum materials and student achievement cannot ignore what actually occurs in classrooms. This necessity was acknowledged by the NRC (2004) panel on evaluating curricular effectiveness:

> A standard for evaluation of any social program requires that an impact assessment is warranted only if two conditions are met: (1) the curricular program is clearly specified, and (2) the intervention is well implemented. Absent this assurance, one must have a means of ensuring or measuring *treatment integrity* [emphasis added] in order to make causal inferences.
>
> (p. 100)

Nevertheless, the documentation of treatment integrity poses numerous methodological challenges in the context of curriculum evaluation studies involving large numbers of students and teachers, different schools, and different types of middle-grade curriculum materials in use.

We began to design our study by consulting the literature to determine how other researchers had conceptualized large-scale studies on the use of curriculum materials and the methodologies they used. We found that the term "fidelity of implementation" was problematic for a variety of reasons. We found, for instance, that researchers have different definitions, perspectives, and purposes related to this construct, and consequently study it differently (Stein, Remillard, & Smith, 2007). The term has been described as the extent to which there is a match between the written curriculum and what teachers do in the classroom (Remillard, 2005). However, some researchers use definitions of fidelity that are strict and dualistic (i.e., curriculum was either implemented as intended or not) whereas others consider degrees or levels of fidelity (e.g., Hall & Loucks, 1981). Still others take a different perspective – acknowledging that the intended and implemented curricula may differ, and adaptation is expected as teachers are seen as active implementers (Ben-Peretz, 1990; Huntley, 2006) or curriculum is constructed within the classroom by teachers and students through participation in a sociocultural context (Remillard, 2005). Not surprisingly, researchers designing studies from these different perspectives have pursued different research questions and designs. Moreover, some have pursued research questions focused on describing the nature of fidelity whereas others have used extent of fidelity as an independent variable in evaluating curricular effectiveness (Remillard, 2005).

In addition to different approaches to defining and conceptualizing fidelity of implementation, there are also conflicting views on how fidelity of implementation should be measured. Teacher and student interviews, classroom surveys, and observations are the most frequent data-gathering techniques (NRC, 2004). Less frequent techniques include teacher logs or diaries of curricular coverage, feedback from teachers at the end of each textbook chapter or end of the school year, and student surveys (NRC, 2004). However, observations are infrequent and typically with small numbers of schools and classes, due to feasibility and cost. The field lacks economical and effective ways of measuring teachers' use of curriculum materials in large-scale, comparative studies examining curricular effectiveness. Researchers continue to develop and refine instruments to address these needs (Cai et al., 2007; Huntley, 2006).

As a result of these controversies and challenges, we concluded that the term "fidelity of implementation" was problematic because there is not agreement regarding whether it is worthy of study (Snyder et al., 1992), how it should be conceptualized (Fullan & Pomfret, 1977; Remillard, 2005; Snyder et al., 1992), how it should be measured (Ruiz-Primo, 2005), or whether it is even a useful construct (Cho, 1998; Remillard, 2005).

Our study involved 70 middle-grade teachers and 4,000 students from 11 schools in six different states, using programs funded by the National Science Foundation (*Connected Mathematics Project* [CMP], *Mathematics in Context* [MiC], *Math Thematics* [MT]) and commercially-developed textbooks published by Glencoe, Saxon, Prentice Hall, Houghton Mifflin, Southwestern, Harcourt, and Addison Wesley. Based on this context, our research questions, a review of the literature, and our experiences collecting and analyzing data, we conceptualized an alternative construct that we defined as *textbook integrity*. We define *textbook integrity* as the extent to which the district-adopted textbook serves as a teacher's primary guide in determining the content, pedagogy, and the nature of student activity over an identified period of time. We identified three essential components of textbook integrity: (a) regular use of the textbook by the teacher and students over the instructional period (in our case, the school year); (b) use of a significant portion of the textbook to determine content emphasis and instructional design over the school year; and (c) utilization of instructional strategies consistent with the pedagogical orientation of the textbook. In the following section, we use data from our study to illustrate each of these components and the instruments we used to measure them. We argue further that, although all three components are necessary, no single component is sufficient for determining textbook integrity. We use our study as an illustrative case to examine considerations, challenges, and limitations in conceptualizing, measuring, and analyzing textbook integrity.

Operationalizing Textbook Integrity

When designing measures to address the three components of textbook integrity, we grappled with several conceptual and methodological issues. For example, for the purposes of our study, textbook integrity was not intended to be a variable to be used as a predictor for student achievement, but as a *threshold* to determine whether student data from particular teachers' classrooms should be included in the analyses. It was clear that, if a teacher never used a textbook to teach mathematics, then data collected from that classroom should not be analyzed in order to determine the effect the program had on student achievement. However, it was not apparent where to set the minimum threshold. We debated whether using the textbook 50 percent, 60 percent, 75 percent, or 80 percent of instructional days was sufficient for inclusion in the data analyses. In addition, we also debated where to set the minimum threshold for the other two components: use of a significant portion of the textbook and utilization of instructional strategies consistent with the pedagogical orientation of the textbook.

In addition to conceptualizing textbook integrity, we needed tools to measure the three components that were cost-effective yet sensitive to the variability across classrooms, schools, and districts. Given the number and location of teachers in the study, we also needed to develop practical and feasible tools that required modest levels of effort from teachers. We recognized that practical and feasible instruments would pose limitations in understanding how materials were implemented and we will discuss these constraints below. In the following sections, we describe the tools that we used to measure the three components.

Regular Use

For many teachers, the textbook is the primary resource used to teach mathematics. Other teachers use the textbook less frequently, drawing instead on other materials, published or self-developed. Thus, we created a *Textbook-Use Diary* to document the first component: regular use. Teachers completed this diary for ten-day intervals in October, January, and March, describing their use of the textbook for a total of 30 days of instruction. Teachers completed one row of the table following each lesson. They noted the resources (including textbooks and supplemental materials) they used in (a) planning instruction, (b) enacting instruction, and (c) assigning homework. Additionally, teachers recorded the specific page numbers of the student and teacher edition used by them and their students.

Figure 5.1 presents an excerpt from a *Textbook-Use Diary* completed in detail. Teachers provided information about each lesson in relation to (a) general topic of lesson, (b) what the teacher did to plan the lesson, (c) what materials the teacher used to plan the lesson, (d) textbook pages used by the teacher, (e) textbook pages used by students, (f) assigned homework from textbook, and (g) other print materials used by the teacher and students. Teachers extended different levels of effort in completing the diaries, and many were less detailed than

7th Grade

> Warm-Up is a daily computation review assignment. I have created them myself using several different resources. I have enclosed an example.

Textbook-Use Diary

Teacher: ███████ School: ███████ MS City: ███████ State: ██

Use this "textbook" diary to record use of materials to support instruction and learning in your 2nd math class of the day. "Textbook" as used below refers to the district-adopted mathematics textbook. Continue this diary until you have 10 entries (10 consecutive lessons). If there is a day when you are absent or have some other interruption (e.g., school assembly), skip that day but continue with the log until you have 10 entries.

Date	General topic of lesson?	a) What did you do to plan this lesson? b) What materials did you use?	Textbook pages used by TEACHER (unit & pages)	Textbook pages used by STUDENTS during the lesson (unit & pages)	Homework from textbook assigned (unit & pages)	Other print materials used by TEACHER	Other materials used by STUDENTS
10-07-03	To learn that the areas of an object is the number of unit squares needed to cover it + that perimeter is the number of units of length needed to surround it.	a) Read TM p. 6-9 and 18a-c b) Covering + Surrounding TM	Covering + Surrounding TM p. 6-9 and 18a-c	Covering + Surrounding p. 6-9	none	none	square tiles grid paper
	• Addition of Fractions (1st Review Lesson)	a) Prepared 3 lessons to review add/sub fractions. This lesson focused on estimation w/ benchmarks. b) various resources including materials	None	None - students took notes	none	Warm-Up	None
10-9-03	To understand what two figures with the same area may have different perimeters - vice versa.	a) Read TM p. 10-11 and 18c-f b) Covering + Surrounding TM	Covering + Surrounding TM p. 10-11 and 18c-f	Covering + Surrounding p. 10-11	none	none	None
	• Addition of Fractions (2nd Review Lesson)	a) Prepared 3 lessons to review add/sub fractions. This lesson focused on estimation again. also why 3/4 + 3/4 can't be 6/8. b) (Adding num + denom. won't work)	None	None - students took notes	None	Warm-Up	None
10-13-03	To visualize what changes when tiles forming a figure are rearranged, added or subtracted.	a) Read TM p. 12 and 18f-j b) Covering + Surrounding TM	Covering + Surrounding TM p. 12 and 18f-j	Covering + Surrounding p. 12	Covering + Surrounding ACE 2-5,10,11 p.14-15	none	square tiles grid paper
	• Addition of Fractions (3rd Review Lesson)	a) Prepared 3 lessons to review add/sub fractions. This lesson focused on estimation and the algorithm. b) see above	None	None - students took notes	None	Warm-Up	None
10-15-03	To develop techniques for estimating areas + perimeters of non-geometric figures.	a) Read TM p. 19-20 and 28a-c b) Covering + Surrounding TM	Covering + Surrounding TM p. 19-20 and 28a-c	Covering + Surrounding p. 19-20	none	none	grid paper string
	No skills lesson	—	None	None	None	Add/Sub Fractions Practice Sheet Warm-Up	None
10-17-03	To develop techniques for estimating areas + perimeters of non-geometric figures.	a) Read TM p. 19-20 and 28a-c b) Covering - Surrounding TM	Covering + Surrounding TM p. 19-20 and 28 a-c	Covering + Surrounding p. 19-20	Covering - Surrounding ACE 3-7, 9-15 p. 22-24	none	grid papers string
	No skills lesson	—	None	None	None	Add/Sub Fractions Practice Sheet Warm-Up	None

University of Missouri (MS)2 Study (8/02/02)

Figure 5.1 Example of *Textbook-Use Diary* completed with detail.

the example shown. Still, the tool enabled the researchers to determine how often the teacher and the students used the district-adopted textbook during the 30 days of monitored instruction.

After collecting the diaries, we determined the percentage of days that the textbook was used as reported by each teacher. Of course, this method is not necessarily sensitive to the fact that teachers may use the book for only a short time during a given lesson.

Figure 5.2, derived from the textbook-use diaries, shows the percentage of days the textbook was used by each teacher, grouped by textbook. The teacher who reported not using the textbook confirmed during an interview that neither she nor her students used the district-adopted textbook. Thus, this teacher failed to satisfy one of our components for textbook integrity and, consequently, we did not include student data from this teacher's classroom in subsequent analysis relating student learning to textbook use. As shown in Figure 5.2, all but three of the teachers in the study used the textbook more than 60 percent of the 30 days of instruction documented in the diary. The data suggest some variability within each of the textbooks, although the sample per textbook is small.

Use of a Significant Portion of the Textbook

A *Table-of-Contents Implementation Record* provided data on the second component of textbook integrity: use of a significant portion of the textbook. In this case, we were interested not in how often the textbook was used, but rather how much of it was used over the course of a school year. This instrument consisted of a photocopy of the Table of Contents from each textbook. Teachers used a highlighter to indicate lessons from the textbook that were a focus of classroom

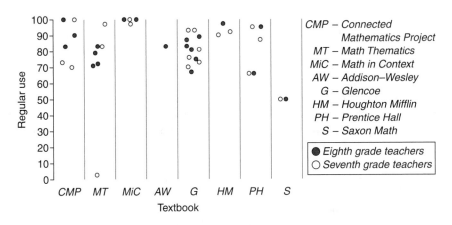

Figure 5.2 Regular use of the textbook.

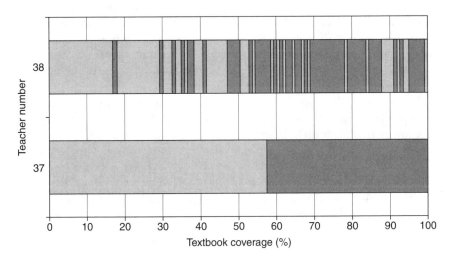

Figure 5.3 Lessons taught/omitted by two teachers using *Saxon*.

instruction. These records were collected four times during the academic year. Figure 5.3 represents data from two teachers who completed the *Table-of-Contents Implementation Record* for textbooks published by Saxon Publishers.

The horizontal bar shown for each teacher indicates the set of lessons ordered from the first page to the last page of the textbook. The dark gray segments indicate omitted lessons and the light gray segments represent taught lessons as documented by the teacher using the *Table-of-Contents Implementation Record*. Teacher 37, a novice teacher, began with the first lesson in the textbook and utilized each subsequent lesson, stopping about halfway through the textbook when the school year ended. As a result, Teacher 1 taught approximately 58 percent of the textbook lessons. Teacher 38, an experienced teacher, made different choices about which lessons to teach, skipping through the textbook; however this teacher covered an equivalent amount of the textbook (58 percent). In these two cases, the teachers made vastly different decisions about which lessons to teach.

Figure 5.3 indicates that only measuring regular use, using the *Textbook Use Diary* discussed above, is not sufficient for determining textbook integrity. In other words, capturing only the number of days the textbook was used does not reflect the distribution of lessons taught apparent in Figure 5.3. Moreover, imagine two other teachers who reported using the textbook on 100 percent of the days recorded in the *Textbook Use Diary*; however, one teacher moved at such a slow pace that he or she covered a minimal amount of the textbook over the course of the year, while the other teacher used tasks from the textbook only during the "warm-up" portion of the lesson, again only using a minimal amount of the textbook over the course of the year. These examples illustrate the need for the second component in examining textbook integrity: use of a significant portion of the textbook. Research studies investigating teachers' use of textbooks should measure the extent of use as well as the distribution of lessons taught. We found the *Table-of-Contents Implementation Record* to be a practical and useful tool for documenting this important aspect. We also found this instrument to be flexible in measuring the distribution of lessons taught in a variety of contexts, including districts with contrasting policies.

In contrast to the teachers represented in Figure 5.3, we found different patterns in other districts where the local policy explicitly dictated the pacing and sequencing of units from its adopted curriculum program. In these districts, we found the graphs for teachers within a grade level to be similar. These examples suggest that it is important for researchers to consider and collect information about district policies when investigating teachers' use of textbooks. These examples also illustrate the flexibility of the *Table-of-Contents Implementation Record* as a tool that can measure the distribution of lessons taught in a variety of contexts.

Consistency with the Pedagogical Orientation of the Textbook

The first two components enabled the researchers to determine whether teachers were regularly using their textbooks and which portions of the textbook they used. However, these components did not allow us to determine whether teachers were using their textbooks in a manner consistent with the pedagogical orientation of the textbook – the third component for textbook integrity. Here we were interested in the extent to which teachers used pedagogical practices consistent with those suggested in the teacher's guides.

To measure this aspect of textbook integrity in classrooms using NSF-funded curriculum programs, we used a *Classroom Observation* protocol. The instrument, adapted from an observation tool used by the Wisconsin Longitudinal Study (Romberg & Shafer, 2004), was designed to measure *Standards*-based instructional practices as reflected in the *Standards* of the National Council of Teachers of Mathematics [NCTM] (1989, 1991, 1995, 2000). Financial constraints limited the number of classroom observations we conducted for each teacher. However, even though teachers were observed only three times (October, February, and April), data from the observations were consistent across observations and appeared to be typical of their instruction. In addition to the observations, we conducted individual teacher interviews to triangulate our analyses. From the observation protocol, we identified five features that indicated whether teachers were using *Standards*-based instructional strategies:

1. The lesson provided opportunities for students to make conjectures about mathematical ideas.
2. The lesson fostered the development of conceptual understanding.
3. Students explained their responses or solution strategies.
4. Multiple perspectives/strategies were encouraged and valued.
5. The teacher valued students' statements about mathematics and used them to build discussion or work toward shared understanding for the class.

For each observation, the researcher determined the extent to which these five features were present and assigned a 1, 2, or 3 based on a rubric (for more details related to this process and inter-rater reliability, see Tarr et al., 2008). After the three observations were completed, we summed the three observation scores for each teacher for each feature. Hence, a feature assigned ratings of 1, 1, and 1 had a sum of 3, and a feature assigned ratings of 2, 2, and 3 had a sum of 7. For each feature, sums of 7, 8, or 9 were classified as high incidence, sums of 5 or 6 as medium, and sums of 3 or 4 as low incidence. To obtain a composite code for all five features for each teacher, we subsequently assigned each high rating a 2, medium rating a 1, and low rating a 0, and then summed the five incidence codes.

This process allowed us to compile the data from three classroom observations for each teacher into one composite score for teachers using NSF-funded curriculum programs. We refer to this composite score as a *Standards-Based Learning Environment* (SBLE) index (0–10 point scale). The first three columns

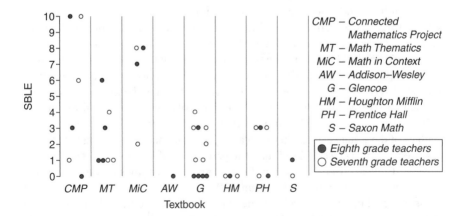

Figure 5.4 Standards-Based Learning Environment index for each teacher by textbook.

in Figure 5.4 display the SBLE indices for each teacher who used NSF-funded curriculum programs, CMP, MT, and MiC.

For the 16 teachers (one of them taught more than one grade) who used NSF-funded curriculum programs, the SBLE indices ranged from 0–10, displaying the variability of the use of *Standards*-based instructional strategies. That is, some of the teachers in the sample who used *Standards*-based textbooks also used *Standards*-based instructional practices. However, using a *Standards*-based textbook did not ensure use of *Standards*-based instructional strategies, as noted in Figure 5.4 (for more discussion of this, see Tarr, Chávez, Reys, & Reys, 2006). We found that the SBLE index was sensitive to the variability of classroom practices within each of the three NSF-funded curriculum programs as well as across the three programs.

The five columns on the right in Figure 5.4 represent the SBLE indices for the teachers using publisher-developed textbooks. It is not surprising that the SBLE indices for the teachers in the publisher-developed textbook columns ranged from 0–4 due to the fact that the five features captured in the SBLE index were not necessarily consistent with what was emphasized in these textbooks. In other words, even though teachers using publisher-developed textbooks were less likely to use *Standards*-based instructional strategies, they may in fact have been adhering closely to the pedagogical orientation of their textbook.

We chose not to describe or measure adherence to the pedagogical orientation in textbooks other than the NSF-funded programs, in part due to the wide range of textbooks used within the study and because of the difficulty in identifying a stated philosophy in the materials. Thus, based on the data we collected, we could only consider textbook integrity for teachers using NSF-funded curriculum materials.

Determining Textbook Integrity

Each of the three instruments used in our study posed potential limitations. For example, we recognized that the *Textbook-Use Diary* and the *Table-of-Contents Implementation Record* involved teacher self-report data. However, we did not use these three data sources in isolation but rather in concert in order to corroborate findings and minimize the inherent limitations of each instrument. As a set, the three instruments captured differences in textbook use and considerable variation across teachers, and enabled us to identify teachers who met a minimum threshold to determine whether student data from particular teachers' classrooms should be included in the analyses. In this section, we demonstrate how we determined the degree of textbook integrity using the three components.

Table 5.1 provides a summary of the data collected from the three instruments for teachers using NSF-funded curriculum materials. It includes the percentage of days that each teacher indicated using the materials during the 30 days reported on the *Textbook-Use Diary*, the percentage of lessons highlighted in the *Table-of-Contents Implementation Record*, and the composite rating for the *Standards-Based Learning Environment* (SBLE).

As depicted in Table 5.1, all but one of the teachers used their district-adopted programs frequently (at least 70 percent of the documented days), which is consistent with the literature (Grouws & Smith, 2000; Whittington, 2000). The

Table 5.1 Indicators of Textbook Integrity for Teachers Using NSF-Funded Curriculum Materials

Teacher no.	District-adopted Textbook	Grade	Regular Use (%)	Significant Portion (%)	SBLE Index
1	CMP	7	73	27	1
2	CMP	7	70	30	6
3	CMP	8	83	40	3
4	CMP	8	90	50	0
5	CMP	7 & 8	100	61 (7th) 74 (8th)	10
6	Math Thematics	7	0	0	1
7	Math Thematics	8	79	61	6
8	Math Thematics	7	83	80	4
9	Math Thematics	7	97	78	1
10	Math Thematics	8	71	84	1
11	Math Thematics	8	72	96	3
12	Math Thematics	8	83	87	1
13	MiC	7	97	66	2
14	MiC	7	100	72	8
15	MiC	8	100	87	8
16	MiC	8	100	89	7

average for all 16 teachers was 81 percent. After removing the outlier (0 percent), the average for the remaining 15 teachers was 87 percent. This rate of use did not necessarily correlate to using a significant portion of the textbook, as seen in the case of Teacher 1 who reported using the textbook 73 percent of the time and teaching 27 percent of the available textbook lessons. Nine of the 16 teachers taught at least 70 percent of the lessons in their textbooks, and only one of the teachers taught more than 90 percent of her textbook. One of the teachers reported not using her district-adopted textbook at all. With regard to use of *Standards*-based instructional strategies, the SBLE rating ranged from 0 to 10, and only six teachers had a SBLE index of 6 or higher.

The data in Table 5.1 provide several cases that underscore the importance of each of the three measures. For example, Teacher 2 indicated regular use of the textbook (70 percent) and had an SBLE composite of 6. However, over the course of the school year, students in this teacher's classroom had an opportunity to study only 30 percent of the curriculum outlined for a year of study. Therefore, this classroom had low textbook integrity. Similarly, Teacher 9 indicated using the book 97 percent of the time and taught over three-fourths of the lessons, but did not exhibit the five features consistent with the pedagogical orientation associated with NSF-funded curriculum materials, receiving an SBLE composite rating of 1. These two examples, for different reasons, illustrate that a causal connection between students' learning outcomes and the district-adopted textbook would be difficult to justify. On the other hand, there were four teachers who indicated using the curriculum materials 100 percent of the time, had high SBLE composite ratings (10, 8, 8, 7), and used a significant portion of the materials. In these four cases, there is high textbook integrity. For students in these four teachers' classrooms the textbook is a significant contributor to their opportunity to learn mathematics, and therefore it is appropriate to include the textbook as a variable in examining student learning outcomes.

Table 5.2 includes a summary of the three measures we collected on the 22 teachers who used publisher-developed curriculum materials. Interestingly, these 22 teachers also reported teaching from the textbook on average 81 percent of the time. Figure 5.2 shows how similar all 38 teachers were in terms of their regular use of the textbook. Teachers using the publisher-developed textbooks also varied, but to a lesser degree than the teachers using NSF-funded programs, in the amount they used their textbooks over the course of a full school year (31 percent to 97 percent). As stated earlier, the SBLE indices for the teachers in the publisher-developed textbook columns ranged from 0–4, and this is not surprising since the five features captured in the SBLE index are not necessarily consistent with what is emphasized in these textbooks. As a result, we were limited to data on two, rather than three, components in considering the relationship between teachers' use of curriculum materials and student achievement for this group.

Our research team faced numerous challenges in designing and conducting a study to examine the association between textbooks and student learning outcomes. (For a detailed discussion, see Chval, Reys, Reys, Tarr, & Chávez, 2006.) For example, in collecting and analyzing the data, we recognized challenges due to (a) the small numbers of teachers who satisfied the minimal threshold for all three components that constitute textbook integrity, and (b) an even smaller number of teachers satisfying the components over two years. As we began to follow students over two years, we found that most students did not have access to minimal textbook integrity for two consecutive years using the same curriculum. For example, some students were in classrooms with high textbook integrity in sixth grade, but not in seventh grade. Other students used NSF-funded curriculum materials in seventh grade and then publisher-developed textbooks in eighth grade. Another challenge emerged when students were assigned to different types of courses, such as remedial, regular, and accelerated. In these cases, a teacher may have high textbook integrity while teaching an accelerated class, but not while teaching the remedial classes. In one school, there were 636 sixth-graders in three different types of classes: remedial, regular, and accelerated. The resulting nine different trajectories that they took into seventh grade illustrate the complexity of examining relationships between student achievement and textbook integrity over multiple years.

Researchers need to anticipate this potential complexity in collecting and analyzing data related to textbook integrity, and devise methods to track student course assignment. In addition, it is critical to collect data from each track that a participating teacher teaches so that it is not assumed that the measure of textbook integrity is equivalent across the different types of mathematics courses he or she teaches.

Table 5.2 Data for Teachers Using Publisher-Developed Textbooks

Teacher No.	District-Adopted Textbook	Grade	Regular Use (%)	Significant Portion (%)	SBLE
17	*Mathematics – Applications and Connections Glencoe (MAC-Glencoe)*	7	81	79	2
18	MAC-Glencoe	7	76	84	1
19	MAC-Glencoe	8	87	73	0
20	MAC-Glencoe	8	89	45	0
21	MAC-Glencoe	7	70	66	4
22	MAC-Glencoe	7	73	77	3
23	MAC-Glencoe	7	93	91	1
24	Addison-Wesley *Middle School Math*	8	83	78	0
25	Addison-Wesley *Middle School Math*	8	75	94	0
26	MAC-Glencoe	8	83	97	0
27	Prentice Hall *Mathematics*	7/8	87 & 66	61 & 89	3
28	Prentice Hall *Mathematics*	7	95	83	0
29	Prentice Hall *Mathematics*	8	95	64	0
30	Houghton Mifflin *Mathematics Experience*	7	92	65	0
31	Houghton Mifflin *Mathematics Experience*	7	90	59	0
32	*Mathematical Connections* Houghton Mifflin	8	97	58	0
33	MAC-Glencoe	7	93	66	3
34	MAC-Glencoe	7	93	58	4
35	MAC-Glencoe	8	81	48	3
36	MAC-Glencoe	8	67	31	0
37	Saxon *Math 87*	7	50	58	0
38	Saxon *Algebra 1/2*	8	50	58	1

Conclusion

In today's political context, there is a call to assess the effects of various curriculum programs on student achievement. Yet doing so is problematic if such comparisons are predicated on assumptions about whether and how teachers are using the textbooks. Moreover, too often there is an expectation that if a given textbook is used in a high-achieving district or school, then adoption of that same textbook in another district will yield similar success. This naïve assumption overlooks other important variables (e.g., teacher professional development and teacher decision-making) that affect student outcomes, and ignores the complexities that our data illustrate. Teachers, even when under strict district policies, still have a certain margin of decision-making related to how they use their district-adopted textbooks. Documenting and understanding the resulting variations in textbook integrity is required to illuminate the interpretation of student performance data.

We described our approach for collecting and analyzing data related to textbook integrity; however, other approaches would be appropriate depending on the research purposes and contexts. The most problematic component to measure was the extent to which the teacher utilized instructional strategies consistent with the pedagogical orientation of the textbook. The NSF-funded and publisher-developed textbooks in our study provided different levels of detail regarding the expectations and descriptions of how to use the materials. Furthermore, even though MiC, CMP, and MT are based on the NCTM *Standards*, their pedagogical orientations differ (Huntley, 2006). Researchers pursuing an investigation of textbook integrity in classrooms using publisher-developed textbooks would require either specific observation protocols for each textbook or a common classroom observation protocol focused on broad features. Given the different pedagogical orientations of currently available textbooks, it is important that this receives greater attention in future studies.

In this chapter, we discussed issues and decisions we made in designing and conducting a large-scale research study on the use of middle school curriculum materials and its relation to student achievement. We introduced the construct of textbook integrity, identified its three critical components, and described methods for measuring textbook integrity. Taken together, examining all three components captured differences in textbook use and considerable variation across teachers. Based on our work, we believe that the construct of textbook integrity is a unique contribution to the field that differs from fidelity of implementation in important ways. Even though researchers have offered different interpretations and definitions for the concept of fidelity of implementation, they focus their efforts primarily on characterizing the degree to which teaching practices *match* a standard (i.e., either the authors' intent or the written curriculum materials), implying a desired exactness. On the other hand, researchers examining textbook integrity would not try to determine if teaching practices match the standard. Rather, they would focus their efforts on documenting how teachers *use* the district-adopted textbook in order to determine whether it primarily influences the content, pedagogy, and the nature of student activity. Without measuring textbook integrity, associations between student learning outcomes and textbooks are simply unwarranted.

Acknowledgments

The study was funded by the United States Department of Education (no. R303T010735) and the Center for the Study of Mathematics Curriculum (NSF award no. ESI-0333879).

References

Ben-Peretz, M. (1990). *The teacher–curriculum encounter: Freeing teachers from the tyranny of texts.* Albany, NY: State University of New York Press.

Cai, J., Grouws, D. A., Kehle, P., Kilpatrick, J., Lambdin, D. V., Moyer, J. C. et al. (2007, March). *Designing longitudinal studies of curricula: Insights from three NSF-funded projects.* Presented at the research presession of the Annual Meeting of the National Council of Teachers of Mathematics, Atlanta, GA.

Cho, J. (1998, April). *Rethinking curriculum implementation: Paradigms, models, and teachers' work.* Paper presented at the Annual Meeting of the American Educational Research Association, San Diego, CA.

Chval, K., Reys, R., Reys, B., Tarr, J., & Chávez, O. (2006). Pressures to improve student performance: A context that both urges and impedes school-based research. *Journal for Research in Mathematics Education, 37*(3), 158–166.

Fullan, M., & Pomfret, A. (1977). Research on curriculum and instruction implementation. *Review of Educational Research, 47*(1), 335–397.

Grouws, D. A., & Smith, M. S. (2000). NAEP findings on the preparation and practices of mathematics teachers. In E. A. Silver & P. A. Kenney (Eds.), *Results from the seventh mathematics assessment of the National Assessment of Educational Progress* (pp. 107–139). Reston, VA: National Council of Teachers of Mathematics.

Hall, G. E., & Loucks, S. F. (1981). Program definition and adaptation: Implications for inservice. *Journal of Research and Development in Education, 14*(2), 46–58.

Huntley, M. (2006, April). *Using CBAM theory to study implementation of two middle-grades mathematics curricula: Connected Mathematics and Math Thematics.* Paper presented at the research presession of the Annual Meeting of the National Council of Teachers of Mathematics, St Louis, MO.

Kilpatrick, J. (2003). What works? In S. L. Senk, & D. R. Thompson (Eds.), *Standards-based school mathematics curricula: What are they? What do students learn?* (pp. 471–488). Mahwah, NJ: Lawrence Erlbaum.

Lambdin, D. V., & Preston, R. V. (1995). Caricatures in innovation: Teacher adaptation to an investigation-oriented middle school mathematics curriculum. *Journal of Teacher Education, 46*(2), 130–140.

National Council of Teachers of Mathematics. (1989). *Curriculum and evaluation standards for school mathematics.* Reston, VA: Author.

National Council of Teachers of Mathematics. (1991). *Professional standards for teaching mathematics.* Reston, VA: Author.

National Council of Teachers of Mathematics. (1995). *Assessment standards for school mathematics.* Reston, VA: Author.

National Council of Teachers of Mathematics. (2000). *Principles and standards for school mathematics.* Reston, VA: Author.

National Research Council. (2002). *Scientific research in education.* Committee on Scientific Principles for Education Research. R. J. Shavelson, & L. Towne (Eds.). Washington, DC: National Academy Press.

National Research Council. (2004). *On evaluating curricular effectiveness: Judging the quality of K-12 mathematics evaluations.* Committee for a Review of the Evaluation Data on the Effectiveness of NSF-Supported and Commercially Generated Mathematics Curriculum Materials. J. Confrey, & V. Stohl (Eds.). Washington, DC: The National Academies Press.

No Child Left Behind Act of 2001, Pub. L. No. 107–110, 115 Stat. 1425 (2002).

Remillard, J. T. (2005). Examining key concepts in research on teachers' use of mathematics curricula. *Review of Educational Research, 75*(2), 211–246.

Romberg, T. A., & Shafer, M. C. (Eds.). (2004). *Purpose, plans, goals, and conduct of the study (Mathematics in Context Longitudinal/Cross-Sectional Study Monograph # 1)*. Madison, WI: University of Wisconsin, Wisconsin Center for Education Research.

Ruiz-Primo, M. A. (2005, April). *A multi-method and multi-source approach for studying fidelity of implementation.* Paper presented at the Annual Meeting of the American Educational Research Association, Montreal, Canada.

Senk, S. L., & Thompson, D. R. (Eds.). (2003). *Standards-based school mathematics curricula: What are they? What do students learn?* Mahwah, NJ: Lawrence Erlbaum.

Snyder, J., Bolin, F., & Zumwalt, K. (1992). Curriculum implementation. In P. W. Jackson (Ed.), *Handbook of research on curriculum: A project of the American Educational Research Association* (pp. 402–435). New York, NY: Macmillan.

Spillane, J. P., & Zeuli, J. S. (1999). Reform and teaching: Exploring patterns of practice in the context of national and state mathematics reforms. *Educational Evaluation and Policy Analysis, 21*(1), 1–27.

Stein, M. K., Remillard, J. T., & Smith, M. S. (2007). How curriculum influences student learning. In F. K. Lester Jr. (Ed.), *Second handbook of research on mathematics teaching and learning* (pp. 319–369). Charlotte, NC: Information Age.

Tarr, J. E., Chávez, O., Reys, R. E., & Reys, B. J. (2006). From the written to the enacted curricula: The intermediary role of middle school mathematics teachers in shaping students' opportunity to learn. *School Science and Mathematics, 106*(4), 191–201.

Tarr, J. E., Reys, R. E., & Reys, B. J., Chávez, O., Shih, J., & Osterlind, S. (2008). The impact of middle grades mathematics curricula and the classroom learning environment on student achievement. *Journal for Research in Mathematics Education, 39*(3), 247–280.

Whitehurst, G. J. (2003, April). *The Institute of Education Sciences: New wine, new bottles.* Paper presented at the Annual Meeting of the American Educational Research Association, Chicago, IL. Retrieved October 15, 2003, from http://www.ed.gov/rschstat/research/pubs/ies.pdf.

Whittington, D. (2002). *2000 national survey of science and mathematics education: Status of middle school mathematics teaching.* Chapel Hill, NC: Horizon Research.

6

Part II Commentary
Considering What We Know About the Relationship Between Teachers and Curriculum Materials

Janine T. Remillard

What do we understand about the relationship between curriculum materials and teaching? Taken together, the chapters in this book offer new insights into how teachers interpret, use, respond to, and learn from mathematics curriculum materials as well as factors that influence their use. They also uncover questions that need further investigation. The chapters in Part II offer conceptual and methodological frameworks that can help the field interpret these findings and guide future research. To a large extent, the four chapters in this part of the book offer starting points in the development of much needed theory that can serve as a foundation for research on the relationships among teachers, teaching, and curriculum materials.

I say "much needed" because, at present, the field of research on teachers' use of mathematics curriculum materials lacks a theoretical and conceptual base. As a field, we do not have – or have not been explicit about – theories that underlie and explain the relationships that are central objects of study. As a result, the field has not produced a body of knowledge about the teacher–curriculum material relationship that is generalizable across teachers, materials, or contexts, or that can inform the work of policy-makers, curriculum decision-makers, and curriculum material designers in substantive ways.

Theory is vital to a body of research because it frames the questions asked and the way they are asked. It also helps us understand and explain what we see. John Dewey (1929) once referred to theory as the most practical of all things. Even though they are often tacit, theories guide our actions and the decisions that underlie them. As Thompson (1994) put it, "Theory is the stuff by which we act with anticipation of our actions' outcomes and it is the stuff by which we formulate problems and plan solutions to them" (p. 229). In this sense, theory allows us to see both what we know and what we still need to understand.

In order to undertake and build on empirical research, a field needs theory to define and characterize the constructs under study, generate explanatory models for how these constructs interact, and develop procedures for examining and measuring their interactions. Moreover, new theories need to draw on existing and related models and theories. For instance, curriculum theorists have long offered frameworks for considering the differences in and the relationships among curriculum as outlined in policy documents, written in curriculum guides, and enacted or experienced in the classroom (Doyle, 1992). But there is limited conceptual clarity about what curriculum guidelines or printed materials *are* in relation to teaching practice. Even curriculum guides that specify pedagogy are not merely the enacted curriculum captured on the page. Then what are they? What do they comprise, and how do they communicate their intent to the teacher using them?

On the other side of the coin, how are teachers and the work of teaching conceptualized in this research, and how can these conceptualizations inform understandings of teachers in relation to curriculum materials? Over the years, researchers have looked to cognitive, social, and sociocultural theories to characterize teaching as intellectual work driven by knowledge and beliefs, as practical action, as mediated human activity, and as guided by habitus. How do these theories explain the process by which teachers read, follow, or use curriculum resources, and the influential factors that matter in this process?

The chapters in this part represent initial steps in the needed work of theoretical and conceptual development about teachers' interactions with curriculum materials. The authors identify and describe constructs and offer frameworks for how these constructs relate to one another. These frameworks, in turn, have implications for what we study about teachers and curriculum materials and how we do so. In the remainder of this commentary chapter, I synthesize the constructs and frameworks offered in the four chapters of Part II to build a conceptual map of the terrain of primary concern to research on teachers and curriculum materials. I then use this map to consider areas that need further conceptual or empirical work.

Theory Building

Drawing on sociocultural theory, Brown conceptualizes curriculum materials as cultural artifacts that mediate human activity. His Design Capacity Enactment Framework locates teacher and curriculum resources in an interactive relationship to one another, illustrating Wertsch's (1998) irreducible tension in examining agent–tool relationships: "Any attempt to reduce the account of mediated action to one or the other of these elements runs the risk of destroying the phenomenon under observation" (p. 25). By conceptualizing teaching as design, Brown (Chapter 2) frames the work of interpreting and using curriculum materials to plan and enact instruction as reflective of the teacher's agency while mediated by the particular features of the materials.

Stein and Kim (Chapter 3), as well as McClain, Zhao, Bowen, and Visnovska (Chapter 4), extend and elaborate the theoretical groundwork laid out by Brown. Stein and Kim use their comparative analysis of two curriculum programs to specify some of the features of curriculum materials that are likely to mediate the way teachers use them, such as their organization, the nature of the tasks, and the embedded supports for teachers. At the same time, acknowledging the irreducible tension between agent and tool, Stein and Kim's analysis considers how particular resources of the teacher, as individuals and as part of social networks, influence the mediational process by which teachers use materials. Brown introduced the term *pedagogical design capacity* (PDC) to characterize a teacher's "ability to perceive and mobilize" the pedagogical ideas embedded in curriculum resources in the process of crafting instruction. Stein and Kim's analysis sheds light on the variation in what we might call *designable* features of curriculum materials – components about which program designers have made explicit or tacit decisions. Further, they have considered how these features make the ideas in the materials available to particular teachers and less so for others, depending on their individual and system-wide pedagogical design capacities, to use Brown's term. By exploring particular dimensions of human and social capital as they play out in curriculum material use, Stein and Kim have identified one approach to measuring Brown's PDC construct for individual teachers and networks of teachers.

McClain and her colleagues focus their analysis on the teacher as agent in the teacher–text relationship and seek to understand the ways in which features of the institutional context – features that Stein and Kim might categorize as measures of social capital, influence the relationship. Like Stein and Kim, McClain et al. view curriculum materials and textbooks as boundary objects (Wenger, 1998) that carry meaning and authority between different communities of practice; however they focus their analysis on the ways that relationships between communities, particularly those of district decision-makers and teachers, influence teacher–textbook interactions. The critical, influential factors that McClain et al. identify (*teachers' instructional reality, agency*, and *teachers' professional status*) can be viewed as dimensions of what Stein and Kim have referred to as social capital. McClain et al. add detail to the notion of social capital by including both the extent to which teachers are positioned by others as having instructional authority in the classroom, and the extent to which teachers see themselves as possessing authority over the textbook. McClain et al.'s dimensions of social capital treat the entire school system or district as a complex social network and highlight the importance of relations across communities of practice within it, whereas Stein and Kim focus on the social relations and networks within communities.

In their analysis of the impact of institutional contexts on teacher–textbook relationships, McClain et al. identify an important teacher characteristic not necessarily specified in human capital (as described by Stein and Kim) or PDC (introduced by Brown); these two constructs focus on what an individual knows or is able to do. The characteristic identified by McClain et al. might be labeled as disposition, orientation (Remillard & Bryans, 2004), or professional identity (Spillane, 2000), and refers to how individual teachers situate themselves in relation to authority, what they are inclined to do, and what they see themselves as able to do in a particular institutional setting.

Chval, Chávez, Reys, and Tarr (Chapter 5) also focus on teacher–text interactions, but not on the factors that influence these interactions. Instead, they are interested in characterizing the extent to which teachers use the textbook as the basis for "determining the content, pedagogy and the nature of student activity over an identified period of time." They refer to this construct as *textbook integrity*. Here, the emphasis is on the role of the textbook as a guide rather than on the degree of match between the text and instruction. Although they argue that textbook integrity can include other dimensions, they focus on three components: (a) regular use of the textbook, (b) use of a significant portion of the textbook to determine content emphasis and instructional design over the school year, and (c) utilization of instructional strategies consistent with the pedagogical orientation of the textbook. In identifying these three components, these researchers offer an implicit conceptualization of dimensions of textbooks that matter for examining the extent of use – mathematical content *and* pedagogical and instructional emphases.

The model in Figure 6.1 represents my attempt to bring the constructs described in each chapter and discussed above together in one synthetic representation of the teacher–curriculum material terrain. I began with Brown's Design Capacity Enactment Framework, which represents the teacher and tool in a mediational relationship. I added to this model influential characteristics of both the teacher and curriculum resources specified by the chapters, including Brown's construct *pedagogical design capacity* (PDC). (See the ovals surrounding the teacher and curriculum resource circles.) Drawing on Stein and Kim's analysis, I added *human* and *social capital* to the teacher resources. The decision to identify social capital as having *local* and *global* components takes into account Stein and Kim's focus on local teacher networks as well as McClain et al.'s finding that global social systems and relationships within a district matter for teachers' curriculum use. I used McClain et al.'s terms *agency* and *professional status* to refer to how teachers locate themselves within a school system and the authority with respect to curriculum decision-making that accompanies these locations. Chapters 2, 3 and 5, by Brown, Stein and Kim, and Chval et al., respectively, all describe aspects of what the curriculum resource includes. (These are represented in the ovals surrounding the curriculum resource.) They all speak to inclusion of mathematical topics and tasks that are structured in deliberate ways. Stein and Kim also highlight the presence of embedded supports for the teacher to guide pedagogical decision-making. Chval and her colleagues identify the presence of a pedagogical orientation or emphasis embedded in instructional strategies and lesson structures.

The textured rings that surround the teacher and curriculum represent features of the institutional contexts (discussed by Stein and Kim and McClain et al.) that contribute to the influence of these factors, including the structure of social relationships within the system, and the instructional authority granted to teachers and curriculum materials through policy and practice. The instructional outcomes – namely the content covered, the mathematical tasks used, and the pedagogical emphasis – result from the interaction between the teacher and the curriculum resources in a particular setting, the focus of analysis for Chval and her colleagues.

Certainly, this model is partial and is ripe for further development. In building it from the synergies in the four chapters, I took care to avoid adding to it from other research and frameworks. As I mentioned earlier, one of the potential

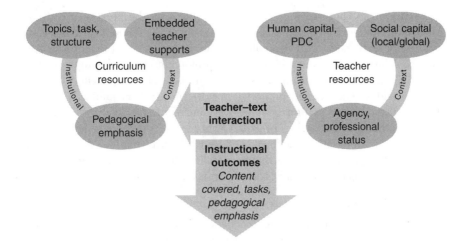

Figure 6.1 Conceptual model of teacher–curriculum interactions and relationships portrayed in the four chapters in Part II.

uses of models is to take stock of what one is and is not attending to, both conceptually and empirically. For instance, integrating the frameworks offered by these chapters illuminates the variety of related characteristics of the teacher and the curriculum resource that need to be taken into account. Moreover, this model highlights the significance of a number of contextual features in which the teacher–text relationship occurs. The model also makes visible dimensions of the curriculum–teacher relationship that merit further attention. I discuss several below.

Areas in Need of Further Development

Teacher–Curriculum Material Interactions

The teacher–curriculum material relationship is at the center of the model. (See the double-sided arrow between the teacher and the curriculum resources.) It is a pivotal component of the relationship between curriculum resources and classroom practice. As a set, the chapters in this part of the book reiterate the fact that there is not a direct line between a curriculum guide and classroom instruction. Teachers read, interpret, adapt, follow, improvise, or ignore the curriculum guide as a result of many individual and contextual factors. What the curriculum guide contains and how it is organized and positioned within a school system mediate this process. But what *is* this process? We know little about how teachers interact with curriculum resources. What verbs best describe teachers' work in curriculum use: following, reading, interpreting, transacting with, participating with? The chapters in this part offer insights into the factors that influence the teacher–text relationship, but provide few details about its nature.

A promising starting place for inquiry into this question is Brown's construct of pedagogical design capacity – a teachers' "ability to perceive and mobilize" the pedagogical ideas captured in a curriculum resource in the process of crafting instruction. Both verbs – perceive and mobilize – have implications for the nature of the work teachers do with curriculum resources, but much of this process has yet to be delineated. Work in this area will be profoundly challenging to undertake well, as it gets at some of the most individual and invisible components of teaching. That said, several chapters in this volume describe teachers' joint curriculum-planning that involves examinations of the contents of curriculum resources in light of the needs and capacities of particular students in a process referred to by Roth McDuffie and Mather (Chapter 21) as *curricular reasoning* (see also Chapters 9, 17, and 20). Analyses of the activity of teachers in groups such as these could offer initial insights to guide studies of teacher–text interactions.

Differentiating Curriculum Features

Much of the research regarding teachers and curriculum materials has focused on examining the personal resources teachers bring to and draw on when using curriculum materials. We know much less about curriculum materials themselves. Stein and Kim's analysis and Brown's conceptualization of curriculum resources represent work in another under-developed area of analysis – differentiating among curriculum features.

When distinctions are made among curriculum programs, they tend to be in broad strokes. This is evident in the way that all *Standards*-based curriculum materials tend to be treated as the same in many studies, just as all commercially-developed materials tend to be treated as the same. When components or features of the curriculum materials are analyzed, the focus tends to be on the mathematical structures and representations and the pedagogical emphasis (Schmidt, Jakwerth, & McNight, 1998; Stein, Remillard, & Smith, 2007). Even though *Standards*-based curriculum materials share a similar alignment with the agenda of the *Standards* (National Council of Teachers of Mathematics, 1989), they represent these ideas in different ways. Their authors made different choices about organizational structure, use of representations and applications, and classroom activities. They made different decisions about how and what to communicate to teachers, and what sorts of pedagogical and mathematical supports to provide. They made different decisions about how to organize their guidance in the books and on the page. Of course, some of these decisions were not the authors' alone, but resulted from compromises made with publishers. Regardless of how these decisions were made, the fact remains that each curriculum program has a number of features (some of which may seem trivial to the researcher or developer) that might figure significantly in how a teacher interacts with it. Beyond the work of Brown and of Stein and Kim (and Herbel-Eisenmann, 2007), we lack conceptualizations of what these features might include, which are needed before we can study how these features matter.

Alternatives to Measuring Fidelity

Another area in need of further conceptual work is how the relationship between teacher–text interaction and the curriculum that is enacted in the classroom is characterized and studied. There is considerable interest in the policy and research arenas in examining *curriculum fidelity*, a term used to refer to the extent to which the curriculum enacted in the classroom matches what is represented in the curriculum guide either in terms of specific instructional tasks or intended learning goals. In Chapter 5, Chval et al. point to a number of problems with this approach, including the challenge of determining from written curriculum materials a specific image for classroom instruction. Instead, these researchers offer a different construct, *textbook integrity*, which considers the extent to which the teacher has drawn on the textbook as the "primary guide" in designing instruction, including the topics covered, the student activities used, and the pedagogical approach employed. This construct places primary emphasis on the process of using, rather than following, a curriculum resource.

As a field, it is critical that we continue to develop approaches to describe the relationship between curriculum materials and the enacted curriculum that are both practical and reflective of its complexity. Chval and her colleagues have made initial steps in this terrain. However, there is much more work to be done.

Keeping an Eye on the Aim

As Dewey's assertion about the practicality of theory reminds us, theoretical progress in these (and other) domains would contribute immensely to how the field understands and studies the relationship between written and enacted curricula. Specifically, empirical and conceptual analyses that result in frameworks for describing and examining key features of and influences on the curriculum process are essential in answering our most important practical questions.

Acknowledgments

I would like to thank Beth Herbel-Eisenmann and Gwendolyn Lloyd for their helpful comments on earlier versions of this chapter.

References

Dewey, J. (1929). *The sources of a science of education.* New York, NY: Liveright Publishing.

Doyle, W. (1992). Curriculum and pedagogy. In P. W. Jackson (Ed.), *Handbook of research on curriculum* (pp. 486–516). New York, NY: Macmillan.

Herbel-Eisenmann, B. A. (2007). From intended curriculum to written curriculum: Examining the "voice" of a mathematics textbook. *Journal for Research in Mathematics Education, 38*(4), 344–369.

National Council of Teachers of Mathematics. (1989). *Curriculum and evaluation standards for school mathematics.* Reston, VA: Author.

Remillard, J. T., & Bryans, M. B. (2004). Teachers' orientations toward mathematics curriculum materials: Implications for teacher learning. *Journal of Research in Mathematics Education 35*(5), 352–388.

Schmidt, W., Jakwerth, P. M., & McNight, C. C. (1998). Curriculum sensitive assessment: Content *does* make a difference. *International Journal of Educational Research, 29,* 503–527.

Spillane, J. P. (2000). A fifth-grade teacher's reconstruction of mathematics and literacy teaching: Exploring interactions among identity, learning, and subject matter. *Elementary School Journal, 100*(4), 307–330.

Stein, M. K., Remillard, J. T., & Smith, M. S. (2007). How curriculum influences student learning. In F. K. Lester Jr. (Ed.), *Second handbook of research on mathematics teaching and learning* (pp. 319–369). Charlotte, NC: Information Age.

Thompson, P. W. (1994). Images of rate and operational understanding in the fundamental theorem of calculus. *Educational Studies in Mathematics, 26*, 229–274.

Wenger, E. (1998). *Communities of practice. Learning, meaning and identity.* Cambridge: Cambridge University Press.

Wertsch, J. V. (1998). *Mind as action.* New York, NY: Oxford University Press.

7

Part II Commentary

A Curriculum Decision-Maker's Perspective on
Conceptual and Analytical Frameworks for Studying
Teachers' Use of Curriculum Materials

Matthew R. Larson

Today, nearly every conversation among K-12 teachers and school administrators concerning the teaching and learning of mathematics eventually involves the No Child Left Behind Act of 2001 (NCLB, 2002). NCLB requires schools to improve student achievement in mathematics (and reading) annually. As the authors in Part II of this book point out, mathematics education has a long history of faith in curriculum programs and their implementation as a means to improve student achievement. Consequently, school practitioners first look to implement new curriculum programs as the primary vehicle by which to accomplish these ever-increasing required levels of student achievement. The issues raised by the authors of Part II of this book have direct implications for individuals charged with making curriculum decisions and providing implementation support to teachers at the K-12 level.

Unwavering Faith in Curriculum Materials Leads to the Quest for Fidelity at the School Level

Because the vast majority of curriculum decision-makers (e.g., district directors of curriculum, subject-specific curriculum supervisors and specialists) charged with improving student achievement believe deeply in the power of curriculum materials, we also tend to place high value on teachers' fidelity to "official" curriculum materials. The K-12 textbook implementation process is premised, as McClain, Zhao, Bowen, and Visnovska point out in Chapter 4, "on the belief that teachers can be trained to implement instructional texts with fidelity and that fidelity to the curriculum will lead to increased student achievement." These assumptions are not only universally accepted at the school level, they are also embedded in a great deal of federal education legislation, such as NCLB and Reading First, reinforcing our adherence to this basic model of implementation. As practitioners, we have a strong predisposition, as McClain and her colleagues argue, to give the agency, or the mathematical authority for students' learning, to the curriculum materials; in mathematics instruction, this typically means the textbook.

Chval, Chávez, Reys, and Tarr (Chapter 5) define text integrity as including three essential components: (a) teachers and students regularly use the officially adopted text, (b) teachers use a significant portion of the text to determine instruction, and (c) teachers utilize instructional strategies consistent with the pedagogical orientation of the text. This theoretical definition is not only consistent with the typical K-12 operational definition of fidelity, but the degree to which these three conditions are met is also often used to define and measure a successful curriculum program implementation.

Therefore, implementation support efforts at the district level, as McClain et al. point out, consequently focus on two questions. First, are the curriculum materials being implemented as intended? Second, what factors facilitate or hinder implementation as planned? Implementation support then takes the form of sharing successful teachers' implementation strategies with struggling teachers, and working to remove or resolve barriers to successful implementation. Having recently overseen the implementation of a district-wide mathematics curriculum program at 36 elementary sites with over 1,000 teachers, I can testify to the importance of these questions to both district and building administrators. Our entire first-year implementation support structure was built around these two questions. (In subsequent years, we shifted our emphasis to in-depth content and content-specific pedagogy professional development.) McClain and colleagues refer to this focus on implementation as intended as a "fidelity approach to implementation," in which, at the extreme, adherence to the text becomes the goal of teaching, as opposed to a process of design in which the text is a resource teachers use to help craft instruction.

Are There Unintended Consequences in the Quest for Fidelity?

McClain et al. argue that a teacher's "instructional reality" is greatly influenced by the degree to which administrators, designers, and teachers hold a fidelity view toward implementation. Their chapter should lead thoughtful curriculum decision-makers to reflect on the following questions: (a) What level of fidelity do we really want to seek? (b) Are there potentially negative consequences for requiring strict fidelity to the curriculum materials? When district curriculum administrators' professional development implementation efforts focus (at least initially) on how to use the text, we unintentionally leave some teachers with the impression that simply following the text is equivalent to teaching with a "new orientation." A disconnect is created when observation indicates teachers are not implementing recommended instructional practices as intended, but teachers believe they are simply because they are "using the text." Frustration is only increased when mathematics teachers are organized in collaborative or lesson study groups for instructionally oriented staff development, and we find that teachers have difficulty discussing the details of their instruction. Is the teachers' difficulty in discussing mathematics instruction rooted in the fact that we have communicated that the text is the authority on effective teaching practices? If the text holds all agency for student learning, what is there, from the teachers' perspective, to discuss?

As Chval et al. point out, even teachers who appear to use the curriculum materials may not actually enact the intended instructional philosophy. This finding raises additional questions: If building-level principals are the primary monitors of curriculum program implementation, do they know what instructional strategies they are looking for, or are they just looking for the physical presence of certain curriculum artifacts? Can professional learning communities (DuFour, DuFour, Eaker, & Karhanek, 2004), a concept increasingly implemented by schools to respond to student learning needs, provide a vehicle by which teachers could effectively monitor and support their own successful implementation of the curriculum materials? Would these learning groups be more effective if they were intentionally designed to include "asymmetrical expertise," as Stein and Kim (Chapter 3) suggest?

McClain et al. argue that when teachers face a fidelity approach to textbook implementation, their sense of professionalism may be threatened. Under McClain et al.'s framework, there are three levels of curriculum program adherence at the school level: (1) the curriculum is defined by the district, and the task of administrators is to ensure that teachers follow the curriculum; (2) teachers work from the district curriculum, but have some professional capacity to make professional decisions; (3) the text is viewed as a tool, and the teachers use it as a tool to design instruction. Their argument is that teachers' sense of professionalism increases as the level of program adherence moves from level one to level three.

Given today's accountability demands, however, more and more districts find themselves requiring level-one curriculum program adherence. Elementary teachers' professional lives, in particular, are made even more difficult when different levels of adherence to their curriculum materials are expected in the different subjects they teach. For example, what happens to elementary teachers' sense of coherence if the district-level reading instruction policy places all agency for student learning on the curriculum materials, but the mathematics program expects level-two adherence? Are teachers willing to place the agency for learning in different locations for different subjects, making professional decisions in one curriculum area, but not another? Differential agency by subject may potentially have a greater negative impact on teachers' overall sense of professional well-being than consistent expectations for program adherence no matter what level of adherence is expected, simply as a function of district incoherence.

The Importance of Considering "Instructional Realities"

Curriculum program selection at the school and district levels has always considered the curriculum program's organization and structure, but this has typically been limited to cosmetic concerns, such as pacing and generic "teacher friendliness." Stein and Kim argue that the nature of the curriculum program's mathematical tasks, its transparency, its structure (integral or modular), and how these factors interact with the district's organizational conditions contribute to teachers' ability to implement a particular curriculum program successfully and learn from it themselves. Social capital (the teachers' ability to access resources through relationships with others), Stein and Kim speculate, has a major effect on teachers' ability to implement the curriculum program. They argue that successful implementation of an integral curriculum program places high demands on the social capital of a building and district. Consideration of the district's social capital, however, is seldom a component of a district's curriculum program selection criteria. They warn that "leaders who disregard the need for social capital among teachers who are implementing challenging curriculum programs ... do so at a risk."

Too often, individuals at the school level charged with making curriculum decisions make those decisions in a theoretical vacuum, only asking "Which program is better?" We do not ask the more complex question raised by Stein and Kim, "Which program is better under what conditions?" I would suggest these conditions include not only consideration of the district's human capital and social capital, but in addition the teachers' beliefs, teachers' content knowledge, content-specific pedagogical knowledge, available planning time, as well as parental expectations and building administrative instructional expertise and support. Together, these conditions constitute a district's "instructional reality." It is this failure to appreciate the interaction of the district's instructional reality in relation to the nature of the curriculum program that may, in some cases, explain the failure of district-wide program implementations that worked when piloted in limited sites with high social capital.

Another argument Stein and Kim offer is that curriculum materials can be educative for teachers if the developers' rationales for including particular tasks are visible to teachers and if curriculum materials help teachers anticipate what students may think about or do in response to instructional tasks. They refer to materials that do this as "transparent." It is not uncommon today to see districts' curriculum program review criteria including "mathematics background" for the teacher, but "transparency" captures something more complex than merely attempting to enrich teachers' personal understanding of mathematics. Transparent materials not only provide mathematics background; they also connect this background to the instructional strategies, creating a synergy that may lead to enriched content-specific pedagogical knowledge.

Re-Conceptualizing the Operational Definition of Fidelity

Brown (Chapter 2) proposes that teachers' interactions with instructional materials can be understood in terms of different degrees of instructional appropriation of those materials: (a) *offloading*, when the materials are used as is, (b) *adapting*, when the materials are used but modified as necessary, and (c) *improvising*, when teachers minimally rely on the materials. Brown argues that this scale does not relate to teacher expertise and that it is value-neutral, but in many schools the reality is that administrators define fidelity as offloading. They look for use of the curriculum materials "as is," and end up using this framework in an evaluative way. An administrator who defines fidelity as offloading may unintentionally further the deprofessionalization of teachers and block highly effective teachers from appropriately adapting or improvising the curriculum to the benefit of students.

Brown argues that the scale is value-neutral because it reflects the fact that teaching cannot be reduced to recipe-following, that it is by definition a process of design. This is a reasonable claim. Anyone who has ever implemented a curriculum program at the K-12 level knows that implementation, including our perception of teachers' fidelity to the curriculum materials, is at best an uneven process. As Brown states, even between two highly skilled teachers "no two renditions of practice are exactly alike." At the school level, this unevenness has traditionally been attributed to the effectiveness of the implementation support structures. But this interpretation may overlook other possible explanations.

Accepting that teaching is a design process raises an additional consideration for the selection of a curriculum program, and calls into question our operational definition of fidelity. Rather than selecting a curriculum program and expecting all teachers to implement the curriculum materials with the same level of instructional appropriation, typically offloading or with minimal adaptation, we need to consider materials that support different modes of use by diverse teachers over time. The materials need to be robust enough to accommodate offloading, adapting, and improvising. However, because teachers clearly have different skills at effectively using curriculum materials, there is a need to determine and explicitly share with teachers the parameters for adapting and improvising curriculum materials. Can only certain teachers adapt and improvise? And if the answer the previous question is yes, then how do we allow for differential levels of freedom with respect to curriculum material appropriation and use? These questions are often dilemmas for curriculum decision-makers, because implementation plans are typically designed as one-year initiatives (e.g., this year mathematics and next year science). One-year implementation timeframes tend to force district and building administrators toward an offloading and strict curriculum materials adherence model, as it makes the evaluation of the implementation straightforward. However, if implementation is viewed not as a one-year time-bound event but instead as an open-ended continual process, then it may be possible to design a long-range implementation plan that would intentionally and gradually increase the degree of freedom teachers are given to adapt and improvise over the life of the curriculum materials while simultaneously providing teachers with the professional development necessary to enable them to do so in ways consistent with the district's goals for student learning.

Brown introduces the concept of "pedagogical design capacity" (PDC) to refer to "a teacher's capacity to perceive and mobilize existing resources in order to craft instructional episodes." This concept can help explain why two highly skilled teachers can enact the same curriculum program in very different ways. PDC appears to be an overlooked component of effective teaching that is not attended to during the implementation process in most districts. PDC raises more questions for the curriculum decision-maker to consider. Can we develop PDC in teachers? If so, how? If PDC emerges over time, as Brown suggests, what conditions accelerate its acquisition? Is it possible that PDC can be developed more readily with teachers in buildings with high social capital, using more transparent materials? If, as Brown suggests, curriculum customization tasks are embedded within professional development activities, does this increase a teacher's PDC? Do teachers with higher levels of PDC actually create learning contexts that lead to improved student achievement? Again, it may be possible to address these questions with a non-time-bound implementation process.

It seems reasonable to expect that teachers with high PDC will, at varying times, appropriately offload, adapt, and improvise, and that they will do so to craft highly effective and "dynamic instruction" to meet the needs of their students and improve student achievement. As school administrators, this would seem to be our ultimate goal, and we should seek to develop this skill in teachers as a component of their instructional practice. If this is one of our goals, then we have to be willing to re-conceptualize our operational definition of fidelity to mean something beyond strict adherence to the curriculum materials "as is." We must consider fidelity to mean use of the text as a tool that results in student learning consistent with the district's learning goals for students. Such a definition permits more flexible use of the curriculum materials while maintaining expectations for student learning of district objectives, thereby reducing the tension between a district's desire to control the curriculum and teacher autonomy to adapt and improvise. As administrators, we need to support different teacher appropriations of instructional materials, if done effectively by teachers with high PDC, as being consistent with our definition of fidelity. Our dilemma as curriculum decision-makers is, as Brown writes, to be "sufficiently open ended to accommodate flexible use, yet sufficiently constrained to provide coherence and meaning with respect to its [the curriculum's] intended uses" to ensure student learning consistent with our goals for students.

Implications for Curriculum Decision-Makers

The pressures of accountability have made the selection of mathematics curriculum programs and the supervision of implementation a high-stakes enterprise for school administrators. A common reaction to this pressure has been to define the curriculum program narrowly and require teachers to adhere strictly to it. This approach has assumed that every teacher can implement the curriculum program in the exact same manner, as if it were merely a matter of following a recipe. The authors of Part II of this book offer explanations for why this strategy has more often than not resulted in teacher resistance and disappointing results. But their work does more than this; it also points to specific actions curriculum decision-makers might consider to improve the selection and implementation of mathematics curriculum programs. When selecting curriculum programs, curriculum decision-makers should consider the "transparency" of the materials as a component of the selection criteria as well as the degree to which the materials support teaching as a process of design. When structuring and supporting the implementation of new materials, curriculum decision-makers should carefully weigh the district's instructional realities alongside consideration of the nature of the curriculum materials. Further, district curriculum leaders need to define clearly what fidelity means, and articulate parameters for acceptable curriculum program and material adaptation and improvisation. Further, implementation processes are likely to be more successful if these leaders adopt a broad operational definition of fidelity to include flexible use of adopted materials over time when such use is consistent with goals for student learning, and attend to the need to develop teachers' Pedagogical Design Capacity.

References

DuFour, R., DuFour, R., Eaker, R., & Karhanek, G. (2004). *Whatever it takes: How professional learning communities respond when kids don't learn.* Bloomington, IN: National Education Services.

No Child Left Behind Act of 2001, Pub. L. No. 107–110, 115 Stat. 1425 (2002).

III
Understanding the Relationships Among Teachers, Mathematics Curriculum Materials, and the Enacted Curriculum

8

How Can Curriculum Materials Support Teachers in Pursuing Student Thinking During Whole-Group Discussions?

Theresa J. Grant, Kate Kline, Carol Crumbaugh,

Ok-Kyeong Kim, and Nesrin Cengiz

With the availability of new curriculum materials that emphasize and build upon students' reasoning, greater demands have been placed on teachers to facilitate work around this reasoning. Studies have cited the challenges teachers face to engage effectively with students about their reasoning, particularly during whole-group discussions (e.g., Cobb, Wood, Yackel, & McNeal, 1992; Grant & Kline, 2002, 2004). This may be due in part to the fact that instruction based on student thinking will necessarily leave some aspects of any lesson undetermined. While one may have a sense of how a discussion might unfold by anticipating certain strategies and lines of reasoning, a teacher still has to consider in the moment which ideas would be most productive for that group of students to discuss, and how to consolidate their thinking. Some researchers have suggested that in order for teachers to navigate this terrain, the curriculum materials themselves must contain information specifically designed to help them learn as they use the materials (Ball & Cohen, 1996; Davis & Krajcik, 2005).

One such curriculum program, *Investigations in Number, Data, and Space* ("*Investigations*"; TERC, 1998), heeds this recommendation by embracing the notion that curriculum materials must be educative for teachers (see Russell, 2007). In particular, the *Investigations* curriculum materials include information for teachers embedded within lessons as well as in unique additional features that describe student thinking and illustrate sample classroom conversations. The intention is that this information will support teachers as they make the kinds of decisions necessary to encourage students to reason about mathematics. The question that follows, then, is how useful are curriculum materials designed specifically to be educative for teachers? In the study described in this chapter, we set out to investigate this issue by analyzing how the *Investigations* curriculum materials support teachers to enact one of the most challenging aspects of teaching – engaging with student thinking during whole-group discussion – in order to understand the efficacy of this novel approach to supporting teachers.

Our efforts to analyze both the curriculum materials and the ways teachers engaged with student thinking were greatly influenced by the work of Fraivillig,

Murphy, and Fuson (1999). Fraivillig and colleagues studied classrooms in which "exemplary" teachers were using a set of *Standards*-based curriculum materials, and distinguished among instructional moves teachers made when they paid attention to student thinking. Their framework of instructional moves included supporting, eliciting, and extending. *Supporting* actions were those focused on "supporting children in carrying out solution methods that were within their current cognitive capabilities" (p. 157). This category included actions such as restating and/or recording student thinking, providing background information, and asking a different student to rephrase or elaborate a peer's solution. *Eliciting* actions were those that provided students with an opportunity to express their mathematical thinking (e.g., asking for different solutions to a problem, providing sufficient wait-time, and encouraging elaboration). Finally, *extending* actions were those that pushed students to move beyond their individual solution strategies (e.g., asking students to try alternative solution methods, and encouraging generalization across concepts).

Fraivillig and her colleagues found that *supporting* actions were the most common of the three; furthermore, the authors conjectured that these actions might be "easier" for teachers because they were the closest to didactic teaching. Based on our experience with hundreds of teachers implementing the *Investigations* curriculum program, we would further conjecture that *extending* student thinking is the most difficult for teachers. In particular, we have found that teachers often find it difficult to move beyond sharing solutions in order to consider the mathematical rationale for those solutions, and rarely consider the generalizability of those solutions.

Based on these conjectures, we chose to study closely teachers' efforts to *elicit* and *extend* student thinking in the context of whole-group discussion. Although it is not possible to completely isolate the impact of curriculum materials on teachers' efforts in this area, we carefully chose teachers for this study in order to heighten the potential impact. First, we chose to study teachers who were implementing particular units from the *Investigations* curriculum program for the first time, and thus were less likely to have had any prior experiences with the particular activities or discussions. Furthermore, we chose to study teachers who were *thorough piloters* (Remillard & Bryans, 2004) of the curriculum materials – that is, their intention was to use the curriculum materials as their sole guide in planning instruction.

In this chapter we provide specific classroom examples of *eliciting* and *extending* student thinking, along with an analysis of the curriculum materials designed to support these lessons. We believe that this will contribute to our understanding of the kinds of information that may or may not be helpful to teachers as they use a set of educative curriculum materials and undertake the challenging work of engaging with student thinking.

Context

The study upon which this chapter is based involved teachers who were implementing units from *Investigations* for the first time. These six teachers were members of the mathematics curriculum committee for their elementary school, and were asked to identify mathematics curriculum materials that matched their magnet school theme of learning through exploration. After the committee determined that the *Investigations* curriculum program seemed to meet their needs, the entire committee chose to pilot one *Investigations* unit and to participate with the authors in a study of that pilot process. There were two main goals for the study of this pilot: (a) to ascertain what students learned during the unit, and (b) to consider the ways in which the curriculum materials supported the teachers to engage with student thinking. Portions of these data were used by the curriculum committee in making their report and recommendations to the entire school about the pilot and potential adoption of the materials.

Following the pilot, the school chose to continue with *Investigations* and gradually to proceed to full implementation. The teachers decided to begin by implementing the number and data units at all grade levels, with a plan to add geometry and measurement units in the following year. During this first full year of implementation, two of the original committee members, Danielle and Carly, agreed to participate in the continued study of their use of the curriculum materials. This chapter is based on data collected as Danielle and Carly enacted two different *Investigations* units for the first time.

Each teacher was interviewed at the start and at the end of each of the two units, and was observed six times during each unit. The interviews provided an indication of the teachers' views about using curriculum materials in general, as well as their perceptions about using the *Investigations* curriculum materials. The analysis of the enacted lessons focused on identifying episodes where student thinking was *supported, elicited,* or *extended,* and understanding the ways in which the teachers engaged with student thinking, particularly during whole-group discussion. For this chapter, we focused on episodes in which students' thinking was *elicited* and/or *extended,* as previous research identified these actions as occurring less frequently than *supporting* actions (Fraivillig et al., 1999). Analysis of the teachers' moves during these episodes was followed by an analysis of the support provided in portions of the curriculum materials relevant to the observed lessons. This latter analysis allowed us to describe the ways in which the curriculum materials may have supported the teachers' efforts to pursue student thinking. Finally, as a result of comparing the analyses of the curriculum materials and the teachers' moves, and then reflecting on our prior experiences with other teachers implementing *Investigations,* we suggest additional kinds of support that might have been helpful.

The Support Materials in *Investigations*

Given the central role of student thinking and teacher decision-making based on student thinking in the *Investigations* curriculum program, it would be impossible for support materials to prepare teachers for every possible classroom scenario that may emerge and, therefore, very difficult for the authors to determine the content and form of this support. Thus we begin by considering the various kinds of support provided for teachers in *Investigations.* At the start of the teacher's edition for each unit, there is a brief essay describing the important mathematical ideas that form the focus of the unit. Each individual lesson description includes a plethora of information for teachers, including suggestions for ways to introduce activities, questions to pose to students, and what to focus on when observing students at work. *Investigations* also includes two unique support features throughout each unit: Teacher Notes (TNs) and Dialogue Boxes (DBs). TNs describe the importance of particular content, explain various strategies students may use and why they work, or discuss connections among mathematics topics. These notes have the potential to prepare teachers for the student thinking they may observe, and the mathematical concepts that underlie such thinking. The DBs also provide teachers with examples of student thinking through sample dialogues a teacher may have with a student or group of students about a particular mathematical idea. Thus, the DBs also provide an image of the role of the teacher as a questioner whose main purpose is to pursue student thinking.

When asked how they utilized the curriculum materials, both teachers stated that they relied most heavily on the bolded questions provided in the lesson descriptions, as well as the DBs that contain sample discussions among teacher and students. Danielle used the DBs as a way to stimulate her thinking just before teaching a lesson. She stated:

> looking at those Dialogue Boxes makes me think more, "Oh, yeah, that is typically – " you know, it kind of lets me troubleshoot the poor responses or the poor interpretations of the questions I ask. It makes me think about them more. So the Dialogue Box, I'm finding, that's usually the last thing I read when I'm all done, when I pretty much have a plan, I'll read that and then go back and usually make a little adjustment and then I read that one more time right before [teaching].

Yet, both teachers also felt that they would benefit from more support from the curriculum materials about asking students productive questions. As Carly said:

> What I am always afraid of is that I am going to give kids the answer instead of letting them find ways. Well, I am going to say do this and I am going to tell them how to do it instead of them finding a way to do it.

Both teachers expressed a need for more examples of discussions that included thought-provoking questions by the teacher. Danielle noted that the DBs tend to include excellent "first" questions to get the discussion going, but there weren't enough examples of good second and third questions, because, she explained, "It is difficult to come up with the next question without giving it away."

Supporting Teachers' Efforts to *Elicit* and *Extend* Student Thinking

In contrast with the teachers studied by Fraivillig et al. (1999), some of whom *elicited* no student solutions during an observed lesson, Carly and Danielle made efforts to *elicit* student thinking as part of the whole-group discussion in every lesson we observed. Efforts to *extend* student thinking were also observed in both teachers' classrooms; however, unlike efforts to *elicit* student thinking, efforts to *extend* student thinking were not observed in every lesson. That we observed many efforts to *elicit* student thinking, and even some efforts to *extend* student thinking, is particularly noteworthy given both Fraivillig's results and the fact that these teachers were implementing *Investigations* for the first time. In the sections that follow, we provide in-depth discussion of two related lessons from the same teacher (Danielle) in order to highlight issues in *eliciting* and *extending* student thinking, and illustrate the ways in which the curriculum materials seemed to support the teachers' efforts to pursue student thinking. The next two sections each contain discussions of a particular lesson and the support provided for that lesson in the curriculum materials; a portion of whole-group discussion from the teachers' enactment of that lesson, including connections to Fraivillig and colleagues' (1999) notions of *supporting, eliciting,* and *extending* student thinking; and suggestions for how the curriculum materials might have better supported the teacher in facilitating student learning.

A Lesson with Support Material for Eliciting Student Thinking

The lesson *Factor Pairs from 100 to 1,000* occurs in the second week of a six-week unit on whole number computation (Kliman, Tierney, Russell, Murray, & Akers, 1998). As described in the curriculum materials, it is a three-day lesson with several related activities involving the exploration and analysis of factor pairs of multiples of 100. The final activity in this multi-day lesson is a whole-group discussion in which students: share the factor pairs of 1,000 that they found and explain how they found them; continue doing so until all factor pairs of 1,000 are accounted for; discuss how they know that they have all the factor pairs of 1,000; and step back to consider this complete list to discuss how they know that each of these pairs represents different rectangles with 1,000 squares. Prior to this lesson, students have been generating rectangular arrangements for various numbers and their factor pairs, and identifying relationships among factor pairs.

One of the main forms of support provided by the curriculum materials is information about the ways students may generate factor pairs. First, the curriculum materials contain multiple references to the "tools and approaches" that have been used thus far in class and that might be helpful in finding factor pairs, such as graph paper, square tiles, calculators, and skip counting (p. 35). Beyond the more "brute force" approach of generating factor pairs by skip counting, either with a calculator or a 300s chart, the curriculum materials highlight two particular strategies that focus on mathematical relationships. The first strategy provides a way to generate factor pairs of multiples of 100 by using known factor pairs for 100. For example, if 50×2 is a factor pair of 100, then you can double one number to generate a factor pair of 200 (e.g., 100×2). The second strategy provides a way to generate factor pairs for any number, by using a known factor pair for that same number: if 10×100 is a known factor pair of

1,000, you can generate a second factor pair by doubling one factor and halving the other factor, yielding either 5×200 or 20×50.

The Enacted Lesson

During the whole-group discussion at the end of this three-day lesson, Danielle *elicited* several factor pairs of 1,000, including 1000×1, 20×50, 4×250, and 2×500. One student, Ryan, explained that he generated 8×125 by using the factor pair 4×250, by halving one factor and doubling the other. The following discussion ensued:

TEACHER: Pay attention to see if you understand Ryan's thinking. Ryan started with this one. 4×250. So, we have four 250s. 250 here, 250, and 250 and 250. We know that's 1,000. Okay. One more time, how did you go from here [4× 250]?

RYAN: I multiplied the four times two and I divided the 250 by two.

TEACHER: So, you multiplied this [pointing to the 4] by two and then you divided this [pointing to the 250] by two?

RYAN: Yes.

TEACHER: So, you doubled this and cut that one in half. And it still worked out. Do you see?

Following this elaboration of Ryan's strategy, Danielle posed a general question, "Do you see?", to the rest of the class, which drew another student, Susan, into this conversation.

SUSAN: You can do that for every one of them.

TEACHER: Well, give me another one that works.

SUSAN: You could do 1,000 by one, which is two times 500.

TEACHER: Okay. Because...¹ tell me that again. Because I think I have it. To go from here 1,000, 1,000×1...

SUSAN: Cut 1,000 in half.

TEACHER: Cut this one [1,000] in half...

SUSAN: ...and...

TEACHER: and then you do what?

SUSAN: and double this one.

TEACHER: You double this one, right? You double this one [the one] and cut that one [the 1,000] in half. So, you have twice as much times half as much, and it still works out. So, we see a pattern between these two [4×250 and 8× 125] and the same pattern between these two [1,000×1 and 500×2]. Are there any others like these two, you can divide one, you can cut in half and double the other one?

In considering the moves made in this episode in light of the framework from Fraivillig et al. (1999) for pursuing student thinking, it is apparent that the teacher *elicited* several factor pairs for 1,000. At the start of the episode, she *sup-*

ported Ryan's thinking by rephrasing the starting point of the strategy by saying "Ryan started with this one. 4×250. So, we have four 250s. 250 here, 250, and 250 and 250. We know that's 1,000." In this way, Danielle drew attention to the strategy. Danielle then asked Ryan to elaborate on his strategy for finding factor pairs, thus simultaneously *eliciting* Ryan's thinking and potentially *extending* the thinking of the rest of the class by exposing them to a strategy they may not have considered. Finally, Danielle further *extended* the thinking of the entire class by having them consider the generalizability of Ryan's strategy.

There are several notable points about this series of moves by the teacher. With each successive move, Danielle made a decision to make student thinking more central to the conversation. In particular, Danielle's move of *extending* student thinking by engaging others in considering the generalizability of a strategy is one that we have not often seen in our experience with teachers implementing *Investigations*. That said, it is important to point out that Danielle might have further *extended* students' thinking by having students consider *why*, for a pair of factors of 1,000, the product of twice one factor and half the other factor is 1,000. In retrospect, and to external observers, these kinds of missed opportunities are often easier to recognize than when engaging with students. They are important to recognize, however, because they help teachers consider what might be done differently next time, and help curriculum developers understand what might be included in curriculum materials to support teachers' efforts to bring about student learning.

Exploring the rationale for the doubling/halving strategy could provide a context for students to grapple with important mathematical issues. For example, if one utilizes an area model of multiplication, one can imagine the factor pair (4, 250) as a rectangular array that is four units wide and 250 units long. Doubling one number and halving another can be interpreted in this context as cutting the array in half (creating two 4 by 125 pieces), and then rearranging these two new arrays to form a larger array with dimensions 8 and 125. Engaging students in the pursuit of such thinking accomplishes several mathematical goals, including reinforcing a particular meaning of multiplication and understanding the conditions under which area is conserved. Although Danielle did not have students pursue these ideas themselves, she later demonstrated this approach to help students understand one way to justify the strategy.

Revisiting the Support from the Curriculum Materials

To consider the ways in which the curriculum materials may have supported Danielle's decision-making during this episode, we begin by speculating about why she may have chosen to focus on Ryan's strategy. We can imagine that the decision to pursue a particular student's thinking can be made for several reasons – for example, the teacher may recognize that the student's thinking has mathematical significance which merits discussion, she may tend to pursue any student thinking offered, or she may not fully understand the student's thinking and want to know more about that process. In this case, there were two factors that indicated that the curriculum materials may have played a role in Danielle's decision: (a) the materials highlighted Ryan's strategy multiple times, both in a DB and in the lesson itself; and (b) Danielle repeatedly stressed the important role the DBs played in influencing her decision-making.

Her decision to continue to pursue this strategy and consider its generalizability may also have been influenced by a DB in which the teacher asked students to apply a student strategy to a new set of numbers. Finally, the decision to provide a demonstration for a particular rationale for the doubling/halving strategy may have been influenced by the curriculum materials. The curriculum materials hint at the use of rectangles as being an important model for understanding the doubling/halving strategy. The materials, however, do not provide any mention of how one might justify this particular strategy, nor do they provide support for engaging students in pursuing this rationale. It is interesting to note that Danielle reverted back to a didactic demonstration rather than pursuing a discussion with her students in this instance in which there was no support in the curriculum materials for such a pursuit.

A Lesson with Support Material for Extending Student Thinking

A few days after the *Factor Pairs* lesson discussed above, students began another three-day lesson, *Multiplication and Division Clusters* (Kliman et al., 1998, pp. 55–65), in which they were asked to utilize the number relationships they had been investigating to reason about clusters of multiplication and division problems. One goal of cluster problems is to encourage students to use what they know to solve harder problems. For example, in order to solve 46×25, students are asked to describe how they might use any or all of the following: 4×25, 20×25, 6×25, 10×25, 50×25. As with the *Factor Pairs* lesson, a major form of support provided by the curriculum materials is a consideration of the ways students may solve the cluster problems. Five specific strategies are offered as examples of *how* students may solve 46×25:

- Breaking the problem into 40×25 and 6×25 and adding the two results
- Breaking the problem into 50×25 and 4×25 and subtracting one from the other
- Skip counting by 25s up from 40×25
- Skip counting down from 50×25
- Transforming the problem by halving one factor and doubling the other, twice, first making 23×50, then 11.5×100, which is easy to multiply mentally. (p. 57)

Unlike the *Factor Pairs* lesson, however, this lesson contains several references to *why* these strategies work. For example, consider the following suggestion for dealing with a potential student difficulty:

If a student can solve 3×50 and 20×50, but not 23×50, you might follow a line of questioning like this: You wrote down 1,000 for the answer to

20×50. How did you find that answer? If you have one more 50 – that is, twenty-one 50s – how much would you have? (p. 56)

The Enacted Lesson

When we observed this lesson in Danielle's classroom, the students were discussing solutions to a multiplication cluster in which the problem to be solved was 23×4=__. Danielle asked Cali, who used 25×4=100 as her first step, to come to the board and describe her strategy. The following discussion ensued as the teacher worked to make explicit the reasoning behind this strategy.

TEACHER: Now, my question for you out there is, she chose – instead of thinking about 23 times four, she decided to think about it like 25 times four, which was one of the suggested problems. She said she chose 25 because it was a landmark. It's an easy number. You know about quarters and money. And 25 times four is a nice number. It's a hundred. Now, is this the answer?

STUDENTS: No.

TEACHER: No. Because. Is the problem 25×4?

STUDENTS: No.

TEACHER: No. What's the problem?

STUDENTS: 23×4.

TEACHER: 23×4. So she knows that this number [points to the 100] is not right. My question for you is: This number is 100, it's not right. So, is it too big or too small for the final answer?

STUDENTS: Too big.

TEACHER: Too big. Why is it too big? It's too big. Why? Anna?

ANNA: Because 23, I mean 25, is more than 23.

TEACHER: Exactly. This is 23 fours and she did 25 fours. So, this answer is too big. Now, this next question is: How much too big is it? It's too big. How can I get from here [the answer to 25×4] to the actual answer? I know that I am doing it too big. I'm doing it too big 'cause I like to work with that number. But now I know my answer is not right. It's too big. How can I change it to be the right answer? How can I change it? James, how can I change it? This is the hard part to explain, so go ahead. You can do it because I know you know it. I know you can do it. [Student does not respond.] So this is 23 and this number is 25. So James, how much bigger is this [points to 25] to start with?

JAMES: Two.

TEACHER: This is two too big, right? This number is two too big. Now, should I just subtract two from here [100] and that's my answer?

As with the *Factor Pairs* episode, Danielle asked students to consider one particular student's strategy. Rather than simply focusing on *how* the strategy worked, however, in this case she *extended* student thinking by engaging the entire class in considering the rationale for the strategy. Danielle did this in several ways. First, she did not allow the entire strategy to be shared. Rather, she asked students to consider the first step (25×4) by asking them to determine whether this would yield a larger or smaller result than 23×4. Although it may have been fairly easy for students to identify that 25 was bigger than 23 and that it was 2 bigger, students were pushed further to consider "how much too big" the answer was. By posing this question, Danielle heightened the potential to *extend* student thinking by encouraging students to determine why one should not just subtract the 2.

As the discussion continued, Danielle posed additional questions, such as "It's two what too big?" to try to encourage the students to think about the fact that the two actually referred to two groups of four. Students' responses to these questions could have indicated a lack of understanding of the solution method or an inability to understand the connection between the question posed and the solution method. Then Mitch offered a suggestion, and the following exchange occurred:

MITCH: There's eight too many for 100.
TEACHER: How do you know?
MITCH: Because you subtract 100 'til you get to 92.
TEACHER: But, how do you know it's 92? How did you know to stop at 92?
MITCH:: Because that's what's the answer.
TEACHER: If I didn't know the answer already, how do I know that I am supposed to subtract eight?

The essence of Mitch's argument was that he knew the answer to the problem was 92 (presumably through using a different strategy) and he used this knowledge to justify why it made sense to subtract eight from 100. Although he seemed confident with the method he used, as observers, we did not have access to that strategy. In any case, his argument was a classic one – use a known solution, of which you are reasonably confident, to justify why you might do something that really does not build on the current strategy under investigation. This was a difficult situation for the teacher in that she needed to acknowledge the use of the correct answer, yet help students recognize that this did not justify why subtracting eight made sense in the context of this particular solution.

Revisiting the Support from the Curriculum Materials

How might the curriculum materials have supported Danielle in facilitating this discussion? As in the previous episode, the curriculum materials provided her with examples of the kinds of strategies that students were likely to use to solve the multiplication clusters. However, Danielle chose to engage students in the process of justifying their thinking, rather than applying that thinking to other problems (as she did in the *Factor Pairs* lesson). There are several possible explanations for Danielle's different approaches. Although both lessons provided examples of student strategies, the *Multiplication and Division Clusters* teacher materials also included multiple references to the meaning of the problems being solved, which is crucial to justifying a particular strategy. For example, in this episode the students were trying to solve $23 \times 4 = \underline{\quad}$ by starting with $25 \times 4 = 100$. By considering the meaning of these computations, one can reason that we have 25 fours, but only want 23 fours, thus we need to subtract 2 fours (or 8). Without this kind of explicit attention to the meaning of these computations, students may not be able to determine what should be done after $25 \times 4 = 100$, let alone be able to justify this next step. The multiple references to the meaning of the problems in the *Multiplication and Division Clusters* teacher materials may have been a factor in Danielle's decision to engage students in justifying their thinking.

Discussion

We set out to explore the ways in which teachers, new to a curriculum program, were able to engage with student thinking during whole-group discussions, and how the curriculum materials supported them in their efforts to do so. The two examples described previously illustrate the ways in which the curriculum materials supported teachers to both *elicit* and *extend* student thinking. In many ways, the teacher's engagement with student thinking aligned with the foci of those two lessons. In other words, when sufficient support was provided for either *eliciting* or *extending* student thinking, the teacher was able to do so. However, the teacher was more challenged to *extend* student thinking. These findings were consistent across all of the lessons we analyzed for both teachers, along with the caveat that, in general, both teachers were more challenged to *extend* student thinking. This may be due in part to the emphasis of the support materials in the lessons we analyzed; they were fairly consistent in providing teachers with information about student strategies/ideas they might expect during a particular lesson. This kind of information occurred both within the text of the lesson plans, as well as in the separate TNs and DBs. The lessons we analyzed were less consistent, however, in providing teachers with information on the kinds of rationales they might see for student strategies/ideas, or in describing how to orchestrate conversations in which such rationales might be pursued.

With respect to the more general issue of support around questioning, it seemed that the lessons we analyzed conveyed a somewhat general image of the role of the teacher as questioner and facilitator of student discussion, and provided teachers with good starting questions, both within the description of a particular activity and in the DBs. There were few instances, however, in which teachers were provided with examples of questions designed to pursue student thinking. In fact, a closer examination of the DBs revealed a pattern of sample dialogue that may be unrealistic: typically, the teacher asked a question, which prompted a discussion dominated by students spontaneously offering strategies and ideas in a fairly articulate way.

Consider, for example, a portion of a DB shown in Table 8.1 (Kliman et al., 1998, p. 42), which accompanied the *Factor Pairs* lesson described previously. The DB began with the teacher asking: "What did you discover for factor pairs of 200 and 300? Did you find a way to use what you know about factor pairs of 100?" (p. 42). A student offered the idea of "doubling one side" to get from a

Table 8.1 Excerpts from the Dialogue Box *Finding Factor Pairs of Multiples of 100*

Let's look at another factor pair of 100 – what about 25 × 4? Can you get to 200 starting with 25 × 4?

JEFF: 27 × 4, because it's twice as much so you go up by 2.

AMIR: No, you added. You need to double. It would work for 50 × 4.

MEI-LING: It wouldn't work because 27 is not a factor of 100.

CARA: Sometimes that doesn't matter. You also need to check other numbers, like 3, 4, 6, 7, 8, 9 … Like 8 works for 200, but it doesn't work for 100.

How could we find a factor pair for 400 starting with 25 × 4?

DANNY: 25 × 16, because 25 times 4 is 100, and all you had to do is keep going with the 4s tables and keep going up by 4s.

ALANI: You go 4, 8, 12, 16. The first is 100, 8 is 200, 12 is 300, and 16 is 400.

Can you make 25 × 4 into a factor pair for 900?

CARA: 36, because you go 4 × 9 – so 36 × 25.

---

factor pair of 100 to a factor pair of 200. The rest of the DB consisted of the teacher asking students to apply this idea to generate factor pairs for multiples of 100.

This DB could be useful to teachers in a variety of ways. It suggests *extending* student thinking by asking the class to take one student's idea for generating factor pairs for 200 by using factor pairs for 100, and then applying the idea in order to generate factor pairs for multiples of 100. More generally, the DB clearly implies that teachers are to encourage and use student thinking during discussions. In this DB, however, there are no examples in which the teacher's initial attempts at *eliciting* and/or *extending* student thinking were unsuccessful. In other words, no examples of how a teacher might further probe student thinking under these circumstances are included. The discussion that is illustrated is ideal in the sense that students are contributing important mathematical ideas, talking to each other, and are not off task. These findings from our analysis support the teacher's observations about the DBs as well.

It is also likely that the teachers' efforts to pursue student thinking were influenced by a host of factors beyond the curriculum materials. For example, Danielle was a gregarious and boisterous person with a clear love of mathematics and a fast-paced conversational style, evident both inside and outside of the classroom. These personal attributes may have contributed to her difficulty relinquishing more control to her students. When discussing her implementation of the *Factor Pairs* lesson, for example, Danielle stated how excited she was that students used the doubling and halving strategy. This excitement may have contributed to her decision to demonstrate why the doubling and halving strategy worked, rather than engaging students more actively in this pursuit.

Finally, we recognize that teachers' efforts to *extend* student thinking in the context of whole-group discussions is only one indicator of their use of curriculum materials. However, it is one of the more challenging aspects of teaching, and, as a result, one of the more difficult aspects for curriculum developers to support. The challenge is determining how to support teachers to navigate the complexities of orchestrating whole-group discussions focused on student thinking.

Implications

It would appear self-evident that, in order to productively pursue and use student thinking as a basis for decision-making in the classroom, teachers must be knowledgeable about the kinds of thinking that will likely be *elicited* and the mathematical rationale underlying that thinking. Our analysis of the lessons used in this study and our experience with the *Investigations* curriculum materials more generally suggest that these materials are fairly consistent in providing examples of the kinds of strategies and ideas that are likely to arise in response to the curriculum activities, but not as consistent in providing support for the kinds of justifications that might be appropriate. Although it is impossible to anticipate all student thinking that might occur in a particular circumstance, it would seem that a more consistent focus on the mathematical reasoning underlying student thinking would be an important way that curriculum materials might support teachers to pursue student thinking.

Beyond this, there are perhaps more global issues of questioning and the teachers' role in a *Standards*-based classroom that impact teachers' facilitation of whole-group discussions. Implicit in the *Investigations* materials is the view of teachers and students as collaboratively engaging in rich mathematical dialogue, thereby repositioning mathematical authority as a jointly constructed phenomenon. As Herbel-Eisenmann (Chapter 10) illustrates, this repositioning is not so simple. In the case of the *Investigations* units we examined, students' strategies and ideas, not teacher questions and talk, dominate the DBs, implying that teachers are to encourage and use student thinking during discussions. However, *how* to do so may not be as well articulated as it could be. As mentioned previously, the examples given in the DBs include conversations that appear to occur smoothly and effortlessly. Although both Danielle and Carly expressed an appreciation for the sample questions and dialogues provided in the curriculum materials, they also mentioned the need for more support in following up on students' initial responses to their questions. This is consistent with findings from other research (Brodie, 2007) where teachers were challenged to both sustain and end conversations so that mathematical learning was optimized. Brodie contends that teachers need support in how to listen carefully to student contributions (rather than evaluating what they say) in order to relate contributions to each other and to the question being discussed. The issue is how to provide support for situations that are typically dependent upon the context of each specific situation.

One approach is to provide teachers with more direct and explicit discussion of their roles in facilitating these conversations. Thus, support materials might include examples in which teachers' first questions are not initially successful and adjustments to questions are illustrated. Alternatively, dialogue could be provided with a commentary by the teacher that highlights the thinking behind his or her orchestration of the discussion. It is interesting to note that the authors of *Investigations* have already recognized some of these issues related to their sample dialogues. For several years they have been revising the curriculum, and in their Pre-Publication Report (Bastable et al., 2006) the authors described changes to the sample dialogues for teachers:

> In the development of the revised curriculum, we worked to make the purpose and course of each discussion clearer. We provide a clear statement of the discussion focus, initial and follow-up questions that can support student thinking, and a sense of the discussion direction and outcome, including examples of possible student responses.
>
> (p. 7)

Additional information that might be helpful for teachers involves what they face when using *Standards*-based curriculum materials. For example, along with examples of what can occur in the classroom, it might be useful to provide teachers with a discussion of the framework of instructional strategies developed by Fraivillig et al. (1999), along with the results of that study. In particular, it could be shared that *eliciting* and *extending* moves may be more difficult initially in that they push teachers toward using student thinking as the basis of their teaching. This kind of framework may increase teachers' awareness of the moves they make as they interact with their students, and thus enable them to better reflect on their role in the classroom.

Although we believe these recommendations could help improve the support provided to teachers, we also recognize the limitations of providing such information in written curriculum materials. There is no guarantee that teachers will read all of the support provided; they may rather pick and choose those aspects in which they have a greater interest (Remillard, 2000). This suggests that it may be necessary to consider how curriculum programs can support teachers with information that is communicated in a format other than printed text. Much as a play can be difficult to visualize when reading it, watching it is a totally different experience that allows for the consideration of verbal and non-verbal cues, and can inspire thoughts that the written text may not be able to do. In the same way, the use of video formats of teaching may enhance written text in curriculum materials and provide a forum for teachers to visualize whole-group discussions and explore more deeply many of the issues we have discussed previously in this chapter.

We see great potential in combining the relatively young, but growing, bodies of research on teachers' enactments of *Standards*-based curriculum programs and teachers' use of their support materials. In this study, we chose to target two particular issues: teachers' pursuit of student thinking during whole-group discussion, and their use of curriculum materials. Prior research has indicated that teachers are particularly challenged to engage effectively with students about their reasoning, and thus it would follow that curriculum designers sympathetic to these findings and to the suggestions for making curriculum materials educative would necessarily address these issues in their design. In many ways, the authors of *Investigations* may be considered innovators in the ways in which they support teacher learning, considering the development of these materials occurred over ten years ago. It is reasonable that a first-generation curriculum program would focus on *eliciting* student thinking. Yet we believe that continuing to develop and study ways to support teachers to *extend* student thinking more consistently will help move us forward in both more effectively focusing instruction on student thinking and supporting teachers in their efforts to do so.

Acknowledgments

The chapter is based on work supported by National Science Foundation grant ESI-0333879. The opinions expressed are those of the authors and do not necessarily reflect the views of the National Science Foundation. A version of this paper was presented at the Annual Meeting of the American Educational Research Association, April 2006.

Note

1. The ellipsis is used to indicate a pause in speaking.

References

Ball, D. L., & Cohen, D. K. (1996). Reform by the book: What is – or might be – the role of curriculum materials in teacher learning and instructional reform? *Educational Researcher, 25*(9), 6–14, 18.

Bastable, V., Bloomfield, K., Cochran, K., Economopoulos, K., Horowitz, N., Murray, M. et al. (2006). *Greater than: A pre-publication report.* Cambridge, MA: TERC. Retrieved March 6, 2006 from http://www.investigations.scottforesman.com/.

Brodie, K. (2007). Teaching with conversations: Beginnings and endings. *For the Learning of Mathematics, 27*(1), 17–23.

Cobb, P., Wood, T., Yackel, E., & McNeal, B. (1992). Characteristics of classroom mathematics traditions: An interactional analysis. *American Educational Research Journal, 29*, 573–604.

Davis, E. A., & Krajcik, J. S. (2005). Designing educative curriculum materials to promote teacher learning. *Educational Researcher, 34*(3), 3–14.

Fraivillig, J. L., Murphy, L. A., & Fuson, K. C. (1999). Advancing children's mathematical thinking in Everyday Mathematics classrooms. *Journal for Research in Mathematics Education, 30*(2), 148–170.

Grant, T. J., & Kline, K. (2002). Developing teachers' knowledge of content and pedagogy through implementation of a Standards-based mathematics curriculum. In E. M. Guyton & J. Rainer (Eds.), *Teacher education Yearbook X: Meeting and using standards in the preparation of teachers* (pp. 67–80). Dubuque, IA: Kendall/Hunt.

Grant, T. J., & Kline, K. (2004). Embracing the complexity of practice as a site for inquiry. In R. N. Rubenstein & G. W. Bright (Eds.), *National Council of Teachers of Mathematics 2004 Yearbook: Perspectives on the teaching of mathematics* (pp. 195–206). Reston, VA: National Council of Teachers of Mathematics.

Kliman, M., Tierney, C., Russell, S. J., Murray, M., & Akers, J. (1998). *Mathematical thinking at grade 5.* Cambridge, MA: Dale Seymour.

Remillard, J. T. (2000). Can curriculum materials support teachers' learning? Two fourth-grade teachers' use of a new mathematics text. *The Elementary School Journal, 100*(4), 331–350.

Remillard, J. T., & Bryans, M. B. (2004). Teachers' orientations toward mathematics curriculum materials: Implications for teacher learning. *Journal for Research in Mathematics Education, 35*(5), 352–388.

Russell, S. J. (2007). The case of *Investigations in Number, Data, and Space.* In C. R. Hirsch (Ed.), *Perspectives on the design and development of school mathematics curricula* (pp. 23–35). Reston, VA: National Council of Teachers of Mathematics.

TERC. (1998). *Investigations in number, data and space.* Menlo Park, CA: Dale Seymour.

9

On the Unique Relationship Between Teacher Research and Commercial Mathematics Curriculum Development

The El Barrio-Hunter College PDS Partnership

Writing Collective

The Purposes

Our chapter addresses an insufficiently considered aspect of the relationship between mathematics curriculum materials and teachers of mathematics: the place of teacher research in the development of commercial curriculum materials. We approach this issue not as disinterested truth-seekers, but as advocates of the stance that classroom teacher researchers should have influence into all aspects of such curriculum materials. We stake our case on the story of five years' worth of teacher research into adapting the *Everyday Mathematics* (University of Chicago School Mathematics Project, 2004) materials for our children. The telling of this story occupies the heart and soul of our chapter.

A no-less-important purpose is simply to have teachers' voices and perspectives heard, listened to, validated, and incorporated in the cacophonous conversation about mathematics curriculum materials. Renée Sillart, a teacher in our collective, speaks to this objective: "Action research has given me a voice. It's a voice that speaks volumes, not just for one, but for several. It's non-negotiable! Teachers *must* be heard!"

In this chapter, we use our voices to speak to curriculum developers.[1]

The People

Who We Are

We are 13 teacher researchers representing New York City's El Barrio-Hunter College Professional Development School (PDS) Partnership. This partnership's flagship site is PS 112, an early-childhood (PK-2) school in East Harlem. Our names are Raquel Corujo, Priscilla Gelinas, Patricia Maiorano, Fadwa M. Nacel, Christine Passarelli, Laura Sebel, Renée Sillart, Esther Robles Soto (PS 112 classroom teachers); Elaine Funches and Gloria Whatts (paraprofessionals at 112); Irma Colón (PS 112 mathematics coach); and Bill Rosenthal and Jenny Tuten (professors in the Hunter College School of Education and PDS co-directors). We speak as a communal voice whenever possible. The use of plural personal pronouns to express a belief signifies a consensus as determined by Bill Rosenthal, who compiled and edited our work. Direct quotations are attributed to the individuals who expressed them.

Passions and Preconceptions

We are, first, passionately committed to the education of our students according to child-centered, progressive educational principles and practices. Our students are (a) prekindergarteners through second-graders at PS 112; and (b) students in Hunter College's School of Education. On account of the vast amount of time the professors spend at PS 112 and the school's pre-eminent role in teacher preparation at Hunter, we all regard ourselves as teachers of both categories of students.

We are passionate about starting with high-quality curriculum materials and making them better for our children. It is this enthusiasm that has brought us here. Although we had no say in choosing *Everyday Mathematics* (EDM), our relationship with it resembles an arranged marriage at its best. We have grown to love many qualities of the materials, particularly their treatment of our students as mathematical thinkers rather than would-be human calculators. However, since the EDM authors do not know our children, these materials cannot be a perfect partner for them. Hence we have undertaken both to modify the materials and to render our relationship non-exclusive by drawing upon other sources. Our teacher research concerns the influences of these modifications and supplementations upon our children's learning, our teaching practices, and our professional selves.

We are passionate about teacher research. One of us, Patricia Maiorano, captures our collective's disposition toward teachers' conducting research on our own practices:

> Researchers have to understand that teachers are our own researchers. Day in and day out we research in our classrooms how to teach our students most effectively. We can only do that successfully if we create inquiries and carry them out.

Raquel Corujo punctuates this principle with one of her own: "Teachers should be considered *first-hand researchers.*"

Here we intertwine two complementary senses of teacher research. On the one hand, we believe in the axiom that because all teaching *is* research by its very essence, all teachers *are* researchers. Here we stand with inspiring teacher-scholars such as Eleanor Duckworth (1987), Ann Berthoff (1987), and Vivian Gussin Paley (1986). The teacher-as-researcher's other hand then conducts teacher research by engaging in deliberate, systematic problem posing; data collection, analysis, and interpretation; and, in teacher *action* research, action taking (Cochran-Smith & Lytle, 1990).[2] The relationship of our teacher research to the written curriculum differs from that of teacher-scholars such as Karen Gallas and Ruth Heaton, with whom we might be identified. We generally do not think in terms of "giv[ing] up some control of the content ... to students" (Heaton, 2000, p. 102) or "developing an informal curriculum" of our own making (Gallas, 1995, p. 70). Our children are better served when we maintain a commitment to the EDM materials and defer to disciplinary experts in determining mathematical content. We are content with conducting research on the manifestations of the smaller-scale, less dramatic alterations we make.

Ms Corujo's pronouncement, "Teachers should be considered *first-hand researchers*," displays our healthful skepticism toward research that is educational research other than teacher research. Although we are not hostile to such modes of inquiry and have learned much from them, we have far more faith in the outcomes of research we ourselves conduct. As the word "first-hand" suggests, we believe that teachers' very closeness to the research setting confers legitimacy upon teacher research. The high value we place on closeness – on intimacy – is a characteristic of the feminist teacher research (Hollingsworth, 1994; Howes, 2002) to which our work is similar. Elaine Funches testifies to how closeness to students legitimizes our research.

> A lot of people believe that teacher action research isn't "hard-core" or "rigorous" enough to be legitimate. If you are not a teacher and don't work in a classroom, I would say that you are not qualified to make that statement. We are the ones who are there every day working with the children. We know the children. We work with the children each and every day. That should be "hard-core" enough.

Two features of our rigorous, hard-core research are especially worth noting. First, we operate primarily by studying our children's work. Teachers create mathematical tasks meant to supplement those in the EDM materials – often due to a determination that, for certain topics, EDM does not adequately meet the needs of *our* children. The children's work on these tasks becomes our primary data source. Our passion for studying children's work is apparent in the following quotes from, respectively, Bernice Arricale (PS 112 literacy coach), Eileen Reiter (the school's principal), and co-author Christine Passarelli:

> The very act of looking at students' work is wonderful and powerful.

> It's *all* about studying children's work.

> Children's work is so filled with truth.

The second striking feature of our teacher action research is that it occurs in grade-level groups. Although individual teacher research can be advantageous, we feel that these advantages are outweighed by the value of intellectual companionship in a complex and uncertain endeavor. Fadwa M. Nacel and then

Priscilla Gelinas testify to the power of more-than-one in our brand of teacher inquiry:

> Coming together as teachers grade-wide helped us to understand a larger population of children and what was common to all.

> I was surprised about how looking at other students' work (other than your own students) can really be very insightful because when you constantly look at your own students' work, sometimes you miss things that another teacher can see. Kind of like looking at things through another set of lenses.

Ms Passarelli provides a vivid example of Ms Gelinas's assertion:

> After I videotaped a student playing the Parking Lot Game, the kindergarten teachers watched and studied the tape together. When I had viewed the tape on my own, I came to the conclusion that my student was beginning to clump numbers (reading them on a domino). A few other teachers observed this same student and pointed out to me that they believed she was not *subitizing* (*clumping*) but possibly *tagging with her eyes*. I had completely missed this! It is just like when you try to proofread your own paper. Someone else has to look at your work before you can say that it has been fully checked, because there is always a chance that someone will be able to see what you are missing.

In the following section, we describe the context in which our work takes place to set the scene for the telling of our teacher-research story.

The Research Setting

PS 112

Public School 112M, also known as the José Celso Barbosa School, is located on 119th Street in easternmost East Harlem. The school has a parkway for its eastern border, and sits a block away from a large trapezoid of public housing ("the projects"). Across 119th Street, a three-square-block construction site has been cleared and is being readied for a big-box retailer. Gentrification of the neighborhood is slowly but surely proceeding.

PS 112 serves approximately 425 children from prekindergarten to second grade, and houses an assortment of other programs for children and parents. The school is the recipient of numerous accolades, including recognition from New York State in 2003 for outstanding early-childhood education. Approximately 95 percent of its students are Black, Latino, or both; 99 percent or more are eligible for free lunch. After completing the second grade, most go on to PS 206, the upper-elementary school with which 112 shares a building and a paved playground. Principal Eileen Reiter, a lifelong New York City teacher and administrator steeped in child-centered education, came to the school in September 2001, when the first week of classes was interrupted by the destruction of the World Trade Center.

The El Barrio-Hunter College PDS Partnership

On September 21, 2001, four representatives of New York City's Community School District 4 met with four faculty members from the Hunter College School of Education. The stated purpose of the meeting was to commence an exploration of the feasibility of formalizing the longstanding close, fruitful relationship between the district and the School of Education into a professional development school partnership. So eager were the participants to move forward that, by the end of the meeting, an agreement in principle had been forged for the partnership's establishment. PS 112 was designated as the flagship school site.

Informed by the national PDS movement (Abdal-Haqq, 1998; Holmes Group, 1990; Teitel, 2001), those responsible for molding the partnership made teacher inquiry a "non-negotiable"[3] condition from day one. During our partnership's first half-decade of life, teacher inquiry has been its strongest suit. It took some time to get the inquiry groups started; there have been times during which the PS 112 inquiry process has stumbled or stalled; and our passion for teacher research has waxed and waned. Yet teacher inquiry has lived on in PS 112, putting down roots that will not easily be dislodged in the wake of systemwide mandates, potentially paralyzing changes in personnel, and inconsistent support from the higher-education side of the partnership.

In the following section, we offer a more thorough history of collaborative classroom inquiry at PS 112 as we build our case for strengthening the relationship between teacher research and the development of commercial mathematics curriculum materials.

Five Years of Teacher Action Research at PS 112

Year One: 2001–02

The same month that teacher inquiry was declared a non-negotiable activity, PS 112 adopted the EDM curriculum materials at the behest of Deputy Superintendent Gyles, who holds a PhD in mathematics education and was a founding co-director of the partnership. These two tributaries – the elevation of teacher inquiry to the partnership's marquee activity and the advent of EDM at 112 – would soon join to form the river of teacher research that this chapter traverses.

Not for some time, however. Practitioner inquiry at PS 112 would have to wait its turn. Principal Reiter had first to establish herself at the school, and the PDS partnership needed to cultivate goodwill and credence to obtain an informed, non-begrudging buy-in from as many teachers as possible. Late in 2001, the partnership was awarded an Eisenhower grant from the New York State Education Department. Our DDE grant required a focus on mathematics, science, or technology. Given this external constraint, the teachers' strongly expressed desire for more professional development with EDM (pacing and spiraling were urgent issues), and both co-directors' expertise in mathematics education, the decision made itself. Teacher action research would be about *mathematics* teaching, curriculum, assessment, and learning. That momentous decision made, the informal committee responsible for PDS planning followed it up by opting to defer the start of the research process until the next school year.

Year Two: 2002–03

On the Friday before the first day of that next school year, the partnership held a "kick-off retreat" at which teacher inquiry took center stage. A contingent of Hunter professors joined the majority of the PS 112 faculty for a program featuring a scholarly pep talk on teacher inquiry by Nicholas Michelli, the CUNY-wide dean of teacher education; a session on EDM planned and led by Ms Colón and Ms Corujo; a panel of "more-experienced others" in classroom research from the Teachers College PDS Partnership; and a brainstorming session on developing inquiry questions. By all accounts, the retreat was instrumental in sparking teacher research in 2002–03 and beyond.

We took the rest of calendar year 2002 for planning. The PDS Advisory Committee was constituted, and assumed responsibility for overseeing inquiry. Six paid teacher and paraprofessional representatives on the committee would become inquiry-group leaders. Ms Colón and Fran Dixon, a retired district administrator hired as PDS inquiry coordinator, would mentor these teachers. Both mentors would consult with Dr Rosenthal as needed.

Sometime during this fall, another momentous decision was made: children's work would become the principal data source for our research. Thus, data analysis and actions taken on the basis thereof would – somehow – center on the study of children's work on mathematical tasks. In early November, Ms Colón and Dr Rosenthal primed the pump by conducting a workshop in which they followed an overview of our plans by engaging the entire PS 112 faculty in on-the-spot analyses of children's mathematical work.

Teacher research commenced early in 2003. Three grade-level groups (kindergarten, first grade, and second grade) engaged in inquiry over the rest of the school year. Only the second-grade group conducted formal teacher action research. Ms Dixon created a protocol for inquiry-group sessions and a systematic process for data collection and analysis. Ms Colón and Ms Arricale assumed lead supporting roles in designing, facilitating, and documenting the research. In June, the second-grade team presented their work to the entire PS 112 faculty.

This work's substance sprang from a key premise that coalesced in the second-grade inquiry group early in the year. The teachers identified the EDM materials as inadequate for their children's learning opportunities with *problem-solving*, generally meaning *story problems*. They then formulated three inquiry questions: What are the children's problem-solving skills and abilities? How do the children solve problems that present multiple concepts? How do the children deal with integrating information to solve problems? The group responded to these questions by analyzing their children's work on tasks designed to elicit details of children's problem-solving strategies and introduce them to new situations and modes of solution. The facilitators devised the tasks with the aid of teacher input, which increased throughout the year.

To render the analysis manageable, each teacher chose three of her students on whom to focus – one whose understanding of problem-solving she deemed "beginning" in terms of grade-level expectations, one child at the "developing" level, and one considered "secure" (the categories are those of EDM). Each teacher kept structured notes on her three children and studied their work with the guidance of questions developed by the facilitators. At the group's meetings, which occurred either monthly or twice-monthly, the participants dug more deeply into their children's strategies and collectively decided upon the resulting "action" of their action research. Prominent actions that they took were to revise and re-administer the task; to create a similar but pointedly different task; and to teach a particular child's strategy to the entire class.

It is this last action that was perhaps the group's most significant finding of its first assay into inquiry – that is, the instructional value of using one child's successful problem-solving strategy as the centerpiece of whole-class instruction. A second key finding was that the categories "beginning," "developing," and "secure" are not fixed for each child. It was a revelation for some second-grade teachers to learn, through analyzing children's work, that a child deemed to be "beginning" relative to one concept could be "developing," even "secure," with another.

Year Three: 2003–04

We followed the previous year's precedent by placing teacher inquiry on hold until the beginning-of-year upheaval settled down. Always an adventure, the school-year start-up was all the more tumultuous due to a reorganization of the New York City school system. In early October, Ms Reiter decided that the inquiry groups would not convene until after the completion of the citywide early-childhood literacy assessment. In early December, the PS 112 staff, a few people from Hunter, and many student teachers convened by grade level to develop inquiry questions. Although all three groups profited from this mini-retreat, the kindergarten team made a leap that still resonates to this day. It was here that the group pinpointed *number sense* as a curricular area on which to focus. Paraprofessional Elaine Funches turned her colleagues' attention to this topic when she mentioned encounters with second-graders whose number sense was not as advanced as she thought it should be. The group reached consensus that, with regard to the number-sense needs of PS 112 children, EDM did not provide enough questions, activities, tasks, and, especially, games. Recognizing the paramount importance of *games* for kindergarteners' mathematical learning, the teachers conjectured that their time and energy would best be invested in experimenting with supplementing EDM's games.

When January arrived, teacher research commenced with some surprises. The first-grade team, which had settled on the topic of *money sense*, suspended its plans due to its leader's medical leave of absence. The second-grade team organized itself and changed its focus from problem-solving to integrating science with mathematics. In January, teacher leader Claudia La Touche exclaimed, "I can't believe that we've come together so quickly and that we're already monitoring ourselves." Around the same time, Ms Sillart, her co-teacher, proclaimed, "We're declaring our ownership of the inquiry group." The group maintained its *modus operandi* of developing tasks with the dual purposes of shoring up the curriculum materials and eliciting children's mathematical strategies, with the teachers now responsible for creating the tasks.

The kindergarten team adopted this approach, including teachers' designations of focus children as "beginning," "developing," and "secure" relative to a concept or skill. The research was headed by the question: *What specific games or activities support the development of number sense in kindergarten students?* This inquiry question had matured from that which had been hurriedly posed at the mini-retreat ("Are the games of EDM addressing number sense?"). Aided by their three mentors, the teachers adapted and created games relating to number sense. They chose or made each game for its potential to mediate the learning of a particular number-sense skill or concept (or more than one). For instance, the teachers transformed an EDM game called the Track Game into the "Teddy Bear Game." In one variation of this game, two children take turns rolling a die and stacking the corresponding number of Unifix® cubes in a line of squares leading to a teddy bear's large head. When both children make it into the head, each counts his or her cubes and the child who has more wins. Teachers designed, used, and revised the Teddy Bear Game to address four number-sense strategies: counting on, magnitude, one-to-one correspondence, and subitizing (or clumping). Ms Colón devoted inquiry-group time to an in-depth treatment of these and other elements of young children's number sense. This theoretical consideration of number sense (later extended to the other grades) was crucial in enabling the group to correlate choices and adaptations of games with targeted skills and concepts.

Writing on behalf of the entire group, teacher leader Laura Sebel speaks of the kindergarten teachers' findings from their first year of practitioner inquiry:

> We now have an organized way to assess our students and increase their math skills. Teachers can recognize which parts of the *Everyday Mathematics* program need adaptation. This is what needs to change: more resources in Spanish, a program that doesn't spiral as much, more supportive games and materials. We will continue to work together to change and improve the math program.

Ms. Sebel's comment concerning spiraling encapsulates three years' worth of PS 112's faculty's tussling with this core feature of EDM The kindergarten teachers, many of whom specialize in special education, reported an additional result: their research enabled them better to tailor games for special-needs children. We were all struck by their finding that modifications made for these children often improved the games' instructional potential for other children as well. At the kindergarten team's year-end presentation, teacher leader Esther Robles Soto told the PS 112 faculty:

This is *inquiry*. This is *research*. So that means that it's a process and we're working on it. We didn't have plans for individualized instruction and we have them now. We've learned that what special-needs children need, all children need.

Year Four: 2004–05

The second-grade group started the year powerfully, gathering itself for 7.15-am meetings without any outside mentoring. It is sad that the team could not sustain its momentum and, midway through December, chose to let go of its mathematics inquiry for the year. In early December, the kindergarten group picked up with its research into aligning games with specific number-sense concepts and skills. The group's teacher leaders took over much of the responsibility for planning and facilitation. The value of video in documenting and analyzing young children's mathematical work became prominent. Most significant among the outcomes was the strengthening of the prior year's preliminary findings of the efficacy of teacher research for differentiating instruction. We shall soon have quite a bit more to say about this result.

The first-grade teachers' first year of formal practitioner inquiry began in December. Taking a cue from their kindergarten peers, they selected number sense as the arena of study. The group then narrowed in on a ubiquitous tool for developing number sense with young children, and formulated the inquiry question *How can we use the 100s grid to teach number sense to our first-graders?*, emphasizing the connections among counting, addition, and subtraction. The team inherited the inquiry process established two years earlier in the second-grade group. Ms Colón introduced the "tuning protocol" (Allen, Blythe, & Powell, 1996), which proved a popular means by which to structure the communal study of student work. Perhaps due to a two-month gap in meetings resulting from the loss of contractual professional development time and two canceled meetings due to snowfalls, the group was hesitant to state any research results.

Year Four-and-a-Half: Inquiry Summer 2005

In May 2005, Hunter College President Jennifer J. Raab awarded the PDS partnership a grant supporting collaborative reflection on, documentation of, and writing about our teacher research. "Inquiry Summer" was a July week during which Dr Rosenthal developed writing prompts and we were off and writing. When the week was done, he compiled all the writings and wrote a summary, which the teacher leaders later shared with their constituencies. Follow-up prompts and discussions during the next school year produced additional data. The 13 participants in Inquiry Summer became this chapter's authors.

The first outcome of Inquiry Summer arrived about 15 minutes into the week. The act of gathering kindergarten, first-grade, and second-grade teachers in a room to write about their research made it clear that we should be connecting inquiry more strongly across the grade levels. A second result began to show

a day later. It was then that we first came to a collective conscio
value of teacher research in enabling us to *differentiate instructi*
that drove much of the work in 2005–06, and provides specifi
cacy of a larger role for teacher research in large-scale curriculum deve....

Year Five: 2005–06

In contrast to past years, PS 112 inquiry groups convened almost from the day school opened. The previous year's success with the tuning protocol led Ms Colón to use it with all three grade levels. The second-grade group again changed direction and, in so doing, reclaimed some of its passion for inquiry. Motivated by their children's difficulty with mastering mathematical vocabulary, second-grade teacher researchers studied the interactions between language use and mathematics. Both the kindergarten and first-grade teachers picked up where they had left off in June, modifying their inquiry questions to enhance attention to differentiating instruction. Pursuing the hypothesis that, because many of the school's children reside in neighborhoods in which dominoes are popular, domino games might be a fertile medium for mathematical learning, the kindergarten team devoted special attention to such games.

So ends our saga of five years of teacher action research at PS 112. Next, we put on display a fuller account of some particular areas of our thinking and our practice. We start with our research's paramount outcome: growth in our ability to differentiate instruction so that our teaching can meet every child where she or he is.

Teacher Research and Differentiating Instruction

Raquel Corujo and then Priscilla Gelinas set the mood for this section:

> As a researcher (through action research), I can tell math curriculum developers that differentiating instruction is crucial to effective teaching.

> I believe that as an inclusion classroom teacher, I should have a bigger role in creating and revising math curriculum like *Everyday Math*. Many students with special needs are unable to process the "spiraling." This area is where I could contribute by providing input on differentiating the instruction in math.

Before presenting two cases of how we have differentiated instruction via teacher action research, we have one alert. We cannot demonstrate to you that our progress in differentiating instruction is due to the research. There was no control group of teachers who refrained from researching their own practices so we could make comparisons. We know that without developing tasks expressly for our purposes and having both a definite process and peer group to study children's work, our insights would have been shallower and our curricular modifications less effective. We hope that, along with our story of the inquiry process, the examples below convince you of the research's influence.

We have mentioned that the kindergarten group devoted considerable attention to games with dominoes. It was with the domino games that we have made perhaps the clearest (and best-tested) differentiations of the same activity. With certain games, having many dominoes visible at the same time was over-stimulating to some children, so the teachers learned when it was beneficial to cover up some of the dominoes. Not incidentally, this inadvertent over-stimulation is reminiscent of a finding the second-grade team made at the very beginning of their research in 2003. The first task (developed by the facilitators) involved snowballs, and was presented on a page with an ornate border depicting the scenario. Not only did teachers observe many children over-attending to the border, but some students used the pictures in their solutions. Subsequent tasks dispensed with such distracters.

Through much experimentation (and, of course, collective analysis of the outcomes), the kindergarten team formulated a set of guidelines for differentiating domino games. Paraprofessional Elaine Funches summarizes:

> When a child is at the secure level, we use little dominoes and have the child work with more than one at a time. These children can answer questions involving larger numbers because they're more advanced with tagging, clumping, and counting on. With children at the developing stage, we can use the smaller dominoes but only one at a time. Children who are beginning do better with the big wood domino. Then they can see the pips and *touch* them, too. One boy in my room was able to play the game with the big domino, but with the little one, he just counted the pips over and over.

The kindergarten teacher researchers made similar modifications with dice games. They amended games whose instructions called for two dice so that children with a less-developed number sense or whose motor skills were less developed could play with a single die. Larger dice came in handy for some children. Students who were having difficulty recognizing numerals used dice whose faces showed the numerals 1–6 instead of pips.

Before engaging in practitioner inquiry, we were all aware of the effects the non-mathematical features of a task – a domino's size, a page's border, and so on – could have on children's ability to engage with that task. Our research has heightened our understanding of how we might amend and vary tasks for different children so that these aspects of an activity do not sabotage their learning opportunities. Paraprofessional Gloria Whatts speaks to the blend of observation, documentation, and reflection that, at our best, we use to differentiate instruction:

> The inquiry has helped me to see children's needs. When you record the children from each class playing the games and compare what strategies they are using, it helps you more to see all the kinds of strategies that are being used. When we played the game, I would see in what areas the

children needed help and I would go home to think of a way to help them master the game and make it fun for them.

Our second case, from the first-grade team, illustrates how inquiry has enabled us to zoom in closely on a single student's mathematical thinking – and, through this kind of investigation of one child's cognition, devise curricular modifications applicable beyond that one child. On May 16, 2005, the team met after school for 90 minutes. The agenda centered on analyzing two children's work on a worksheet from commercial materials other than EDM (Greenes et al., 2002). The teachers decided to go outside of EDM because, as one said, "The EDM worksheets on this topic are too much." The Spanish-language worksheet they used included the following questions.

Count by 10s.

3. <u>70, , , 100, , , , , .</u>

5. <u>36, 46, , , , , , 106, .</u>

6. <u>92, 102, , , , , , .</u>

We now offer an edited excerpt of the group's analysis of the thinking of a boy with the pseudonym Miguel. The teacher presenting Miguel's work is Yolanda Raimundi (her real name) – for short, Ms Y. Other teachers are identified by initials. Ms C is Math Coach Irma Colón, the group's facilitator. Please keep in mind that this group's inquiry question was "How can we use the 100s grid to teach number sense to our first-graders?"

MS Y: I *thought* that Miguel was secure, but – I put down in my notes that I consistently had to tell him to use the number grids. But these seemed to confuse him. The number grids and number line confused him. When he did it mentally, he could always get the correct answer. I kept telling him, "Look at the number line. Look at the number grid." He lost it on #6. He didn't use the number line.
MR T: How fluent was he?
MS Y: He had a hard time. When we do it orally, he answers real quickly because his father owns a store. It's funny. When we do it orally, he never uses the number line and he's the first to get it right.
MS C: We should look at what the child *does* know.
MS J: He knows how to count by 10s up to 100.
MR T: And not just on the even 10s.
MS M: Starting at any number.
MS J: He knows place value.
MS G: I'm not sure.
MS J: 90 to 100 is wrong.

MR T: He started counting by 100s.

MS C: How can we use this tool to help teach counting by 10s in the 100s?

MS J: Make a new 100s grid from 100 on.

MR T: Can I put out the whole idea of metacognition – asking the child to look at his work and notice for himself? Where does the awareness come in? Saying it out loud – would it sound right to him?

MS C: Interesting because we've spoken about getting the song, the rhythm.

MS M: Ms Y told us she thought Miguel was secure and that he's the first one to answer. Maybe he didn't pay attention to the number line because he knows the numbers. The number line threw him off. He may not pay attention to the number line because he already knows it from the store. Kids may not want to learn a new strategy if they already know how to do it.

MS W: What if instead of giving so many blank boxes, we start slowly so it doesn't become overwhelming? Then maybe in 3–4 days we can throw this one in.

MS C: Great idea. This is using your expertise and knowledge of children.

We wish to comment on two aspects of this discussion. First, the first-grade teachers' analysis replicates the creation of the type of small yet crucial modifications the kindergarten team made with domino and dice games (e.g., Ms W's "What if instead of giving so many blank boxes...?"). We also see the discussion as laying the groundwork for deepening our understandings of complex general issues in children's mathematical cognition (the interplay between school mathematics and such other forms of mathematical knowledge, such as Miguel's store-developed calculation strategies).

Before speaking directly to our EDM colleagues in the finale, we close this section with an assertion by a kindergarten teacher whose identity has been lost, followed by a reflection from teacher-researcher-author Christine Passarelli:

> Having done action research makes me feel more qualified to give advice to mass-market curriculum developers. Action research has enabled me to actually see that there is progress in students' playing number sense activities a number of times. A teacher who has done action research is prepared and knows what math skills to be aware of, and knows how to adapt games for different levels in math.
>
> Action research has helped me to differentiate instruction and make small-group instruction more meaningful. Through action research, I am looking at one math game and not thinking to myself – Whom can I use this game with? Instead, I am taking math games and thinking – How can I modify this game so all my students can play it? How can I make it work for students at all levels?

An Open Letter to Our *Everyday Mathematics* Colleagues

July 31, 2006

To Our Colleagues in *Everyday Mathematics*,

> During Inquiry Summer 2005, PDS co-director Jenny Tuten wrote,

> I think that teachers' voices need to be much louder in educational research. This was a struggle I went through with my doctoral study. I continue to try to create frameworks relevant to academics but that allow participants' voices to emerge.

This chapter is an attempt to create one such framework for scholarly research and writing. We reiterate that *knowing the children* is of supreme importance to our research methods and results. Knowing the children works for us in two directions. The simpler direction is that what we learn about the children adds to what we know about them. Inquiry teaches us more than we would otherwise be able to learn about their thinking and learning needs. What may be more relevant to your work is that it works the other way, too – what we know about the children contributes to what we learn about them from our research. Look, please, at the disconnect between Miguel's ability to count on the number line and in his family's store. Had Ms Raimundi not known so much about Miguel, we would never have made this precious research finding.

All of which brings us to the fundamental tension between what we do and what you do. Teacher research is localized, specific, and personal; you write curriculum programs for millions of children. This tension is the uniqueness to which we refer in our "unique relationship." Why *should* you attend to our findings about one boy in one classroom in one school in one Latino neighborhood? How *can* you possibly attend to Miguel and not leave other children behind?

In her comprehensive review of science teacher research, Kathleen J. Roth (2007) asserts that "teacher research produces knowledge," and she asks,

> What kind of knowledge is being produced by science teacher research? In what ways might this knowledge be of interest beyond the individual teacher researcher and her/his immediate collaborative group or school?
> (p. 1,228)

These questions live at the epicenter of the unique relationship between your work as commercial curriculum developers and ours as teacher researchers. It will take talking with you rather than writing at you to formulate a satisfactory response. We'll start the conversation now:

> Differentiated instruction must be a huge problem for people who create curriculum programs for the millions. We who differentiate only for the dozens do not envy you your daunting job! Less conscientious curriculum writers would pass the buck to teachers and mathematics specialists. In particular, we greatly appreciate the "Adjusting the Activity" component of your materials.

Nevertheless, there is only so much that you can do. Upon learning of our work, Susan Jo Russell remarked, "It's *impossible* for the curriculum to differentiate instruction because the curriculum writers can't put in all the details for all the different groups and students. The best case is, 'Here is what we teachers can do'" (personal communication, February 15, 2006). We have shown you what we can do. Thousands of other teacher researchers are doing similar work, many on implementing your materials. Imagine what you could do with the findings from hundreds of teacher-research experiments with dice and domino games, the outcomes of thousands of variations on your problem-solving tasks, and the results of plumbing the minds of millions of Miguels.

The generality of your work and the specificity of ours mean that the relationship between teacher research and commercial mathematics curriculum development is unique insofar as the distance separating the two parties at the outset. It mustn't remain so. Our collective's Gloria Whatts tells us how to come together, right now: "Doing the research helps us to focus on things that we never paid mind to." We suspect that you've not paid mind to the things thousands of us have thought about courtesy of the uniquely beneficial methods of teacher research. When we pay mind to these things together, our relationship will become uniquely close.

PS 112 principal Eileen Reiter is forever exhorting her faculty to "take it to the next level." Please help teacher researchers help you to take *Everyday Mathematics* to the next level.

We look forward to your response. On behalf of our entire partnership, we remain…

Collegially yours,

The members of the El Barrio-Hunter College PDS Partnership Writing Collective (Raquel Corujo, Priscilla Gelinas, Patricia Maiorano, Fadwa M. Nacel, Christine Passarelli, Laura Sebel, Renée Sillart, Esther Robles Soto, Elaine Funches, Gloria Whatts, Irma Colón, Bill Rosenthal, and Jenny Tuten).

Acknowledgments

We are grateful to Project Manager Sue Marsa for her many contributions to our work, particularly her persistence in spurring us to write. Thanks also to Dr Bob Gyles, who conceived of the Inquiry Summer project from which this chapter developed, and to Donna Balter-Meislin for her support. Finally, our gratitude goes out to Hunter President Jennifer J. Raab for buying into our efforts, both figuratively with her faith in us and literally with a generous grant.

Notes

1. Mindful that all teachers develop curriculum in practice, we nevertheless use the term "curriculum developers" throughout this chapter as shorthand for "developers of curriculum programs."
2. It has become commonplace to use the terms "teacher research" and "action research" interchangeably despite their being distinct modes of inquiry. Our variety of practitioner inquiry

falls within *both* traditions. Although it is proper to brand our work "teacher action research," we typically shorten it by dropping either "teacher" or "action." Zeichner and Noffke (2001, pp. 300–306) describe five "traditions" of practitioner research, of which our approach is primarily a mélange of the British teacher-as-researcher and North American teacher research traditions.

3. We took the term "non-negotiable" from Superintendent Evelyn Castro and Deputy Superintendent Robert Gyles, who had formulated a short list of "non-negotiable" policies for school improvement. Top-down though these requirements may sound, they were reasonable policies, such as "Children's work will be displayed in the hallways."

References

Abdal-Haqq, I. (1998). *Professional development schools: Weighing the evidence.* Thousand Oaks, CA: Corwin Press.

Allen, D., Blythe, T., & Powell, B. S. (1996). *A guide to looking collaboratively at student work.* Cambridge, MA: Harvard Project Zero.

Berthoff, A. (1987). The teacher as REsearcher. In D. Goswami & P. R. Stillman (Eds.), *Reclaiming the classroom: Teacher research as an agency for change* (pp. 28–39). Portsmouth, NH: Boynton/Cook.

Cochran-Smith, M., & Lytle, S. L. (1990). Learning from teacher research: A working typology. *Teachers College Record, 92*(1), 83–103.

Duckworth, E. (1987). Teaching as research. In M. Okazawa-Rey, J. Anderson, & R. Traver (Eds.), *Teachers, teaching, and teacher education* (pp. 261–275). (*Harvard Educational Review* Reprint Series No. 19.) Cambridge, MA: Harvard Educational Review.

Gallas, K. (1995). *Talking their way into science: Hearing children's questions and theories, responding with curricula.* New York, NY: Teachers College Press.

Greenes, C., Larson, M., Leiva, M., Shaw, J. M., Stiff, L., & Vogeli, B. R. (2002). *Matemáticas.* Boston, MA: Houghton Mifflin.

Heaton, R. M. (2000). *Teaching mathematics to the new standards: Relearning the dance.* New York, NY: Teachers College Press.

Hollingsworth, S. (1994). *Teacher research and urban literacy education: Lessons and conversations in a feminist key.* New York, NY: Teachers College Press.

Holmes Group. (1990). *Tomorrow's schools: Principles for the design of professional development schools.* East Lansing, MI: Holmes Group.

Howes, E. V. (2002). *Connecting girls and science: Constructivism, feminism, and science education reform.* New York, NY: Teachers College Press.

Paley, V. G. (1986). On listening to what the children say. *Harvard Educational Review, 56*(2), 215–224.

Roth, K. J. (2007). Science teachers as researchers. In S. K. Abell & N. G. Lederman (Eds.), *Handbook of research on science education* (pp. 1,205–1,259). Mahwah, NJ: Erlbaum.

Teitel, L. (2001). *How professional development schools make a difference: A review of research.* Washington, DC: National Council for the Accreditation of Teacher Education (NCATE).

University of Chicago School Mathematics Project. (2004). *Everyday mathematics* (2nd Edition). Chicago, IL: SRA/McGraw-Hill.

Zeichner, K. M., & Noffke, S. E. (2001). Practitioner research. In V. Richardson (Ed.), *Handbook of research on teaching* (Fourth Edition, pp. 298–330). New York, NY: Macmillan.

10

Negotiating the "Presence *of* the Text"

How Might Teachers' Language Choices Influence the Positioning of the Textbook?

Beth A. Herbel-Eisenmann

In the *Professional Teaching Standards*, the National Council of Teachers of Mathematics (NCTM, 1991) called for a shift in authority in mathematics classrooms – away from the teacher and textbook as the primary determinants of mathematically correct answers and toward students' own mathematical reasoning. The ways in which this shift in authority might take place in a mathematics classroom, however, are not clear or straightforward. For example, merely telling teachers "not to tell" is not helpful (Chazan & Ball, 1999). Furthermore, once a textbook is added to the teacher–student interaction, there are additional complexities. As Thom (1973) pointed out: "As soon as one uses a textbook, one establishes a didacticism, an academicism, even if the book be so written as to promote individual research" (p. 196). Given Thom's assertion, it is interesting to note that, although the NCTM document suggested a shift away from the textbook as authority, one policy response was to fund curriculum materials that could support teachers in helping students learn mathematics in deeper and more meaningful ways. The juxtaposition of NCTM's position on textbooks and the subsequent policy response compels us to think about how teachers might manage a shift in authority with the use of "new" (*Standards*-based) textbooks.

With some exceptions (e.g., Wilson & Lloyd, 2000), in most studies in which students determined the validity of their mathematical reasoning without relying on the teacher or textbook, textbooks were not present in the classroom (e.g., Cobb, Wood, Yackel, & McNeal, 1992; Cobb, Yackel, & Wood, 1993; Schoenfeld, 1992). Instead, the teacher and researchers developed lessons and tasks to be used in particular contexts based on what happened in the class each day. Yet, textbooks more commonly have a pervasive presence in mathematics classrooms and can impact what and how teachers teach and students learn (Begle, 1979; Tobin, 1987). In fact, when McNeal (1995) followed a student from one of the previously described classrooms where the textbook was not physically present into the next school year, she found that the student "abandoned his self-generated computational algorithms in favor of less understood conventional procedures" (p. 205). She claimed that the teacher's *use* of the textbook was partly responsible, although she did not carefully examine how this happened.

In this chapter, I draw on examples from two classrooms to conceptualize issues about authority and language choice as they relate to how textbooks are used and referred to[1] by mathematics teachers. The specific words that people speak (i.e., their "language choices," which are not necessarily conscious) when referring to and using a textbook can influence the ways in which people and textbooks are positioned as responsible for mathematical knowledge. I begin the chapter with relevant literature related to authority and language choice. I then offer three illustrative examples of textbooks being used in two classrooms and explain how the language choices in those examples "position" the teacher, students, and textbook in particular ways. I argue that teachers' choice of language when using mathematics textbooks can undermine or support instructional goals for students' engagement with mathematics.

A Lens for Interpreting the Examples

> "authority" *c.*1230, *autorite* "book or quotation that settles an argument," from O.Fr. *auctorité*, from L. *auctoritatem* (nom. *auctoritas*) "invention, advice, opinion, influence, command," from *auctor* "author" (see *author*). Meaning "power to enforce obedience" is from 1393; meaning "people in authority" is from 1611.
>
> (*Online Etymology Dictionary*, 2006)

As the above excerpt indicates, there is a direct etymological link between the words "authority" and "author": one of the listed definitions of "authority" originates from the word "author." This raises the following question: how might teachers' use of an authored text like a mathematics textbook influence its authority in a mathematics classroom? Authority is one of many resources teachers employ for control (Metz, 1978), and has been defined in an educational context as "a social relationship in which some people are granted the legitimacy to lead and others agree to follow" (Pace & Hemmings, 2007, p. 6). It needs to be emphasized that this relationship is a highly negotiable one. Students rely on a web of authority relations with friends and family members as well as with the teacher (Amit & Fried, 2005). I focus here, however, on the student–teacher–textbook relationship. In this section, I provide a lens to interpret the upcoming examples, drawing on literature related to authority, language choice, and positioning.

Teacher Authority

Much educational research related to teacher authority describes different types of authority. (For detailed discussions about these, see Amit & Fried, 2005; Pace & Hemmings, 2007.) The distinctions that are most relevant here are the ones authors make between being an authority because of one's *content knowledge* and being an authority because of one's *position* (e.g., Skemp, 1979). Basically, these researchers describe teachers as being *"an* authority [of content] *in* authority [by virtue of position]" (Russell, 1983, p.30). Some researchers (e.g., Pace, 2006) argue that the former is more relevant to teachers because it emphasizes their ability to reach their educational goals. Although these distinctions are made for analytic purposes, Pace (2003) has shown that the types of authority become blended as participants interact in classrooms.

Skemp (1979) pointed out the inherent tension in the fact that when authority is gained by position, authority is imposed: the teacher commands, students obey, and instructions are perceived as orders. In contrast, authority by knowledge involves being more like a "mentor." The authority is vested in the person by virtue of his own knowledge; instruction is sought and is perceived as advice. Pace and Hemmings (2006) recognized how rival and conflicting values complicate authority relations because they are socially constructed in the service of a moral order. Moral order, in this case, was defined as "shared norms, values, and purposes" (p. 21).

Regardless of what kind of authority seems to be at play, teachers need to develop an internal sense of authority, or a sense of agency, rather than rely on external forces in order to develop their own "pedagogical authority" (Wilson & Lloyd, 2000).[2] Furthermore, as Wilson and Lloyd point out, a parallel argument can be made for how teachers help students develop their own sense of mathematical authority. That is, the same kind of reliance on internal authority can help students learn mathematics with meaning. As Schoenfeld (1992) pointed out, however, the development of internal authority is rare in students, who have "little idea, much less confidence, that they can serve as arbiters of mathematical correctness, either individually or collectively" (p. 62).

Teachers can unknowingly undermine their intentions to develop this kind of mathematical authority in their students. For example, Forman, McCormick, and Donato (1998) examined authority patterns in a classroom in which the teacher was working toward the vision described in the *Standards* (NCTM, 1989, 1991) documents. The authors found evidence that although the teacher wanted to solicit, explore, and value multiple solution strategies, some of her discourse practices undermined this goal. They argued that the teacher asserted her authority through the use of tacit language patterns like overlapping speech, vocal stress, repetition, and expansion. Despite the fact that three students in her class presented mathematically correct and different solution strategies, the teacher overlapped a student's explanations *only* when the student was *not* using the procedure the teacher recently taught.

Up to this point, I have briefly discussed authority relationships between teachers and students. In mathematics classrooms, however, another pervasive presence that influences what and how mathematics is taught is the textbook. Most research on authority in classrooms has focused on teacher authority and briefly mentions that the textbook may have played a role in authority relationships in classrooms (Amit & Fried, 2005; Haggarty & Pepin, 2002; Hamm & Perry, 2002; McNeal, 1995). Some of this research has occurred in the context of teachers' use of *Standards*-based curriculum materials (e.g., Wilson & Lloyd, 2000). None of those authors, however, have seriously considered the interactions among the teacher, textbook, and students in their inquiries, perhaps because, as Olson (1989) argued, textbooks "are taken as the authorized version of a society's valued knowledge" (p. 192).

Textbook Authority

In current literature, there exist at least three (overlapping) perspectives on the source of a textbook's authority. Although these perspectives agree that text-books are an authoritative presence in the classroom, each highlights a different factor that is important to the positioning of the textbook as an authority. Two of these perspectives, in particular, are pertinent here.

First, Olson (1989) argued that the authority of the textbook is an intrinsic property of the structure of the text. The separation of the author from the text as well as the particular linguistic characteristics of a textbook helped to instanti-ate the textbook as an authority:

> Textbooks, thus, constitute a distinctive linguistic register involving a particular form of language (archival written prose), a particular social situation (schools) and social relations (author-reader) and a particular form of linguistic interaction.
>
> (p. 241)

In mathematics education, authors have referred to examining characteristics of textbooks in this way as focusing on the "presence *in* the text" (Love & Pimm, 1996).

In fact, examining the textbook in this way can help to show how the text-book is also in some ways *an* authority *in* authority. For example, a textbook[3] provides particular topics in a particular order and offers particular representa-tions of mathematical concepts and skills. A textbook is a codified version of what content is valued at a given point in time; it is a message from the math-ematical community far removed from any particular school, teachers, and stu-dents about both what knowledge is necessary and the ways in which that knowledge should be organized and taught (Apple, 1986; Stray, 1994). Thus, it acts as *an* authority on mathematics. In the teacher's edition, the textbook also provides suggestions about how to organize activities, what kind of lesson format to use (e.g., small-group explorations vs whole-group summarizing), and how to teach particular mathematical ideas. In this way, it provides information to the teacher about how to organize the students' social behaviors.

Second, Baker and Freebody (1989) contend that the authority of the text is the result of pedagogy. They argued that most research on the authority of the textbook primarily stems from theoretical arguments. Their perspective, however, takes as central actual classroom interactions, and the authors empiri-cally investigate how "text-authorizing practices ... may be observed in the course of classroom instruction" (p. 264), as well as how these practices evolve in relation to the authority of the teachers. To illustrate these practices, they exam-ined the kinds of questions teachers ask and the ways teachers respond to stu-dents' answers to their questions. They sought to "describe the intimate connections between talk around text and the social organization of authority relations between teachers and students. Teachers may be shown to use various practices to assign authority to the text and simultaneously to themselves"

(p. 266). In this chapter, I seek to understand teachers' negotiation of the presence *of* the text (Love & Pimm, 1996) by looking at teachers' "talk around text."

Language Choice and Positioning

Language is an important component of the teaching-learning process because it can help establish routines and regularities within which learning can take place (Voigt, 1985; 1995). For instance, Mehan (1979) described a hierarchical arrangement of lessons he found in his research: "lessons" can be broken down into "phases" that are comprised of "topically related sequences" (pp. 73–74). Language also is used for many other purposes in classrooms. For example, Cazden (2001) provided many important reasons for focusing on spoken language in classrooms. The one most relevant here is that, in contexts like schools and classrooms,

> one person, the teacher, is responsible for controlling all the talk that occurs while class is officially in session – controlling not just negatively, as a traffic officer does to avoid collisions, but also positively, to enhance the purposes of education.
>
> (p. 2)

As Cazden alluded to above, some perspectives on language in classrooms make a distinction between language that is used to focus on the content understandings being developed (i.e., "to enhance the purposes of education") and language that is used to control social behaviors (i.e., "to avoid collisions"). The distinction Cazden made about language in classrooms parallels nicely the literature on teacher authority. Not only is a teacher *an* authority *in* authority, but a teacher also deploys language forms that can be used for each of these purposes. For example, Christie (1995) more explicitly differentiated between an "instructional register" and a "regulative register" when she addressed pedagogical discourse. The instructional register is related to the content area or subject matter being taught (e.g., "The equation of a line can be written in the form $y = mx + b$."), whereas the regulative register relates to the overall goals of the activities and to the sequencing of the teaching-learning behaviors (e.g., "If you want to share your conjecture, you need to raise your hand first."). In their work with a middle school mathematics teacher related to her classroom discourse, Nathan and Knuth (2003) found that the teacher maintained a central *social* scaffolding role in order to promote student interactions. They also found, however, that in the process that she inadvertently reduced her role as *an* authority in the classroom. Although the teacher was successful in increasing students' interactions with one another, the discussions lacked mathematical accuracy. This study made clear the complexity involved in trying to balance these two registers in order to promote student learning.

Christie (1995) argued that these two registers help us see how students are

> apprenticed into behaviors, skills, attitudes, procedures, and forms of knowledge which enable them to achieve particular pedagogic subject

positions, and hence to acquire aspects of the "common knowledge" that is an important part of schooling.

(pp. 222–223)

Like Christie, many authors who study language assume that language choice is important because it indexes a particular set of values, dispositions, and ideologies (e.g., Lemke, 1990; Morgan, 1996). Whenever a speaker speaks, she makes (often unconscious) choices about the particular words she will use and how she will organize those words. These choices affect the functions of the words and the meanings that others may make of those words. A speaker has a "set of resources which constrain the possibility [of specific language choices], arising from her current positioning within the discourse in which the text is produced" (Morgan, 1996, p. 3).

For every phrase a person utters, a multitude of alternative phrases could be spoken that carry essentially the same meaning. The particular words that are chosen, however, carry additional messages about who we are and what we are doing. For example, in one classroom I heard students use the following two phrases to refer to the fact that a graph was exponential: "that graph shows a swoopy curve," and "that graph shows an exponential relationship." The first phrase had meaning only in the specific classroom in which it was generated, whereas the latter phrase would be recognized by the broader mathematical community. If students were to use the term "swoopy curve" outside of the context in which it was developed, they may not position themselves as being mathematically knowledgeable.

As the Morgan quotation above highlights, the notion of "positioning" is important because it recognizes that authority and power are dynamic constructs. That is, if we consider that teachers, textbooks, and students all have some agency within a classroom environment, at different moments in time, each of these participants might be privileged in different ways and may take on different responsibilities for the teaching–learning process. All participants are involved in the constitution of positioning. As Davies and Harré (1990) explained,

[positioning] is the discursive process whereby selves are located in conversations as observably and subjectively coherent participants in jointly produced story lines. There can be interactive positioning in which what one person says positions another. And there can be reflexive positioning in which one positions oneself. However, it would be a mistake to assume that, in either case, positioning is necessarily intentional.

(p. 48)

As these authors pointed out, in some cases, people can be positioned by others (e.g., "Carl's smart and he got that answer, so it must be right.") or they may position themselves in different ways (e.g., "But that answer is the same as the one I gave a little bit ago.").

In subsequent sections, I elaborate some of the ways the teacher, textbook, and students can be positioned through language choices, and illustrate how these positionings index authority at various points in time. The teacher, students, and textbook are all potential sources of knowledge that can take on responsibility for learning. The ways in which the teacher and students draw on, use, and refer to the textbook influence its position and privilege as a source of knowledge. And, through this positioning, language choice also allows the teacher and students to position themselves and one another.

Positioning in Three Classroom Examples

The following three examples come from two different eighth-grade classrooms in which the teachers, Josh and Karla, were both using the *Standards*-based curriculum materials from the *Connected Mathematics Project* (CMP) (Lappan, Fey, Fitzgerald, Friel, & Phillips, 1998a). This context is important to investigate, because balancing goals of social order and content engagement are more difficult in the middle school than in elementary school due to the fact that middle school students tend to shift from typically going along with adults to stronger loyalty to peers (Pace & Hemmings, 2007). For a detailed description of the teachers and students in these classrooms and the context in which they were situated, see Herbel-Eisenmann (2000).

In these particular examples, the teachers were working with a unit on mathematical modeling, *Thinking with Mathematical Models* (TMM)[4] (Lappan, Fey, Fitzgerald, Friel, & Phillips, 1998b). At least two different kinds of modeling experiences are included in TMM: (a) experiences in which students are asked to collect the data themselves and then represent and analyze it; and (b) experiences in which students are given data, graphs, or equations from an existing modeling situation. One recurring context in TMM has students measure the breaking weight of paper bridges by loading pennies into a cup until the bridge "crumples." The first time this context appears, students vary the thickness of the bridges; the second time, they vary the length of the bridges. Students are also asked to compare their own bridge-breaking experiences to those of a class in Maryland who did this problem during the pilot phase of CMP. Most of the situations in TMM can be modeled by a line, and some (e.g., when they vary the length of the bridge) can be modeled by a curve.

The first two examples come from one class period in Josh's classroom. The third example comes from Karla's classroom. Although all three examples are fairly routine examples of textbook use, there are subtle differences in what is being done and said. In the interpretation of the examples, I highlight how the ideas of language choice, positioning, and authority uncover substantially different potential meanings in the examples. In the transcripts, I use "J" or "K" to indicate that Josh or Karla is speaking. Any other names that appear indicate specific students who were speaking and all names are pseudonyms. When it was difficult to tell who was speaking, I use "Ms" and "Fs" to recognize the gender of the student and "Ss" is used whenever a group of students was calling something out. I also use italicized text to indicate words that were read verbatim from the textbook. After each example, I interpret the teacher's language choice with respect to positioning and authority.

Example 1

The transcript for the first example is displayed in Table 10.1.

   This example highlights the positioning and repositioning of the textbook and the teacher, illustrating how authority and positioning are fluid in classroom interactions. Josh began the interaction by calling on a student to read from the textbook. After Cory read a section of the textbook (lines 002–005), Josh re-read a portion of what Cory read (lines 006–008). Reading directly from the text – especially with little or no interpretation (and then a re-reading) of it – is privileging the wording of the textbook (or Privileging the Textbook). The teacher did not authorize the text, but rather, from his position *in* authority, he deferred to the text as authoritative, tacitly suggesting that his students also should defer

Table 10.1 Example 1

---

001 J: Let's go ahead, read on.
002 Cory: *The class then made a graph of the data. They thought the pattern looked*
003 *somewhat linear, so they drew a line to show this trend. This line is a good model for*
004 *the relationship because, for the thicknesses the class tested, the points on the line are*
005 *close to points from the experiment.*
006 J: Okay, now, let's look at that line again: *This line is a good model for the relationship*
007 *because for the thicknesses the class tested, the points on the line are close to the*
008 *points from the experiment.* Take a look at what they did. Now, their data was a little
009 bit scattered, a little more scattered than ours was. But, they still were able to draw a
010 line that seemed to fit the data pretty well.... That's sometimes called a line of best
011 fit. We're gonna use that term an awful lot. Cory read on.
012 Cory: *The line that the Maryland class drew is a graph model for their data. A graph*
013 *model is a straight line or curve that shows a trend in a set of data. Once you fit a*
014 *graph model to a set of data, you can use it to make predictions about values between*
015 *and beyond the values in your data.*
016 J: Okay, I don't have a vocabulary chart yet ... I'll get it up later. But, there's a good
017 definition for a graph model. It's one of your vocabulary words. It's *a straight line or*
018 *curve that shows a trend in a set of data.* It models the data, it shows the path....
      [three speaking turns later]
019 J: ... Remember what a graph model is – *it's a straight line or curve that shows a trend*
020 *in a set of data,* it fits the data. So that all the points are pretty close. Um, I don't know.
021 Why do we do this? What's the purpose of a graph model? [Abram's hand goes up
022 immediately] Abram, what's the purpose?
023 Abram: To show the linear relationship
024 J: Yeah. I could maybe see that it's linear just from looking at the table or if just
025 looking at the way the points are plotted. Why did I draw the line in? Just to show the
026 pattern? Christy?
027 Christy: To get a better look at what the data is trying to tell you?
028 J: Well, maybe that's part of it. Look back at your definition for a graph model. Look
029 at your definition of a graph model. What does it say? Read that last paragraph to
030 yourself on page seven. Lance, what's the purpose here? Why do we even bother
031 doing this?

---

to the textbook's authority. In this case, the textbook was authorized to introduce and define particular mathematical terms.

When a teacher reads from a textbook or a student is called on to read from the textbook, the talk in the classroom is similar to talk that occurs in church rituals when the congregation is asked to read from or repeat a text. As Olson (1989) has pointed out:

> ritual utterances radically restrict the linguistic options at the lexical, syntactic, and intonational levels ... such restricted propositional content gain their illocutionary force through the limited options they provide for dissent ... formalized language of ritual involves a different relation between the speaker and the message than does ordinary oral conversation ... [a] speaker ... is not speaking his own words but the words of elders [or in this case, the words of textbook authors]; the orator does not simply express his personal view but rather acts as a spokesman or messenger.
>
> (p. 235)

This practice authorizes the textbook as the authority because a ritualized form of reading requires a person to speak words that do not originate with him- or herself, but rather with someone else.

Josh stepped back and commented on the textbook's words (line 008). He pointed out that the data given in the text were different from the data that they collected in class. That is, the data from the book were a little more "scattered." "But," he continued, "they still were able to draw a line that seemed to fit the data pretty well," indicating that if the class from Maryland was able to draw a line of best fit, then his class should be able to do so, also. In this segment of the transcript, there was a shift from Privileging the Textbook to a positioning of the teacher and textbook as having a privileged subjectivity (or Teacher–Textbook Aligned). The teacher, in this case, positioned himself as someone who can interpret the text and images for his students.

In lines 010–011, there was another shift in positioning when Josh introduced a term that the textbook did not use, "line of best fit," and told students that this was a word they would use "an awful lot." By doing so, Josh shifted his positioning to having the authority to introduce mathematical terms that were not even introduced in the textbook (or Privileging the Teacher).

A shift back to Privileging the Textbook took place when Josh called on Cory to read from the book a second time. Josh further privileged the textbook's definition of graph model when he said that the book gave a "good definition" and provided a third reading of the graph model definition (lines 017–018). Josh asked students what the purpose of finding a graph model was. Both Abram and Christy attempted to answer his questions. When their answers seemed to be not quite what Josh was looking for (e.g., "I could maybe see that..." (line 024) and "Well, maybe that's part of it" (line 028)), he directed students' attention to the specific page number in the book and instructed students to "Read that last paragraph to yourself" so that they could answer his question appropriately.

Josh's questions and imperatives (or commands) positioned the textbook as both something that determined the purpose of classroom activity and something in which students could find answers to his questions. Interestingly enough, there were instances in the larger set of classroom data that indicated that students came to understand that the textbook was a place in which they were to find answers to Josh's questions. In some cases, when Josh asked students a question and then asked "How do you know?," students said, "It's in the book," as a form of justification.

Example 2

The transcript for the second example is displayed in Table 10.2.

Similar to the first example, Example 2 included a combination of reading from the textbook followed by the teacher's interpretations of the textbook information. In this example, however, the reading of the textbook was to inform the class what materials they needed to use for the bridge experiment they were about to do. Josh's comments on the activity positioned him as someone who had been part of the classroom community but who also had the right to tell students what they would be doing next. He pointed out that this experiment was "similar to the problem *we* did about a week and a half ago" (line 035), but that this time students (who he referred to as *you*) were going to vary the lengths of the bridges rather than the thickness. Josh then shifted his positioning again when he said, "The book says to … [*but*] we're going to…" (lines 039–040). In this case, he shifted to Privileging the Teacher, positioning himself as someone who had the authority to change an activity given in the book and thus mediated the textbook's authority and highlighted his own.

Table 10.2 Example 2

---

032 J: If you look at the directions, it says we're, you're gonna need *eight 4-inch wide strips*
033 *of paper with lengths 4 inches, 5 inches, 6, 7, 8, 9, 10, and 11 inches, two books of the*
034 *same thickness, a small paper cup and about 50 pennies.* Now this sounds very similar
035 to the problem we did about a week and a half ago, right? This time every bridge you
036 make is only going to be one layer thick, one sheet of paper. What we're going to vary
037 are the lengths. One thing you're going to change on this right now. Instead of bridge
038 thickness, you're going to have bridge length. You're still going to have breaking weight.
039 The book says to start with a bridge 4 inches long, we're going to start with bridge
040 that is 5 inches long because when you do the one-inch overlaps, you only have two
041 inches in the middle and I'm not positive your cups would even fit on that. So, start with
042 a bridge five inches and then go 6, 7, 8, where do we stop?
043 Ms: 11.
044 J: 11 inches? Okay you're going to need to do some measuring, and a couple things
045 to watch: make sure the only thing that differs from one test to the next is the length of
046 the bridge, make sure you place your cups in the middle, make sure you place the
047 pennies in, make sure you have one inch overlap on your books. Most people who
048 screwed up last time, that's what you screwed up. Alright, any questions?

When Josh first used TMM, he found that the cups were too wide to be placed on four-inch long bridges, so he told his students to "start with a bridge that is five inches." His last turn in this segment of transcript had a series of commands related to what he wanted students to "make sure *you*" do (lines 045–047). All of these commands related to mistakes students made when they did the first bridge experiment (or in past school years when Josh did this unit with other students). Pointing out that "most people screwed up" reinforced Josh's authority to structure the classroom activity; he highlighted the fact that, drawing on the way the problem was stated in the textbook, students made many mistakes. Therefore, he needed to clarify the process so that students could avoid mistakes of the past.

Example 3

The example from Karla's classroom came from the day after the students had a difficult time with the following question on a quiz:

> To plant potatoes, a farmer cuts each potato into about 4 pieces, making sure each piece has an "eye." The eye contains buds that will become new plants. Each new plant will produce 5 potatoes. Thus, a single potato will yield 20 potatoes.
> A. Make a table and a graph model that show how the number of potatoes grown depends on the number of potatoes cut and planted.
> B. Write an equation that describes this situation.
> (Lappan et al., 1998b, p. 64)

Subsequently, the discussion shown in Table 10.3 took place when Karla handed back the quiz.

Unlike Josh's language choices for the textbook as "it" (lines 029 and 032) and "the book" (line 039), in Example 3 Karla used the pronoun "they" to refer to

Table 10.3 Example 3

049 K: The potato problem, they gave more information than we needed to know. I've heard
050 this – to try to get you to sort through the information that was necessary. All they wanted
051 to know was that if I plant an old potato, about how many new potatoes are going to
052 grow from it? All that stuff about cutting it up and dividing some from each piece and
053 all that, that was just some background information about how if you wanted to go home
054 and do this, you could do this.
055 Ms: It was easy.
056 Sammie: I was confused.
057 K: I know [to Sammie].
058 [Ss comment – overlapping speech]
059 K: [inaudible] 20 potatoes. So then two potatoes and we could get 40 and three,
060 hopefully 60. So, your table is going to increase that way. Why did they use the word
061 "graph model" when the data seemed perfectly linear?… [Comment regarding student
062 behavior] They used the word graph model when it seemed to be a perfect fit.…

the textbook. The background and context of the use of "they" are important. In this particular instance, Karla referred to the textbook as "they" after students did not do well on a particular quiz problem. She often used the word "they" in a context of differing interpretation (e.g., when the students seemed to interpret something differently than the authors of the curriculum materials suggested they might in the teacher's edition). This strategy allowed her to act as an interpreter for her students, distancing herself from the authority of the textbook and the authors and aligning herself as part of the classroom community (or Teacher–Students Aligned).

The language of the quiz problem was absolute and precise ("will produce," "will yield") and may have been confusing to students because when students collected their own data or when they were given data that had been collected by someone else, the increases were *not exact* increments to account for errors in the data collection process. Furthermore, students seemed to have come to understand "graph models" as not being completely regular or precise because they referred in class to mathematical models as "kinda linear," "almost linear" or "sorta linear." In fact, both Karla and the students used the word "perfect" to distinguish data that was exactly linear from a modeling situation. Karla mediated this disjuncture by using language that was hypothetical ("if," "could") and vague ("about," "seemed," "hopefully"). To deal with this conflict of language use, Karla used "they" to identify the authors of the textbook as a third party, positioning herself away from the textbook's external authority.

Hamm and Perry (2002) noticed that the teachers in their study "distanced themselves from the domain of mathematics by reference to the text with deference" (p. 135), saying things like "they want us to" and "they tricked us." I contend, however, that the context in which these words are spoken needs to be considered before claims can be made that these phrases indicate deference. A phrase like "they want us to" could position the textbook as something that has agency to dictate activities that are done in the classroom, highlighting the textbook's authority to do so. A phrase like "they tricked us," however, seems to align the teacher and students, and mitigates the authority of the textbook. Although I agree with the authors that "the incidental and routine comments that teachers make about their own place" (p. 135) (and, I would argue, the place of the textbook) might influence the classroom practices, I maintain that detailed analysis of the classroom discourse (which includes close attention to context) is needed to make such claims. In fact, although Romberg (1997) reported that teachers using *Standards*-based curriculum materials (*Mathematics in Context*) could not fall back on the use of *they* in the same ways as previously might have occurred (e.g., when using commercially-developed textbooks), his claim appears to be in need of further empirical investigation.

Permutations of Positioning

In summary, there are at least four categories of positionings illustrated in these classroom examples: (a) Privileging the Textbook, (b) the Teacher–Textbook Aligned, (c) Privileging the Teacher, and (d) the Teacher–Student(s) Aligned.

Each of these positionings authorizes or privileges particular ways of taking responsibility for learning. And, as the examples clearly show, these positionings are constantly changing and shifting as people interact. When the textbook is read from, it is authorized to do and say things in particular ways. When the teacher adds interpretation and comments to the textbook reading, these words can be examined to see if the teacher and textbook are aligned or if the teacher is positioning herself as an authority that can change the textbook. Finally, the teacher and students can be aligned, for example, through particular references to the textbook as "they."

Each illustration of these positionings that appeared in the examples is only one point on a continuum of practices within each of the categories of positionings. For example, a more extreme illustration of Privileging the Teacher might occur when a teacher enters the classroom, turns her back on the students and begins to speak to the board, virtually ignoring the students in the room. A more extreme version of Privileging the Textbook could appear when a teacher changes his or her approach to a problem because it does not match a solution in the back of the book (see Johansson, 2007). In the case of the Teacher–Students Aligned, it is possible that the authority could be shared so that "dialogic discussion" (Nystrand, 1995) is taking place. Alternatively, the textbook may be completely absent from any of the classroom activity. An extensive investigation of a larger database could help to develop a more nuanced understanding of the range of practices within each type of positioning described here.

Furthermore, there are at least two other potential positionings that did not appear in the examples: (e) Student(s)–Textbook Aligned, and (f) Privileging the Student(s). These absent categories are important because they suggest that students can be active agents in these positionings, too. These two positionings could occur in the classroom, but they are seldom captured in mathematics education research. Student(s)–Textbook Alignment might occur when a teacher lacks knowledge of a particular content area. For example, a teacher may state that a square is not a rectangle, and a student in the class may refer to the textbook as evidence that the teacher was incorrect. A more extreme case could occur when a student disrespects a teacher and takes serious study only of the textbook, ignoring anything the teacher has to say.

Instances of Privileging the Student(s) may be more prevalent in small-group settings than in whole-class discussions due to the removal of the teacher from the interaction. For example, students have been shown to take on teacher roles in small groups, positioning themselves as having a privileged voice (female students, in particular, have been shown to do this more often than male students) (Tholander & Aronsson, 2003). One form this type of positioning might take in whole-class discussions is that of student(s)–teacher debate. In his extensive research on science classrooms, however, Lemke (1990) reported that teacher–student debates occurred very infrequently. It is possible that in a domain like mathematics, student(s)–teacher debates would be even less frequent due to a pervasive belief that mathematical knowledge is absolute and infallible. Privileging the Student(s) appeared in Oyler's (1996) account of how a first-grade teacher followed students' initiations rather than controlling them. This kind of teacher-following allowed students to "bring their knowledge to bear in ways that challenged the authority of texts and occasionally that of the teacher" (Pace & Hemmings, 2007, p. 20).

Purposeful Positioning

In this chapter, I have shown that language choice can position the teacher, students, and textbook in different ways. I contend that the words spoken in relationship to the textbook matter when supporting students' learning. The unconscious nature of language choice and positioning make it imperative that they become a focus of reflection and inquiry in mathematics teaching and learning. In 1968, Jackson described the centrality of authority to classroom life, naming the rules, routines, and regulations he observed "the hidden curriculum." Some scholars (e.g., Bloom, 1972) have argued that the impact of the hidden curriculum is even greater than the content-related curriculum because it is so pervasive. Teachers' language choice is integrally related to the hidden curriculum (Gayer, 1970). Although authority is a social construction that is mutually negotiated by the teacher and students, teachers tacitly have more control over social and content language patterns than students do. Consequently, language choice is a critical part of the hidden curriculum and can undermine goals explicitly held for students.

When teachers, textbooks, and students come into contact with one another, there is the potential for each of these "participants" in the classroom to take on responsibility for the introduction and development of mathematical knowledge. Attention to how this responsibility is enacted and where this responsibility lies is important to the learning process, and can be seen through the lens of language choice and positioning. Who (the teacher or students) or what (the textbook or mathematical reasoning) is considered responsible for the development and justification of mathematical knowledge impacts who or what is seen as an authority. A teacher's language choice when using and referring to textbooks influences how the textbook is constructed as both *an* authority and *in* authority. These language choices shape how teachers, textbooks, and students are positioned as being responsible for learning mathematical terms, definitions, skills, and concepts. If students come to see the teacher or textbook as *the* source of authority too often, it may be detrimental to them developing agency as mathematical knowers.

The ways in which teachers might consciously negotiate the teacher–textbook–student relationship needs to be further examined. Textbooks are written to guide, shape, and inform classroom practice. How might teachers navigate the challenge of using a textbook to guide in this way without undermining the development of authority of the students? There are mathematical ideas and understandings that have been developed by the mathematics community that most people agree students should learn. A critical component of mathematical learning involves students making sense of these ideas, learning how to reason mathematically, and determining the correctness of their mathematical solutions rather than relying on a "greater" authority to do so. How might the teacher balance these two perspectives that, in some ways, seem to contradict one another? Can these two perspectives co-exist? When would it be reasonable to have students consult the text? For example, mathematical terms are "arbitrary" (Hewitt, 1999) in the sense that, at some point in time, the mathematical community decided to adopt particular words for specific ideas. In order to know mathematical terms, students need to be told them. As I pointed out earlier, if students thought "swoopy curve" was the only way to talk about exponential graphs, they may not be recognized as being mathematically knowledgeable. In this situation, it would make sense for a teacher or textbook to be *an* authority and offer the appropriate terminology – certainly someone must. Understanding the ideas associated with mathematical terms, however, is more complicated because the ideas are multi-faceted, connected to other ideas, and can be represented in multiple ways. The language choices related to mathematical ideas and processes may matter more to student learning than they do in the context of offering mathematical terminology.

Although readers of this chapter could interpret my argument as saying that all textbook use undermines student learning, I want to make clear that this is not the case. Rather, the argument put forth here is that textbook use and associated language choices are complicated. We need to better understand what kinds of positionings are productive for students' learning, and in what contexts. My inclination would be to propose that when the textbook too often determines mathematical processes and concepts rather than being consulted as *an* authority of convention, over-reliance on the textbook could be unproductive. This hypothesis, however, needs to be investigated empirically.

I have made a shift from suggesting that teachers should be conscious of their language choices to saying that students may become aware of their language choices, impacting in some ways their learning experience in mathematics. Other researchers (e.g., Love & Pimm 1996; Morgan, 1998) have made a similar shift in their writings about language choice in mathematics education. Ultimately, our goal as mathematics educators is to help students learn mathematics in ways that are meaningful to them. Part of this learning should include ways of seeing the nature of authority in the discipline and, as the *Standards* (NCTM, 1989) suggest, helping students see themselves as able to use mathematical reasoning to justify their mathematical thinking. As Wagner (2007) has pointed out, however, these kinds of practices are not straightforward. Although some mathematics educators (e.g., Chazan and Ball, Cobb and colleagues, Schoenfeld) have shown that teachers can consciously work toward deflecting mathematical authority, there is much we still need to learn about what language practices might be most helpful and identify ways to enact them in order to offer powerful educative experiences for students. These are issues that should be taken up by the mathematics education community if we are going to continue improving mathematics classroom practices.

Acknowledgments

The writing of this chapter was supported by the National Science Foundation under Grant Number 0347906 (Beth Herbel-Eisenmann, PI) and the Center for the Study of Mathematics Curriculum. Any opinions, findings, and conclusions or recommendations expressed in this piece are those of the author and do not necessarily reflect the views of NSF or CSMC. I would like to thank Janine Remillard, Gwen Lloyd, Dave Wagner, David Pimm, Corey Drake, and CSMC Graduate Student Fellows for engaging in conversations about this work with me.

Notes

1. I distinguish between "referring to" and "using" because in some cases the textbook is being talked about but may not be physically present (e.g., a teacher might say, "Yesterday we looked at fractions in your textbook") and in other cases the textbook is a physical presence in the ways it is being used (e.g., when it is read directly from).
2. As shown in Chapter 4 of this volume, by McClain et al., many of these issues related to agency also occur at the broader district level.
3. In this wording, I give agency to the mathematics textbook because I see the teacher–textbook relationship as a "participatory" one (Remillard, 2005). As Brown (Chapter 2) points out, the teacher shapes the textbook when he or she uses it *and* the textbook can influence the teacher's knowledge, beliefs, skills, etc.
4. In Herbel-Eisenmann (2007), I used linguistic theory to analyze the voice *in* the unit (TMM), and showed some of the ways authority is structured in this text.

References

Amit, M., & Fried, M. N. (2005). Authority and authority relations in mathematics education: A view from an 8th grade classroom. *Educational Studies in Mathematics, 58,* 145–168.

Apple, M. W. (1986). *Teachers and texts.* New York, NY: Routledge & Kegan Paul.

Baker, C. D., & Freebody, P. (1989). Talk around text: Constructions of textual and teacher authority in classroom discourse. In S. de Castell, A. Luke, & C. Luke (Eds.), *Language, authority and criticism: Readings on the school textbook* (pp. 263–283). New York, NY: Falmer Press.

Begle, E. G. (1979). *Critical variables in mathematics education: Findings from a survey of the empirical literature.* Washington, DC: Mathematical Association of America.

Bloom, B. (1972). Innocence in education. *School Review, 80,* 333–352.

Cazden, C. (2001). *Classroom discourse: The language of teaching and learning* (2nd Edition). Portsmouth: Heinemann.

Chazan D., & Ball, D. (1999). Beyond being told not to tell. *For the Learning of Mathematics, 19*(2), 2–10.

Christie, F. (1995). Pedagogic discourse in the primary school. *Linguistics and Education, 7,* 221–242.

Cobb, P., Wood, T., Yackel, E., & McNeal, B. (1992). Characteristics of classroom mathematics traditions: An interactional analysis. *American Educational Research Journal, 29*(3), 573–604.

Cobb, P., Yackel, E., & Wood, T. (1993). Theoretical orientation. In T. Wood, P. Cobb, E. Yackel, & D. Dillon (Eds.), *Rethinking elementary school mathematics: Insights and issues, Journal for Research in Mathematics Education, Monograph #6.* Reston, VA: NCTM.

Davies, B., & Harré, R. (1990). Positioning: The discursive production of selves. *Journal for the Theory of Social Behaviour, 20*(1), 43–63.

Forman, E. A., McCormick, D. E., & Donato, R. (1998). Learning what counts as a mathematical explanation. *Linguistics and Education, 9*(4), 313–339.

Gayer, N. (1970). On making morality operational. In J. R. Martin (Ed.), *Readings in the philosophy of education: A study of curriculum* (pp. 264–273). Boston, MA: Allyn & Bacon.

Haggarty, L., & Pepin, B. (2002). An investigation of mathematics textbooks and their use in English, French and German classrooms: Who gets an opportunity to learn what? *British Educational Research Journal, 28*(4), 567–590.

Hamm, J. V., & Perry, M. (2002). Learning mathematics in first-grade classrooms: On whose authority? *Journal of Educational Psychology, 94*(1), 126–137.

Herbel-Eisenmann, B. A. (2000). *How discourse structures norms: A tale of two middle school mathematics classrooms.* Unpublished doctoral dissertation, Michigan State University, East Lansing, MI.

Herbel-Eisenmann, B. A. (2007). From intended curriculum to written curriculum: Examining the "voice" of a mathematics textbook. *Journal for Research in Mathematics Education, 38*(4), 344–369.

Hewitt, D. (1999). Arbitrary and necessary part 1: A way of viewing the mathematics curriculum. *For the Learning of Mathematics, 19*(3), 2–9.

Jackson, P. W. (1968). *Life in classrooms.* New York, NY: Holt, Rinehart and Winston.

Johansson, M. (2007). Mathematical meaning and textbook tasks. *For the Learning of Mathematics, 27*(1), 45–51.

Lappan, G., Fey, J., Fitzgerald, W., Friel, S., & Phillips, E. (1998a). *The Connected Mathematics Project.* Palo Alto, CA: Dale Seymour.

Lappan, G., Fey, J., Fitzgerald, W., Friel, S., & Phillips, E. (1998b). *Thinking with mathematical models, Teacher's edition.* Menlo Park, CA: Dale Seymour.

Lemke, J. (1990). *Talking science: Language, learning, and values.* Norwood, NJ: Ablex.

Love, E., & Pimm, D. (1996). "This is so": A text on texts. In A. J. Bishop, K. Clements, C. Keitel, J. Kilpatrick, & C. Laborde (Eds.), *International handbook of mathematics education, Part 1* (pp. 371–410). Dordrecht: Kluwer Academic.

McNeal, B. (1995). Learning not to think in a textbook-based mathematics class. *Journal of Mathematical Behavior, 14*, 205–234.

Mehan, H. (1979). *Learning lessons.* Cambridge, MA: Harvard University Press.

Metz, M. H. (1978). *Classrooms and corridors: The crisis of authority in desegregated secondary schools.* Berkeley, CA: University of California Press.

Morgan, C. (1996). "The language of mathematics": Towards a critical analysis of mathematics texts. *For the Learning of Mathematics, 16*(3), 2–10.

Morgan, C. (1998). *Writing mathematically: The discourse of investigation.* Bristol, PA: Falmer Press.

Nathan, M. J., & Knuth, E. J. (2003). A study of whole classroom mathematical discourse and teacher change. *Cognition and Instruction, 21*(2), 175–207.

NCTM. (1989). *Curriculum and evaluation standards.* Reston, VA: Author.

NCTM. (1991). *Professional standards for teaching mathematics.* Reston, VA: Author.

Nystrand, M. (1995). *Opening dialogue: Understanding the dynamics of language and learning in the English classroom.* New York, NY: Teachers College Press.

Olson, D. R. (1989). On the language and authority of textbooks. In S. de Castell, A. Luke, & C. Luke (Eds.), *Language, authority and criticism: Readings on the school textbook* (pp. 233–244). Philadelphia, PA: Falmer Press.

Online Etymology Dictionary. (2006). Authority. Retrieved January 25, 2006, from http://www.etymonline.com/index.php?search = authority&searchmode = none

Oyler, C. (1996). *Making room for students: Sharing teacher authority in room 104.* New York, NY: Teachers College Press.

Pace, J. L. (2003). Using ambiguity and entertainment to win compliance in a lower-level US history class. *Journal of Curriculum Studies, 35*, 83–110.

Pace, J. L. (2006). Saving (and losing) face, race, and authority: Strategies of action in a ninth-grade English class. In J. L. Pace & A. Hemmings (Eds.), *Classroom authority: Theory, research, and practice* (pp. 87–112). Mahwah, NJ: Lawrence Erlbaum.

Pace, J. L., & Hemmings, A. (2006). Understanding classroom authority as a social construction. In J. L. Pace & A. Hemmings (Eds.), *Classroom authority: Theory, research, and practice* (pp. 1–31). Mahwah, NJ: Lawrence Erlbaum.

Pace, J. L., & Hemmings, A. (2007). Understanding authority in classrooms: A review of theory, ideology, and research. *Review of Educational Research, 77*(1), 4–27.

Remillard, J. T. (2005). Examining key concepts in research on teachers' use of mathematics curricula. *Review of Educational Research, 75*(2), 211–246.

Romberg, T. (1997). Mathematics in Context: Impact on teachers. In E. Fennema & B. S. Nelson (Eds.), *Mathematics teachers in transition* (pp. 358–380). Mahwah, NJ: Lawrence Erlbaum.

Russell, T. (1983). Analyzing arguments in science classroom discourse: Can teachers' questions distort scientific authority? *Journal of Research in Science Teaching, 20*(1), 27–45.

Schoenfeld, A. H. (1992). Reflections on doing and teaching mathematics. In A. H. Schoenfeld (Ed.), *Mathematical thinking and problem solving* (pp. 53–70). Hillsdale, NJ: Erlbaum.

Skemp, R. (1979). *Intelligence, learning and action.* New York, NY: John Wiley and Sons.

Stray, C. (1994). Paradigms regained: Towards a historical sociology of the textbook. *Journal of Curriculum Studies, 26*(1), 1–29.

Tholander, M., & Aronsson, K. (2003). Doing subteaching in school group work: Positionings, resistance and participation frameworks. *Language and Education, 17*(3), 208–234.

Thom, R. (1973). Modern mathematics: Does it exist? In A. G. Howson (Ed.), *Developments in mathematical education: Proceedings of the Second International Congress on Mathematical Education* (pp. 194–209). Cambridge: Cambridge University Press.

Tobin, K. (1987). Forces which shape the implemented curriculum in high school science and mathematics. *Teaching and Teacher Education, 3*(4), 287–298.

Voigt, J. (1985). Patterns and routines in classroom interaction. *Recherches en Didactique des Mathematiques, 6,* 69–118.

Voigt, J. (1995). Thematic patterns of interaction and sociomathematical norms. In P. Cobb & H. Bauersfeld (Eds.), *The emergence of mathematical meaning: Interaction in classroom cultures* (pp. 163–201). Hillsdale, NJ: Lawrence Erlbaum.

Wagner, D. (2007). Students' critical awareness of voice and agency in mathematics classroom discourse. *Mathematical Thinking and Learning, 9*(1), 31–50.

Wilson, M., & Lloyd, G. M. (2000). Sharing mathematical authority with students: The challenge for high school teachers. *Journal of Curriculum and Supervision, 15*(2), 146–169.

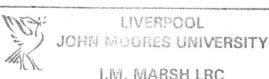

11
Similarities and Differences in the Types of Algebraic Activities in Two Classes Taught by the Same Teacher

Tammy Eisenmann and Ruhama Even

Recently, studies of curriculum enactment have suggested that different teachers enact the same written curriculum materials in different ways (Cohen & Ball, 2001; Manouchehri & Goodman, 2000). The literature, however, provides little information about the enacted curriculum in different classes of the same teacher, and even less about the *mathematical ideas* enacted in different classes of the same teacher. Are students exposed to the same mathematical ideas when a teacher enacts the same written curriculum materials in different classrooms? This study explores this question in the context of algebra, an important school mathematics subject. The aim of this study is to examine how algebraic ideas may change when the one teacher enacts the same written curriculum materials in different classes.

Relevant Literature

Curriculum materials such as textbooks and teacher's guides can be regarded as mediators between a general intention of the intended curriculum and classroom instruction (Schmidt, McKnight, Valverde, Houang & Wiley, 1997; Stein & Kim, Chapter 3 of this volume). Curriculum materials are regarded as the *potential* enacted curriculum because they include mathematical items (e.g., problems, exercises) for teachers to use in their instruction, and often suggestions for mathematical activities, recommendations on how to structure classroom lessons (e.g., time allocation), pedagogical strategies, and instructional approaches.

Some studies show that the enacted curriculum is not identical to the written curriculum (Cohen & Ball, 2001; Manouchehri & Goodman, 1998; McClain, Zhao, Bowen, & Visnovska, Chapter 4 of this volume). The discrepancies have been historically attributed to deficiencies in teacher subject-matter knowledge, inadequate acquaintance with the new curriculum program, and little understanding of the new curriculum program (its rationale, content, and instructional strategies) (Freeman & Porter 1989; Manouchehri & Goodman, 1998; Remillard, 2005). Recently, studies of curriculum enactment have explained the differences between the enacted curriculum and the written curriculum materials by giving a prominent role to teacher decision-making (Clandinin & Connelly, 1992; Clarke, Clarke, & Sullivan, 1996; Drake & Sherin, 2006; Lloyd, 1999).

The findings of more recent studies show that different teachers enact the same curriculum materials in different ways (Cohen & Ball, 2001; Lloyd, 1999; Manouchehri & Goodman, 2000; McClain et al., Chapter 4 of this volume; Tirosh, Even, & Robinson, 1998). Studying the enacted curriculum in different classes of one teacher, however, has only now started to be the focus of research studies. Even and Kvatinsky (2007) examined the content, instructional practices and classroom interactions in high-school classes having different levels taught by the same teacher – investigating the nature and sources of differences. Herbel-Eisenmann, Lubienski, and Id-Deen (2006) studied the instructional practices of one teacher who taught two eighth-grade mathematics classes using different curriculum materials in each of the classes. Lloyd (2008) studied a high school mathematics teacher's decisions about classroom organization and interactions during his first two years using new curriculum materials. These studies highlight contextual factors that contribute to the enacted curriculum (e.g., student/parent expectations). Still, seldom did the teacher in these research studies use the *same* written materials in the different classes, and the focus in these studies was mostly on pedagogy and rarely did they examine the mathematics in the enacted curriculum in different classes of one teacher. This study addresses this deficiency in the context of school algebra.

Algebra is a central topic in school mathematics. In the past two decades, alternative ways of conceptualizing school algebra and algebraic thinking have been suggested and discussed (e.g., Bednarz, Kieran, & Lee, 1996; Kieran, 2007; NCTM, 1989, 2000; Usiskin, 1988). These novel approaches and theoretical discussions aimed to pinpoint what is important in school algebra and to provide meaning to the various activities students are experiencing when learning algebra. Recently, revisiting the question of what should comprise the core of school algebra, Kieran (2004) built on those ideas and suggested that it would be useful to approach algebra as an activity. She developed a model of algebraic activity that we find to be useful as a framework for organizing school-level algebra activities. The framework distinguishes among three types of school algebra activities:

1. *Generational activities.* These activities involve the forming of expressions and equations that are the objects of algebra (e.g., writing a rule for a geometric pattern). The focus of generational activities is the representation and interpretation of situations, properties, patterns, and relations. Much of the initial meaning-making of algebra (i.e., developing meaning for the objects of algebra) occurs within generational activities.
2. *Transformational activities.* These include "rule-based" algebraic activities (e.g., collecting like terms, factoring, substituting). Transformational activities often involve the changing of the form of an expression or equation in order to maintain equivalence. It is important to note that meaning-building is not related solely to generational activities, as transformational activities can also involve meaning-building for equivalence, and for the use of properties and axioms in the manipulative processes.

3. *Global/meta-level activities.* These are activities that are not exclusive to algebra. They suggest more general mathematical processes and activities in which algebra is used as a tool. They include activities that require students to problem-solve, model, generalize, predict, justify, prove, and so on.

Unlike some frameworks that distinguish between lower and higher cognitive demand of mathematical tasks (e.g., Stein, Grover, & Henningsen, 1996), this framework focuses only on the type of algebraic activity and not on the cognitive level of the activity. Thus, all three types could relate to high-level tasks. Nevertheless, transformational activities often appear in conventional textbooks in relation to low-level tasks.

The assignment presented in Figure 11.1, which guides an exploration of the "match train" problem situation, illustrates the three types of algebraic activity described above. The work includes the examination of concrete cases involving small numbers (task a) and large numbers (tasks b, c, and f), inverse substitution

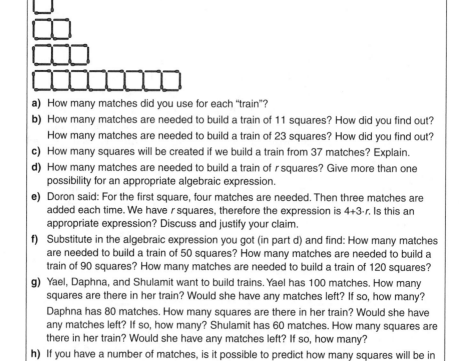

Let's make "trains" from matches.

a) How many matches did you use for each "train"?

b) How many matches are needed to build a train of 11 squares? How did you find out? How many matches are needed to build a train of 23 squares? How did you find out?

c) How many squares will be created if we build a train from 37 matches? Explain.

d) How many matches are needed to build a train of r squares? Give more than one possibility for an appropriate algebraic expression.

e) Doron said: For the first square, four matches are needed. Then three matches are added each time. We have r squares, therefore the expression is $4+3 \cdot r$. Is this an appropriate expression? Discuss and justify your claim.

f) Substitute in the algebraic expression you got (in part d) and find: How many matches are needed to build a train of 50 squares? How many matches are needed to build a train of 90 squares? How many matches are needed to build a train of 120 squares?

g) Yael, Daphna, and Shulamit want to build trains. Yael has 100 matches. How many squares are there in her train? Would she have any matches left? If so, how many? Daphna has 80 matches. How many squares are there in her train? Would she have any matches left? If so, how many? Shulamit has 60 matches. How many squares are there in her train? Would she have any matches left? If so, how many?

h) If you have a number of matches, is it possible to predict how many squares will be in the train? Would there be any matches left? If so, how many? Discuss and explain.

Figure 11.1 The "match train" assignment (Robinson & Taizi, 1997, pp. 8–9).

(tasks c, g, and h), forming an algebraic expression for a general "match train" (task d), examination of an unsuitable algebraic expression (task e), manipulating algebraic expressions (tasks f and g), and predicting, justifying, and analyzing relationships based on previous work (task h).

The assignment is composed of eight related tasks that include all three types of algebraic activity. Some tasks (tasks a–e, g, h) involve the forming of, and building meaning for, expressions that describe the generality arising from the geometric pattern of the "match trains" (generational activities). There are also tasks (tasks f–h) that involve substituting numerical values into the constructed or given expressions (transformational). Finally, there is one task (task h) that requires predicting, justifying and analyzing relationships – general mathematical activities that are not specific to algebra (global/meta-level). This task belongs to all three categories, as working on the task also combines forming expressions and developing a meaning for them (generational) and manipulating algebraic expressions (transformational).

The aim of this chapter is to use Kieran's framework of algebraic activities to examine how a teacher enacts the same algebra curriculum materials in two different classes. We first analyze the types of algebraic activities in the written curriculum materials, and then in the enacted curriculum in the two classes. For the latter we examine both the differences in the types of algebraic activities when moving from the curriculum materials to the enacted curriculum, and the differences between the enacted curriculum in the two classrooms.

Methods

This is a case study of one teacher, Sarah (pseudonym), who taught two seventh-grade classes, each in a different school (Carmel and Tavor – pseudonyms). Sarah used the same curriculum materials (i.e., textbook and teacher guide) in both classrooms.

Participants and Setting

Sarah had a B.Ed degree with emphases in mathematics and biblical studies from a teacher's college. She taught for eight years in the upper elementary grades, including fifth- and sixth-grade mathematics and other subjects. She then decided to go into teaching at the junior-high school level and registered for a two-week summer workshop intended for junior-high school teachers. The workshop was conducted by the team who developed the curriculum materials that were the focus of this study (intended for seventh and eighth grades). In an interview, Sarah described this experience as transformational: "At the workshop I actually felt that my eyes were opened." She became fond of the curriculum materials, feeling that they "make mathematics meaningful," (Sarah's Interview, July 2003) and decided that she wanted to use them in her teaching. In the year preceding this research project, Sarah spent her sabbatical year working once a week with the team that developed the curriculum materials, becoming well acquainted with the rationale, goals and intentions, the mathematical content, course outlines, textbooks, teacher guides, and other learning, teaching and assessment materials. The year of the study was Sarah's first year teaching seventh grade, her first year teaching with the new curriculum materials, and her first year teaching in the two focus schools.

One of the schools in which Sarah taught, Carmel, was a selective Jewish religious girls' junior-high school. Observations in the seventh-grade class (with 20 students) that participated in the research showed an active participation of most students both when working on assigned work in small groups and during whole-class work. The students shared and discussed their mathematical work, and responded to the teacher's questions. These characteristics were observed in the mathematics lessons as well as in lessons other than mathematics, and were also observed in other classes in the school. Carmel's written guidelines emphasized cognitive skills and quality of instruction rather than the coverage of topics. Sarah, as other teachers in the school, had autonomy in planning her lessons and constructing her exams.

The other school, Tavor, was a secular junior-high school located in a rural area. Observations in the mathematics lessons in the seventh-grade class (with 27 students) that participated in the research revealed that the class was noisy and that there were many disciplinary problems. These characteristics were specific to Sarah's mathematics lessons, and were not observed when the same class studied other subjects with other teachers. In Tavor, it was the head of the mathematics department's responsibility to plan the teaching sequence for all the mathematics classes and to construct uniform exams that were taken at the same time by all classes in the same grade level. Thus, at Tavor, Sarah had less autonomy in planning her lessons and exams. Both Carmel and Tavor were categorized by the Ministry of Education to be in the upper thirtieth percentile in the socioeconomic index (SES).

The curriculum materials Sarah used in both classes were part of *Everyone Learns Mathematics* (Robinson & Taizi, 1995–2002), one of the innovative seventh-grade mathematics curriculum programs developed during the 1990s in Israel. This curriculum program has many of the characteristics described in *Standards*-based curriculum programs in the United States (Even, Robinson, & Carmeli, 2003). One of the main characteristics of the *Everyone Learns Mathematics* curriculum materials was that students were to work cooperatively in small heterogeneous groups for much of the class time, investigating algebraic problem situations. Following small-group work, the curriculum materials suggested a planned whole-class discussion aimed at advancing students' mathematical understanding and conceptual knowledge.

Data Collection

Data collection was conducted during one school year (2002–03). The main data sources included: (a) video-taped observations of Sarah's teaching the beginning of the topic *equivalent algebraic expressions* (resulting in 19 lessons of 45 minutes in Carmel and 15 lessons of 45 minutes in Tavor where the researcher was a non-participant observer [Sabar, 2001]), and (b) an audiotaped interview with Sarah that was conducted after all observations were completed. The observations focused on the enactment of the curriculum materials and on the context of enactment; the interview focused on Sarah's view of the written curriculum materials and their enactment in the two classes. In order to provide additional information on the curriculum enactment and the context of enactment, data were collected from other sources as well, including additional lesson observations (more than 30 mathematics and non-mathematics lessons taught by Sarah and other teachers in the research classrooms and other classes in the schools), teacher and student interviews, and informal conversations.

Data Analysis

The data were analyzed both quantitatively and qualitatively. First, we coded the written curriculum materials. The beginning of the topic *equivalent algebraic expressions* was divided into 15 units in the curriculum materials, each of which was expected to be a 45-minute lesson. Of these units, 11 were enacted (fully or partially) in Carmel and 10 in Tavor. For the purpose of this study, only the 11 units that were enacted in at least one of the classes were analyzed. The units were composed of several assignments. In general, each unit started with a multi-task assignment for small-group work (e.g., the problem in Figure 11.1), followed by another multi-task assignment for whole-class work. Some of the units also included single- or multi-task assignments that could be assigned to the whole class or to specific students by the teacher as needed (e.g., to low- or high-achieving students in order to slow or advance them). The 11 units analyzed included a total of 46 assignments. We coded these assignments into one or more of Kieran's categories (generational, transformational, and global/meta-level algebraic activity) by analyzing their potential. We focused on the potential type of a written item because the enacted activity may not realize the task's potential (e.g., justification may not be provided even though it was requested in the item). We also found the sum of the time suggested by the written materials for class work for each assignment.

Almost all the assignments were composed of several related smaller tasks (e.g., the assignment in Figure 11.1 is composed of eight smaller tasks); the 46 assignments included a total of 367 tasks. We also coded these 367 tasks into one or more of the above categories. The assignments and tasks with which Sarah supplemented the written curriculum materials were also categorized. Four other researchers in mathematics education participated in the categorization of about 15 percent of the data. All disagreements were resolved by discussion until consensus was reached on each categorization.

We examined the class videotapes and field notes to check which assignments and which tasks were enacted in each class and the time spent on each assignment (using Z test to compare). Using a Chi-square test, we compared between the distributions of algebraic activity types (a) in the written curriculum materials and in the enacted curriculum for each of the two classes, and (b) in the enacted curriculum between the two classes. Comparisons were made between the total number of assignments and tasks in each category (taking into consideration that the categories were not distinct) and the total time spent on assignments in each category, because these were important indications of the nature of students' algebraic experiences in class. Next, we compared the written and enacted sequence of assignments and tasks based on the three types of algebraic activity. Finally, we examined the nature of the class activity and the realization of the potential of the algebraic types, as well as Sarah's view of that.

Types of Algebraic Activity in the Curriculum Materials

The 11 units we analyzed comprised 46 assignments. The recommendation in the curriculum materials was that most of these assignments would be given to all students and a few would be assigned simultaneously to different groups of students according to their needs (e.g., more advanced or students with difficulties). Consequently, the number of assignments suggested in the written materials for each student to work on during the teaching of the 11 units was 35–38 assignments (made up of 263–321 tasks). Table 11.1 presents the distribution of assignments, time, and tasks, included in the written curriculum materials, into the three types of algebraic activity. Assignments and tasks that were coded as more than one type of algebraic activity were included in each category. For example, the assignment in Figure 11.1, which is both generational and global/meta-level, was counted twice (as generational and also as global/meta-level), and so was its respective suggested time. Similarly, the last task of the assignment in Figure 11.1 (task h) was counted three times, as generational, as transformational, and as global/meta-level.

As can be seen in Table 11.1, most assignments and tasks in the written materials – about three-fourths – were transformational, and a related amount of class time was suggested to be devoted to these assignments. The written curriculum materials also included quite a few generational and global/meta-level activities. About one-half of the assignments were generational, and a similar amount of the class time was suggested to be devoted to them. Moreover, almost one-third of the assignments were global/meta-level and more than 40 percent of the class time was suggested to be devoted to them. The discrepancy between the percentage of global/meta-level *assignments* (more than 30 percent) and that of global/meta-level *tasks* (less than 10 percent) is due to the fact that often an overarching assignment was global/meta-level whereas none of its individual tasks was. In other words, it was the assignment as a whole, but not its individual parts, that reflected a global/meta-level type of

Table 11.1 Distribution of Assignments, Time, and Tasks in the Written Materials

	Generational		Transformational		Global/Meta-level	
	n	*%*	*n*	*%*	*n*	*%*
Assignments (35–38)	17	45–59	28–30	79–80	11–12	31–32
Time (495 min)	250–265	51–54	375	76	215	43
Tasks (263–321)	95–100	31–36	190–244	72–76	23–25	8–9

algebraic activity (e.g., problem-solving). There were, however, a few cases when a global/meta-level task was part of an assignment that was not global/-meta-level. For example, sometimes students were asked to justify an answer they got in one task, but justification was rather minor to the entire activity, so the assignment as a whole did not reflect a global/meta-level type of algebraic activity.

As already mentioned, not all 46 assignments were intended for every student. Some were suggested to be assigned only to some students. No statistically significant differences were found, however, among the distributions of types of algebraic activities suggested for individual students. Furthermore, an analysis of the suggested sequence of assignments and tasks showed that all three types appeared throughout the teaching of the beginning of the topic *equivalent algebraic expressions*. This illustrates how the curriculum materials focused on problem-solving, examining connections, hypothesizing, generalizing, and justifying throughout the activities and not only at the end of them.

Most generational activities appeared in the first part of the teaching sequence. This reflected the structure of the curriculum materials, in which the first units included problem situations that required students to find rules for different patterns and to form suitable general expressions. The "match train" problem in Figure 11.1 is a typical problem situation from the beginning of the teaching sequence of the topic *equivalent algebraic expressions*.

The second part of the teaching sequence included mainly transformational activities. This reflected the emphasis in the curriculum materials on the development of "the ability to investigate the expression, the ability to 'change' the expression in order to 'obtain' required properties," as stated in the teacher's guide (Robinson, Inbar, & Koren, 2001, p. 24). As exemplified in this quotation, transformational activities in the curriculum materials often developed meaning for equivalence and the use of properties in the manipulative processes.

Types of Algebraic Activity in the Enacted Curriculum

We begin this section with a presentation of the types of algebraic activity that characterized the assignments and tasks that the teacher chose to *assign* to students. For this, we combined small-group and whole-class activities. Yet classroom observations suggested that, in Tavor, students often did not work on their assigned small-group activities but instead chose to engage in other non-mathematical activities. Also in Carmel, some of the students were not always on task during small-group work. Thus, an analysis that combines small-group and whole-class activities does not necessarily reflect the activities that were *actually worked on*. Therefore, in the second part of this section we examine separately the whole-class work, which included only activities actually worked on in class. The whole-class activities were especially important because, according to the written materials, their aim was to advance students' mathematical understanding and conceptual knowledge. Whereas the first part of the section includes findings from a quantitative analysis, only the second part reports findings from both quantitative and qualitative analyses.

Types of Assigned Activities

Analysis of the enacted curriculum in each of the two classes showed that Sarah only used assignments from the curriculum materials and rarely used tasks that were not from the curriculum materials (only in a few cases of whole-class work). Still, not all of the assignments and tasks from the written curriculum materials were used, either in Carmel or in Tavor. As shown in Table 11.2, about two-thirds of the assignments and the tasks from the written materials were used in Carmel and about one-half of them were used in Tavor.

Table 11.2 shows also that although not all of the assignments and tasks included in the written materials were used in the classes, in Carmel statistically significantly more time was devoted to the teaching of the materials than either the time suggested in the curriculum materials or the time devoted to the teaching in Tavor.

An analysis of the types of algebraic activity of the assignments and the tasks used in the two classes, and of the class time devoted to the different types, showed that in spite of the above mentioned differences in the coverage of the materials, there were no statistically significant differences between Carmel or Tavor in their overall emphasis on the different types of algebraic activity. Table 11.3 presents the distribution of assignments, time, and tasks – those included in the written curriculum materials, and those used in the classes Carmel and Tavor – into the three types of algebraic activity. As mentioned earlier, assignments and tasks that were coded as more than one type of algebraic activity were included in each category.

As can be seen from Table 11.3, all three types of algebraic activity appeared in both enacted curricula in a similar proportion to that of the written curriculum materials. Transformational activities were again more dominant (about three-fourths of the activities), and generational and global/meta-level activities also played a considerable role, with generational activities being more frequent. The analysis showed that, overall, the relative distribution of the types of algebraic activities assigned was similar in the two classes and it was also similar to the distribution in the curriculum materials. In the following, we examine separately the whole-class work which, according to the written curriculum materials, is to be used to advance students' mathematical understanding and conceptual knowledge.

Table 11.2 Comparisons of Assignments, Time, and Tasks Among Carmel, Tavor, and the Written Curriculum Materials

	Curriculum Materials	*Carmel*	*Tavor*
Assignments	35–38	30–31	21–22[a]
Time (in min)	495	525–635[a, b]	444[b]
Tasks	263–321	235–271[b]	152–178[a, b]

Notes

a. Significant difference was found between the written curriculum materials and the enacted curriculum (Z test, $P \leq 0.05$).

b. Significant difference was found between Carmel and Tavor (Z test, $P \leq 0.05$).

Table 11.3 Distribution of Assignments, Time, and Tasks in the Written Materials and in the Classes Carmel and Tavor into Types of Algebraic Activity

		Curriculum materials 35–38 assignments 495 minutes 263–321 tasks		Carmel 30–31 assignments 625–635 minutes 235–271 tasks		Tavor 21–22 assignments 444 minutes 152–178 tasks	
		n	%	n	%	n	%
Generational	Assignments	17	45–49	14–15	45–50	11–12	52–54
	Time (min)	250–265	51–54	352–372	55–60	252	57
	Tasks	95–100	31–36	82–84	30–36	59–66	37–39
Transformational	Assignments	28–30	79–80	24–25	80–81	16	73–76
	Time (min)	375	76	475–485	76	306	69
	Tasks	190–244	72–76	171–209	73–77	107–127	70–71
Global/meta-level	Assignments	11–12	31–32	11	35–37	9–10	43–45
	Time (min)	215	43	287	45–46	208	47
	Tasks	23–25	8–9	24	9–10	10–13	7

Notes
The frequency of the variables was compared using χ^2 test, $P \leq 0.05$.

Types of Whole-Class Activities

Analysis of the whole-class work showed that a lesser percentage of global/meta-level activities was enacted in Tavor during whole-class work (three out of 10 assignments, and one out of 48 tasks) compared with Carmel (six out of 11 assignments, and nine out of 51 tasks). Those differences were statistically significant (χ^2 test, $P \leq 0.05$). The three global/meta-level assignments and one task enacted in Tavor during whole-class work occurred during the first teaching units of the topic *equivalent algebraic expressions*. In Carmel, the global/meta-level activities during whole-class work occurred during the same time period but also were included in additional activities in later units. Thus, Tavor's students not only worked during whole-class time on fewer global/meta-level activities than Carmel's students, but they did it only during the first part of the teaching sequence whereas Carmel's students did it throughout the teaching of the topic.

In addition to omitting the global/meta-level activities from the whole-class work during the second part of the teaching sequence in Tavor, there were several instances when the same assignment or task was enacted in Carmel as a global/meta-level activity but not in Tavor. We include an illustrative example from our qualitative analysis to demonstrate this difference. In both classes, as suggested by the written curriculum materials, Sarah started the whole-group work on the "match train" assignment (see Figure 11.1) with a task that was similar to task e:

> Doron said: "For the number of matches required to build a train with r squares, the algebraic expression $4 + 3 \cdot r$ is suitable." Is this algebraic expression suitable? Use substitution to check. How many numbers need to be substituted to determine that this algebraic expression is not suitable?
>
> (Robinson & Taizi, 1997, p. 10)

Analysis of the types of algebraic activity showed that the potential of this task was all three types of algebraic activity. To check the suitability of the algebraic expression $4 + 3r$ one may, for example, reconstruct the hypothetical process Doron used to form it: four matches for the first wagon, and three matches for each of the other wagons, resulting with an extra set of three matches (generational). Another way to check would be to substitute a specific number in the given expression, build and count the number of matches in the corresponding train, and compare the two results (transformational). The last part of the task, according to the written materials, should be used to initiate an examination of the role of examples and counter-examples in mathematics proof and refutation (global/meta-level). As often happened, Sarah enacted this task differently in the two classes. In the following section, we describe the main mathematical teaching sequence of each enactment and analyze it by means of the types of algebraic activity.

ENACTED TASK IN CARMEL

Sarah followed the teacher-guide's recommendation, and started the whole-class work by posting on the board three five-wagon trains that illustrated different ways of counting the number of matches (Figure 11.2). She then invited students to post their small-group products for task d in Figure 11.1. Students posted 11 algebraic expressions (e.g., $1+3 \cdot r$, $4+3 \cdot (r-1)$, $2 \cdot r + 1 \cdot r + 1$).

Sarah asked the students what they thought about Doron's claim that the algebraic expression $4+3 \cdot r$ was suitable. One student, Yael, objected almost immediately and suggested using, as an example, the case of a five-wagon train to show that it was wrong. Yael claimed that if they removed one match from the train in part (a) of Figure 11.2, then they should multiply the number of wagons by three, but using Doron's suggestion there would be an extra square.

Sarah (denoted by "T" below) used Yael's suggestion to check the specific case of five to explain an important mathematical principle – the role of a counter-example in refutation:

T: Okay, let's check Yael's answer. She said it correctly but I want us to explain ... The method Yael used is correct. It is called, when we want to prove that something is incorrect, I can give a counter-example. Counter-example means that I – it is enough that I provide one example where this is not correct, in this case what Doron says, then, Shani, it is sufficient for saying that it does not work out, that it is probably wrong. And in the example that Yael said, if indeed we have five wagons [writes five above Doron's algebraic expression: $4+3 \cdot (r-1)$], then we have, according to that [Doron's algebraic expression], three times five, which is fifteen, plus four is nineteen. Do five wagons have nineteen matches?

Several students immediately shouted "No!" and claimed that the number of matches in a five-wagon train was 16. The class then analyzed Doron's mistake and constructed a suitable algebraic expression:

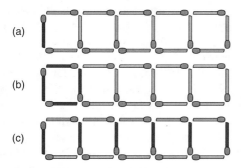

(a)

(b)

(c)

Figure 11.2 Different ways of counting matches.

T: Then what is Doron's mistake?

S: You have to take 1 off *r*, because [inaudible]

T: ... *r* is related to that there are here five wagons. What is four matches? It is actually the first wagon, right? According to what Doron says, there is one wagon that I count twice. I count the first wagon both as four separate matches and also as one of these five wagons. Therefore this is wrong. If you want to do it like Doron then you really have to

S: Take off one.

T: Take off one, and say, here, I took the first wagon separately. This is the first wagon. I already counted it. Therefore, I'll multiply the three with one less wagon, not these five wagons, but four. And this is what you actually wrote in this algebraic expression [points at $4 + 3 \cdot (r-1)$, which is one of the algebraic expressions on the board]. Which group wrote this expression?

S: We did.

T: Great. Then this algebraic expression is what is described here ... This is what we say, that we have four separate wagons [matches] and we add to them, ah, the three matches that repeat themselves one time less than the number of wagons.

The whole-group work described above included all three algebraic activity types. Led by the teacher, the class examined a situation and formed suitable expressions (a generational activity). By analyzing the hypothetical process Doron used to form his algebraic expression, the teacher showed that his suggestion was inappropriate. Working on the task also included substitution in Doron's expression ($r=5$) to enable a comparison between the numerical result of the substitution (19) and the actual number of matches in a five-wagon train (16) (a transformational activity). Finally, the teacher explained and named an important method of refutation in mathematics (counter-example), which also made this activity a global/meta-level one.

ENACTED TASK IN TAVOR

Sarah also invited students at Tavor to post their small-group products for task (d) in Figure 11.1. This time, however, only four expressions were posted ($r \cdot 3 + 1$, $4 + 3 \cdot (r-1)$, $r \cdot 4 - (r-1)$, $3 \cdot r + 1$). In contrast with Carmel, Sarah did not post ready-made wagon trains that illustrated different ways of counting the number of matches. Instead, she stated that there was a problem with the expression Doron suggested, and started to explain the hypothetical process Doron used to form his algebraic expression: four matches for the first wagon and three for each of the other wagons. Sarah accompanied her explanation with a drawing of a six-wagon train (similar to part (b) in Figure 11.2), using blue for the first square and red for the others, emphasizing the addition of three matches for each additional wagon. Throughout Sarah's teaching, the class was very noisy and Sarah continually stopped talking to deal with disciplinary problems. Sarah concluded, like Doron: "Therefore, this is $4 + 3 \cdot (r - 1)$" and immediately questioned this conclusion: "Then what Doron says is fine?" She then used the six-wagon train to examine this:

r is the number of wagons. Here I have one, two, three, four, five, six – six wagons. And then we do four plus three times six. This is the number of matches. Does everyone agree with this? ... If I have here four and three times the number of wagons, three times six, 18, plus four. How much is it? Twenty-two.

Sarah invited one student to come to the board to count the number of matches used for the six-wagon train drawn on the board. To the surprise of some students, the counting resulted with the number 19: "Yhu, how come this is wrong?" one student asked. Sarah pressed for a decision: 22 or 19? One student suggested that the first square was counted twice, and Sarah explained that this was true. It was once counted as "four," and then also when the total number of wagons was multiplied by three. Realizing that in the case of a six-wagon train they needed to multiply three by five and not by six, the class reached the expression: $4+3(r-1)$. Again, the students were noisy and Sarah stopped talking to deal with disciplinary problems.

In contrast with Carmel, the whole-group work on this task included only two algebraic activity types. Again, led by Sarah, the class examined a situation, formed suitable expressions (a generational activity) and, by analyzing the hypothetical process Doron used to form his algebraic expression, showed that his suggestion was inappropriate. An important component of the work on the task in Tavor was substitution in Doron's expression ($r=6$) to enable a comparison between the numerical result of the substitution (22) and the result of the actual counting of the number of matches in a six-wagon train (19) (a transformational activity). Unlike the work in Carmel, however, the class activity did not include a global/meta-level aspect. Neither Sarah nor the students incorporated more general mathematical processes and activity, such as the role of examples in mathematical proof and refutation.

The difference in emphasis on global/meta-level activities between the two classes seemed to be related to the different characteristics of the two classroom environments – namely, discipline problems and lack of student cooperation with Sarah at Tavor. At the end of the year, Sarah explained how this caused her to change her instructional strategy to implement less thinking-related activities and more basic and practice activities during whole-class work:

I: When you planned a lesson, did you plan the same thing for the two classes?
T: Yes, although sometimes I had considerations of, eh, additional considerations when I chose, if I had to choose whether to do something or not. There are things, there are things that require more thinking and more, eh. In Tavor sometimes I gave up on them. More so, later in the year, but, eh.
I: Overall, would you have sought to do the same lesson? In theory would you have liked to prepare the same lesson, but actually in practice?
T: Yes, in Tavor I chose a more concrete direction. Later on. It was not like this at the beginning. But when I realized what is going on there, then, yes, I went in the direction of more.

I: What is concrete?

T: From the material aspect – and I also went in the direction, eh, that it might be less – of things that require more practice, or practice that is more important for equivalent expressions. That means less the direction of thinking and new things in the same topic, but more to strengthen what they have learned already.... The direction, the choice, I knew that not everything could work there. And I also saw that they need these enforcements, from the material aspect.

I: Not everything could work there because?

T: Because of the problems that, discipline problems, problems of students' cooperation.

(Sarah's Interview, July 2003)

Observations at Tavor indeed indicated that, during the whole-class work, there were many discipline problems that caused interruptions in the mathematics activity. An examination of the percentage of time in the whole-class work devoted to mathematical activity vs non-mathematical activity (mainly discipline interruptions) showed that in Carmel there were rarely any discipline problems (about 2 percent of the whole-class time) that caused interruptions in the mathematical activities. In Tavor, however, the case was quite different; in every lesson during the whole-class work there were interruptions to the mathematical activities, totaling 20 percent of the whole-class work time.

Furthermore, as mentioned earlier, Tavor's students, in contrast to Carmel's, often did not complete the assigned small-group work. Therefore, at Tavor, tasks intended for the small-group work were repeated during whole-class work. Since mathematical work at Tavor was interrupted many times, either because of discipline disruptions or because of unfinished small-group work, Sarah found it more difficult to enact whole-class activities that required higher-order thinking. Some of these activities were of the global/meta-level type. For example, the class in Tavor did not get to generalize all the algebraic expressions that the students generated during the small-group work to a "family" of algebraic expressions with the same character and/or structure, nor did they get to demonstrate general mathematical principles, such as refutation by using counter examples. Consequently, most of the global/meta-level activities recommended to be enacted during whole-class work were enacted only in Carmel and, as we saw earlier, there were cases when the same assignments/tasks were enacted in Carmel as a global/meta-level activity but not so in Tavor.

Conclusions

Sarah taught the topic *equivalent algebraic expressions* using the same curriculum materials and teaching sequence, covering by and large the same teaching units, in two seventh-grade classes in two different schools. Even though fewer activities were enacted in both classes than recommended in the written curriculum materials, all three types of algebraic activity were enacted in both schools in similar proportions and order. In fact, the proportion and order of the types of activities that were enacted in both schools were similar to their proportion and order in the written curriculum materials. Transformational activities were more dominant (about three-fourths of the activities), but generational and global/-meta-level activities also played a considerable role.

In both classes, most enacted generational activities appeared in the first part of the teaching sequence, reflecting the structure of the curriculum materials, in which the first units included problem situations that required students to find rules for different patterns and form suitable general expressions. Similarly, in both classes, the second half of the teaching sequence included mainly transformational activities, reflecting the emphasis in the curriculum materials on the manipulative processes (frequently with emphasis on developing meaning). Furthermore, global/meta-level activities were assigned in both classes from the beginning of the teaching of the topic, reflecting the emphasis in the curriculum materials on problem-solving, examination of connections, hypothesizing, generalization, and justification throughout the teaching of the topic and not only at the end.

An analysis that combines small-group and whole-class activities suggested that there was no statistically significant difference in the types of algebraic activities that Sarah *assigned* to the students in her two classes. Yet, an examination of the whole-class work only showed that both generational and transformational activities were given a similar emphasis in the two classes. In Tavor, Sarah enacted fewer global/meta-level activities during the whole-class work than in Carmel. Generational and transformational activities are often considered to be the heart of school algebra, and are the main focus of school algebra textbooks. Thus, it may seem that Sarah provided students in the two schools with similar algebraic activities. However, the fact that Tavor students had fewer opportunities to engage in global/meta-level algebraic activities during whole-class work cannot be ignored. This type of algebraic activity is an integral component of algebra. Knowledge about mathematics (i.e., general knowledge about the nature of mathematics and mathematical ways of work) is not separate from but rather an essential aspect of knowledge of any concept or topic (Even, 1990). As Kieran (2004) emphasized:

> Attempting to divorce those meta-level activities from algebra removes any context or need that one might have for using algebra. In fact, from the point of view of the curriculum, the global/meta-level activities cannot be separated from the other activities of algebra.
>
> (p. 24)

Thus, Tavor students were learning a different algebra than Carmel students during whole-class work – algebra that, in contrast with Carmel's algebra, included less hypothesizing, justifying, and proving.

Why might Tavor students have learned a different algebra than Carmel students during whole-class work? Sarah believed that the written curriculum materials helped make the mathematics meaningful, and used the same textbook in both classes. She also attempted to enact in both classes global/meta-level activities during whole-class work of the first half of the teaching sequence of the topic *equivalent algebraic expressions*. After discontinuing the enactment of global/meta-level activities during whole-class work in Tavor, Sarah continued to assign students in Tavor small-group work that included global/meta-level activities, as she did in Carmel. But it appeared that the lack of students' cooperation and frequent lesson discipline interruptions caused Sarah to omit global/meta-level activities from whole-class activities in Tavor and, because of that, changed the kind of algebra the students were learning.

Several research studies have linked the enactment of curriculum materials and the teacher's perception of the curriculum materials and of mathematics teaching and learning (e.g., Even & Kvatinsky, 2007; Lloyd, 1999; Manouchehri & Goodmann, 2000; Remillard, 1999). Some studies have suggested additional factors that impact and shape the enactment of curriculum materials, such as the school's support for the pedagogical approach of the curriculum materials (e.g., Cuban, Kirkpatrick, & Peck, 2001; Roehrig, Kruse & Kern, 2007), parental expectations and demands of their children's mathematics studies (Gallego & Cole, 2001; Herbel-Eisenmann, Lubienski, & Id-Deen, 2006), the need to prepare for external evaluation exams (e.g., Freeman & Porter, 1989; McClain et al., Chapter 4 of this volume), and classroom norms (Hershkowitz & Schwarz, 1999; Lloyd, 2008). This study adds to this growing literature on curriculum enactment by showing that another factor (namely, discipline problems) may cause the mathematical ideas to change even when the same teacher enacts the same written curriculum materials in different classes. It also further supports Herbel-Eisenmann, Lubienski, and Id-Deen's (2006) suggestion that, in order to make trustworthy claims about the enacted curriculum of a single secondary mathematics teacher who is teaching more than one section of mathematics, we must examine multiple class periods that he or she teaches.

Acknowledgment

This research was supported in part by the Israeli Science Foundation.

References

Bednarz, N., Kieran, C., & Lee, L. (Eds.). (1996). *Approaches to algebra: Perspectives for research and teaching*. Dordrecht: Kluwer.
Clandinin, D. J., & Connelly, F. M. (1992). Teacher as curriculum maker. In P. W. Jackson (Ed.), *Handbook of research on curriculum* (pp. 363–401). New York, NY: Macmillan.
Clarke, B., Clarke, D., & Sullivan, P. (1996). The mathematics teacher and curriculum development. In A. J. Bishop, K. Clements, C. Keitel, J. Kilpatrick, & C. Laborde (Eds.), *International handbook of mathematics education* (pp. 1,207–1,234). Dordrecht: Kluwer.
Cohen, D. K., & Ball, D. L. (2001). Making change: Instruction and its improvement. *Phi Delta Kappan, 81*(1), 73–77.
Cuban, L., Kirkpatrick, H., & Peck, C. (2001). High access and low use of technologies in high school classrooms: Explaining an apparent paradox. *American Educational Research Journal, 38,* 813–834.
Drake, C., & Sherin, M. G. (2006). Practicing change: Curriculum adaptation and teacher narrative in the context of mathematics education reform. *Curriculum Inquiry, 36,* 153–187.
Even, R. (1990). Subject matter knowledge for teaching and the case of functions. *Educational Studies in Mathematics, 21,* 521–544.

Even, R. & Kvatinsky, T. (2007, August). *Teaching mathematics to low-achieving students: enhancement of personal or traditional teaching approach?* Paper presented at the 12th Biennial Conference of the European Association for Research on Learning and Instruction (EARLI), Budapest, Hungary.

Even, R., Robinson, N., & Carmeli, M. (2003). The work of providers of professional development for teachers of mathematics: Two case studies of experienced practitioners. *International Journal of Science and Mathematics Education, 1,* 227–249.

Freeman, D. J., & Porter, A. C. (1989). Do textbooks dictate the content of mathematics instruction in elementary schools? *American Educational Research Journal, 26,* 403–421.

Gallego, M. A., Cole, M., & The Laboratory of Comparative Human Cognition (2001). Classroom cultures and cultures in the classroom. In V. Richardson (Ed.), *Handbook of research on teaching* (4th Edition, pp. 951–997). Washington, DC: American Educational Research Association.

Herbel-Eisenmann, B. A., Lubienski, S. T., & Id-Deen, L. (2006). Reconsidering the study of mathematics instructional practices: the importance of curricular context in understanding local and global teacher change. *Journal of Mathematics Teacher Education, 9*(4), 313–345.

Hershkowitz, R., & Schwarz, B. B. (1999). The emergent perspective in rich learning environments: Some roles of tools and activities in the construction of sociomathematical norms. *Educational Studies in Mathematics, 39,* 149–166.

Kieran, C. (2004). The core of algebra: Reflections on its main activities. In K. Stacey, H. Chick, & M. Kendal (Eds.), *The future of the teaching and learning of algebra; The 12th ICME study* (pp. 21–33). Boston, MA: Kluwer.

Kieran, C. (2007). Learning and teaching algebra at the middle school through college levels. In F. K. Lester, Jr. (Ed.), *Second handbook of research on mathematics teaching and learning* (pp. 707–762). Charlotte, NC: Information Age.

Lloyd, G. M. (1999). Two teachers' conceptions of a reform curriculum: Implications for mathematics teacher development. *Journal of Mathematics Teacher Education, 2,* 227–252.

Lloyd, G. M. (2008). Teaching mathematics with a new curriculum: Changes to classroom organization and interactions. *Mathematical Thinking and Learning, 10,* 163–195.

Manouchehri, A., & Goodman, T. (1998). Mathematics curriculum reform and teacher: Understanding the connections. *The Journal of Educational Research, 92,* 27–41.

Manouchehri, A., & Goodman, T. (2000). Implementing mathematics reform: The challenge within. *Educational Studies in Mathematics, 42,* 1–34.

National Council of Teachers of Mathematics. (1989). *Curriculum and evaluation standards for school mathematics.* Reston, VA: Author.

National Council of Teachers of Mathematics. (2000). *Principles and standards for school mathematics.* Reston, VA: Author.

Remillard, J. T. (1999). Curriculum materials in mathematics education reform: A framework for examining teachers' curriculum development. *Curriculum Inquiry, 29,* 315–342.

Remillard, J. T. (2005). Examining key concepts in research on teachers' use of mathematics curricula. *Review of Educational Research, 75,* 211–246.

Robinson, N., & Taizi, N. (1995–2002). *Everybody learns mathematics: Mathematics for heterogeneous classes* (A series of textbooks for grades 7–8). Rehovot: The Weizmann Institute of Science (in Hebrew).

Robinson, N., & Taizi, N. (1997). *Everybody learns mathematics: Mathematics for heterogeneous classes, on the algebraic expressions 1.* Rehovot: The Weizmann Institute of Science [in Hebrew].

Robinson, N., Inbar, Y., & Koren, M. (2001). *On the algebraic expressions: Teacher's guide.* Rehovot: The Weizmann Institute of Science [in Hebrew].

Roehrig, G. H., Kruse, R. A., & Kern, A. (2007). Teacher and school characteristics and their influence on curriculum implementation. *Journal of Research in Science Teaching, 44,* 883–907.

Sabar, N. (Ed.). (2001). *Qualitative research: Genres and traditions in qualitative research.* Tel Aviv: Zmora Bitan [in Hebrew].

Schmidt, W. H., McKnight, C. C., Valverde, G. A., Houang, R. T., & Wiley, D. E. (1997). *Many visions, many aims: A cross-national investigation of curricular intention in school mathematics* (Vol. 1). Dordrecht: Kluwer.

Stein, M. K., Grover, B. W., & Henningsen, M. A. (1996). Building student capacity for mathematical thinking and reasoning: An analysis of mathematical tasks used in reform classrooms. *American Educational Research Journal, 33,* 455–488.

Tirosh, D., Even, R., & Robinson, N. (1998). Simplifying algebraic expressions: Teacher awareness and teaching approaches. *Educational Studies in Mathematics, 35,* 51–64.

Usiskin, Z. (1998). Conceptions of school algebra and uses of variables. In A. F. Coxford (Ed.), *The ideas of algebra, K-12* (pp. 8–19). Reston, VA: National Council of Teachers of Mathematics.

12

High School Teachers as Negotiators Between Curriculum Intentions and Enactment

The Dynamics of Mathematics Curriculum Development

Steven W. Ziebarth, Eric W. Hart, Robin Marcus, Beth Ritsema, Harold L. Schoen, and Rebecca Walker

This chapter investigates secondary mathematics teachers' interactions with authors of curriculum materials *as the materials are being developed*. We focus our attention on the ways in which the *intended curriculum*[1] is negotiated by highlighting how teachers participate in the curriculum development process – beginning with the authors' initial conceptions of teaching and learning sequences (i.e., their "intentions") as reflected in early drafts of written materials, and following the evolution of the curriculum materials into a final, published and viable commercial product. The term *negotiation* can connote both a hard (i.e., to settle a contract) and soft (i.e., to confer with another in order to come to agreement) definition, depending on the context in which it is used (Costello & Pritchard, 1994). We use the softer definition as a descriptor throughout this chapter. We identified three types of negotiation and conversation that produced changes as the curriculum materials evolved: (a) author point of view negotiation, in which authors of the curriculum materials negotiate changes with teachers in order to help teachers see and test new ideas that challenge their existing ideas about teaching and learning and the mathematical content; (b) teacher point of view negotiation, in which teachers negotiate changes with authors of the curriculum materials to help make materials more teachable and relevant to local situations; and (c) discussions of how to develop and teach the curriculum materials to help users better understand the core principles behind the curriculum project.[2] Although all negotiations described in this chapter included some aspects of each of these three types, typically one or another was more apparent in a particular negotiation context or setting.

We begin this chapter with an overview of some relevant literature in an attempt to situate our research within the field of curriculum program development studies and to delimit our particular data and implications. We then provide illustrative examples where the three types of negotiation categories noted above helped to define the relationships between teachers and curriculum developers as they existed within the five-year development process of the second-edition of *Core-Plus Mathematics*[3] (Hirsch, Fey, Hart, Schoen, & Watkins, 2008), an NSF-funded high school curriculum program. We conclude with some implications of our research for teachers and developers of curriculum materials.

Relevant Literature

A review of the literature shows a variety of assumptions about the role of teachers in the curriculum development process. One common perception amongst mathematics educators today is that teachers are primarily "implementers" of curriculum materials, in the sense that they are *receivers* of published (or pre-published) material. That is, the teachers are not involved in the curriculum development process, and they enact those curriculum materials as best they can in their unique school environments. This view of teachers as "faithful implementers" of curriculum materials suggests that there is a "right way" of using curriculum materials, designed by others, and that teachers have little autonomy when using them with students.

A counter-position argues that this view makes little sense in the real world, noting that curriculum materials, once in the hands of teachers, undergo many transformations, depending on teacher idiosyncrasies and external factors over which teachers have little control. A third position puts teachers at the heart of the curriculum writing process, as important and essential collaborators with other types of experts, and brings to the table teachers' wealth of experiences and classroom wisdom. We briefly elaborate on these positions below, as each has characteristics that played a role in our experiences with teachers during the curriculum writing process.

The perception of teacher as faithful implementer is well grounded in the many studies of curriculum enactment during the past decade, especially with NSF-funded curriculum projects (see National Research Council, 2004). In these studies, the metaphor of teacher as conduit is prominent and has its roots in related studies that date to the early 1900s. As Clandinin and Connelly (1992) acknowledge: "this literature is almost exclusively one in which the distinction between means and ends is maintained and in which the conduit metaphor is the dominating intellectual structure" (p. 370). Much of the current research that focuses on *fidelity of implementation* (see, for example, Chapter 5 of this volume) can be viewed as an extension of this line of thinking. The teacher's role in such studies is one of faithful implementer of the "ideal" curriculum that represents a "pure" interpretation of author's intended designs for teaching and learning sequences as seen in the materials they are asked to implement. From this perspective, curriculum materials are viewed as vehicles of reform for teacher practices as much as they are opportunities for presentation of new content or alternative views of student learning and assessment. In such cases, the curriculum materials will likely have a pedagogical model advocated as a part of the curriculum and are aligned with research on teacher as facilitator as described in the *Standards* documents (National Council of Teachers of Mathematics [NCTM], 1989, 1991, 2000).

Clandinin and Connelly (1992) use the conduit metaphor as an organizing theme for this most dominant line of curriculum research, but also trace a second line of research back to such educators as Dewey (1938), who viewed teachers as *curriculum makers* with an "active and creative role" in picking or developing the best of materials for use in their classrooms. Teachers were seen as experimenters who constantly modify curriculum materials to fit new groups of students in new situations as times change. Recently, the contrast of these first two positions was discussed by Remillard (2005).

The third view of teachers' role in curriculum development may be described as an offshoot of the curriculum-maker model, and can be seen in the active participation of teachers in the writing and testing of curriculum materials. In this model, teachers are viewed as essential collaborators alongside university mathematicians and mathematics educators (and often others from a variety of disciplines) as part of writing teams. Such a model can be seen in some of the large curriculum projects of the 1950s and 1960s, most prominently that of the School Mathematics Study Group (SMSG) (Wooten, 1965).

The three different roles of teachers in the curriculum development process are perhaps better viewed as points on a continuum, because the role of any given individual can change as projects evolve (Connelly & Ben-Peretz, 1980). Within a single project, all participants' roles may vary depending on many factors – for example, the strand of mathematics being emphasized, the grade level for which the material is intended, or the types of students who may be the primary audience for the published materials (see Garry, Connelly, & Dittman, 1975). This more dynamic view of teachers' roles in curriculum materials development suggests that a single description of teachers' roles within the process may be inadequate (Howson, Keitel, & Kilpatrick, 1981). In many respects, our experience concurs with this viewpoint.

Many of the more comprehensive research summaries of curriculum development and focused studies of curriculum implementation (see below) make special note of the numerous factors affecting teachers' roles in the development process, including their use of field-test materials and the feedback they give or are able to give to authors (assuming a conduit or equal-participant model) based on their classroom expertise. Such advice is tempered by many variables, including teacher content knowledge, teachers' beliefs about pedagogy and student learning, local demographics and constraints, cultural norms, state assessments, and national policy directives, to name a few (see EDC, 2005, and Lloyd, 1999, 2002, for specific projects; Clandinin & Connelly, 1992, Howson, Keitel, & Kilpatrick, 1981, and Remillard, 2005 for general summaries; and Clarke, Clarke, & Sullivan, 1996, for an international perspective). It should be noted that the mathematics educators and mathematicians involved in the development process face these same issues and influencing factors as they develop curriculum materials, albeit oftentimes in different proportions.

For the developers of curriculum materials, the complexity of the teachers' environment is but one factor that determines what ultimately becomes their version of the intended curriculum. Curriculum writers, while relying heavily on teacher feedback, must also balance that feedback with their own teaching and scholarly experiences that guide their thinking – those of colleagues within their projects, along with advice from colleagues within the broader communities of mathematics and mathematics education, advice from different kinds of advisory boards linked directly with curriculum development projects, as well as publishers' concerns. Because of these varying influences within the curriculum development process and the sometimes uncertain dynamics affecting those influences, we suggest that the term *intended curriculum,* as referenced at the outset of this chapter, is not as well-defined as some authors (e.g., Clarke, Clarke, & Sullivan, 1996; Remillard, 2005) may indicate. As we show, the *intended curriculum* is not a fixed entity that existed in the curriculum authors' minds at the inception of the development process. A major part of the authors' intent is to negotiate curriculum materials that are effective in terms of student outcomes and meet with the approval of stakeholders and advisors. The form of the curriculum materials at any stage in the development can be viewed as the present best approximation of the *intended curriculum.*

Guiding Questions

Our goal in the remainder of this chapter is to describe the ways in which teachers and developers of materials worked together during the development process of the second edition of Core-Plus Mathematics Project curriculum materials. The negotiation dynamics that we describe will help to illustrate the complexities inherent in the term *intended curriculum.* In terms of a set of guiding questions, we investigate the following:

1. How might we characterize curriculum development (i.e., writing) as a negotiation among curriculum authors, field-test teachers, and other professional stakeholders?
2. In what ways do specific teacher and school characteristics (i.e., beliefs, extensive use of "first edition" materials, and individual school environment) play a role in the curriculum development process?

We address these questions by focusing our discussions on specific examples drawn from evaluation data collected during the writing of major parts of the curriculum: student materials, teacher guides, and assessments. In doing so, we identify and discuss instances in which the three types of negotiations are present: author-negotiated changes, teacher-negotiated changes, and discussions focused on understanding and implementing aspects of the curriculum representing core principles of the author development team. We argue that this process more accurately describes the *intended curriculum* under the paradigm in which teachers are involved in the curriculum development process, and suggest that it can be represented by the product at a given point in time, of negotiations and compromises on the part of all parties involved. The intended curriculum always involves authors as decision-makers and dilemma managers, analogous to similar teacher roles in the classroom (see Lampert, 1985), trying to manage tensions and make informed decisions from amongst multiple options that result in a viable improved curriculum.

Background on Second-Edition *Core-Plus Mathematics*

CPMP Authors and Design Principles

During the 1990s, the National Science Foundation funded 14 projects that developed curriculum materials consistent with the recommendations of the NCTM *Standards* documents (1989, 1991, 1996). The Core-Plus Mathematics Project (CPMP) (Hirsch et al., 2008) is a high school curriculum program developed at that time, and it has more recently undergone revisions. The writing team consisted of three co-directors who are also authors of the curriculum materials, five additional authors, and a number of technical and support staff responsible for duties ranging from page layout and graphics design to developing solution keys and producing teacher support material. Because the curriculum program is integrated by topic across grade levels, the group was organized into author teams with primary responsibility for the main mathematical ideas within each of four content strands: algebra and functions, geometry and trigonometry, probability and statistics, and discrete mathematics. Each team was also responsible for proofreading and critiquing other strands, and for providing connecting exercises that link all strands together. A separate team was responsible for writing assessments, and another for developing teacher support material. Most of the strand authors responsible for writing the revisions were involved in writing the first edition of *Core-Plus Mathematics*. Classroom teachers were involved primarily after a first draft of the curriculum materials was written. They piloted the materials and provided feedback to the author team.

According to CPMP co-directors Fey and Hirsch (2007), the writing of first-edition *Core-Plus Mathematics* adhered to five key design principles:[4]

1. Mathematical content is integrated across major strands of mathematics and is designed to develop student understanding and skill in mathematical modeling, mathematical habits of mind, and mathematics as a sense-making activity.
2. Sequencing and organization of content reflect author "judgments of what would be most important for students to know if that was to be their last formal experience in school mathematics" (p. 131).
3. "Students would have ready access to only graphing calculators" (p. 131).
4. The instructional design is intended "to support problem-based, student-centered classroom activity" (p. 132) that focuses on problem contexts and encourages small-group investigation and experimentation and student-student dialogue.
5. Assessment is an integral part of the instructional model and is embedded throughout the curriculum material as opportunities for ongoing monitoring of student progress.

These five principles guided the writing of the first-edition materials, and were the foundation of the second edition. The core principles were communicated to the teachers and refined but not negotiated to the same extent as other curriculum project content. The CPMP co-directors noted that their design principles were revised slightly based on extensive first-edition field-test data and changes in education policy factors at the local, state, and national levels. They noted, in particular, that high-stakes testing, better communication about benefits associated with using the CPMP curriculum, and enhancing the support materials were all issues that were addressed in the revision. The project directors were also mindful of advances in technology and its availability, and the general push to have most students study more algebraic ideas at earlier grade levels. All of these issues had an impact on what content appeared in units and courses and its sequencing, while maintaining overall coherence across the entire set of curriculum materials.

Teacher Negotiation in CPMP Curriculum Development

Approximately 20 teachers (from five high schools and, in year 1, two middle schools) who participated in the revision were included in this study. The schools served a diverse mix of students from various socioeconomic backgrounds, and included rural, urban, and suburban settings. Students represented a wide range of achievement levels as measured by the Iowa Test of Educational Development subtest *Ability to do Quantitative Thinking*. Schools were selected to participate in the CPMP revision field-test based on a number of conditions, including feeder middle schools that implemented a *Standards*-based middle school curriculum program and extensive use of first-edition CPMP materials but no involvement in the development of those materials. The authors sought to recruit a new set of teachers to react to new material, with the goal of gathering fresh perspectives related to the curriculum materials revision process.

The criteria for selection of teachers and conditions set by the project for participation in the CPMP revision locates the assumptions of the curriculum project within the teacher-as-conduit literature, since in many ways these teachers represented a best-case scenario for implementing authors' vision of their intended curriculum. However, within the general parameters of this vision, authors encouraged the teachers to become more engaged as collaborators. This proved somewhat frustrating in that, despite encouraging teachers to think about and provide advice about the inclusion and development of topics or different content organization, their comments were most often only about fine-tuning the materials on a page-by-page or problem-by-problem basis. Furthermore, authors acknowledged the reality that teachers' curriculum implementation decisions were strongly influenced by educational policies, personal philosophies, and powerful socioeconomic factors present in their classrooms, schools, and communities. Thus, all three models of curriculum development discussed previously – teacher-as-conduit, teacher-as-collaborator, and teacher-as-curriculum-maker – can be seen in the development of the CPMP curriculum program.

The authors thought that the teachers, despite having variation in experience levels and professional development participation, represented a strongly committed cadre of implementers of first-edition curriculum materials. CPMP authors appreciated the role of these field-test teachers because they were the ones being asked to deal with the "challenge of implementing radical change and giving the new ideas a fair chance to succeed" (Fey & Hirsch, 2007, p. 135) within their local contexts of implementation. For changes such as those reflected in the CPMP curriculum to occur, fidelity of implementation is important in the feedback loop of the curriculum development process, but adaptation is recognized as inherent in the process. More explicitly, some of the issues teachers have wrestled with in implementing revised curriculum materials are the following:

> Field-test teachers often report puzzling over the level of mastery expected on topics in the new curriculum, since their experiential reference points have been knocked askew by the new content development. They also find it challenging to let students struggle a bit with open-end problem tasks. As a result, particularly in the first classroom testing of a new unit or course, it is unlikely that the material is taught as the authors envisioned.
>
> (p. 135)

In the next section, we explore several examples from the CPMP writing process that illustrate how curriculum materials envisioned by authors changed and developed, some factors that seemed to be at play in those changes, and the role of field-test teachers in that process.

Examples and Discussion

Organizational Notes

The examples in this chapter are drawn from three of the more prominent aspects of the curriculum materials: student materials, teacher-support materials, and assessment features. Each example illustrates and analyzes the negotiation between authors and teachers in the curriculum development process, and the roles played by teacher and school characteristics. We highlight different issues faced by the teachers and the authors as the curriculum materials were revised and renegotiated until a compromise acceptable to all involved was reached. Examples are drawn from a variety of data sources: archived curriculum materials representing different stages of development, teacher-annotated versions of pilot- and field-test materials, detailed field notes and transcriptions from author/teacher focus group meetings and summer workshop sessions, author and teacher interviews, and classroom observations of teachers using revised materials.

Revisions Requiring Little Negotiation

When revising curriculum materials, authors need to blend some of their favorite features of first-edition curriculum materials with new local demands and national trends, such as those related to pacing, algebraic skills coverage, review exercises, and state testing requirements. CPMP authors also saw opportunities for trying new ideas based on evidence from previous use of earlier materials and the evolution of their own thinking about teaching and learning. The process of writing a multi-year curriculum program involved decisions at all points, and advice from field-test teachers was sought at each of the different structural levels of the materials. There were also decisions about larger elements (i.e., courses and units) of the integrated curriculum program, such as those related to course focus (i.e., total number of units and number by mathematical strand) and unit sequencing, and decisions that focused attention on issues related to smaller elements involving lessons, investigations, problems, and tasks.

Although some negotiations involved the larger structural elements, teacher input often confirmed what appeared to be current national trends in mathematics education. For example, in response to teacher feedback and national trends calling for more algebra earlier, CPMP authors changed the lead unit of the first edition, which focused on data collection and interpretation, to a unit titled *Patterns of Change* that focused more on algebra content. Also, an additional algebra unit was added into Course 1. These changes gave the revised *Core-Plus Mathematics* Course 1 a more prominent algebra flavor. Field-test teachers responded positively to the large element changes in the curriculum materials with little need for negotiation. In the following examples, we provide details of the three types of negotiation where teacher negotiation was prominent.

Author-Point-of-View Negotiation: An Example from CPMP Assessment Material

Near the beginning of the revision process, conversations with the field-test teachers made clear the power that the assessments had in shaping how they viewed what was important in the curriculum materials and what was important to do in the classroom. In focus group meetings, teachers indicated that they often looked at the assessments to determine what students were expected to learn during the unit, and used the assessments to help guide how they would teach a unit and what topics they decided to emphasize. This happened most explicitly when the mathematics or the approach to the mathematics in a unit was unfamiliar to the teachers. For example, teachers indicated that they were unsure of the level of mastery expected during the *Patterns of Change* unit of Course 1, and so they used the assessments to help them set their expectations for students. They also talked about considering the assessments when they were teaching the *Patterns of Shape* unit of Course 1. During this unit they used the assessments to help them determine the level of formal reasoning that students were expected to have developed by the end of the unit. According to the teachers, the assessment items defined what the outcomes of the curriculum should be.

There was an ongoing tension between the teachers and the curriculum developers about what types of items were appropriate to place on formal end-of-lesson or end-of-unit assessments. The curriculum developers believed that students should focus on problematic situations as well as grapple with different contexts and open-ended problems during assessments. The teachers raised questions and concerns about this in several ways. Some of the teachers changed the contexts of problems to match what was used in the text or removed the open-ended problems when compiling their own set of test items. Others said they did not use a problem because the context was too different or the problem was quite different from those that students completed during the unit. CPMP authors developed different problems in order to challenge students in new ways because they believed that students should be able to apply their knowledge and skills to contexts and problems that were different from those they encountered in the unit (see the CPMP design principle 1 above). Thus, many assessments included some items that not all students could be expected to complete successfully. Many teachers had difficulty adjusting to this view of assessment, and were more comfortable with assessment items that were accessible and familiar to all students in their classes.

One set of teachers voiced this concern by saying that "the items on the quizzes and tests did not assess the big ideas of the units." When asked what this meant, the teachers found it difficult to elaborate. To further explore this concern, several CPMP authors examined the assessments this group of teachers chose to use. The teachers had deleted the more open-ended items and those that might be considered more difficult for the students. This group of teachers seemed to want the assessments to focus on only the core ideas from the unit, and wanted those ideas assessed using questions similar to those students had worked on in the unit. Asking students to use knowledge to solve a new type of problem on assessments seemed to make some teachers uncomfortable. When field-test teachers at other locations used some of the more open-ended and unfamiliar problems, however, they were quite surprised at how well their students performed on the problem. They found their students could apply their knowledge in novel ways, and that they could solve an unfamiliar problem.

Despite conversations at focus group meetings, and one-on-one conversations, the development team did not find an effective way to get all teachers to recognize the advantages of using assessment items that were different from the problems that students encounter in the unit. This was an ongoing source of conversation and negotiation between the teachers and the developers. In some instances, the authors changed the context of problems and types of problems to ones that teachers indicated would be more familiar to the students. In other instances, the authors tried to help the teachers understand the importance and value of using different types of items on formal assessments. At the same time, because the assessments were supplied to teachers electronically, teachers who continued to be uncomfortable with such items on end-of-lesson quizzes or end-of-unit tests simply deleted or changed them. In this way, the decision to provide the assessments electronically allowed the teachers more control over the assessment items that they used to assess their students.

Negotiation-Across-Types: An Example from Geometry

This example involves the evolution of student material in a curriculum unit. The unit arose in part from a critique by teachers and mathematician consultants of the first edition; that is, standard geometry theorems about chords, tangents, and inscribed angles in circles were not in the curriculum materials. Yet, it was argued, this was important mathematics often tested on college entrance exams and state tests.

The author team agreed that some of these theorems would be in the second edition. The authors did not consider the development and proof of the circle properties important enough, however, to warrant more than a lesson (that is, perhaps a week of instructional time). These decisions led to the need to answer two important questions: Where did a lesson on properties of circles fit? What topics already in the curriculum were most closely connected to these properties so that the unit would be coherent?

Traditionally, circle theorems are several of many theorems situated in a course on synthetic geometry. Whereas some of the earlier synthetic geometry theorems are prerequisites to the proofs of circle theorems, circles are also important in other areas of mathematics, including circular functions in trigonometry. In an integrated curriculum program, these areas provide choices for where to place circle theorems. In *Core-Plus Mathematics* Course 2, the sine, cosine, and tangent were developed as functions of angle measures in both rectangular coordinates and right triangles. The synthetic geometry prerequisites for proving circle theorems were treated in the first half of Course 3, so the mathematical prerequisites for both the circle theorems and the circular functions were in place by the middle of Course 3. The authors decided to develop a two-lesson unit, *Circles and Circular Functions*, to be field tested as Unit 6 of the eight-unit Course 3. Circles would serve as the unifying topic of the unit, and the content would cut across synthetic geometry and circular motion, leading finally to the development of the circular functions. Field-test teachers and mathematician consultants agreed that this made sense.

The first lesson, *Properties of Circles*, was a completely new lesson, whereas the second lesson on circular functions drew substantially from carefully field-tested and evaluated material in the first edition. Following their work through the *Properties of Circles* lesson during a summer workshop, field-test teachers' reactions to the new first lesson were positive. Their most substantial suggestions resulted in adjusting ideas for the design of supporting dynamic geometry software. After minor revisions based on this initial feedback, the teachers tested this version of the unit in their classrooms and again provided feedback to the authors. The classroom field test raised many issues that had not been anticipated, and led to substantial revisions of the first lesson. We describe one of those revisions below, and the negotiations that led to the revisions.

The Inscribed Angle Theorem is one of the most important properties in the first lesson. The usual synthetic proof of this property involves three cases that differ by whether the circle's center O lies on a side of the inscribed angle ABC, in its interior, or in its exterior (see Figure 12.1). In case 1, triangle ABO is an isosceles triangle, so angles ABO (or ABC) and BAO have equal measures. By the Exterior Angle Theorem, the measures of these two equal angles sum to the measure of central angle AOC, so, by definition, the measure of minor arc AC as well. Therefore, the measure of inscribed angle ABC is half the measure of inter-cepted arc AC, so the Inscribed Angle Theorem is proven in this case. In each of the other two cases, students would need to draw the diameter BD that contains the vertex B of the inscribed angle and use case 1, the Angle Addition Postulate, and Arc Addition Postulate to complete the proof.

In the first tested draft of the lesson, students were to explore the relationship between the angle measures of the inscribed angle and its intercepted arc with a dynamic geometry tool and then were to be presented with the steps in the proof of case 1. Students were asked to provide a reason for each step in the proof. The curriculum materials then indicated that this proof does not prove the Inscribed Angle Theorem in general, because it does not apply to cases 2 and 3. Finally, students were asked to share the work of constructing the proofs for cases 2 and 3. When the field-test teachers and the mathematician consultant reviewed the draft unit prior to classroom testing, this approach met with their approval. After classroom testing, however, teachers reported that the students were almost uniformly baffled.

According to the teachers, students seemed to understand the relationship stated in the Inscribed Angle Theorem after some exploration. The students could provide reasons for the given proof of the first case, but they did not understand why this did not prove the theorem. They had had no previous experience with proof by cases, and this proof strategy was more difficult than anyone had antici-pated. Very few students were able to proceed with the proofs of the second and third cases, and fewer still understood that the proofs of the three cases, taken together, proved the Inscribed Angle Theorem. The authors and field-test teachers agreed that additional revision of this material was needed.

In the second draft, the figures illustrating the three cases were explained in more detail. The curriculum authors provided more scaffolding questions

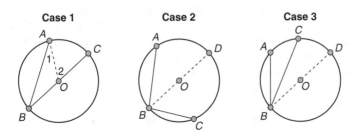

Figure 12.1 Cases involving the inscribed angle theorem.

concerning the three cases, and included reasons why proving all three cases proves the Inscribed Angle Theorem in general. The Angle Addition and Arc Addition properties students needed to prove cases 2 and 3 were inserted in the student materials immediately before the request for proofs.

After testing the second draft in their classes, teachers agreed that these were helpful revisions, but reported that the proof was still difficult for their students. As one teacher said at the teacher/author focus group meeting, "Most students don't see a need for proving the Inscribed Angle Theorem after dynamic exploration convinces them that it is true." All the other teachers agreed, and an interesting discussion ensued about whether to insist on formal proof. Some teachers argued that exploration of the properties via dynamic geometry tools, followed by numerical applications of the properties, resulted in a sufficient level of understanding. Many of the students, the teachers reported, saw the proof process as unrelated to or in conflict with the exploration and application phases of learning.

The authors and some of the teachers, however, argued that proof is an essential part of the process of doing mathematics (see Wu, 1997). In spite of the difficulty, by their third year of high school mathematics, the proponents for including this content believed that students should be developing facility with formal mathematical proof. Although the authors did not agree that they should eliminate proof from the lesson on circle theorems, the teachers who held the opposite belief somewhat influenced their thinking. In the third, and nearly final, version of the lesson, the proofs of cases 2 and 3 of the Inscribed Angle Theorem were moved to homework problems. A compromise between teachers and curriculum developers, this approach was meant to make it easier for teachers to differentiate the level of proof in their course depending on the backgrounds and needs of their students.

This example illustrates some strengths and limitations of negotiations that blend across the three types described earlier. With their previous experience teaching high school students, teachers bring an important perspective when they review draft curriculum materials. As the foregoing example shows, however, even the most skillful and experienced teachers cannot always predict exactly how their students will interact with draft materials. Classroom pilots in a range of target environments are a key test of a lesson, but the pilots cannot be expected to produce a consensus direction for revisions of the tested materials. There is a great deal of variation across target classrooms and across the perceptions and beliefs of teachers about mathematics and how it should be taught and learned. Curriculum developers must mediate their own professional knowledge and beliefs with these variations of field-test teachers and their students, with pertinent student outcomes in response to draft material, with the content of state and national standards and of high-stakes tests, and with the advice of mathematicians and other mathematics educators serving as project consultants. One might also ask, what is the *intended curriculum* in this example? The authors would have preferred that the initial draft would have worked as well as they expected. When it did not, subsequent revisions should be viewed as better approximations of the intended curriculum, not as movements away from some *a priori* intended curriculum existing in the minds of the authors.

Negotiation Reflected in Teacher and Student Materials

In this section, we illustrate how the CPMP development team and field-test teachers negotiated the crucial issue of how much scaffolding should be included in investigations, how this issue is linked to development of the teacher resource material, and the role of teachers in that process. We focus this discussion on a particular investigation in the Course 2 unit, *Matrix Methods*, from the discrete mathematics strand. All three types of negotiation are evident in this example – author point of view, teacher point of view, and discussion of core principles.

In early discussions by the CPMP development team, the vision for the second edition included the possibility of more open-ended problems and a continued emphasis on getting students actively engaged in making sense of the mathematics. A key challenge was to provide the optimum level of scaffolding so that student learning is effectively facilitated but not superficially curtailed. In some cases, mathematician consultants and teachers indicated that sections of the first-edition materials were repetitive or prescriptive. On the other hand, some material seemed to be so open-ended that teachers reported that students tended to give up.

To illustrate the challenges, we consider the "Power of a Matrix" investigation from the *Matrix Methods* unit. This investigation was a familiar one from the first edition. Students investigate matrix operations in the context of an ecosystem "food web" where organisms are linked by predator–prey relationships. Figure 12.2 shows the introduction to this investigation.

At a summer work session with field-test teachers, teachers were asked to examine a more open version of this investigation in terms of whether or not they thought their students could learn the content in this format. Teachers were asked to provide specific written suggestions for improvement of this revised investigation with the hope not only that this would improve the lesson but also that their input during the writing stage of these materials would increase their willingness to teach the investigation the following school year. Teachers offered only minor wording and punctuation changes to the investigation. Teacher's Guide material for the alternative open investigation included questions the teacher might ask as students worked on the investigation. To test the usability of the open format one field-test teacher agreed to teach the investigation in both formats and other teachers agreed to teach one version or the other.

The authors gathered feedback using the questions in Table 12.1 to help determine which version would remain in the student text, which elements would move to the Teacher's Guide, and how much scaffolding would be provided. Additionally, one development team member was able to observe the alternative investigation being taught by two different field-test teachers. The observer took field notes, periodically asked questions of students to help understand their thinking, and carried out a short debriefing with each teacher directly following the class periods.

Pollution in an ecosystem

An ecosystem is the system formed by a community of organisms and their interaction with their environment. The diagram below shows the predator–prey relationships of some organisms in a willow forest ecosystem.

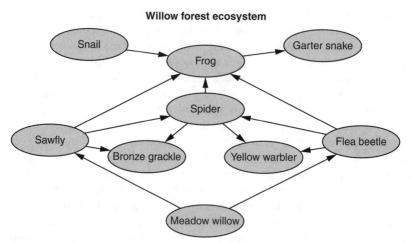

Such a diagram is called a **food web**. An arrow goes from one organism to another if one is food for the other. So, for example, the arrow from spider to yellow warbler means that spiders are food for yellow warblers.

Pollution can cause all or part of the food web to become contaminated. In the following problems, you will explore how matrix multiplication can be used to analyze how contamination of some organisms spreads through the rest of the food web.

Figure 12.2 Introduction to the ecosystem investigation.

Table 12.1 Evaluation Questions for the Matrix Investigation

Matrix models
Power of a matrix – alternative investigation
Feedback questions

1. How much time did it take to complete this investigation?
2. How does the time for teaching the investigation compare with the time you typically use for the published version of this investigation or the one in the current field-test booklet?
3. What differences did you notice in student understanding developed by the two forms of the investigation?
4. Specifically, how were the teacher's notes for the alternative investigation helpful? How could they be more helpful?
5. What improvements to the investigation would you suggest? (Please provide comments on a copy of the investigation and return to CPMP.)
6. Do you think the idea of a few more open investigations in the published version is valuable? Why or why not?

Overall, teachers' responses to the more open investigation were quite positive. Three main issues arose related to student learning and the curriculum materials:

1. Students did not realize that an organism could be contaminated without dying.
2. Students were confused about the meaning of the Paths of Length Two matrix (a partially completed square matrix was provided for students to reason from). In particular, each entry indicates the number of paths of length two between the two corresponding vertices (organisms), not the existence of a path of length two, or the length of a path between the two vertices.
3. Students had a difficult time relating powers of the adjacency matrix to matrices that give the number of paths of length n.

The teacher who taught both versions and the teachers who taught only one version of this investigation found the same issues in all classes, and they did not think the issues were related to the open format of the material.

Authors used information from teacher–author negotiations related to the two teaching scenarios to address all three issues. Issue 1 was just a factual point, and was dealt with by simply clarifying the point in the student material and adding an accompanying instructional note in the Teacher's Guide. Issue 2 concerned building and interpreting a mathematical representation. This was dealt with by using a more explicit title on the matrix, "Number of Paths of Length Two" instead of "Paths of Length Two." Also, clarifying language and additional focus questions were added to the student text and an instructional note was added to the Teacher's Guide. Issue 3 was more problematic, as it is a complex mathematical issue.

According to the curriculum authors, the key question related to issue 3 was: How might we develop the material so that students learn that the nth power of an adjacency matrix gives the number of paths of length n in a digraph? This issue was not new; in fact, it arose with this investigation in the first edition of *Core-Plus Mathematics*. During development of both editions of the curriculum materials, authors considered four possible development strategies:

1. Students could be led to understand the underlying concept: Structure the investigation so that the students find out for themselves why the nth power of an adjacency matrix gives the number of paths of length n in a digraph. (This is a challenging goal, and would probably take a significant amount of class time.)
2. Students could be asked to find and test a pattern: Structure the investigation so that students directly construct some matrices that show numbers of paths of length n, and they also construct an adjacency matrix. Then they are prompted to consider powers of matrices, and they are expected to find and test the connection between powers of an adjacency matrix and matrices that give the number of paths of length n.

3. Students could be given the information and asked to notice and test the pattern: Structure the investigation so that students are given some matrices that show numbers of paths of length n. They are given some powers of the adjacency matrix, are asked to notice that the matrices are the same, and then try some other matrices to see if the pattern holds.
4. Students could be told the fact and then asked to verify it: Students are told that the nth power of the adjacency matrix gives the number of paths of length n in a digraph, then they verify this for some cases.

Strategy 1 was never tried because authors and teachers agreed that, although the use of matrix powers as mathematical models in network situations such as this is a worthwhile part of the curriculum, developing technical understanding of why powers of an adjacency matrix give the number of paths of different lengths is not core material worth the investment of time and work required. Authors and some teachers also agreed that strategy 4 was too low level, not engaging, and thus not worthwhile. In the first edition of *Core-Plus Mathematics*, authors tried several versions of strategy 2. Teachers suggested various alternatives, many of which were tried, but still limited success was reported. Thus, eventually, the investigation was written as described in strategy 3. This version, however, was so tightly structured that a more open-ended version was provided in the Teacher's Guide for optional use. The more open-ended version was used in the teaching experiment described above. Discussions among authors and teachers who had used the more open-ended version resulted in a consensus that the more open-ended version was in fact feasible and more desirable. Thus, for the published investigation, the open-ended version was moved from the Teacher's Guide to the Student Edition and became the final student version. In addition, the technical difficulty of viewing and operating on 9×9 matrices when exploring the relationship between path lengths and powers of matrices was addressed by the development of some custom software.

This example illustrates all three types of negotiations: some teachers negotiated versions that were more structured (suggesting that the materials should just tell students the square of the adjacency matrix represents the numbers of paths of length two); authors and some teachers negotiated more open-ended versions; and the Core-Plus principles of active learning, high cognitive demand, and student-centered approaches were discussed and maintained. This example particularly focuses on how much structure and explicit help students' need for understanding key mathematical ideas. Authors describe this as an ongoing dilemma: "There is constant tension between providing too much scaffolding or not enough."

Core Principles of the Core-Plus Mathematics Program

There have been numerous times during the writing of *Core-Plus Mathematics* where authors have resolved negotiations by appealing implicitly or directly to the design principles described early in this chapter. Issues related to the investigative nature of the curriculum materials, the use of contexts as a basis for the mathematics that is investigated, or the integrated nature of the mathematics within courses have all been addressed many times as information is proposed by authors, teachers, or mathematician consultants during revision iterations. Some ideas are offered and rejected in short order with little teacher input; others are tested and rejected or improved based on negotiations. We offer a final example from the assessments that briefly illustrates how the CPMP authors decided that the design principles did not allow for negotiation about a particular feature of the curriculum materials.

The teachers consistently wanted multiple-choice items on the quizzes and tests. They requested this because of the pressure they face to get students ready to take standardized assessments such as state tests, the ACT and SAT, or college placement tests. Interestingly enough, the teachers involved in the CPMP revision work were more adamant about this than were teachers working with the previous edition, possibly because of the recent increased emphasis on accountability. The developers were unwilling to provide these items as a *regular* feature of the formal assessments. This is one area where the conversation with the teachers resulted in change, but not in the manner in which the teachers requested. The curriculum materials now include four or five multiple-choice items from each unit that teachers can choose to use in the mid-year or end-of-year assessments. Additionally, there is a black line master at the end of each unit consisting of ten multiple-choice items and a test-taking tip as a part of the supplementary teacher's resources. These ten multiple-choice items were not intended to be used as an assessment of the content addressed in the unit, but rather to provide students with an out-of-class opportunity to consider multiple-choice questions and to think about strategies that might be employed when taking multiple-choice tests. In fact, of the ten items, there are usually only one or two that are directly connected to the content of the unit just completed. Although the teachers may choose to add their own multiple-choice items, the authors felt that this compromise gave students the opportunity to consider multiple-choice items while at the same time preserving a core principle of CPMP to support ongoing monitoring of student thinking.

Summary Discussion

This chapter has attempted to describe the curriculum development process through the examination of the process CPMP authors and teachers used in order to develop a better understanding of the idea of "intended curriculum." Our argument is simple: the intended curriculum is the result of a process of ongoing negotiations between authors and teachers, and seldom represents the "pure," first "intentions" that authors put to paper. As the authors of this chapter worked toward a better understanding of the intended curriculum, we described the interactions between CPMP authors and teachers in the process through examining actual examples from the curriculum writing process of second-edition *Core-Plus Mathematics.*

Among the issues highlighted in our examples, several are worth re-emphasizing. Most curriculum literature defines the intended curriculum based on the final product. Our examples illustrated a number of instances in the writing of student materials, teacher materials, and assessment where various levels of negotiation took place. Our lead example illustrated differing views of assessment between authors and teachers, and how authors sought to change existing views of how student thinking should be assessed within the CPMP curriculum. In another example, the negotiation focused on the need for additional scaffolding whereas teachers realized that "less" *can* produce desirable learning outcomes. Another case tested the ability of students to understand an important kind of proof technique where some of the initially intended investigation material ultimately was negotiated into homework exercises. We ended with an illustration that suggests that some parts of the writing process involved very limited negotiation for fear of compromising the core principles that define this particular curriculum program.

The teachers' role in the CPMP curriculum development process was an important one. They provided feedback in many forms at all points of the process and for all parts of the finished curriculum. They brought experience and wisdom of practice to the development and pilot process that often placed a reality check on authors' intentions and helped transform those intentions into something usable in a variety of school settings. The end product was the result of negotiations that sought to mediate between authors' and teachers' points of view. Authors knew that writing good material that pushes the envelope of what mathematics students are able to learn hinges on good feedback from and negotiation with field-test teachers. And despite characterizing teachers as "faithful implementers" of the curriculum materials, the authors recognized that the teachers played a very important, and sometimes little acknowledged, role in the development of quality mathematics materials.

Notes

1. Although definitions of intended curriculum vary in the literature, we use the term to mean the authors' vision of what content will be addressed in the curriculum materials along with the manner in which the curriculum materials will be used in the classroom.
2. See, for example, Hirsch (2007) for perspectives on core design principles for a variety of K-12 curriculum development projects.
3. The lead author of this chapter is an evaluator on the project. The associate authors are CPMP authors responsible for various aspects of the curriculum project.
4. The principles for CPMP are more fully explicated in Hirsch (2007).

References

Clandinin, D. J., & Connelly, F. M. (1992). Teacher as curriculum maker. In P. W. Jackson (Ed.), *Handbook of research on curriculum* (pp. 363–401). New York, NY: Macmillan.
Clarke, B., Clarke, D., & Sullivan, P. (1996). The mathematics teacher and curriculum development. In A. Bishop, K. Clements, C. Keitel, J. Kilpatrick, & C. Laborde (Eds.), *International handbook of mathematics education* (pp. 1,207–1,233). Boston, MA: Kluwer Academic.
Connelly, F. M., & Ben-Peretz, M. (1980). Teachers' roles in the using and doing of research and curriculum development. *Journal of Curriculum Studies 12*(2), 95–107.
Costello, R. B., & Pritchard, D. R. (Eds.). (1994). *The American heritage dictionary* (3rd Edition). New York, NY: Houghton Mifflin.
Dewey, J. (1938). Experience and education. In J. A. Boyston (Ed.), *The later works of John Dewey, 1925–1953*, Vol. 13. Carbondale, IL: Southern Illinois University Press.

Educational Development Center, Inc., & The K-12 Mathematics Curriculum Center. (2005). *The changing mathematics curriculum: An annotated bibliography.* Newton, MA: EDC.

Fey, J. T., & Hirsch, C. R. (2007). The case of *Core-Plus Mathematics.* In C. R. Hirsch (Ed.), *Perspectives on the design and development of school mathematics curricula* (pp. 129–142). Reston, VA: National Council of Teachers of Mathematics.

Garry, R. F., Connelly, M. F., & Dittman, F. (1975). Interpretive case studies of selected projects. In P. Dalin (Ed.), *Handbook of curriculum development* (pp. 55–118). Paris: Organization for Economic Cooperation and Development, Center for Educational Research and Innovation.

Hirsch, C., Fey, J., Hart, E., Schoen, H., & Watkins, A. (Eds.). (2008). *Core-Plus Mathematics: Contemporary mathematics in context: Second edition.* New York, NY: McGraw Hill/Glencoe.

Hirsch, C. R. (Ed.). (2007). *Perspectives on the design and development of school mathematics curricula.* Reston, VA: National Council of Teachers of Mathematics.

Howson, G., Keitel, C., & Kilpatrick, J. (1981). *Curriculum development in mathematics.* Cambridge: Cambridge University Press.

Lampert, M. (1985). How do teachers manage to teach? Perspectives on problems in practice. *Harvard Educational Review, 55*(2), 178–194.

Lloyd, G. M. (1999). Two teachers' conceptions of a reform oriented curriculum: Implications for mathematics teacher development. *Journal of Mathematics Teacher Education, 2*(3), 227–252.

Lloyd, G. M. (2002). Mathematics teachers' beliefs and experiences with innovative curriculum materials: The role of curriculum in teacher development. In G. Leder, E. Pehkonen, & G. Torner (Eds.), *Beliefs: A hidden variable in mathematics education?* (pp. 149–159). Utrecht: Kluwer Academic.

National Council of Teachers of Mathematics. (1989). *Curriculum and evaluation standards for school mathematics.* Reston, VA: Author.

National Council of Teachers of Mathematics. (1991). *Professional standards for teaching mathematics.* Reston, VA: Author.

National Council of Teachers of Mathematics. (1996). *Assessment standards for school mathematics.* Reston, VA: Author.

National Council of Teachers of Mathematics. (2000). *Principles and standards for school mathematics.* Reston, VA: Author.

National Research Council. (2004). *On evaluating curricular effectiveness.* Washington, DC: National Academies Press.

Remillard, J. T. (2005). Examining key concepts in research on teachers' use of mathematics curriculum. *Review of Educational Research, 75*(2), 211–246.

Wooten, W. (1965). *SMSG: The making of a curriculum.* New Haven, CT: Yale University Press.

Wu, H. (1997). The mathematics education reform: Why you should be concerned and what you can do. *The American Mathematical Monthly, 104*(10), 946–954.

13

Part III Commentary

Who Knows Best? Tales of Ordination, Subordination, and Insubordination

David Pimm

The five chapters that form the primary constituents of this part of the book each contain teacher tales worth the telling. We read about teachers at work in their own classrooms, in the presence of new text material in Chapter 8. In Chapter 11, we meet one teacher teaching from the same materials in two different settings. In Chapter 9, we get to eavesdrop on a teacher collective at work, examining their own emergent teacher-researcher practice in relation to classroom mathematics materials. We encounter two more teachers through their ways of referring to the text materials in mid-stream in Chapter 10. Finally, in Chapter 12, we run into teachers recruited as developmental testers for a text-series revision. But we also hear these tales told through the eyes of different tellers, who additionally bring other work and ideas to bear. And the teachers know they are being observed.

There are many differences among them: one is in text materials – *Everyday Mathematics, Investigations in Number, Data and Space, Everyone Learns Mathematics* (from Israel), the *Connected Mathematics Project*, and *Core-Plus Mathematics Project*. Two of the series are under revision, allowing the materials' developmental processes, as well as teachers' ways of working with less familiar resources, to be rendered more visible to an outside eye. Another considerable range is to be found in classroom grade level – K–2, 3–5, 7–8, 8, and high school. In some accounts, teacher voices are more clearly heard than in others, either as reported speech or as authorizing authors themselves. The settings reported on are also varied, as we eavesdrop vicariously on classroom interactions between teachers and students, conversations among a group of teachers in a school (with invited outsiders from a nearby teachers' college) as they look at students' work from their classes grade by grade, between teachers and materials developers and authors, and between teachers and ("second-hand") researchers.

In searching for some commonalities across chapters around which I might offer some connected remarks, however, I kept coming back to the endemic tensions within the classroom situation itself when teachers opt to work with or alongside texts and other pre-prepared materials while working with their students on mathematics. For, as Mr Weasley remarks to his daughter Ginny in *Harry Potter and the Chamber of Secrets,* "Never trust anything that can think for itself *if you can't see where it keeps its brain*" (Rowling, 1998, p. 242; italics in original). Just like Tom Riddle's diary, a mathematics text always has a brain embedded in it, even if precisely where and what its pedagogic nature and intent are may not be immediately apparent. The distinction between text and teacher with regard to which classroom intentions are enacted and how is both real and significant.

For intentions, *pedagogic* intentions especially, are at the heart of each of these chapters, while whose intentions get realized (and how) is a key consideration. The fact that everyone involved, directly or indirectly, has intentions is something that the term "intended curriculum" conveniently masks.[1] The classroom is and has always been a systematic site of struggle around intentions – something that, at some level, every teacher knows. And the formulation of the specific curricular struggle I have chosen to address here is one of "who knows best?"

Is it the state curriculum formulators whose specifications about mathematics have legal force who "know best"? Is it the text authors who are the primary producers of classroom materials that teachers may call upon in some way or other, to a greater or lesser extent, during the school year? (Even though, as is pointed out in Chapter 12, there are also many influences upon these authors too, many competing voices clamoring for their attention.) Is it the classroom teachers themselves, who always teach in a particular present, even though they often attempt to do so in concert with the material traces of the presence of the past – for that is what mathematics texts and materials necessarily are (see Love & Pimm, 1996)? And many of those traces are pedagogic in intent, but the pedagogy may not sit either simply or well with that of the empirical teacher in her or his classroom setting, school, and community – teaching with a text present is always team-teaching. And finally, there are the students themselves, and their wide-ranging intentions about school in general and mathematics class in particular, who are in some significant sense the final arbiters of this whole, complex process, in terms of what is learnt, whether awarely or not. Though they too have their shoulder-dwellers whispering in their ears, struggling for influence (parents, teachers, other students in the class, counselors, siblings, ...). No one is ever alone in a classroom; it is always an over-full, jostling place to inhabit.

So, having announced the theme of crowded conflict and the struggle for whose intentions get attended to in some form, and hence which have the opportunity to be heard above the cacophony, the particular line I wish to explore here involves a curious trio: ordination, subordination, and insubordination. These words evoke other contexts, specifically religious and military ones (and school teaching and learning historically have had considerable interactions with both, specifically with their intents and purposes). But the power of order, as well as the giving and receiving (or taking) of orders, is uppermost in both of these other contexts. I will address these three lexically-linked terms separately as I look across the five chapters, before returning to broader questions of authority at the end.

Ordination

Ordination involves the process of admittance of the new into an existing setting. In a church context, it can involve taking holy orders, with all its consonance with established authority and, perhaps, authoritarianism. What may be sought by or even required of the novice is subordination to the will of another, whether a person, an institution, or even the "Word," as well as questions of fidelity, of faithful following. Questions of active or tacit resistance also arise, leading to the possibility of covert or overt insubordination.

What resonances with these notions do we find in this book? The most obvious instance of ordination is as a new teacher of mathematics ordained into the priestly caste of teachers. We read about one instance at least, albeit in a different part of this book, in Chapter 16. A central issue there has to do with many of the novitiate having insufficient mathematical pedagogic intentions with respect to their charges, and where they might turn for assistance in developing some.

But there are also accounts of the challenges of being a teacher-informant (in Chapter 12) where a particular form of "fidelity" is specifically requested. The "conduit" metaphor, as described Chapter 12, provides one clear view on this question about the proper flow of intention (though not one I wholeheartedly share). The metaphor's confusing complexity is due to uncertainty about the nature of the connectivity among the components, but also about the direction and relative size of the flow (see also Reddy, 1979, for a description of a similar metaphor with regard to linguistic meaning). But that chapter additionally raises the challenge of reading others' intentions from text alone (whether intended for the student or the teacher).

Third, there is the ordination of teachers as action researchers: in the El Barrio-Hunter College collective instance, liberation theology is decidedly at work. An unexamined fourth is that of becoming a researched teacher (e.g., in Chapters 8, 10, or 11). Lastly, there is the ordination of *students* of mathematics, novices to be initiated into its knowledge and mysteries. Who ordains them and how? What practices can we see at work in these classroom settings and discussions of practitioners that reflect attitudes and orientations to where mathematics is to be found and the role of text within them?

Lastly, a text too might metaphorically need to be ordained: again, Chapter 12 offers some insight into this process, although "implementing" a new text or set of materials also has something to offer in this regard.

Subordination

"Subordination" has the ring of a term that is often seen as negative, a result of a hierarchical deployment of power and will (whether individual or institutional). Yet it is many people's experience that the willing subordination of oneself to a powerful teacher (for instance, in psychotherapy) can be a profound and significant experience. And subordinate roles may regularly be accepted. But this is quite different from finding oneself unwillingly framed or made subordinate to someone or something else (e.g., a text, here).

In mathematics education, the word "subordination" is closely tied to the work of Gattegno (see, for example, Gattegno, 1970) on the subordination of teaching to learning. Hewitt (1996) too has written insightfully on a teacher subordinating one mathematical task to another (one that relates to it in particular ways) as a means to work on the acquisition of fluency. Deliberately and covertly directing student attention *away* from the learning that the teacher is focusing on provides a telling instance that counters a commonplace belief in always letting the student in on what the teacher is doing (see also Pimm, 1995).

Within the classroom setting, Chapter 10 addresses privileging and alignment (and hence, indirectly, subordination) among the school's holy trinity of teacher, students, and text. Her two teachers differed in terms of the place they accorded the text in their classrooms: for Josh, the word was to be repeatedly read aloud, both by himself and by his students, whereas Karla regularly interpreted the text for her students. I would want to argue that the valuing of the text is different for these two teachers, and this difference is reflected in their classroom practices, inculcating attitudes and orientations into their students.

But there is also the key question: to what extent is the text to be mediated by the teacher? This issue is at the heart of major schisms in European Christian church history (as well as a major force motivating attempts to eradicate illiteracy, so that the Bible could be read individually – see Ferreiro, 2003). Even the teacher, Josh, despite his close attention to the word of the text, authorizes himself both to comment on and to evaluate it.

Fauvel (1991) has written powerfully on the history of mathematics textbooks, drawing attention to how taken-as-given norms, forms and purposes have been far from constant. Among other examples, he discusses *The Schoolmaster's Assistant*, a mid-eighteenth-century arithmetic textbook written by Thomas Dilworth. Fauvel observes, "There is also a clear conception, embodied in the style of Dilworth's book, of mathematics as a body of content rather close to religious doctrinal truths" (p. 117). Quite apart from the fact that Dilworth deliberately chose the Catholic catechism as a specific didactic-rhetorical model, there are two further features of relevance here. The first is the subordinate positioning of the text implicit in his choice of the word "assistant" for its title. The second has to do with the then-novel feature, claiming in the preface that his was "a very good examining Book."

Interestingly, the theme of text assessment resurfaces in Chapter 12. Ziebarth and his colleagues report teachers' confident assertion of their right to decide about assessment, even while generally being willing to go along as "passive" teacher-informants (as described in some of the other episodes in that chapter), subordinating themselves "faithfully" to their text-author authorities. This seemed to involve them not simply at the level of individual teachers deciding, but in some sense as "representatives" of the profession.

Once the text has died (by being printed), it can no longer change (until its next incarnation). Teachers who subsequently come to it select from it the things they think *will* work. Teacher-developers come to the draft materials primed for the possibility of change, for looking for the things that require revision or excision, things that *do not* "work." In this sense, they are being accorded a different position (whether they take it up or not) from that of "the faithful," the conduit metaphorees.

Lastly, there is the fact that the text is setting itself up to be not only the students' instructor but the teacher's as well. There is no space here to go into this point more deeply, but the history of whom the text addresses and how is an interesting one (see Gray, 1991, for one example).

Insubordination

Even more than subordination, *in*subordination presupposes a hierarchy (e.g., in the military) from which "legitimate" orders devolve. Ziebarth et al.'s mention of the "conduit" signals the delegated flow of such curricular requirements within one view of the proper order of things. Consequently, insubordination involves a deliberate and conscious refusal to carry something out. It can also involve "talking back."

A commonplace instance of curricular insubordination involves a teacher making decisions in the presence of a textbook, skipping material, or explicitly disagreeing with the text to students (e.g., "I don't like the way the book does this") or even pointing out places where it is misguided or erroneous. Insubordination towards the legal curriculum itself could be continuing to teach material (under the guise of "enrichment," perhaps) that is no longer in a particular grade-level's specification (e.g., proper fractions relegated to a higher grade level) or even in the required curriculum at all (e.g., Roman numerals or other numeration systems – Babylonian or Mayan, perhaps). Berdot, Blanchard-Laville, and Bronner (2001) present a fascinating psychological discussion about the effect on French high school mathematics teachers arising from such an institutionally-decreed loss.

The El Barrio-Hunter College piece is rife with joyful instances of insubordination and talking back – it comprises a strong tale of refusal in terms of asserting the right of teachers to determine their own classrooms, of finding ways not to be solely subordinate to text material. Action research both amplified and strengthened these teachers' voices, voices that would not be silenced when faced with the text. The moral became one of "adapting" materials for their children, in light of their work as "first-hand researchers."

Insubordination fundamentally raises the issue of disagreeing and how to do so in different contexts (e.g., by instituting classroom rules), as well as a need for trust. Many chapters contained instances of disagreement: in classrooms (Chapter 8), with textbooks (Chapter 10), with text authors (Chapter 9). But if students are to have intellectual autonomy, they must learn to argue. And the same is true for teachers, too: how do they resist the hypnotic power of the text, to refuse as well as to accept on occasions the model roles laid out in teacher's guides?

Author, Authorize, and Authority

Who knows best? And could we, as an informed jury of readers, decide? Is this even a democratic question? What does "knowing best" involve, and about what:

those with the clearest or noblest intentions or with the most specific knowledge of the classroom setting; those directly involved or those with the positional power and authority,…? What about those who know about mathematics itself, about teaching mathematics to school-age students, about learning mathematics, about creating productive tasks,…? Teachers know most about their specific setting, but may not have a more general eye to the district or state as a whole, about the other grade levels, about mathematics: their focus is rightly specific and particular, as the El Barrio teachers' comments reveal. Wider and differently informed external perspectives also have their place, but there is necessary and significant turbulence in the conduits.

Especially with mathematics and its teaching and learning, the question of authority is never far away; neither is asking whence this authority derives. With these queries comes an exploration of possible reasons why this or that authority should or might be heeded in certain circumstances. Robert Record, one of the earliest and most prolific mathematics textbook authors to write in English, chose a conversational dialogue form for most of his books. This style was not intended as representative of "model" classroom discussion, but rather framed the reader-learner as an eavesdropper on a conversation between a fictional "Master" (teacher) and "Scholar" (student).

Master and Scholar make their appearance, discussing why numbering is a good thing; the Scholar says he wants to learn, to which the master responds:

MASTER: I am very glad of your request, and will do it speedily, since that to learn it you be so ready.

SCHOLAR: And I to your authority my wit do subdue; whatsoever you say, I take it for true.

MASTER: That is too much; and meet for no man to be believed in all things, without showing of reason. Though I might of my Scholar some credence require, yet except I show reason, I do not it desire.

(quoted in Fauvel, 1989, p. 2)

So within this dramatized context, Record as textbook author is also working on creating his model reader, one who likewise requires reasons for belief. (See Love & Pimm, 1996, for a discussion of Umberto Eco's notion of model reader in a mathematics education context.)

The clearest examples of this tension between "model" and "actual" come with the example of "Dialogue Boxes" from the materials discussed in Chapter 8; dialogues which serve to conjure both a model teacher and a model student. But what is to be learnt from them? Are they an ideal? A "should"? A "might"? Is the empirical response one of recognition, puzzlement or curiosity? Are they "real" (in the sense of deriving from an "actual"), and does it matter? Am I as teacher-reader being asked to subordinate my actual to someone else's imagined or virtual?

Mathematics teachers offer tasks. They always have, they always will. Many have always adopted/modified them to suit their situation, finding them where they may. The sources of these tasks (increasingly via the Internet) and the con-comitant authority with which they come, as well as modifications made and reasons for selecting them, are all important. As indicated by the title of this part of the book, the relationships among teachers, curriculum materials, and what happens in actual classrooms are diverse and complex, as these chapters have indicated. For myself, materials and texts are at best seen as one starting point; they usually require teachers to be thoughtful, aware, and autonomous to use them successfully. To what extent do the texts themselves help to bring this state of affairs about? Is a text's role to make itself redundant for the reader? Are text materials created so as to render themselves unnecessary for a teacher? For a student? How do they, how can they, in Eco's (1979) terms, serve to create their own *model reader*? Do they endeavor to encourage self-confidence or depend-ence, autonomy or subservience? And who knows best how to achieve these intended ends?

Note

1. Neither is a curriculum simply "enacted". Curriculum, in Varela's (1992, p. 255) resonant image, *emerges* as "a path that does not exist but is laid down in walking" – or here, perhaps, "in talking." It appears from individual teachers in conjunction with their students, in class-rooms, every day.

References

Berdot, P., Blanchard-Laville, C., & Bronner, A. (2001). Mathematical knowledge and its relation to the knowledge of mathematics teachers: Linked traumas and resonances of identity. *For the Learning of Mathematics, 21*(1), 2–11.
Eco, U. (1979). *The role of the reader: Explorations in the semiotics of texts.* Bloomington, IN: Indiana University Press.
Fauvel, J. (1989). Platonic rhetoric in distance learning: How Robert Record taught the home learner. *For the Learning of Mathematics, 9*(1), 2–6.
Fauvel, J. (1991). Tone and the teacher: Instruction and complicity in mathematics textbooks. In D. Pimm & E. Love (Eds.), *Teaching and learning school mathematics* (pp. 111–121). London: Hodder and Stoughton.
Ferreiro, E. (2003). *Past and present of the verbs to read and to write: Essays on literacy.* Toronto, ON: Douglas and McIntyre.
Gattegno, C. (1970). *What we owe children: The subordination of teaching to learning.* New York, NY: Outerbridge and Dienstsfrey.
Gray, E. (1991). The primary mathematics textbook: Intermediary in the cycle of change. In D. Pimm & E. Love (Eds.), *Teaching and learning school mathematics* (pp. 122–136). London: Hodder and Stoughton.
Hewitt, D. (1996). Mathematical fluency: The nature of practice and the role of subordination. *For the Learning of Mathematics, 16*(2), 28–35.
Love, E., & Pimm, D. (1996). "This is so!" A text on texts. In A. J. Bishop, K. Clements, C. Keitel, J. Kilpatrick, & C. Laborde (Eds.), *International handbook of mathematics education, Part I* (pp. 371–409). Boston, MA: Kluwer Academic.
Pimm, D. (1995). *Symbols and meanings in school mathematics.* London: Routledge.
Reddy, M. (1979). The conduit metaphor: A case of frame conflict in our language about language. In A. Ortony (Ed.), *Metaphor and thought* (pp. 284–324). New York, NY: Cambridge University Press.
Rowling, J. K. (1998). *Harry Potter and the chamber of secrets.* Vancouver, BC: Raincoast Books.
Varela, F. (1992). Whence perceptual meaning? A cartography of current ideas. In F. Varela & J. Dupney (Eds.), *Understanding origins* (pp. 235–263). Dordrecht: Kluwer Academic.

14

Part III Commentary
Teachers and the Enacted Curriculum

Marty J. Schnepp

Each of the chapters in this part of the book touches on or explicitly discusses the literature on the roles teachers play in the curriculum process. I will mention here some details of these discussions that stand out in my mind and that I will draw on as I share my reactions to the chapters using my particular lens as a practicing high school teacher.

Ziebarth et al., in Chapter 12, explicitly detail themes in the literature on curriculum. They discuss views that position teachers as "faithful implementers" or "conduits" of curriculum materials, other notions of teachers as "curriculum makers," and they themselves offer a third perspective of teachers as "collaborators alongside university mathematicians and mathematics educators (and often others from a variety of disciplines) as part of writing teams." Other authors in this part discuss or carefully put forth the position that curriculum materials are subject to interpretation by teachers. Knowledge of the theoretical perspectives and accurate images of individual views that researchers find in their practitioner subjects are critical to understanding this complex world of intended, enacted, and attained curriculum.

Teachers Position Themselves in Relation to Curriculum Materials

I believe that one of the most significant factors in teachers' use of curriculum materials is how they position themselves in relation to those materials. The labels and concepts in the literature that researchers use to describe their practitioner subjects establish a common language to help us understand what happens when curriculum materials are placed in the hands of individual teachers. But something that I am intrigued by is the spectrum of roles teachers see for themselves. The spectrum has implications for student learning and for the day-to-day professional work of a group of teachers working together.

Students at a given school using a given curriculum program will experience more than a single classroom (or two) as examined in the research chapters in this part of the book. As a result, the learning experiences of students progressing through a set of curriculum materials will be varied. I can only wonder about the end result of students moving among experiences with teachers who act as conduits of the authors and experiences with teachers who rarely use the materials designed by outside authors. What might there be to learn about students' learning in such a setting?

I teach in a mathematics department in which various personal views are held. "Faithful implementers" in my department express confidence in published curriculum materials and are reluctant to make changes to what they believe are intricately sequenced activities and topics. On the other end of the spectrum are "curriculum makers." These are colleagues who believe it is their professional obligation to be writers of the curriculum program, and that published materials are simply a resource from which to draw. Many teachers fall somewhere in between. And I think it is accurate to say that not everyone (myself included) maintains a consistent position. The existence of a spectrum of ways teachers position themselves in relation to curriculum materials impacts how we work together now, and in the future will have an impact on the execution of our curriculum program.

Michigan has recently adopted the Michigan Merit Curriculum, and the topic lists for recommended mathematics courses do not align well with any published curriculum materials. Departmental meetings to prepare upcoming courses are filled with tension. Some teachers want to adopt and teach as much as possible from a published curriculum program and then fill in topic gaps by supplementing from other published materials. Other teachers want to establish predetermined curriculum objectives and sequencing, believing that published curriculum materials should be used only after they are shown to include concepts (and pedagogy) that provide a means to those predetermined ends. Working and making decisions with such varied views is difficult.

At the end of this work, one of those two approaches will lead us to some sequence of topics and some set of curriculum resources. And, once decisions are finalized, there will be teachers whose perspective differs from the chosen path. I believe the effectiveness of the curriculum materials and program will be lessened to some degree as a result. I cite Herbel-Eisenmann's account of how teacher's language choices can undermine learning goals of curriculum materials as support for my belief and as an example of one possible mechanism by which effectiveness will be reduced. A teacher who is not comfortable or is unhappy with the chosen curriculum materials or program will convey that disposition in the classroom. There are, no doubt, other mechanisms by which effectiveness is diminished when a course is designed from a perspective different from the one held by the teacher of the course.

Teachers Adapt to Instructional Context

The unique opportunity to study a single teacher using the same curriculum materials in two different school settings allowed Eisenmann and Even (Chapter 11) to bring to light an unsettling reality that the context of curriculum enactment, including the particular students involved, plays a significant role in curriculum enactment. I would argue that the dissimilarity of school context does not have to be as stark as the two schools, Trevor and Carmel. Although not carefully researched, I know and will concede that there are different enacted curriculums in classes I teach in the same school. Different class periods respond to curriculum materials and pedagogy in different ways. As a simple example, first-period classes are often quiet and discussions are hard to elicit, whereas last-period classes are often unfocused and difficult to work with. In general, though, "lack of students' cooperation" (Eisenmann's and Even's tactfully chosen words) is pervasive with some groups of students. I have worked with groups of students who are reluctant or downright mutinous when pushed to work harder or think more deeply. The very next class period, for what seem to be unknowable reasons, students are eager to engage in difficult content and complex tasks requiring higher-order thinking.

Chapter 11 makes me uncomfortable because I see in my own teaching what they have documented in their research. My discomfort stems from recalling times when I was not as successful as I would have liked at shifting student dispositions toward inquiry and sense-making. When faced with groups of students who are reluctant or simply having difficulty, I have broken difficult tasks down into less open-ended tasks. "Scaffolding" activities as a means of opening up points of access, if done well, can be a good teaching maneuver. At times, rather than assigning group work, requiring presentations, and holding whole-group discussion for an activity designed for such a process, I have assigned individual work and studied the student work in hope of finding model responses to share or to find a substantive discussion prompt. I could cite other examples of alterations to curriculum materials that I have made with the best of intentions, many of which would be considered good teaching (some admittedly not so good), only to see, through Eisenmann and Even's example, that students from the different sections were presented with different curricular experiences.

Curriculum Adaptation is Inevitable and Difficult

Several authors posit that curriculum materials are subject to interpretation. I have argued that interpretation is subject to how individual teachers position themselves in relation to curriculum materials. Eisenmann and Even show that interpretation can be prejudiced by school context. Therefore, it is clear that altering, supplementing, and implementing curriculum materials while maintaining or improving quality is difficult. In my experience, even with excellent materials, working alone can too easily lead to misaligned or misguided implementation. In the chapters of this part of the book, I see two clear models for how teachers can prudently engage in the process of adaptation of materials, and some implied approaches.

Model 1: Front Line Field Testers

Chapter 12 describes a unique role that teachers play in their curriculum materials revision work, that of "front line field testers." The window to the curriculum process that Ziebarth et al. provide readers will be of great value to curriculum developers and possibly teachers who sign onto a project in this role and want to know what to expect. However, in my day-to-day teaching and curriculum work, I recognize that teachers selected for these positions are afforded opportunities that the typical teacher is not. Direct access to program designers is a great luxury. Opportunities to probe the goals and intentions of the creators of a curriculum program better prepare teachers to act as "faithful practitioners" simply because they can be thoroughly informed of the multi-faceted goals of activities. Furthermore, elevating the teachers' status to equal that of designers in the revision process prepares them especially well to play the role of curriculum adapter.

I have experienced a role similar to what Ziebarth et al. describe as a part of the NSF-funded SIMCALC project. I worked directly with the designer of a pedagogical software environment connected to physical devices and, together with his team of researchers, we studied classroom activities that I designed (Schnepp & Nemirovsky, 2001). Among the best learning experiences for students in my classroom are lessons that came from this work. Unfortunately, access to curriculum designers is a luxury available to few teachers. Yet all teachers adapt curriculum materials.

Model 2: Collaboration

The action research model of curriculum adaptation, illustrated by The El Barrio-Hunter College PDS Partnership Writing Collective, holds promise for mitigating unplanned consequences of changes made by teachers who do not have direct access to designers of curriculum materials. In-depth discussion among collaborative members focused on activities or student work is a means by which advantages and disadvantages of altering activities, resequencing topics, or altering pace can be better predicted. Bringing to bear a wide range of expertise and experience in thinking through these matters, providing time for this kind of analysis and for deliberate, informed decision-making is a vast improvement over what would typically be decisions made by a solitary teacher. I believe very strongly in this kind of work because of the positive impact I have seen it have on student learning.

In my experience, this kind of action-research is the most fruitful way to work at school-based curriculum materials implementation. The school I teach in was a Professional Development School (PDS) affiliated with Michigan State University during the 1990s. At the time *Standards*-based curriculum materials (UCSMP) were being used, and, later, function-based curriculum materials were created on site. During this era, time and other resources were dedicated to creating opportunities for observing other teachers using these materials, analyzing videotape of teaching using these materials, analyzing student work, and discussing the development of lessons. When we used collaborative teacher research to guide instruction, and curricular supplementation and alteration, different perspectives on a teacher's role in using curriculum materials became a moot point. In the face of student work and discussions, our work became understanding the results of our teaching and improving learning.

I believe this way of working raised expectations and the level of performance in classroom activities. Additionally, this kind of work helped to keep activities and assessment consistent with curricular goals. One teacher's move to alter an activity could be scrutinized by others to ensure the change does not work contrary to other aspects of the curriculum. For example, choosing to replace one problem context with another may be problematic if that context is used again for other purposes later in the course.

However, PDS-based action research groups are another luxury not unlike direct access to designers. The affiliation my school once shared with Michigan State University ended nearly a decade ago. Alone, it is a difficult task to walk the tightrope of carefully designed differentiated instruction (the kind described by El Barrio-Hunter College); it is too easy to fall off into an abyss of less rigorous enacted curriculum materials (as illustrated by Eisenmann and Even in Chapter 11).

Are There Other Models?

Without direct access to designers of curriculum programs and materials or PDS affiliations, what are the rest of us to do? How do we adequately discern the goals and intentions of carefully designed *Standards*-based (or other) curriculum programs before we make changes in our classrooms? How do the rest of us become practiced in the inquiry-based teaching methods that so many *Standards*-based curriculum programs rely on?

Lurking in the background of the study of supporting materials by Grant, Kline, Crumbaugh, Kim, and Cengiz (see Chapter 8) is the potential for lowering the quality of enacted curriculum if teacher moves in discussion do not anticipate and respond to students in a manner that elevates the level of thinking. And, as Herbel-Eisenmann notes, a teacher's language choice when using and referring to textbooks can support or undermine these goals. She argues that, "These language choices shape how teachers, textbooks, and students are positioned as being responsible for learning mathematical terms, definitions, skills, and concepts" (Chapter 10).

Are curriculum materials an adequate method for conveying designer intentions, for helping teachers to become experts at facilitating discussions that strive for higher order thinking to be expressed, or for becoming deliberate in choosing language suited to their purposes? Grant et al.'s study of the Teacher Notes (TNs) and Dialogue Boxes (DBs) features included in the *Investigations* materials sheds light on teaching aids that are better than any I have seen as a part of published materials. Designers who have made an effort to help teachers learn and plan to "elicit and extend" student thinking rather than simply find "the answer" or anticipate common student calculation errors impress me. However, I believe printing possible scenarios for teachers to read is not adequate support. Does professional development exist for the development of such expertise? In my opinion, yes! Grant et al., in Chapter 8, suggest that "video formats of teaching may enhance written text in curriculum materials and provide a forum for teachers to visualize whole-group discussions." Quoting Susan Jo Russell, the El Barrio-Hunter College Collective asserts, "It's impossible for the curriculum to differentiate instruction because the writers can't put in all the details for all the different groups and students." They go on to argue, "The best case is thousands of other teacher researchers doing similar work." That is, asking researchable questions about implementation of curriculum materials, discussing in collaborative groups, videotape and student work, and the like. I would add to this list: studying and practicing the arts of language use and discussion facilitation.

Opportunities to engage in the type of work described by El Barrio-Hunter College and Ziebarth et al. have helped me develop as a professional more than any traditional form of professional development. University classes, workshops from textbook publishers, and most of the other activities that garner state-sanctioned continuing education credit have done little to help me take on the complex tasks of contemporary mathematics instruction compared to facilitating the sort of discussions Grant et al. describe in Chapter 8. I cannot imagine how traditional professional development formats could ever approach the subtleties involved in the language issues raised by Herbel-Eisenmann in Chapter 10. I can, however, imagine reading her chapter and some of the literature she referenced, watching videos of teachers working with students, and holding discussions with experienced teachers as a means of developing understanding of the issues to which she calls attention. I can imagine a follow-up session some time later in which members of the discussion group share video or other evidence of the impact the initial discussions had on their use of curriculum materials in their actual classrooms. This kind of work could be adapted to various aspects of teachers' use of curriculum materials: understanding designers' intents, facilitating discussions, adapting curriculum materials, and differentiated instruction using a set of curriculum materials, to name a few. I believe there are ways to do this work without direct access to curriculum designers or PDS affiliation. The million-dollar questions are: What are those ways to make it happen? How do we make this replace ineffective modes of professional development? And, finally, how do we make it easier to get credit for continuing education from it?

Reference

Schnepp, M., & Nemirovsky, R. (2001). Constructing a foundation for the fundamental theorem of calculus. In A. A. Cuoco (Ed.), *The role of representation in school mathematics (2001 Yearbook)* (pp. 90–102). Reston, VA: National Council of Teachers of Mathematics.

IV

Teachers' Use of Curriculum Materials at Different Stages of Implementation and at Different Points on the Professional Continuum

15

Factors Influencing Student Teachers' Use of Mathematics Curriculum Materials

Stephanie L. Behm and Gwendolyn M. Lloyd

I feel like the teacher's guide is a script, so I always have it with me because I never have it memorized. I just feel like if I miss a paragraph in the book then that will throw the lesson off. It's too much information.

Heather, first-grade student teacher

It's brief what they [the authors of the curriculum materials] tell you to do, so it's a lot of make up your own approach. Sometimes I write myself notes, but otherwise, I just get it in my head and can go from there.

Anne, kindergarten student teacher

I had to use the workbook that you saw the students using. I needed to use that for every new thing that I did.... The truth is, I have to use what they're giving me, but I add to it where I think it's lacking.

Bridget, kindergarten student teacher

In this chapter, we describe three elementary student teachers' uses of mathematics curriculum materials and propose potential factors that may have worked together to contribute to their ways of using the materials. As the above quotations highlight, student teachers' ways of using mathematics curriculum materials can vary tremendously. Heather aimed to follow closely the suggestions of her *Standards*-based curriculum materials, Anne made adaptations to her *Standards*-based materials, and Bridget followed selected components and supplemented her commercially-developed textbook. What factors might have influenced these student teachers to use their curriculum programs in different ways? Attention to this question has the potential to expand our current understandings of teachers' relationships with mathematics curriculum materials and the ways teachers are prepared for their initial instructional experiences. Because preservice teachers' field experiences are likely to involve textbooks or curriculum materials intended to guide the design of instruction, understanding the nature of and factors influencing these first encounters with curriculum materials for teaching are undoubtedly important.

Teachers' Use of Textbooks and Curriculum Materials

Over several decades, researchers have set out to define, characterize, and understand teachers' work during various phases of their professional lives – from novice teachers to mid-career teachers to experienced and expert teachers (Berliner, 1986; Steffy, Wolfe, Pasch, & Enz, 2000). Yet, within the realm of teachers' use of mathematics textbooks and curriculum materials, research about the professional continuum is in its infancy. Two recent studies reported that beginning teachers appear to appreciate and rely on the explicit guidance about what and how to teach that mathematics textbooks can offer (Kauffman, Johnson, Kardos, Liu, & Peske, 2002; Remillard & Bryans, 2004). These studies suggest that beginning and experienced teachers may use mathematics textbooks and curriculum materials differently. For instance, Remillard and Bryans noted that the beginning teachers in their study

> tended to read and use all parts of the curriculum guides in their teaching... they sought to follow all the lessons as suggested in the guide, studying, and sometimes struggling with, all or most of the information provided for the teacher.
>
> (p. 377)

In contrast, most of the experienced teachers in the study "regularly adopted mathematical tasks from the curriculum guides, but drew on their own strategies and approaches to enact them in the classroom" (p. 374). The field is in need of additional studies that investigate the particular ways that teachers at different points on the professional continuum use curriculum materials for mathematics instruction. We also need to understand how and why differences in teachers' use of mathematics curriculum materials develop.

In the present chapter, we briefly describe three student teachers' ways of using curriculum materials for the design and enactment of mathematics instruction. Then we propose multiple factors that may have contributed to these student teachers' use of mathematics curriculum materials. We suggest that these factors warrant further examination by researchers interested in understanding the influences on teachers' initial use of mathematics curriculum materials.

Preservice Teachers and Mathematics Curriculum Materials

Most teachers view the student-teaching internship as the most valuable and beneficial part of their preparation (Feiman-Nemser, 1983; Guyton & McIntyre, 1990), claiming that much of what they know comes from first-hand teaching experience (Feiman-Nemser & Buchmann, 1985). Preservice teachers' interactions with curriculum materials are an important aspect of their first mathematics teaching experience. Twenty years ago, Ball and Feiman-Nemser (1988) discussed the experiences of teachers who emerged from teacher education programs with the impression that good teachers do not follow textbooks or rely upon teacher's guides. The authors described this finding as "a significant dilemma for preservice teacher education" created by the following two competing facts:

> On the one hand, textbooks are widely criticized for their content, their biases, and their implicit views of teaching and learning. Logically, this suggests that new teachers should not be encouraged to use them. On the other hand, many beginning teachers are hired by school districts where such textbook materials are mandated.
>
> (p. 419)

Two decades later, teacher education faces some similar dilemmas as well as new ones. Increasingly, student teachers are placed in schools where mathematics textbooks are adopted by districts as a strategy for improving student achievement (Corcoran, 2003). Indeed, some student teachers are asked to use textbooks "widely criticized for their content" or "curriculum that is controlled through objectives and standardized testing" (Ball & Feiman-Nemser, 1988, p. 421). Since the publication in the 1990s of over a dozen mathematics curriculum programs designed to align with the *Standards* (National Council of Teachers of Mathematics, 1989), many student teachers have been placed in classrooms where *Standards*-based mathematics curriculum materials are in use (e.g., Van Zoest & Bohl, 2002). Although mathematics curriculum programs are a common component of student teachers' experiences and some teacher educators have begun to explore the use of mathematics textbooks and curriculum materials as learning tools in teacher education coursework (e.g., Hjalmarson, 2005; Lloyd, 2006; Lloyd & Behm, 2005; Tarr & Papick, 2004), our knowledge about how preservice teachers' experiences with curriculum materials might influence their future instruction is quite limited.

Investigating student teachers' uses of mathematics textbooks and curriculum materials is critical to understanding teachers' curriculum use across the professional continuum and to improving teacher education. This chapter aims to (a) describe briefly student teachers' use of the mathematics curriculum materials of their internship sites, and (b) propose a set of factors that may have contributed to the student teachers' ways of using their curriculum materials.

Research Context

The participants in this study were three white undergraduate preservice elementary teachers in their early twenties – Heather, Anne, and Bridget.[1] Data collection occurred during the last seven weeks of Heather, Anne, and Bridget's ten-week student-teaching internships when they were teaching mathematics full-time in spring 2004. The majority of the data were collected through classroom observations and informal and semi-structured interviews. Methodological details can be accessed in reports of the individual teachers (Behm & Lloyd, 2008; Lloyd, 2007, 2008). Our focus in this section is on the context in which the study took place.

The university that these preservice teachers attended is located in the Mid-Atlantic region of the United States in a small town in Jameson County. Heather and Anne completed their student-teaching internships in Jameson County at a school approximately three miles from the university. The area surrounding the school contains rural and suburban regions, and has a predominantly white student population. The *Standards*-based *Everyday Mathematics* (EM) curriculum program (University of Chicago School Mathematics Project, 2001) was used in all elementary schools in Jameson County. Heather was placed in Ms Greene's first-grade classroom, and Anne worked with Ms Roy and Ms Jones in their combined kindergarten classroom across the hall.

Bridget completed her internship at Walnut Street School in the urban Coopersburg Schools, located 45 miles from the university. Bridget was placed in Ms Barrett's kindergarten classroom, which was composed of 13 African American students and one Asian student. During the 2003–04 academic year, 93 percent of the students attending Walnut Street were eligible for free or reduced-cost lunch programs. For mathematics instruction, the teachers utilized materials from the commercially-developed *Silver Burdett Ginn* (SBG) (Fennell et al., 1999) textbook series. In addition, administrators and teachers at Bridget's school viewed the state mathematics framework as a critical curriculum guide to be followed closely.

The Student Teachers' Ways of Using Their Curriculum Materials

In this section, we briefly describe the student teachers' use of mathematics curriculum materials for the design and enactment of instruction during their student-teaching internships.

Heather's Use of Standards-Based Curriculum Materials

Each weekend, Heather prepared for the upcoming week's mathematics activities using a copy of the EM teacher's guide to develop general plans for her lessons: "On the weekend I'll do an outline for the week and write down roughly what I'm going to do.... These [*handwritten notes in her planning book*] aren't really detailed." Heather explained that she looked at the teacher's guide again each morning before teaching: "During specials or snack time, I'll just review the lesson for that day." Heather felt that detailed lesson plans were unnecessary because when she taught, she had "the teacher's manual up there." Although Heather typically planned on her own as she read through the lessons in the teacher's guide, she also occasionally consulted her cooperating teacher: "I would ask [Ms Greene] about any questions that came up when I was planning, like about different games or just questions that come up.... She's really helpful."

Typically, Heather attempted to conduct her mathematics lessons in the specific ways recommended by the four- to five-page lesson plans found in the first-grade EM teacher's guide. She used the guide during instruction to refer to specific tasks and questions to ask students, as well as the overall organization of lessons. Heather explained that she tended to rely on the book during instruction because of the detailed, scripted nature of the information contained in the teacher's guide: "I feel like the teacher's guide is a script, so I always have it with me. A lot of times, I feel like if I miss a paragraph in the book then maybe that will throw the lesson off." When Heather adapted the recommendations, her changes usually related to the amount of time to spend on each lesson component. She often experienced difficulty carrying out her lessons in the timeframe she had allotted, and as a result she sometimes changed the nature of the activities to "make up time." For example, during a lesson titled *Data Landmarks*, students spent the majority of class time collecting and recollecting data, taking more time than she had planned. After the data were collected, Heather asked the students to "act out" the process of finding the range of the data, an activity she was initially excited to allow students to explore and discuss. However, with limited time remaining in class, Heather "really rushed through [it]. I said, 'Subtract the smallest from the biggest. What is it?' And they knew it, so I said, 'Okay, just fill it in.'" Heather commented, "I would have felt much better if we had gotten to discuss it more." Although after teaching this lesson and most others Heather identified aspects of her instruction that she wished had been different, and attempted to think of alternative approaches, her future lesson plans were typically driven by the presentation of the next lesson in the EM guide.

Anne's Use of Standards-Based Curriculum Materials

During mathematics time in Anne's large kindergarten classroom, each teacher (Ms Roy, Ms Jones, Anne, and another student teacher) taught one-fourth of the students. Groups of eight to ten students rotated among the four teachers so that each child saw each teacher, and did each mathematics activity, once during a four-day period. Because Anne taught each lesson four times, she had the opportunity to adapt her lessons multiple times and to consult with Ms Roy and Ms Jones between lessons to develop instructional ideas. (Due to the classroom structure, however, neither Ms Roy nor Ms Jones was able to observe Anne's mathematics instruction directly.)

Each week, Anne met with Ms Roy and Ms Jones to decide what activities from the EM curriculum program would be taught, and by whom. During planning meetings, the cooperating teachers offered short commentaries about their previous experiences teaching particular lessons. After each meeting, Anne was given (or made herself) photocopies of the pages that she needed from the EM teacher's guide – a book with half-page lessons that Anne described as "activity ideas, briefly written so you can quickly grab it and see, 'Oh, here's what I need to do today.'"

As Anne used the photocopied pages to plan her lessons, she began to make adaptations to EM's written suggestions. She explained, "It's a lot of make up your own approach. I make notes to myself, sometimes just underlining and sometimes it's actually writing out what I'm going to need to do." For example, when she read the EM recommendations for a lesson titled "Bead String Name Collections," she felt that the lesson was "pretty simple" and "wouldn't take a whole half hour in the way it's written." For this particular lesson Anne planned to alter the physical materials (to make bracelets using pipe cleaners and beads instead of using buttons and string) and the mathematical emphasis (to intro-duce number sentences involving addition instead of continuing exploration of equivalent names for numbers). These changes to extend the duration of the proposed activities and increase the mathematical sophistication of the chil-dren's work were apparent in many of Anne's lesson adaptations.

During instruction, Anne rarely consulted her plans or pages from the EM book. Prior to instruction, she concentrated on learning details that would allow her to conduct her lesson without a book or notes: "I try to remember little hints [from the lesson plan], but otherwise I tend to wing it and do what feels right and go wherever the kids are going with it." Most adaptations that Anne made during instruction were related to student behavior after students had completed or lost interest in an activity or game. For example, during her first time teaching the "Disappearing Trains" lesson (an addition and subtraction game with linking cubes), Anne spent a fair amount of class time redirecting students who were off-task. She commented, "There will definitely be a modification tomorrow. I need to find a new thing to do."

When making adaptations, Anne sometimes addressed classroom manage-ment issues that had emerged during her first attempt at teaching a lesson (as was the case in the "Disappearing Trains" lesson described above), but she more frequently made adaptations to the *mathematical content* of the lesson – she emphasized key ideas more explicitly and emphatically in subsequent lessons. For example, we observed that, in contrast to her first time teaching it, Anne emphasized addition to a greater extent in her second and third iterations of "Bead String Names Collection" by introducing addition number sentences that were not part of the EM lesson description. After teaching one of her lessons four times, Anne remarked that there were "lots of adjustments, but it got pretty good by the end for having them think deeply."

Bridget's Use of a Commercially-Developed Textbook

During her internship, Bridget used the workbook component of the SBG cur-riculum program and supplemented the workbook with additional tasks and activities. Each week, Bridget met with three other kindergarten teachers to plan for upcoming lessons. The focus of these planning meetings was on the selection of SBG workbook pages and worksheets: "I've been told several times that I needed to make sure that [the students] are getting plenty of paperwork." Bridget perceived that the other components of the SBG curriculum did not "fit" the school, and she described that the teachers "never used any full lessons" from the SBG guide. Instead, the teachers used a year-long curriculum plan to identify which pages of the SBG workbook could be used to address the state curriculum standards. Bridget explained that "the principal likes to know what [state stand-ards] we're covering which day."

Although Bridget found the planning meetings to be helpful, she consistently made her own plans after the meetings. As Bridget explained, "The truth is, I am trying to use what they're giving me and add to it where I think it's lacking." For each lesson, Bridget evaluated the SBG workbook offerings according to her informal assessment of students' knowledge, the objectives presented in the state curriculum framework, and her own visions of mathematics instruction. Typically, Bridget extended workbook lessons to allow students to "move around" and use physical materials or manipulatives. To develop new mathematics activities for use in conjunction with the SBG worksheets, Bridget first consulted the state curriculum framework to identify specific mathematical content and then tapped other resources for instructional ideas that would address the needs of her students.

For example, after teaching with some of the SBG worksheets related to coins, Bridget created her own additional worksheets: "I was actually really disappointed with how they did money in the book. So I made a few sheets and we did a lot of that together because I didn't feel like the book really did it at all." The sheets Bridget created were based on pictures of coins and activities that she found in "stuff from *Everyday Math* that [she] copied from teachers in [Jameson] County," and were intended to address mismatches she identified between students' understandings and the emphases of the SBG worksheets. Later in her internship, Bridget was responsible for reviewing "shapes" with her kindergarten class – a topic for which students had already completed the relevant SBG workbook pages. As in the previous example, Bridget designed her lessons about shapes using the state curriculum framework and her informal assessments of students' knowledge. Although she created some new worksheets to satisfy the expectations of her school, the majority of her lessons about shapes were based on her memory of activities from her mathematics pedagogy course at the university.

Student Teachers' Use of Mathematics Curriculum Materials

These descriptions suggest that student teachers' ways of using curriculum materials can vary a great deal from teacher to teacher. Whereas Heather read and used all parts of the EM curriculum guide to structure daily mathematics lessons, Anne consistently made adaptations to the recommendations of her EM materials and Bridget used her SBG materials minimally. The variation we observed across the student teachers' curriculum use is consistent with reports of inservice teachers' use of curriculum materials (Remillard & Bryans, 2004).

However, some aspects of the student teachers' use of curriculum materials appeared to be distinctly different from that of inservice teachers. When the student teachers in our study used their curriculum materials, they did not draw upon "their own strategies and approaches" or "the repetoires they had developed over years of teaching" (p. 374), as did the inservice teachers described by Remillard and Bryans (2004). Instead the student teachers tapped both human and material resources, including their cooperating teachers, peers (other student teachers), their own subject matter knowledge and preservice teacher education experiences, and alternative instructional materials. This finding draws attention to the potential importance of such resources in preservice and beginning teachers' early use of curriculum materials. It also raises the question of whether differences in the availability of human and material resources might contribute, in part, to differences in student teachers' ways of using their curriculum materials.

Potential Factors Influencing Student Teachers' Use of Curriculum Materials

In this section, we propose factors that may have contributed to the student teachers' ways of using of their mathematics curriculum materials. The purpose of proposing these factors and discussing their potential influences on the three student teachers' use of curriculum materials is (a) to offer a tentative set of factors to be explored in future research, and (b) to suggest aspects of teacher preparation that might be adjusted to support teachers' initial use of mathematics curriculum materials. As presented in Table 15.1, these factors include each student teacher's curriculum program, mathematics teacher education coursework, mathematics content knowledge and confidence in teaching mathematics, school accountability status and context, and cooperating teacher.

Although we discuss each proposed factor individually in the sections that follow, our view is that these factors (and likely other factors as well) worked together to influence the student teachers' use of their mathematics curriculum materials. Heather's efforts to follow closely the recommendations of the EM materials were likely influenced by interactions among a variety of factors that may include the detailed nature of the curriculum materials, her focused experiences with EM in her teacher education coursework, her lack of confidence about teaching mathematics, the alignment of her received curriculum with the state curriculum standards, and her cooperating teacher's influence. In Anne's case, the brevity of EM's kindergarten lesson descriptions, her experiences with a variety of *Standards*-based curriculum materials in university coursework, her high confidence in teaching mathematics and mathematical content knowledge, the alignment of her received curriculum with the state curriculum standards, and her opportunity to teach mathematics lessons independently and multiple times with the support of her cooperating teacher might have contributed to her tendency to make adaptations to EM's recommendations. Finally, Bridget's use of the SBG program may have been impacted by the limitations of the SBG workbook as an instructional resource and Bridget's perception of a lack of "fit" of the materials, her past experiences in university courses advocating a variety of resources for mathematics instruction, her explicit attention to the state curriculum standards, her high level of confidence in and content knowledge for teaching mathematics, and her cooperating teacher's minimal guidance.

Curriculum Materials in Use

In her review of research about teachers' uses of mathematics curriculum materials, Remillard (2005) suggested that the "materials themselves matter in teachers' interactions with curriculum materials" (p. 240). Similarly, in a study of four beginning elementary teachers, Kauffman (2002) found that characteristics of the curriculum materials in use were "central to how ... teachers approach[ed] their lesson planning and instruction" (p. 21). Qualities of Heather, Anne, and

Table 15.1. Factors Influencing Student Teachers' Use of Curriculum Materials

	Heather	Anne	Bridget
Curriculum Program	Detailed multi-paged teacher's lesson guide (EM)	Half-page teacher's lesson guide (EM)	Student workbook (SBG)
Mathematics Teacher Education Coursework	1 mathematics course (used a textbook for prospective teachers)	2 mathematics courses (used units of Standards-based curriculum materials)	2 mathematics courses (used units of Standards-based curriculum materials)
	1 mathematics pedagogy course (focused on the EM curriculum materials)	1 mathematics pedagogy course (emphasized an investigative approach)	1 mathematics pedagogy course (emphasized an investigative approach)
Content Knowledge/ Confidence	Medium/Low	High/High	High/High
Accountability Status of School	Fully accredited	Fully accredited	Provisionally accredited
Cooperating Teacher	5 years' teaching experience (4 years using EM), close relationship with student teacher	Veteran (5 years using EM), good relationship with student teacher, no teaching observations	4 years teaching (no prior experience in kindergarten), little curricular guidance for student teacher

Bridget's received curriculum programs – together with additional factors – may have contributed to the ways they used their curriculum materials during student teaching.

Heather's use of the first-grade EM curriculum materials may have been influenced, in part, by her sense that the materials were detailed and what she referred to as "scripted." She described being faced with a great deal of information in the curriculum materials, the majority of which was new to her. Because she focused on enacting the details of the EM lessons, and seemed to understand the "big picture" of her lessons only after teaching them, it may have been difficult for Heather to make adjustments to the written suggestions in the materials. Heather also had a favorable view of the extensive information in the materials. She appreciated and agreed with the pedagogical approaches of the EM materials. This view may have contributed to her inclination to try to follow closely the recommendations of the materials. Only when she experienced difficulty enacting EM's recommendations in her allotted class time did Heather make adjustments to the curriculum materials.

In contrast to Heather, both Anne and Bridget made adaptations to curriculum materials that were either brief or limited as instructional resources. Although Anne used the same curriculum program as Heather, the EM materials for kindergarten consisted of brief lesson descriptions typically spanning half a page. It is possible that the brief nature of Anne's curriculum materials offered opportunities for her to gain a general sense of EM lessons and to make decisions about adjusting the specific activities and mathematical emphases of lessons. Anne's EM lesson pages were not only brief, but they also described lessons that were generally consistent with her own instructional philosophy. Bridget's lessons, too, were based on relatively brief written information – pages from the workbook component of SBG's commercially-developed curriculum program. However, this curricular resource failed to meet either her own goals for mathematics instruction or the objectives of the state curriculum framework. These mismatches likely contributed to Bridget's tendency to adapt and supplement the SBG program.

We remind the reader that it is not our intention to argue that the nature of the curriculum materials, as we have described, can explain some particular aspect of the student teachers' curriculum use. Instead, our aim is to propose ways that the nature of the curriculum materials may have contributed – most likely through interaction with other factors – to the student teachers' curriculum use. For example, we are doubtful that Heather would have adapted the brief EM kindergarten materials in the ways that Anne did, if Heather had been placed in Anne's classroom. Other factors, such as Heather's teacher education experiences and lack of confidence about teaching mathematics, may have contributed to Heather attempting to follow closely the recommendations of the kindergarten materials (as she did with her first-grade materials), unlike Anne. On the other hand, perhaps Heather would have made adaptations to the recommendations of her curriculum materials if she had had the opportunity to teach each lesson multiple times in the kindergarten classroom, as Anne did. Because the student teachers' curriculum use was probably influenced by the contextual and situational characteristics of their internship sites *as well as* personal factors, we would not expect the student teachers to exhibit the same type of curriculum use across different internship sites. We emphasize that, in all likelihood, the factors discussed in this section – as well as others that we have not identified – worked together in complex ways to shape the student teachers' ways of using curriculum materials.

Teacher Education Coursework

A recurring question in teacher education is whether the effects of university coursework are "washed out" by classroom experiences (Ebby, 2000; Raymond, 1997; Steele, 2001; Zeichner & Tabachnick, 1981). In our study, the preservice teachers' internships did not appear to eliminate the impact of prior course experiences – in fact, as we describe below, the student teachers' coursework, in conjunction with other factors, may have contributed to their tendencies to use curriculum materials in particular ways during their internships.

Heather's experiences in mathematics education courses were quite different from those of Anne and Bridget. Anne and Bridget completed two undergraduate mathematics courses for preservice elementary teachers. In these courses, they used a variety of units from different *Standards*-based curriculum programs and worked through the mathematics in these units as learners. Two years later, Anne and Bridget completed a graduate-level pedagogy course that emphasized an investigative approach to mathematics teaching and learning. The preservice teachers were introduced to the EM curriculum program during one three-hour class session.

In contrast, Heather enrolled in one mathematics course for preservice teachers. In that course, she used a college mathematics textbook written for preservice elementary teachers. Less than one year later (during a summer term), Heather's graduate-level mathematics pedagogy course was taught by the mathematics curriculum supervisor of Jameson County (where use of EM was mandatory). The course focused almost exclusively on learning how to implement the EM program effectively. As Heather expressed, "We learned so much. We spent the whole semester using *Everyday Math.*"

Heather's preservice course experiences with the EM materials – experiences that were led by a strong advocate for the series – might have impacted her efforts to implement the curriculum materials closely. For instance, she initially expressed excitement about having been placed in a county that used EM because she assumed that "math would be planned." Anne and Bridget, on the other hand, were more inclined to make adaptations to their curriculum programs. Prior exposure to the mathematics embodied in *Standards*-based curriculum materials (in their mathematics courses) and an investigative approach to teaching and learning (in their pedagogy class) may have contributed to Anne's tendency to make adaptations to her EM materials and Bridget's decision to supplement the SBG workbook pages. Moreover, Anne and Bridget's pedagogy course did not explicitly advocate the use of any one curriculum program in particular, whereas Heather's pedagogy course had a specific focus on implementation of the EM curriculum program. It may be the case that Heather perceived that implementation of EM was the "correct way" to teach mathematics. Such a view would likely contribute to an inclination to adhere to the recommendations of curriculum materials.

Unlike Heather and Anne, who used a *Standards*-based curriculum program during their student teaching, Bridget was expected to use only the workbook component of a commercially-developed curriculum program. Bridget's visions for mathematics instruction, which were likely influenced by her experiences with *Standards*-based materials at the university, appeared to contribute to her dissatisfaction with the SBG worksheets and her decisions to adapt and use alternative resources. Recall that, in the design of several mathematics lessons during her internship, Bridget drew upon activities in the EM materials and from activities she remembered from her mathematics pedagogy course. In Bridget's case, teacher education coursework may have influenced her interpretations of the SBG curriculum program as well as her selection of resources for the design of supplemental activities.

Student Teachers' Content Knowledge and Confidence About Teaching Mathematics

The influence of teachers' conceptions of mathematics on classroom instruction has been widely documented. In the case of student teachers, Borko, Livingston, McCaleb, and Mauro (1988) found that differences in subject matter knowledge and confidence in that knowledge were associated with differences in student teachers' planning and teaching. Those teachers who had strong content knowledge and confidence in their knowledge were more responsive to students while teaching. Similarly, Kahan, Cooper, and Bethea (2003) found that student teachers' mathematical content knowledge affected their preparation and instruction across a wide variety of elements of teaching.

In their mathematics content course for elementary teachers, Anne and Bridget were considered by the course instructor to be two of the strongest mathematics students. Anne described herself as "a math person" and explained, "Math is a thing I was always good at. I was one of those students that it clicked for me. I always liked math." The following year, Heather also performed well in her mathematics course; however, she was not considered to be one of the strongest students mathematically. Moreover, her confidence in teaching mathematics appeared to be significantly lower than that of Anne and Bridget. Heather expressed that she was not confident in her ability to understand the topics or to teach elementary mathematics. She commented on her apprehension about teaching mathematics: "You never know if [the students] are going to get it, or if you are going to be able to explain it."

These differing levels of confidence in teaching mathematics and mathematical abilities may have contributed to Heather's, Anne's, and Bridget's use of their curriculum materials. For example, Heather was observed using her curriculum guide as a resource during most of our observations, holding and reading the book throughout her instruction. In contrast, Anne and Bridget did not use their teacher's guides or lesson notes while they taught. This difference may be related to the varying amounts of information provided in the three student teachers' materials. It may also be related to the student teachers' differing levels of confidence in teaching mathematics and mathematical content knowledge. Although it would be difficult, based on our data, to speculate about the primary influences on Heather's tendency to follow the curriculum program closely and make minimal adaptations to lessons, Anne's inclination to adapt lessons to increase the mathematical sophistication of lessons, and Bridget's decisions to supplement the SBG worksheets with exploratory activities, the student teachers' confidence about teaching mathematics appears to be one of several contributing factors.

School Context

There are many aspects of school context that influence teachers' work with curriculum materials and textbooks. Because our study took place in a state where a detailed curriculum framework specifies standards in four core content areas (including mathematics) and at a time when teachers faced increasing pressures from mandated state testing, we found it interesting to consider how the accountability status of each internship site might have impacted the student teachers' ways of using their curriculum materials.

Kauffman (2002) identified ways that local expectations about teachers' use of mathematics textbooks can be tied closely to school- and district-level implementation of accountability policies. In the case of two of the beginning teachers in his study, "Their principals and curriculum coordinators expect them to adapt and supplement the textbook materials regularly, using them as resources for teaching the state standards rather than relying on them to determine the curriculum" (p. 17). In contrast, two other beginning teachers perceived that "they are expected to use their textbook regularly. The materials themselves constitute the *de facto* curriculum. There is also an expectation that they supplement the materials, but in clearly defined ways and in a limited fashion" (p. 18). Student teachers also receive such messages about curriculum from authority figures, including their cooperating teachers. (See the next section for our discussion of cooperating teachers.)

Bridget's student teaching took place in a school that was identified as "low performing" on state tests. During the year of Bridget's student-teaching internship, as well as the previous year, the school's mathematics test scores were below the passing rate for both third and fifth grades. Bridget received strong messages from teachers and administrators about the importance of addressing the state curriculum objectives to prepare students for state tests. Bridget frequently adapted and supplemented the SBG worksheets that she felt did not adequately address the objectives of the state curriculum framework. The mismatch between the SBG worksheets and the mathematical goals of the state curriculum framework (as well as her personal instructional goals) likely contributed to Bridget's minimal use of the SBG curriculum materials.

Heather and Anne, on the other hand, were placed in a school that was labeled by the state as "Fully Accredited." Teachers at their school used a pacing guide that identified how each state standard was addressed in the EM program. As Heather's cooperating teacher pointed out, "More times than not, EM has a higher expectation than the [state curriculum framework]. We're meeting the [state curriculum framework] needs by using this curriculum." Because students at their school were successful in state mathematics tests and teachers and administrators were assured that the EM curriculum addressed the state curriculum standards, Heather and Anne were positioned to place greater trust in their curriculum programs than was Bridget. In Heather's case, the school's endorsement of the EM curriculum program was underscored by her cooperating teacher's support and by her prior experience with EM at the university.

For the student teachers in our study, alignment between curriculum programs, the expectations of their internship sites, and their own instructional goals appeared to impact their use of curriculum materials. The student teacher who experienced the greatest curricular alignment, Heather, attempted to adhere to the recommendations of her curriculum materials. The student teacher who experienced the least curricular alignment, Bridget, used her curriculum program minimally as she attempted to meet state objectives, satisfy her school's expectations, and fulfill her own goals for teaching mathematics.

Cooperating Teachers

An essential ingredient of a student-teaching experience is a mentor teacher's guidance (Britzman, 1991; Fairbanks, Freedman, & Kahn, 2000; Feiman-Nemser, 2001; Frykholm, 1998). In this section, we consider how the expectations, instructional practices, and mentoring styles of the cooperating teachers might have impacted the student teachers' use of curriculum materials.

Heather's efforts to follow the EM materials closely may have been influenced by the practices of her cooperating teacher. Ms Greene reported that she used the EM teacher's guide to structure mathematics lessons and suggested that the teacher's guide "has so many good questions so I always have [the guide] up there with me. They have some really good examples and stories ... and the book really does help." Heather observed Ms Greene's mathematics instruction for two weeks at the beginning of her internship. When Heather began teaching mathematics full-time, Ms Greene observed all of Heather's lessons and offered regular feedback. Ms Greene spoke to Heather frequently about the difficulties she and other teachers faced in learning how to pace EM lessons. The close relationship between Ms Greene and Heather, and Ms Greene's close adherence to the recommendations of the EM materials, likely influenced Heather's use of the materials and her focus on lesson-pacing.

Anne, on the other hand, worked with Ms Roy in a unique classroom situation in which each of the four teachers taught one-fourth of the students each day. This structure allowed Anne the opportunity to revise and adapt her lessons extensively as she taught each lesson four times. However, because Ms Roy and Ms Jones taught mathematics at the same time that Anne did, Anne's mathematics instruction was never directly observed by her cooperating teachers. Yet Anne's inclination to make adaptations to EM seemed to be supported by Ms Roy and Ms Jones. Their lunchtime conversations offered occasions for Anne to receive assistance in addressing problems she encountered during the lessons. Perhaps their conversations with Anne, encouraging her to modify tasks between each lesson iteration, influenced Anne's more adaptive use of EM. It may also be the case that the classroom structure, in which Anne taught her lessons on her own and unobserved, afforded Anne the freedom to make extensive adaptations to the content and organization of lessons.

Relative to Heather and Anne, Bridget received less guidance from her cooperating teacher regarding her mathematics lessons. Typically, Ms Barrett's guidance related to Bridget's classroom management strategies. Bridget offered that it might have been difficult for Ms Barrett to make suggestions about mathematical content or student learning because of her lack of familiarity with the kindergarten curriculum. (Ms Barrett had no prior experience teaching kindergarten.) With the limited curricular guidance from her cooperating teacher, Bridget turned to a range of alternative resources for instructional ideas.

Conclusions and Implications

Like Christou, Menon, and Philippou (Chapter 16) and Silver, Mills, Ghousseini, and Charalambous (Chapter 17), in this chapter we have discussed teachers' use of mathematics curriculum materials at a particular point on the professional continuum. We have offered preliminary information about how student teachers' use of curriculum materials compares to that of more experienced teachers. Whereas Remillard and Bryans (2004) found that the beginning teachers in their study tended to follow closely the recommendations of their curriculum materials, we found significant variation in curriculum use across our three student teachers – variation that is similar to that across the eight teachers in Remillard and Bryans's study. However, in contrast to the teachers in Remillard and Bryans's study, who drew upon their own instructional repertoires as they interpreted and used their curriculum materials, the student teachers in our study turned to their cooperating teachers, peers, teacher education experiences, and other textbooks and materials. This finding suggests that resources such as these may be critical supports, or safety nets, for student teachers when they use curriculum materials for mathematics instruction for the first time. The potential importance of such resources is underscored by Kauffman et al.'s (2002) portrayal of beginning teachers as "lost at sea" during their initial use of mathematics curriculum materials and textbooks.

We have also proposed and discussed five factors that may have worked together to influence the student teachers' ways of using their curriculum materials. Although we cannot claim to have identified the primary influences on the student teachers' use of their curriculum materials or the key factors that might explain other student teachers' curriculum use, our tentative set of factors can be used to inform the focus and design of future studies. The factors we discussed, and relationships among them, are promising candidates for further investigation of how and why student teachers develop particular ways of using curriculum materials. Understanding the personal and contextual factors that jointly shape teachers' initial use of mathematics curriculum materials may also help teacher educators to provide productive experiences for preservice teachers. Even those factors that are not easily adjusted within teacher preparation programs deserve awareness and attention from those involved in student teachers' experiences.

Drawing on the five factors we have proposed, we put forth the following questions for consideration by researchers and teacher educators:

1. How do *characteristics of mathematics curriculum materials* affect student teachers' initial teaching experiences? How might teacher education activities prepare student teachers to read and interpret the suggestions of different kinds of mathematics curriculum materials and textbooks?
2. How might *preservice teacher education coursework* prepare student teachers to use a variety of curriculum materials and frameworks for mathematics instruction? How might preservice teacher education experiences prepare teachers to identify and use human and material resources available for instructional support?
3. What are the relationships between *mathematical content knowledge and confidence* and student teachers' use of curriculum materials? How might teacher education activities prepare teachers to use curriculum materials for their own learning of mathematics and to increase their confidence in teaching mathematics?
4. How do *policy mandates for state testing and curriculum frameworks* impact student teachers' initial experiences using mathematics curriculum materials for instruction? What can teacher educators do to prepare teachers to engage in productive relationships with state curriculum frameworks?
5. What is the influence of *cooperating teachers* on student teachers' use of curriculum materials? How might teacher educators collaborate with cooperating teachers to support student teachers' initial interactions with mathematics curriculum materials?

Although our study suggested a number of important factors that may influence student teachers' use of curriculum materials, there are additional factors that we have not addressed. For example, in their review of research on learning to teach, Wideen, Mayer-Smith, and Moon (1998) called for more focused attention on how *all* players affect the landscape and process of learning to teach, including supervising teachers, teacher educators, students, and parents themselves. The effects of parents on teachers' use of curriculum materials (Gellert, 2005; Lubienski, 2004) and the role of university supervisors are certainly important considerations (Frykholm, 1998). In addition, longitudinal studies of teachers – from preservice experiences to the early years of teaching – are greatly needed. What factors seem to have the greatest impact on teachers' use of curriculum materials as they gain experience? Investigating these questions will not only provide clearer understandings about teachers and teaching, but might also suggest ways that preservice coursework and internship experiences can be adjusted to support teachers' early encounters with mathematics curriculum materials in the classroom. Because student teachers' experiences have the potential to influence the nature of subsequent professional learning, we must identify and provide supports for teachers' initial curriculum use so that productive interactions with curriculum materials can continue to develop in the future.

Acknowledgments

The work reported in this chapter was funded in part by the National Science Foundation under Grant Number 9983393. Any opinions, findings, and conclusions or recommendations expressed in this publication are those of the authors and do not necessarily reflect the views of the National Science Foundation. The authors wish to thank the editors and other chapter authors of this volume and the members of the mathematics education group at Virginia Tech for their helpful feedback on several previous drafts of this chapter.

Note

1. All names for teachers, schools, and counties are pseudonyms.

References

Ball, D. L., & Feiman-Nemser, S. (1988). Using textbooks and teachers' guides: A dilemma for beginning teachers and teacher educators. *Curriculum Inquiry, 18*(4), 401–423.

Behm, S. L., & Lloyd, G. M. (2008). Piloting the mandated curriculum and adapting an alternative textbook: A student teacher's varying relationships with mathematics curriculum materials. *Manuscript submitted for review.*

Berliner, D. C. (1986). In search of the expert pedagogue. *Educational Researcher, 15*(7), 5–13.

Borko, H., Livingston, C., McCaleb, J., & Mauro, L. (1988). Student teachers' planning and post-lesson reflections: Patterns and implications for teacher preparation. In J. Calderhead (Ed.), *Teachers' professional learning* (pp. 65–83). London: Falmer Press.

Britzman, D. P. (1991). *Practice makes practice: A critical study of learning to teach.* Albany, NY: SUNY Press.

Corcoran, T. (2003). *The use of research evidence in instructional improvement.* Philadelphia, PA: Consortium for Policy Research in Education (CPRE Policy Brief No RB 40).

Ebby, C. B. (2000). Learning to teach mathematics differently: The interaction between coursework and fieldwork for preservice teachers. *Journal of Mathematics Teacher Education, 3*, 69–97.

Fairbanks, C. M., Freedman, D., & Kahn, C. (2000). The role of effective mentors in learning to teach. *Journal of Teacher Education, 51*, 102–112.

Feiman-Nemser, S. (1983). Learning to teach. In L. Shulman & G. Sykes (Eds.), *Handbook of teaching and policy* (pp. 150–170). New York, NY: Longman.

Feiman-Nemser, S. (2001). Helping novices learn to teach: Lessons from an exemplary support teacher. *Journal of Teacher Education, 52*(1), 17–30.

Feiman-Nemser, S., & Buchmann, M. (1985). Pitfalls of experience in teacher preparation. *Teachers College Record, 87*(1), 53–65.

Fennell, F., Ferrini-Mundy, J., Ginsburg, H. P., Greenes, C., Murphy, S., & Tate, W. (1999). *Mathematics: The path to math success.* Parsippany, NJ: Silver Burdett Ginn.

Frykholm, J. A. (1998). Beyond supervision: Learning to teach mathematics in community. *Teaching and Teacher Education, 14*(3), 305–322.

Gellert, U. (2005). Parents: Support or obstacle for curriculum innovation? *Journal of Curriculum Studies, 37*(3), 313–328.

Guyton, E., & McIntyre, D. J. (1990). Student teaching and school experiences. In W. R. Houston (Ed.), *Handbook of research on teacher education* (pp. 514–534). New York, NY: Macmillan.

Hjalmarson, M. (2005). Purposes for mathematics curriculum: Pre-service teachers' perspectives. In G. M. Lloyd, M. R. Wilson, J. L. M. Wilkins & S. L. Behm (Eds.), *Proceedings of the 27th Annual Meeting of the North American Chapter of the International Group for the Psychology of Mathematics Education*. Eugene, OR: All Academic.

Kahan, J. A., Cooper, D. A., & Bethea, K. A. (2003). The role of mathematics teachers' content knowledge in their teaching: A framework for research applied to a study of student teachers. *Journal of Mathematics Teacher Education, 6*, 223–252.

Kauffman, D. (2002). *A search for support: Beginning elementary teachers' use of mathematics curriculum materials.* Paper presented at the Annual Meeting of the American Educational Research Association, New Orleans, LA.

Kauffman, D., Johnson, S. M., Kardos, S. M., Liu, E., & Peske, H. G. (2002). "Lost at sea": New teachers' experiences with curriculum and assessment. *Teachers College Record, 104*(2), 273–300.

Lloyd, G. M. (2006). Using K-12 mathematics curriculum materials in preservice teacher education: Rationale, strategies, and teachers' experiences. In K. Lynch-Davis & R. Rider (Eds.), *The work of mathematics teacher educators: Continuing the conversation, AMTE Monograph 3* (pp. 11–28). San Diego, CA: Association of Mathematics Teacher Educators.

Lloyd, G. M. (2007). Strategic compromise: A student teacher's design of kindergarten mathematics instruction in a high-stakes testing climate. *Journal of Teacher Education, 58*(4), 328–347.

Lloyd, G. M. (2008). Curriculum use while learning to teach: One student teacher's appropriation of mathematics curriculum materials. *Journal for Research in Mathematics Education, 39*(1), 63–94.

Lloyd, G. M., & Behm, S. L. (2005). Preservice elementary teachers' analysis of mathematics instructional materials. *Action in Teacher Education, 26*(4), 48–62.

Lubienski, S. T. (2004). Traditional or *Standards*-based mathematics? The choices of students and parents in one district. *Journal of Curriculum and Supervision, 19*(4), 338–365.

National Council of Teachers of Mathematics. (1989). *Curriculum and evaluation standards for school mathematics.* Reston, VA: Author.

Raymond, A. M. (1997). Inconsistency between a beginning elementary school teacher's mathematics beliefs and teaching practice. *Journal for Research in Mathematics Education, 28*(5), 550–576.

Remillard, J. T. (2005). Examining key concepts in research on teachers' use of mathematics curricula. *Review of Educational Research, 75*(2), 211–246.

Remillard, J. T., & Bryans, M. B. (2004). Teachers' orientations toward mathematics curriculum materials: Implications for teacher learning. *Journal for Research in Mathematics Education, 35*(5), 352–388.

Steele, D. F. (2001). The interfacing of preservice and inservice experiences of reform-based teaching: A longitudinal study. *Journal of Mathematics Teacher Education, 4*, 139–172.

Steffy, B. E., Wolfe, M. P., Pasch, S. H., & Enz, B. J. (2000). *Life cycle of the career teacher.* Thousand Oaks, CA: Sage.

Tarr, J. E., & Papick, I. J. (2004). Collaborative efforts to improve the mathematical preparation of middle grades mathematics teachers. In T. Watanabe & D. R. Thompson (Eds.), *The work of mathematics teacher educators: Exchanging ideas for effective practice, AMTE Monograph 1* (pp. 19–34). San Diego, CA: AMTE.

University of Chicago School Mathematics Project. (2001). *Kindergarten Everyday Mathematics teacher's guide to activities.* Chicago, IL: SRA/McGraw-Hill.

Van Zoest, L. R., & Bohl, J. V. (2002). The role of reform curricular materials in an internship: The case of Alice and Gregory. *Journal of Mathematics Teacher Education, 5*, 265–288.

Wideen, M., Mayer-Smith, J., & Moon, B. (1998). A critical analysis of the research on learning to teach: Making the case for an ecological perspective on inquiry. *Review of Educational Research, 68*(2), 130–178.

Zeichner, K. M., & Tabachnick, B. R. (1981). Are the effects of university teacher education washed out by school experiences? *Journal of Teacher Education, 32*, 7–11.

16

Beginning Teachers' Concerns Regarding the Adoption of New Mathematics Curriculum Materials

Constantinos Christou, Maria Eliophotou Menon, and George Philippou

Research suggests that beginning teachers face serious problems in the areas of teaching and learning in the first few years following their entry into the profession (Bullough, 1992; Calderhead & Robson, 1991). Given that the problems faced by beginning teachers have been linked to job dissatisfaction and turnover, it is important to examine the nature of these problems in an attempt to provide support and guidance to this group. Through this examination, the concerns of beginning teachers can be identified, making it possible to address potential sources of anxiety and dissatisfaction.

The introduction of innovations in the first years of teaching presents an additional challenge for beginning teachers who struggle to cope with the demands of their new positions. Without proper support, beginning teachers may regard an innovation as an additional burden that they are forced to take on. Experienced teachers may also resist a proposed change, especially when they are not convinced that adoption of the innovation will result in significant benefits for themselves and their students (Thompson, 1992). Research suggests that the conceptions people have regarding an innovation may determine the degree of its success to a greater extent than its objective features (Hall & Hord, 2001; van den Berg, 1993).

In Cyprus, recent efforts to reform school mathematics were initiated in the mid-1990s. The Committee of Primary Mathematics Education urged that school mathematics programs be revised and updated to reflect contemporary views and ideas, such as those put forth in the *Standards* (National Council of Teachers of Mathematics [NCTM], 1989). The Committee also called for mathematics curriculum materials (defined here as the textbooks, teachers' guides, and other printed materials that describe the content and the methods of its communication to students) to develop students' mathematical power, feature relevant applications, and foster active student involvement. The reformed national curriculum reached the classroom in the form of new textbooks that teachers were expected to use, without previous systematic professional preparation.

Given the key role of the teacher in the successful implementation of any innovation, a few years after the introduction of the new mathematics curriculum materials we investigated the degree to which Cypriot teachers in general, and beginning teachers in particular, had accepted and felt confident in their ability to use the new materials. We focused on the types of concerns teachers had regarding the innovation, teachers' appraisals of the potential effectiveness of the new materials, and possible differences between beginning and experienced teachers. In this chapter we present the theoretical perspectives of the study by discussing change and reform in mathematics education and its relationship to teacher attitudinal and behavioral variables in general, and to innovation-related concerns in particular. We then focus on concerns that have been reported in research on beginning teachers. A description of the method and findings of the study follows. Finally, we draw conclusions and discuss implications for research and practice.

Theoretical Background

Change in Mathematics Education

In the 1980s, the publication of reports in different countries focused attention on an impending crisis in mathematics and science (e.g., *An Agenda for Action*, NCTM, 1980; *Mathematics Counts*, Cockcroft, 1982). In accordance with the new vision put forward by these publications and subsequent ones (*Curriculum and Evaluation Standards for School Mathematics*, NCTM, 1989; *Professional Standards for Teaching Mathematics*, NCTM, 1991), several local and national reform efforts were initiated in many countries, with the aim of redesigning mathematics curriculum materials in the light of new research findings.

Teachers' Responses to the New Textbooks

Recent studies in mathematics education have placed a great deal of responsibility for the success of educational improvement on the teacher (Christou, Eliophotou-Menon, & Philippou, 2004). In this context, emphasis is placed on mathematical processes such as problem-solving and reasoning, communication and discourse about mathematical topics, and connections within and across content areas. Many of these conceptions of mathematics teaching and learning are new to the typical classroom teacher, and require change at multiple levels to make them a reality (Nelson, 1997; Senger, 1999). Spillane (1999) argued that "the new ideas about practice that teachers encounter through the policy and professional sectors can only work in and through teachers' existing knowledge and beliefs" (p. 169). He introduced the term *zone of enactment* to refer to "the space in which [teachers] make sense of, and operationalize for their own practice, the ideas advanced by reformers ... Differences in teachers' enactment zones are key in understanding their efforts to change the core of mathematics instruction" (p. 159). Research has recently focused attention on teachers' conceptions of mathematics and on their beliefs about the teaching and learning of the subject. The implementation of new curriculum materials in the classroom could create disjunctions between teachers' former knowledge and practice, which require resolution (Romberg, 1997). Such disjunctions can be expected to increase teachers' problems in the implementation of the innovation and lead some teachers to the point of anxiety and frustration.

Innovative curriculum programs argue that more emphasis should be placed on guidance of learning rather than transmission of knowledge, and on the promotion of constructive rather than receptive learning on the part of the students (van den Berg, 2002). Based on the teacher's conception of his or her role, such demands may be experienced in different ways, as limiting and problematic, or as challenging and enriching. The reactions of teachers to externally imposed expectations and changes of internal conditions can often be seen as ambiguous, filled with emotion, and at times even contradictory (Lloyd, 1999). In the light of the current "intensification of the teaching profession" and the increased demands imposed by new curriculum materials, it becomes vital to maintain one's professional identity. Externally imposed decisions may diminish teachers' professionalism and have a negative impact on effectiveness and work ethics (van den Berg, 2002). As long as teachers have worries and feel threatened by the demands of new visions of mathematics teaching, all innovations will continue to be at risk (Vandenberghe, 2002).

Teachers' Concerns

Concerns encompass thoughts, feelings, worries, and reactions that individuals develop in relation to a new program or innovation that is relevant to their daily job (Hall & Hord, 2001). The concept of "concerns" and the associated theoretical framework date back to the late 1960s. In a pioneer study, Fuller (1969) put forward a classification of teachers' concerns consisting of three consecutive stages: self, task, and impact concerns. *Self concerns* relate to the teachers' own anxiety about their ability to perform in the school environment; *task concerns* relate to the daily duties of a teaching job, especially in relation to a number of limitations such as the teaching of large numbers of students and the lack of resources, and *impact concerns* refer to the teachers' apprehension about student outcomes. According to McKinney, Sexton, and Meyerson (1999), individuals move through stages of implementation in a developmental pattern. They first focus on self-stage concerns, then move to task-stage concerns, and finally reach the impact stage.

Fuller's framework has provided the basis for many studies, some of which have focused on concerns regarding the adoption of educational innovations. In Fuller's framework, the stages of concerns include the teachers' state of perceived readiness to cope with new conditions in their work and measure their appraisals of the expected outcomes in relation to student learning. Teachers' concerns may exert powerful influence on the implementation of new curriculum materials and determine the type of assistance that teachers may need during the adoption process. Previous studies have shown that the conceptions of those involved in innovations are of major importance for the success of the process (Lloyd, 2002). Thus, it is useful for administrators and educators to have a picture of teachers' concerns in general, and of beginning teachers' concerns in particular, both before and during the implementation phase of an innovation (Fullan, 1999).

Beginning Teachers' Concerns

Beginning teachers are confronted with two major issues when they start teaching. On the one hand, they feel relief, freedom, and enthusiasm as they realize their goal of becoming teachers. On the other hand, there are concerns associated with becoming a member of the profession (Huberman, 1992); being accepted by peers, administrators, students and parents; being immersed in the school culture; and settling into teaching. Hence, teachers' behaviors, values, and volition to act may be enhanced or inhibited during their early career. The concerns of beginning teachers about new curriculum materials may determine whether they persist with the innovation or withdraw from the teaching of mathematics. Consequently, the identification of these concerns can assist mathematics teacher educators in improving preservice and inservice teacher education programs.

With regard to teachers' emotional responses to educational change, Hargreaves (2005) argued that "age has an impact on how teachers respond to educational change [...] aging is not just a process of chronological accumulation [...] people tend to move through life in stages and passages" (p. 967). These stages may exhibit certain distinctive characteristics, but teachers' careers and lives vary among different kinds of teachers and across cultures and times. Beginning teachers strive to "find their feet as professionals and people" (p. 970), establish their basic confidence and competence, and gain acceptance and respect from students and colleagues. In this respect, studies focusing on concerns that beginning teachers have with respect to change and innovation are indispensable. The first year of teaching can come with a reality shock as the novice teacher is faced with all the role demands and expectations encountered by experienced teachers (Veenman, 1984). Recent research findings (Christou et al., 2004) indicate that teachers who completed their first year of teaching with a high sense of teacher efficacy experienced greater job satisfaction, had a more positive reaction to teaching, and exhibited less stress. Confident novices gave higher ratings to the adequacy of support they had received than those who ended their year with a shakier sense of their own competence and a less optimistic view of what teachers could accomplish. Highly efficacious beginners gave higher ratings to the quality of their preparation and lower ratings to the difficulty of teaching, in contrast to their low-efficacy counterparts.

Mathematics curriculum materials, particularly textbooks and teacher's guides, are central to the work of beginning teachers (Kauffman, Johnson, Kardos, Liu, & Peske, 2002); they are used in most classrooms and address the central activities of students and teachers, making them a "concrete and daily" part of the classroom with a "uniquely intimate connection to teaching" (Ball & Cohen, 1996). It appears that teachers look to their curriculum materials for support in planning and delivering instruction, but they vary widely in their concerns about the materials and the extent to which they feel supported by them.

The literature on the first years of teaching describes a time of extreme challenge and rapid learning (Wideen, Mayer-Smith, & Moon, 1998). Curriculum decisions are among the many challenges new teachers face; they must determine what to teach and how to teach it, often by themselves through trial and error (Kauffman et al., 2002). Making these decisions in mathematics may be especially hard for elementary school teachers, who are typically generalists, teaching several subjects.

The Present Study

The Context

The educational system in Cyprus can be characterized as centralized in the sense that important decisions are made at the level of the Ministry of Education. There are about 400 public primary schools and more than 20 private schools; the former are mostly homogeneous in terms of student language, religion, and sociohistorical background.

Teachers participate in the process of curriculum decision-making through Teacher Union representatives, who represent the teachers in all relevant meetings and discussions. Practicing teachers are informed of new policies through annual day-long seminars delivered by inspectors (higher-rank educators promoted among teachers on the basis of qualifications, experience and ability, and assigned the task of guiding and evaluating teachers). These seminars, however, cannot address wider theoretical and practical issues involved in extensive curriculum change, mainly due to time shortage and the size of the audience.

In Cyprus, the teaching profession is a high-status occupation. Teachers are relatively well paid; they receive the same pay and benefits as most of the other degree-mandatory government positions. Since 1996, all newly appointed teachers are university graduates. The Department of Education is responsible for teacher education, and is one of the most popular destinations for high school students applying for university studies, resulting in strong competition among prospective students. The program of studies of the Department of Education aspires to educate teachers along the social constructivist paradigm; its mathematics education section comprises mathematics content and methods courses as well as two phases of field work, all focusing on developing understanding through using problem-solving activities and group work.

During the early 1990s, the Committee of Primary Mathematics Education designed a new mathematics curriculum program on the basis of the advice of several specialists who adopted the main recommendations of the *Standards* (NCTM, 1989). A major goal was to present thought-provoking situations that involve challenging themes through emphasis on the following: problem-solving and reasoning, communication and discourse related to mathematical topics, use of manipulatives and group work, and new elementary school content (e.g., number sense, algebra, discrete mathematics, probability, and spatial sense). Teachers are urged to see themselves as guides, listeners, and observers rather than as authorities and answer-givers. Students are encouraged to tackle diverse problems, which reflect real-life situations and involve their creative interest, whereas less emphasis is placed on rote memorization and procedure-driven computation (NCTM, 1989). Meaning and understanding are major goals to be achieved with the use of pictures, objects, graphs, and language in an attempt to help the student visualize abstract ideas. A specially developed mathematics textbook series was introduced in the course of six successive years, starting from Grade 1 in 1995, proceeding to Grade 2 in the next year, and so on until 2000, when it covered all primary grades. As a consequence, at the time the study took place, school teachers had different years of experience in teaching with the new curriculum materials. However, previous research showed that using novel curriculum materials for longer periods of time was not a decisive factor in explaining the differences in teachers' concerns (Christou et al., 2004).

The change in the teaching of mathematics embodied in the new curriculum materials is considered one of the most important innovations in primary education in Cyprus in the last 30 years. For the typical classroom teacher, most of the proposed developments represent major departures from standard practices. Yet teachers were expected to implement the new textbooks without substantial professional development. The policy-makers failed to realize the importance of wide-ranging teacher preparation, as they conceived of change as an "event" rather than a "process" (Hall & Hord, 2001); this is clearly reflected in the way they chose to inform and educate teachers regarding the innovation. Specifically, teachers had two-day professional development workshops, after which they were left to implement the curriculum materials in the ways they judged most appropriate. This "event mentality" had serious consequences for teachers' morale and efforts; the pressure to bring about change quickly meant that there was little time to learn about and come to understand the new meanings, and abandon previous practices. Not surprisingly, the innovation generated mixed reactions among teachers and parents alike; they expressed contradictory appraisals, ranging from strong criticism to mild acceptance (Christou et al., 2004). The main complaint on the part of the teachers concerned their limited and inappropriate preparation for meeting the new demands associated with the new curriculum materials.

Aims of the Study

The literature on teachers' use of curriculum materials typically treats curriculum materials as potential sources for teaching content and practice, with no differentiation made between the needs of beginning and experienced teachers. Given the challenges new teachers face in their work, curriculum materials may lead them to develop important concerns about the necessity of the innovation. Thus, in addition to concerns, this study investigated the extent to which teachers considered the new materials as adequate sources for supporting new forms of teaching. The purpose of this study was twofold: first, to identify and examine the concerns that beginning teachers (i.e., teachers with less than two years of experience) expressed about the new mathematics curriculum materials in comparison to concerns of more experienced teachers; and second, to identify the extent to which beginning teachers felt supported by the new textbooks. Thus, the first purpose of the study addresses teachers' concerns and is expected to provide information on the degree to which teachers feel capable of effectively implementing the approaches suggested by the new textbooks. The second purpose of the study addresses an important theme in educational research, which views textbooks as potentially educative for teachers (Ball & Cohen, 1996).

To this end, we investigated teachers' conceptions about the support they received from the new materials along three components: the ease of use of the textbooks (ease of use), the teachers' perceived ability to effectively use the textbooks (efficacy), and the extent to which teachers felt comfortable using the textbooks (anxiety). This study focuses on teachers' experiences and appraisals as they face the task of teaching with new mathematics curriculum materials on a regular basis; we examine in particular the concerns and feelings of teachers of different "ages," and particularly of beginning teachers. The first part of this chapter, which reflects the first aim of the study, analyzes data from 655 teachers about the concerns they exhibited in response to new situations or demands emerging from the adoption of new mathematics curriculum materials. Two research questions were addressed for this purpose:

1. What type of concerns do novice teachers have regarding the innovation in mathematics education associated with the new mathematics textbooks?
2. How do beginning teachers' concerns differ from the concerns of teachers with more than two years of experience in teaching mathematics?

The second part refers to the second aim of the study, and addresses beginning teachers' conceptions about the support they have received from the textbooks they were asked to use.

Research Method

Participants

The participants in this study included 655 teachers from 106 elementary schools, which were selected on the basis of size, location and demographic characteristics. Table 16.1 presents the teachers involved in the study by years of experience and gender; the numbers shown are representative of the population of teachers in Cyprus. Specifically, the sample included four groups of teachers dispersed across the whole range of teaching experience. The relative size of the

Table 16.1 Teacher Participants by Years of Experience and Gender

Years of Experience	1–2	3–10	11–20	>20	Total
Male	10	48	26	71	155
Female	70	229	108	93	500
Total	80	277	134	164	655

female and male teachers' samples reflect the actual proportion of teachers in Cyprus.

Instruments

Data were collected through a self-report questionnaire that was administered at the end of 1999–2000 school year. The questionnaire consisted of two parts. The first part was constructed in such a way as to reflect the Stages of Concern Questionnaire (SoCQ) (Hall & Hord, 2001), and addressed the first aim of the study. Specifically, this part of the questionnaire provided the means for assessing concerns along the following seven stages: Awareness, Informational, Personal, Management, Consequences, Collaboration, and Refocusing. A brief description of each stage is given below.

> *Awareness (stage 0)*: Teachers feel that they have little knowledge of the innovation and have no interest in taking any action.

> *Informational (stage 1)*: Teachers express concerns regarding the nature of the innovation and the requirements for its implementation. At this stage, teachers usually show their willingness to learn more about the specific innovation or reform.

> *Personal (stage 2)*: Teachers focus on the impact the innovation will have on them. They exhibit concerns about how the use of the innovation will affect them on a personal level. They may be concerned about their own time limitations and the changes they will be expected to make.

> *Management (stage 3)*: Teachers express concern over the organization and details of implementation, and the overcoming of difficulties. Time requirements are among the prime management factors.

> *Consequences (stage 4)*: Teacher concerns centre upon effects on student learning. If positive effects are observed, teachers are likely to continue to work on the implementation of the reform.

> *Collaboration (stage 5)*: Teachers express an interest in sharing their ideas and experiences from the implementation of the reform with their colleagues.

> *Refocusing (stage 6)*: Teachers proceed to evaluate the innovation and make suggestions for continued improvements, or consider alternate ideas that would work even better.

The stages of concerns used in the study do not correspond exactly to the original American and Dutch–Belgian stages; adaptations were deemed necessary due to the conditions and context of Cyprus education, and the specific subject domain (mathematics). The first obvious difference between the questionnaires developed in the United States and Europe and the questionnaire used in the present study was the elimination of stage zero. We have not included the stage of awareness because, by the time the study was conducted, all participants were acquainted with the new mathematics curriculum materials – in fact, they had all been involved in the implementation of the new textbooks. Moreover, the present questionnaire included 27 items, whereas the American and the Dutch–Belgian questionnaires involved 35 and 52 items, respectively. Finally, the number and sequence of items within each stage as well as their wording were different to suit the needs of the mathematics domain in which the questionnaire was applied. Teachers' ratings on the 27 items of the questionnaire were made on a 9-point scale ranging from 1 (strongly disagree) to 9 (strongly agree), enabling us to grasp in a more concise way the teachers' concerns; all responses were recoded so that greater numbers indicated stronger agreement.

We piloted the questionnaire in an attempt to retain the structure of the stages of concerns as they were proposed by Hall and Hord (2001). One hundred teachers participated in the pilot phase. Most provided suggestions for rephrasing some statements and mentioned possible teachers' misunderstandings in relation to the meaning of some of the statements. During the pilot phases, factor analysis was conducted to validate the stages of concern. A minimum loading of 0.30 was consistently required for the inclusion of a statement within a particular factor. The six-factor solution produced the most satisfactory description of the underlying factor structure. Factor 1 closely corresponded to the "information" phase of the innovation in the original questionnaire. Factor 2 was described as "personal" and factor 3 was interpreted as "management." Factor 4 closely resembled the stage "collaboration," whereas factors 5 and 6 were interpreted as the "consequences" and "refocusing" dimensions, respectively. The items, the means of teachers' responses, and the loadings of the items on each factor are presented in Table 16.2.

To address the second aim of the study, we developed the second part of the questionnaire, which consisted of nine items. These items were intended to identify teachers' conceptions about the support they had received from the new curriculum materials. An important factor influencing teachers' concerns about the new mathematics curriculum materials was support. The perceived support is considered in three themes that emerged from a synthesis of previous studies (Kauffmann et al., 2002): (a) ease of use, (b) efficacy, and (c) anxiety. Specifically, three items aim at eliciting teachers' conceptions about the *ease of use* of the new curriculum materials (ease of use), three items aim at capturing teachers' concerns and conceptions regarding the instructional effectiveness of the materials (efficacy), and three items aim at measuring teachers' anxiety as a result of the adoption of the materials (anxiety). Altogether, these three themes provide a composite picture of support for each teacher.

Analysis of Data

Data were analyzed using the SPSS 12.0 statistical package. In order to answer the questions related to the first aim of the study, we used Multivariate Analysis

Table 16.2 The Means of the Items in the Questionnaire by Years of Experience and the Loadings of the Items on Each Factor

Concerns	Means by Years of Experience			
	1–2	3–10	11–20	>20
Information	6.49	6.74	6.69	7.14
1. I have very good knowledge of the targeted mathematics outcomes for the class I teach. (0.61)*	7.35	7.74	7.72	7.79
2. I know the content of the new books for the classes that I have taught. (0.59)	8.22	8.38	8.19	8.20
3. I am familiar with the material covered in the new books for the classes I have not yet taught. (0.48)	4.35	4.33	4.48	5.69
4. I am aware of the changes associated with the new books in the mathematics curriculum. (0.47)	6.18	6.33	6.46	6.77
5. I was well informed about the philosophy of the new books at inspector conferences. (0.35)	3.26	4.63	4.67	3.97
6. The training seminars held cover the needs of teachers regarding teaching with the new books. (0.33)	4.53	3.28	3.47	3.07
Personal	6.22	6.48	6.41	6.45
1. The new books require the use of methods that I am sufficiently familiar with. (0.58)	7.30	7.01	7.00	7.12
2. I have no difficulty with the knowledge required by the new mathematics books. (0.49)	7.38	7.16	7.15	7.37
3. I personally make use of all the activities in the book. (0.49)	6.04	8.29	6.01	6.38
4. My role in the class has changed with the introduction of the new books. (0.45)	5.29	5.54	5.67	5.66
Management	5.10	4.93	4.63	4.62
1. The new books have reduced pupils' homework. (0.61)	4.92	4.66	4.46	4.35
2. The structure of the new books allows me to follow the progress of each pupil. (0.45)	4.93	5.16	4.78	5.14
3. For the teaching of some subjects, it is necessary to use equipment and resources that are not available at my school. (0.44)	4.28	4.50	4.63	4.77
4. I can organize my teaching with the new books so as to achieve the set aims. (0.35)	7.23	7.29	7.00	7.43
Collaboration	5.12	5.61	5.69	5.79
1. There is cooperation between teachers and parents for the utilization of the new books. (0.62)	3.44	4.25	459	4.25
2. I often discuss questions relating to the new books with my colleagues. (−0.43)	6.19	7.10	7.16	7.10
3. The frequent communication with the headmaster concerning the new books is useful. (0.38)	6.03	5.81	5.92	6.43
4. The visits of the inspector help improve my teaching of mathematics. (0.30)	4.48	3.61	3.64	3.72

Consequences				
1. I believe that the new books introduce major changes in the teaching of mathematics. (0.57)	6.25	6.037	5.75	5.88
2. The introduction of the new textbooks is not a useless innovation in primary education	6.64	7.07	6.86	6.82
mathematics. (−0.51)	8.82	7.70	7.63	7.79
3. The new books meet the needs of all pupils. (0.45)	4.83	4.34	3.97	4.64
Refocusing				
1. The new books place a lot of emphasis on investigation. (0.78)	5.82	6.02	5.93	5.98
2. I submit my proposals regarding the improvement of the new books to the appropriate officials. (0.59)	6.86	7.30	7.40	7.22
3. Pupils acquire the knowledge and skills expected of them. (0.53)	4.41	4.91	5.13	5.51
4. The knowledge acquired by the pupils through the new books is superficial. (−0.44)	5.81	5.63	5.78	5.65
5. The various activities included in the book finally function at the expense of practice in the four	3.86	4.30	4.22	3.80
operations. (-.33)	5.14	6.17	6.40	5.98
6. The new books place too much emphasis on problem solving. (−0.31)	5.90	5.76	5.99	6.04

Notes

*The numbers in parenthesis indicate the loadings of each item to its respective factor.

of Variance (MANOVA), because there were several dependent variables. We conducted MANOVA with the teachers' "years of experience" as the independent variable and the factors corresponding to the six stages of teachers' concerns as the dependent variables. In the same way, MANOVA was used to address the second purpose of the study, with "years of experience" as the independent variable and factors reflecting "ease of use," "efficacy," and "anxiety" as the dependent variables. Finally, for the post hoc analysis of the data, Tukey's HSD test was conducted to compare all different combinations between the "years of experience" groups in an attempt to obtain statistically significant differences.

Findings

Before addressing the questions of the study, we examine the Cronbach alphas for the six scales that represent the different stages of concern and the three scales that represent the teachers' conceptions about the support they received from the new materials. The Cronbach alphas for all stages were sufficiently high for the total sample of teachers involved in the study. The values of the alphas indicate that the instrument has acceptable reliabilities for the sample of the study. The Cronbach alphas for the last stages are relatively low ($\alpha_{collaboration} = 0.70$, $\alpha_{refocus} = 0.65$, and $\alpha_{consequence} = 0.73$), whereas the alphas for the management stage and the first two stages are considerably higher ($\alpha_{management} = 0.78$, $\alpha_{information} = 0.80$, and $\alpha_{personal} = 0.82$). The Cronbach alphas for the factors of ease of use, efficacy, and anxiety were also high, and comparable with those reflecting the stages of concern ($a_{ease\ of\ use} = 0.70$; $a_{efficacy} = 0.65$; $a_{anxiety} = 0.73$).

Research Question 1: Teachers' Concerns about the Implementation of the New Materials

BEGINNING TEACHERS' CONCERNS

The mean responses of the beginning teachers to each sub-scale of the SoCQ questionnaire (information, personal, management, consequences, collaboration, refocusing) appear in Table 16.2. The highest means occurred in the information, personal, and consequences concerns ($\overline{X}_{information} = 6.49$, $\overline{X}_{personal} = 6.22$, and $\overline{X}_{consequences} = 6.25$). This indicates that novice teachers at this implementation stage perceived themselves as relatively well acquainted with the philosophy and the objectives of the new mathematics textbooks. More importantly, they reported that they had the personal abilities required for the new curriculum materials, and believed that the innovation would have positive outcomes on students' learning. Novice teachers reported that they were familiar with the content and the methods required for the implementation of the innovation ($\overline{X} = 8.22$, $\overline{X} = 7.30$, respectively). Both the information and the personal stages describe the self-concerns of teachers about the new curriculum materials; the means in these two factors were high, indicating that, contrary to expectations, novice teachers felt well informed and confident in teaching mathematics with the new textbooks. In addition, the high value of the consequence factor suggested that beginning teachers did not have, at this point of the innovation, any serious concern about the impact of the textbooks on students' performance in mathematics. On the contrary, they reported that the new textbooks were useful for primary school students (see Table 16.2, $\overline{X} = 8.82$).

The fact that teachers had low concerns regarding the impact of the curriculum materials on students' learning could be explained, at least partially, by the lower values of the management and collaboration means (see Table 16.3). This might be an indication that teachers were more concerned about how to accomplish objectives, follow the progress of each student, get materials together, cover the content of mathematics in the set time limits, and establish themselves as teachers in the educational community. The concerns of beginning teachers about the management factor, as well as about their collaboration with parents, colleagues, and supervisors, support other research findings that suggest that management factors are among the primary factors that create skepticism among teachers in general (Christou et al., 2004). As expected, novice teachers have concerns associated with the process of becoming members of the teaching community (Huberman, 1992). The results suggest that teachers, at this point of the innovation, had fewer concerns about the impact of the innovation on students' performance in mathematics, and more on ways of dealing with daily instructional practices.

The refocusing factor is related to teachers' concerns regarding the evaluation of the innovation. The moderate mean on refocusing ($\overline{X} = 5.83$; see Table 16.3) indicates that novice teachers may not have clear views and new ideas regarding the improvement of the innovation; moreover, the majority do not have real concerns about the evaluation of the textbooks, the specific emphases placed on different subjects, and possible alterations in the teaching materials (see Table 16.2 for mean values of items on refocusing). However, the concerns of beginning teachers cannot be viewed in isolation from the concerns of experienced teachers. A more meaningful picture of beginning teachers' concerns about the new textbooks can be gained by comparing their concerns with those of experienced teachers. In the following section, we compare the concerns of beginning teachers about the new curriculum materials with the respective concerns of experienced teachers, by age or stage of career.

CONCERNS OF BEGINNING AND EXPERIENCED TEACHERS

Previous research suggests that years of teaching experience and the teachers' stage of career affect the way in which they respond to innovations (Hargreaves, 2005). To examine this hypothesis, multivariate analysis of variance was applied with the six stages of concerns used as dependent variables and the years of teaching experience used as the independent variable. To this end, participant teachers were grouped by length of experience as shown in Table 16.1. It should be noted that in this study most of the teachers with more than 20 years of experience were deputy headmasters or headmasters. Therefore, in the following analysis, the comparisons between groups of teachers are differentiated in such a way as to reflect not only the years of experience but also the stages of teachers' careers, since the latter were found to affect the responses of teachers in the case of major changes in the educational system (Hargreaves, 2005). On the basis of the CBAM results (Hall & Hord, 2001), a shift from information and personal concerns towards management concerns, followed by consequences concerns, collaboration and refocusing concerns, was expected to occur as a result of the teachers' experience with the implementation of the new curriculum materials (Hall & Hord, 2001). As a consequence, inexperienced beginning teachers would have been expected to show greater concern about the information and the personal aspects of the innovation than experienced teachers and headmasters. The latter were expected to worry more about the impact of the innovation on students' learning and achievement, and less about self-concerns. However, the results of the multivariate analysis do not support these hypotheses.

As shown in Table 16.3, the results of MANOVA for beginning teachers (one to two years of experience), for teachers with some experience (three to ten years), for the experienced teachers (11–20 years), and for deputy headmasters and headmasters (more than 20 years of experience) revealed significant differences in four factors: information, management, consequence, and collaboration ($F_{(3,595)}$ = 6.13, 3.87, 3.09, 4.55, and P=0.00, 0.01, 0.02 and 0.00, respectively). The significance of the observed differences was further examined on the basis of univariate analyses of variance; it was found that highly experienced teachers (headmasters) scored higher than beginning teachers on the scale measuring the need for information. This result suggests that headmasters exhibited fewer information concerns than beginning teachers. However, no significant difference was found between headmasters and teachers with 3–20 years of experience.

With regard to the task-concern scale relating to management, beginning teachers scored higher than the other groups of teachers ($\overline{X}_{management}$ =5.10), meaning that they saw fewer practical problems in the implementation of the new mathematics curriculum materials than more experienced teachers and headmasters. This difference was not significant between novices and teachers with three to ten years of experience; this result is in contrast with most previous studies, which found that beginning teachers' concerns focus mainly on the management problems when organizing their daily work in the classroom (van den Berg, Sleegers, Geijsel, & Vandenberghe, 2000).

Teachers' concerns about the consequences and collaboration aspects of the innovation differed significantly by years of experience. Specifically, beginning teachers and teachers with three to ten years of experience scored higher on the consequence ($\overline{X}$=6.25, $\overline{X}$=6.03) and lower on the collaboration scales ($\overline{X}$=5.12, $\overline{X}$=5.61, respectively) than the other three groups of teachers (see Table 16.3). It appears that novices and teachers with a few years of experience worried less than more experienced teachers about the consequences for their students of the use of the new curriculum materials; however, novice teachers were concerned about their collaboration with other colleagues and the coordination of their work. No significant difference was found in the mean responses of the groups of teachers participating in this study on the personal and refocusing factors (see Table 16.3). This is an indication that the teachers under study appeared to have

Table 16.3 Multivariate Analysis of Variance of Each Concern Factor by Year of Experience

Concerns	Years of Experience	Mean	F	P
Information	1–2	6.49	6.13	0.00
	3–10	6.74		
	11–20	6.69		
	Over 20 *	7.14		
Personal	1–3	6.22	0.99	0.40
	3–10	6.48		
	11–20	6.41		
	Over 20	6.45		
Management	1–2	5.10	3.87	0.01
	3–10	4.93		
	11–20*	4.63		
	Over 20*	4.62		
Consequences	1–2	6.25	3.09	0.02
	3–10	6.03		
	11–20 *	5.75		
	Over 20*	5.88		
Collaboration	1–2	5.12	4.55	0.00
	3–10 *	5.61		
	11–20 *	5.69		
	Over 20*	5.79		
Refocusing	1–2	5.82	1.45	0.23
	3–10*	6.02		
	11–20	5.93		
	Over 20	5.98		

Notes
* For this concern factor, this group of teachers is significantly different from the group of beginning teachers.

similar concerns about their abilities to deal with the innovation and finding alternative ways of implementing the innovation.

Research Question 2: Teachers' Conceptions of the Adequacy of the New Materials

The second purpose of the study refers to the concerns of beginning teachers in relation to the perceived potential of the new textbooks to support teachers' efforts to improve students' learning. As in the previous section, we first discuss the conceptions of beginning teachers and then compare these conceptions with those of more experienced teachers. Our discussion revolves around the three main constructs previously introduced: ease of use, efficacy, and anxiety. The data for this analysis were collected through the second part of the questionnaire.

BEGINNING TEACHERS' CONCEPTIONS OF THE SUPPORT THEY GET
FROM THE TEXTBOOKS

Table 16.4 summarizes the mean responses of beginning teachers to each item of the second part of the questionnaire in relation to the three constructs of support (ease of use, efficacy, and anxiety). With regard to the first construct, beginning teachers seem to consider curriculum materials, and particularly textbooks, as easy to use; the majority stated that they could easily use all the activities in the textbooks ($\overline{X}=6.04$), and also felt that the textbooks were well laid out ($\overline{X}=7.20$), enabling them to meet the new aims for mathematics instruction. The lowest mean occurred in the first item of the "ease of use" construct ($\overline{X}=2.8$), indicating that beginning teachers used the textbooks and did not feel that they needed to supplement the activities provided in the curriculum materials. Overall, beginning teachers appreciated the structure and the activities provided in the textbooks and considered them "user friendly." This is quite important for elementary school teachers who teach several subjects each day.

With regard to the second construct, beginning teachers seemed to feel confident that using the new textbooks will facilitate student learning in mathematics; this is one of the most important findings of the present study. Specifically, the mean response on the first item in the efficacy construct ($\overline{X}=8.26$) indicates that most beginning teachers believed that the new textbooks allow teachers to help students make progress in learning mathematics. In addition, the majority of

Table 16.4 Means of Items that Constitute the Support Construct for Beginning Teachers

Support Constructs	Items	Mean	SD
Ease of Use	It is necessary to enrich the new textbooks by providing extra worksheets.	2.80	1.65
	It is easy for me to deal with all the activities in the textbooks.	6.04	2.21
	The structure of the new textbooks enables me to organize my teaching so as to cover the aims of the curriculum.	7.20	1.65
Efficacy	I think that the new textbooks in general will improve students' performance.	8.26	1.52
	The new textbooks contribute to the development of students' thinking.	6.80	1.70
	The structure and content of the new textbooks contributes to the improvement of students' performance.	6.86	1.58
Anxiety	The new textbooks decreased my worries for organizing my work.	5.94	2.26
	The activities proposed in the textbooks save time from my preparation.	4.35	2.49
	With the new textbooks, I can cover the mathematics content in time.	3.88	2.55

beginning teachers felt confident that the new textbooks worked well in developing students' thinking ($\bar{X}=6.80$); moreover, they did not express doubts that the organization and structure of textbooks contribute to the improvement of students' performance ($\bar{X}=6.86$). These results seem to deviate from previous studies, which found that most beginning teachers lack confidence in their ability to realize the purposes of proposed reform in education (Kegan, 1994).

The findings with regard to the third construct (anxiety) seem to contradict those of the first two. Thus, despite beginning teachers' praise for the new textbooks because of the "ease of use" of the materials they provide and their professed belief that the textbooks could potentially help student learning, respondents expressed some doubts regarding the effect on teachers' anxiety. Specifically, beginning teachers reported that they were worried that there was not enough time to cover the mathematics content ($\bar{X}=3.88$). Subject matter coverage is a persistent theme in similar research studies and it is one of the most important factors associated with anxiety (Kauffmann et al., 2002).

It is also evident that whereas the textbooks alleviate some of the demands of planning and teaching mathematics lessons, they come with their own demands in terms of the preparation time for beginning teachers. The low mean in the second item in the anxiety construct ($\bar{X}=4.35$, see Table 16.4), indicates that beginning teachers need considerable time for preparing their daily teaching in mathematics, organizing and solving the textbook activities.

In the following section, a comparison between beginning and experienced teachers' feelings regarding the support received from the new textbooks sheds more light on the way these feelings develop, particularly through experience.

BEGINNING AND EXPERIENCED TEACHERS' CONCEPTIONS OF THE
ADEQUACY OF NEW TEXTBOOKS

It was hypothesized that years of experience influence the extent to which teachers feel supported by the new mathematics textbooks. To this end, MANOVA was conducted with the total teaching experience as the independent variable and the constructs of "ease of use," "efficacy," and "anxiety" as the dependent variables (see Table 16.5). Clearly, for the efficacy factor of support, no significant differences were found in teachers' feelings across years of experience ($F=0.54$, $P=0.065$). The high means in each of the items of the efficacy factor suggests that teachers in general are not concerned about the effectiveness of the new textbooks.

However, significant differences were found in both the "anxiety" and "ease of use" factors ($F=3$, $P=0.03$, and $F=5.82$, $P=0.00$, respectively). Although the low means in the anxiety factor do not suggest a high level of anxiety among teachers who use them, and the high means in the "ease of use" factor indicate that the new textbooks can be easily used by teachers, post hoc analysis of the means in these two factors revealed significant differences among teachers. Experienced teachers (11–20 years of experience), in contrast with headmasters, reported fewer concerns about the anxiety the new textbooks created for them ($\bar{X}_{experienced}=3.67$; $\bar{X}_{headmasters}=4.35$). Beginning teachers seemed to have similar

Table 16.5 Means for Each Support Construct and Summary of MANOVA

Constructs of Support	Years of Experience	Mean	SD	F	P
Ease of use	1–2 *	5.36	1.20	5.82	0.00
	3–10	5.71	1.31		
	11–20	5.51	1.25		
	Over 20 *	6.00	1.23		
	Total	5.70	1.28		
Efficacy	1–2	7.31	1.18	0.54	0.65
	3–10	7.38	1.22		
	11–20	7.44	1.10		
	Over 20	7.49	1.22		
	Total	7.41	1.19		
Anxiety	1–2	4.13	1.79	3.00	0.03
	3–10	4.04	1.98		
	11–20 **	3.67	1.91		
	Over 20 **	4.35	1.90		
	Total	4.05	1.93		

Notes
* The group of headmasters has significantly lower concerns than the group of the beginning teachers.
** The group of headmasters has significantly higher anxiety than the group of the experienced teachers.

concerns as other teachers in the anxiety factor. Finally, statistically significant differences were found between beginning teachers and headmasters in the "ease of use" factor. Headmasters reported significantly lower concerns on the "ease of use" of textbooks than did beginning teachers ($\overline{X}_{headmasters} = 6.00$ and $\overline{X}_{beginners} = 5.36$, respectively).

Conclusions and Implications

In the present study, we attempted to explore beginning teachers' concerns regarding the implementation of a series of new mathematics textbooks and to compare beginning teachers' concerns with the concerns of teachers with more teaching experience. In addition, we investigated the extent to which beginning teachers were supported by the new textbooks, and compared their views with those of other teachers who implemented the new textbooks. The findings suggest that beginning teachers accepted the decision to proceed with the change in mathematics curriculum materials and did not seem to have high self-concerns about the innovation. Beginning teachers were not concerned about their abilities in relation to the new mathematics textbooks and, on the contrary, felt capable of meeting the demands of the innovation.

The analysis of the data in the present study also showed that, in general, beginning teachers focused mainly on the management of their work. The management stage exhibited the lowest mean scores, indicating that beginning teachers at this phase of the implementation mainly had concerns about planning instruction and teaching too many students. It seems that the teachers' attention is mainly focused on the processes and tasks involved in using mathematics textbooks, and on issues related to organizing, managing, and meeting time demands (Huberman, 1992). The comparison of teachers' management concerns showed that beginning teachers had fewer management concerns than more experienced teachers, suggesting that beginning teachers operationalize the ideas in the textbooks more efficiently. At first sight, this finding seems to contradict the results reported in previous studies. There is, however, a possible explanation: in our study, all beginning teachers and the vast majority of teachers with up to ten years' experience graduated from university departments, whereas the older generations of teachers are graduates of pedagogical academies. The "younger" teachers had the opportunity to have a professional education with most of their courses emphasizing the philosophy and the practices needed for the successful implementation of the new mathematics curriculum materials. This suggests that the most important factor in explaining teachers' concerns may not always be teaching experience, but the teachers' professional development programs they have attended.

Beginning teachers in this study seemed to worry about their collaboration with other teachers and headmasters, reaffirming in this respect the results of previous studies (Huberman, 1992). The lack of collaboration may result in the abandonment of beginning teachers' ideals and teacher education foundations (Hargreaves, 2005); if they feel isolated and unsupported, they may adjust to the existing culture of the school and the practices and concerns of experienced teachers (Hargreaves, 2005). The fact that beginning teachers appear to have concerns regarding the organizational aspects of their work points to the need for further investigations of these aspects in the innovation adoption process. In general, research on the obstacles faced by new teachers has focused on the problems they face in the areas of teaching and learning and has neglected to examine the role of organizational variables (Weiss, 1999). However, studies of leavers from the teaching profession or dissatisfied teachers in employment have found the main reasons for dissatisfaction and/or turnover to relate to weaknesses in the area of school administration, such as leadership, collaboration, and teacher autonomy (National Center for Education Statistics, 1997). Consequently, the importance of school administration factors for beginning teachers, as reflected in the findings of the present study, points to the need for administrative support measures for new entrants to the teaching profession. Overall, the determination of the nature of concerns of beginning teachers is necessary in order to allow for the design and implementation of intervention strategies appropriate for the relevant stage of concerns. Bearing in mind that "curricular reforms may be fragile and transient" (Senger, 1999, p. 201), educational planners should develop inservice programs supporting the teachers' adoption of the innovation.

The second purpose of the study referred to the teachers' conceptions regarding the support provided by curriculum materials (Grant et al., Chapter 8 of this volume). Support is reflected in the degree to which materials are appraised by

242 · C. Christou et al.

teachers as helping them to teach effectively (efficacy), the degree to which the materials alleviate the demands of planning and teaching ("ease of use"), and the degree to which beginning teachers feel that the materials help them to overcome anxiety in their daily teaching of mathematics. The findings of the study point to new aspects of the use of curriculum materials, at least as far as beginning teachers are concerned. Much of the prior research on the use of curriculum materials focuses on textbooks as determinants of teachers' curriculum decisions (Sosniak & Stodolsky, 1993). This study shows that an important aspect of the usefulness of curriculum materials lies in the support provided (or not provided) to teachers. It is shown that the daily challenges of managing a classroom and the challenge of planning lessons for several subjects make the structured lessons of the mathematics textbooks appealing. Beginning teachers in the present study reported that they could easily use the new mathematics textbooks, and felt confident that students could learn mathematics with these textbooks. However, despite their praise for the textbooks, beginning teachers expressed some worries about the time needed for preparing their daily work. This anxiety was widespread among teachers, with the exception of headmasters.

The results of the present study point to the importance of attending to the concerns and experiences of teachers with respect to new mathematics curriculum materials. It is the responsibility of educational leaders and policy-makers to acknowledge and identify the concerns of teachers in order to increase the prospects of success for educational innovations. In particular, the findings of the study have implications for teacher education programmes and the support of beginning teachers. As regards teacher education, the students' teaching experience module can be modified to allow for the greater involvement of student teachers in the organizational aspects of their work. For instance, cooperating teachers can be expected to have a significant impact on the students' internship experience. More frequent contact with cooperating teachers before, during and after the teaching experience module can help alleviate the collaboration concerns of beginning teachers (see Chapter 15 of this volume).

We also suggest that pre-service teachers receive greater support from headteachers and other administrators before their appointments, to help them adjust to the school culture and avoid feelings of anxiety and isolation. Additional support can be offered to beginning teachers after their appointments. Individuals or small groups can undertake the task of beginning-teacher support at the school level. For this to be effective, experienced teachers must be assigned formal responsibility for beginning-teacher support. Incentives (such as lower teaching loads) can be offered to experienced teachers to encourage them to undertake this role. Moreover, it is important to follow the experience of beginning teachers in an attempt to identify the obstacles and problems they encounter. To this effect, beginning teachers can be encouraged to record their experiences on a daily basis, thus providing information on specific problem areas.

In conclusion, inservice education and administrative support should be provided for beginning teachers with a high level of management and collaboration concerns. Meeting the concerns of teachers is necessary for the recognition of teachers' professional selves and the restoration of working conditions conducive to good teaching performance. Overall, the present study points to the importance of examining teacher concerns in the innovation adoption process. If these concerns are not addressed, teacher satisfaction with and commitment to their career may be negatively affected. This is particularly the case for beginning teachers, who face a difficult adjustment period after their entry into the profession. It is hoped that additional research on the topic will allow for the design of effective support and development initiatives, based on the needs of individual teachers.

References

Ball, D. L., & Cohen, D. K. (1996). Reform by the book: What is – or might be – the role of curriculum materials in teacher learning and instructional reform? *Educational Researcher, 25*(9), 6–8.

Bullough, R. (1992). Beginning teacher curriculum decision making, personal teaching metaphors, and teacher education. *Teaching and Teacher Education, 8*, 239–252.

Calderhead, J., & Robson, M. (1991). Images of teaching: Student teachers' early conceptions of classroom practice. *Teaching and Teacher Education, 7*, 1–8.

Christou, C., Eliophotou-Menon, M., & Philippou, G. (2004). Teachers' concerns regarding the adoption of a new mathematics curriculum: An application of CBAM. *Educational Studies in Mathematics, 57*, 157–176.

Cockcroft, W. (1982). *Mathematics counts*. Report of the Committee of Inquiry into the Teaching of Mathematics in Schools. London: HMSO.

Fullan, M. (1999). *Change forces: The sequel*. London: Falmer Press.

Fuller, F. (1969). *Change forces: Probing the depths of educational reform*. London: Falmer Press.

Hall, G. E., & Hord, S. M. (2001). *Implementing change: patterns, principles and potholes*. Boston, MA: Allyn and Bacon.

Hargreaves, A. (2005). Educational change takes ages: Life, career and generational factors in teachers' emotional responses to educational change. *Teaching and Teacher Education, 21*, 967–983.

Huberman, M. (1992). Teacher development and instructional mastery. In A. Hargreaves & M. G. Fullan (Eds.), *Understanding teacher development* (pp. 122–142). New York, NY: Teachers College Press.

Kauffman, D., Johnson, S. M., Kardos, S. M., Liu, E., & Peske, H. G. (2002). Lost at sea: New teachers' experiences with curriculum and assessment. *Teachers College Record, 104*(2), 273–300.

Kegan, R. (1994). *In over our heads: The mental demands of modern life*. Cambridge, MA: Harvard University Press.

Lloyd, G. M. (1999). Two teachers' conceptions of a reform curriculum: Implications for mathematics teacher development. *Journal of Mathematics Teacher Education, 2*, 227–252.

Lloyd, G. M. (2002). Mathematics teachers' beliefs and experiences with innovative curriculum materials: The role of curriculum in teacher development. In G. Leder, E. Pehkonen, & G. Törner (Eds.), *Beliefs: A hidden variable in mathematics education?* (pp. 149–159). Utrecht: Kluwer Academic.

McKinney, M., Sexton, T., & Meyerson, M. J. (1999). Validating the efficacy-based change model. *Teaching and Teacher Education, 15*, 471–485.

National Center for Education Statistics. (1997). *Job satisfaction among America's teachers: Effects of workplace conditions, background characteristics, and teacher compensation*. Washington, DC: US Department of Education.

National Council of Teachers of Mathematics. (1980). *An agenda for action: Recommendations for school mathematics of the 1980s*. Reston, VA: Author.

National Council of Teachers of Mathematics. (1989). *Curriculum and evaluation standards for school mathematics*. Reston, VA: Author.

National Council of Teachers of Mathematics. (1991). *Professional standards for teaching mathematics*. Reston, VA: Author.

Nelson, B. (1997). Learning about teacher change in the context of mathematics reform: Where have we come from? In E. Fennema & B. Nelson (Eds.), *Mathematics teachers in transition.* (pp. 3–18). Mahwah, NJ: Lawrence Erlbaum.

Romberg, T. (1997). Mathematics in context. In E. Fennema & B. Nelson (Eds.), *Mathematics teachers in transition* (pp. 357–380) Mahwah, NJ: Lawrence Erlbaum.

Senger, S. E. (1999). Reflective reform in mathematics: The recursive nature of teacher change, *Educational Studies in Mathematics, 37,* 199–221.

Sosniak, L. A., & Stodolsky, S. S. (1993). Teachers and textbooks: Materials use in four fourth grade classrooms. *The Elementary School Journal, 93*(3), 249–275.

Spillane, J. P. (1999). External reform initiatives and teachers' efforts to reconstruct their practice: The mediating role of teachers' zones of enactment. *Journal of Curriculum Studies, 31*(2), 142–175.

Thompson, A. (1992). Teachers' beliefs and conceptions: A synthesis of the research. In D. Grouws (Ed.), *Handbook of research on mathematics teaching and learning* (pp. 127–146). New York, NY: Macmillan.

van den Berg, R. (1993). The concerns-based adoption model in the Netherlands, Flanders and the United Kingdom: State of the art and perspective. *Studies in Educational Evaluation, 19,* 51–63.

van den Berg, R. (2002). Teachers' meanings regarding educational practice. *Review of Educational Research, 72* (4), 577–625.

van den Berg, R., Sleegers, P., Geijsel, F., & Vandenberghe, R. (2000). Implementation of an innovation: Meeting the concerns of teachers. *Studies in Educational Evaluation, 26,* 331–350.

Vandenberghe, R. (2002). Teachers' professional development as the core of school improvement (Guest editorial). *International Journal of Educational Research, 37,* 653–659.

Veenman, S. (1984). Perceived problems of beginning teachers. *Review of Educational Research, 54*(2), 143–178.

Weiss, E. M. (1999). Perceived workplace conditions and first-year teachers' morale, career choice commitment, and planned retention: A secondary analysis. *Teaching and Teacher Education, 15,* 861–879.

Wideen, M., Mayer-Smith, J., & Moon, B. (1998). A critical analysis of the research on learning to teach: Making the case for an ecological perspective on inquiry. *Review of Educational Research, 68*(2), 130–178.

17

Exploring the Curriculum Implementation Plateau

An Instructional Perspective

Edward A. Silver, Hala Ghousseini, Charalambos Y. Charalambous, and Valerie Mills

Curriculum materials typically provide tasks and activities that constitute the instructional core for teachers and students in mathematics classrooms, especially in the United States. Curriculum materials also affect the sequencing of mathematics topics and influence the way that mathematical ideas and processes are made available to students. Because of their centrality to mathematics teaching and learning, curriculum materials have long been viewed as critical leveraging tools for instructional reform. The adoption of new curriculum materials, especially those designed to embody innovative ideas and practices, can catalyze changes in teachers' instructional practice and enhance students' opportunities to learn mathematics. A view of curriculum materials as levers for innovation led to ambitious curriculum development efforts during both the "new math" era of the 1960s (see Begle, 1973) and the so-called *Standards*-based curriculum development of the 1990s in response to the publication of *Curriculum and Evaluation Standards for School Mathematics* (National Council of Teachers of Mathematics [NCTM], 1989; see Senk & Thompson, 2003).

Studies of educational innovations of various kinds have noted some general tendencies in the use of an innovation over time. In particular, many studies have found that innovations are difficult to implement and rarely have a long-term impact. For example, Hall and colleagues (Hall, Loucks, Rutherford, & Newlove, 1975) suggested a sequence of eight distinct "levels of use" to encapsulate phases of adopting and enacting an innovation over time, ranging from basic orientation and management of implementation logistics in the early phases to the later phases of refinement, integration and renewal in a well-implemented innovation. Hall et al. note that the use of innovations in education rarely reaches the last three levels of use (p. 53), unless education systems and key actors are supported by interventions specifically intended to help them refine their use of the innovation.

These claims about educational innovation in general resonate with more recent observations by St John, Heenan, Houghton, and Tambe (2001) regarding the adoption and implementation of *Standards*-based mathematics curriculum materials, which constitute a certain kind of educational innovation. They proposed a four-level model based on their analysis of processes associated with the implementation of *Standards*-based curriculum materials. The first two levels in the model (awareness and selection) pertain to a decision to adopt an innovative curriculum program, and the third level is the initial implementation. The fourth level, according to St John and his colleagues, denotes a consistent, masterful use of *Standards*-based curriculum materials. St John et al. noted that *Standards*-based curriculum materials have been put into use in many locations, giving evidence of levels one to three, but examples of attainment of level four were less evident.

As an extensive body of research on educational innovation attests, and as both models given above suggest, innovation is not an all-or-nothing phenomenon. Moreover, the use of an innovation does not usually proceed in an orderly fashion from nothing to everything, despite the wishes of the designers of the innovation or those who decide to use it to leverage change. Based on his analysis of many reform efforts, Fullan (2004) argued that educators should expect to encounter *plateaus* as they enact innovations, but that these perturbations need not be viewed as fatal to reform: "What needs to be sustainable is not particular practices but rather the capacity and process of continuous problem solving and improvement. This is not simply linear improvement" (p. 9).

In general, educators have been more attentive to the early stages of implementation than to the latter stages. For example, when school districts adopt *Standards*-based curriculum materials, it is not uncommon for professional development support to be offered to teachers to familiarize them with basic features of the new materials. New users of the *Connected Mathematics Project* (CMP) (Lappan, Fey, Fitzgerald, Friel, & Phillips, 1996), a *Standards*-based curriculum program, often receive professional development aimed at familiarizing them with the basic CMP lesson structure: the *launching* of a complex mathematics task, its *exploration* and solution, and then the concluding phase of *summarizing* the major ideas encountered in the lesson (Phillips, Lappan, & Grant, 2000). Professional development might also focus on particular instructional units to help teachers become comfortable with the treatment of specific topics in the curriculum materials, and to deepen teachers' understanding of key mathematical concepts (Banilower, Boyd, Pasley, & Weiss, 2006). Such familiarization with newly adopted *Standards*-based curriculum programs has been found to support teachers' initial use of the curriculum materials (Banilower et al., 2006; Schoen, Cebulla, Finn, & Fi, 2003). Although we appear to have some understanding of what is needed to support initial implementation, we know far less about what might be needed to ensure and sustain effective implementation in the long run. If we assume, as Fullan and Hall et al. argue, that implementation will not proceed smoothly and that a plateau will be reached after some time, then it is critical to learn more about the nature of the challenges encountered on the plateau and about what kinds of supports might be needed to help users meet these challenges successfully.

In this chapter, we explicate the notion of a *curriculum implementation plateau* in relation to the use of *Standards*-based curriculum materials. To do this we draw on our experiences in the BIFOCAL (*Beyond Implementation: Focusing on Challenge and Learning*) project, in which we worked with teachers who were users of such materials. Viewing curriculum materials as a key resource for instruction, we attend to the ways in which BIFOCAL teachers talked about the materials and worked to improve their teaching practice in relation to them. Viewed from this perspective, the curriculum implementation plateau can be seen not merely as a technical problem related to fidelity of implementation but rather as an *instructional problem* related to the use of curriculum materials and also (at least somewhat) independent of the specific curriculum materials in use.

Conceptualizing the Curriculum Implementation Plateau: An Instructional Perspective

Our conceptualization of the curriculum implementation plateau incorporates two frameworks that capture key aspects of mathematics instruction. One is the so-called instructional triangle, and the other is the Mathematical Tasks Framework.

The work of a teacher can be conceptualized as that of engaging students in learning about particular content (Lampert, 2001), and this dynamic relationship among students, content to be learned, and the teacher can be rendered as an instructional triangle with each of three interactive elements at the vertices (Figure 17.1a). The vertical arrow in Figure 17.1a draws attention to the teachers' activity in relation to the student-content relationship. The arrow draws attention to the critical influence that teachers have in affecting what students can learn from engagement with particular content. Curriculum materials often play a key role in this interaction between students and content to be learned, because the curriculum materials provide tasks that offer occasions for students to engage with content. As Figure 17.1b suggests, curriculum materials can be seen as important resources for classroom instruction because they occupy a critical mediating position in the interaction between students and their learning of mathematics content. The tasks in the curriculum materials serve as resources for students' learning of content, and the materials also mediate teachers' instructional practice in relation to their students' engagement with content. The critical mediating role of the teacher, in addition to the tasks, is explicitly addressed in the elaboration of the teaching principle in the *Principles and Standards for School Mathematics* (NCTM, 2000):

> Worthwhile tasks alone are not sufficient for effective teaching. Teachers must also decide what aspects of a task to highlight, how to organize and orchestrate the work of the students, what questions to ask to challenge those with varied levels of expertise, and how to support students without taking over the process of thinking for them and thus eliminating the challenge.
>
> (p. 19)

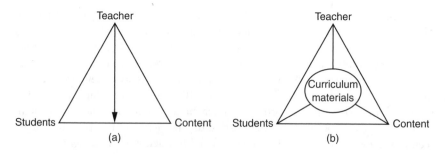

Figure 17.1 Viewing curriculum materials as a resource in the instructional triangle.

According to this view, a teacher has a key role in shaping the interaction between students and mathematical ideas that occurs as students engage with tasks found in curriculum materials. In Figure 17.1b, we convey the mediating role of the curriculum materials by the lines connecting to the students and content vertices, and the key mediating role of teacher by the line connecting to the teacher vertex. This view is similar to that of Brown (Chapter 2 of this volume), who uses the term *pedagogical design capacity* to capture the active role of teachers in deploying and mobilizing curriculum materials and their own personal resources (skills, knowledge, beliefs, and orientations) to assist students to learn worthwhile mathematics.

Viewing teachers as active agents who use curriculum materials as resources to mediate the engagement of students with mathematics content to be learned draws attention to the multiple ways in which teachers can affect learning opportunities. The Mathematical Tasks Framework (Stein & Smith, 1998; Stein, Smith, Henningsen, & Silver, 2000) specifies several points at which a teacher mediates students' engagement with the tasks found in curriculum materials and highlights the ways that task demands may change as a teacher uses them with students (see Figure 17.2). A teacher decides which tasks to assign and which to omit, and he or she may transform tasks substantially when reading and interpreting the curriculum materials, when setting up the tasks during instruction, and while interacting with students during the enactment of these tasks (see Stein, Remillard, & Smith, 2007).

As previous studies suggest, teachers' mediating decisions, and associated actions and interactions with students, can affect student learning. For instance, Stein and Lane (1996) found that students had higher mathematics attainment in classrooms in which teachers selected and enacted challenging mathematical tasks in ways that maintained the challenge. Unfortunately, other research has shown that it is quite difficult for teachers to maintain the cognitive demands of challenging tasks during a lesson, due to many factors that may pressure teachers to reduce the cognitive demand (Henningsen & Stein, 1997; Stein, Grover, & Henningsen, 1996).

How might these two frameworks help us understand why teachers may encounter an implementation plateau after a few years of using *Standards*-based

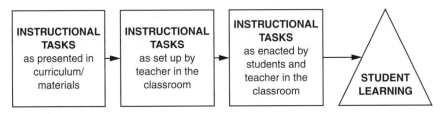

Figure 17.2 The Mathematical Tasks Framework (adapted from Stein & Smith, 1998).

curriculum materials? Initially, the curriculum materials offer a rich supply of worthwhile mathematical tasks and novel topical sequencing. As the novelty wears off, however, the instructional challenges inherent in problem-based mathematics instruction become more apparent – particularly the challenge of supporting students' thoughtful engagement with cognitively demanding mathematical tasks and avoiding the temptation to remove the complexity or pre-empt students' opportunities for thinking. If neither the curriculum materials themselves nor the professional development provided to support initial implementation are sufficient to help teachers address the core instructional challenge, a plateau will likely be reached.

More than a plausible argument, there is also some indirect empirical support for this conceptualization of a curriculum implementation plateau for *Standards*-based curriculum materials. For example, Banilower et al. (2006) analyzed classroom mathematics lessons taught by teachers who received at least 20 hours of professional development on implementing *Standards*-based curriculum materials. The researchers reported that many teachers were able to incorporate challenging curriculum tasks into their lessons, but they often reduced the "investigative nature" of these tasks and they rarely helped their students to develop conceptual understanding of the ideas discussed in the lesson. Similarly, an examination of the instructional practices of elementary teachers implementing *Everyday Mathematics* (Bell et al., 2001; Carroll & Isaacs, 2003) found that only half of the teachers elicited students' explanations and only one-fourth engaged students in sharing and discussing multiple solutions, despite the fact that both practices were explicitly and strongly endorsed by the curriculum materials. Thus, it is clear from these findings that the adoption and initial implementation of innovative curriculum materials does not automatically help teachers to deal with instructional challenges.

It is widely acknowledged that *Standards*-based curriculum materials place heavy instructional demands on teachers (e.g., Clarke, 1997). Good implementation is a non-trivial matter. Designers of these materials intend that they be used in the context of classroom instruction that focuses on the understanding of mathematics concepts and on the posing and solving of complex problems, both of which are features generally absent from US mathematics instruction (Hiebert et al., 2005). Thus, the implementation of *Standards*-based curriculum materials may increase the salience of some inherent and enduring challenges of instruction, as well as introduce new ones. Viewed in this way, a plateau is seen as a consequence of unresolved instructional issues that affect the scope and effi-cacy of implementation. It was this perspective that guided our initial design of BIFOCAL and our ongoing work with teachers.

Context of the Study

In this chapter, we focus primarily on the first year of BIFOCAL (May 2003 to May 2004). During this time, the BIFOCAL team worked with 12 teachers from five middle schools in the Detroit Metropolitan area; all teachers had used *Connected Mathematics Project* middle-grades curriculum program for at least three years.

The project sought to help teachers move beyond the curriculum implemen-tation plateau by drawing their attention to some of the inherent instructional challenges and supporting them as they worked to address these issues in their teaching. The project employed a blend of two professional development approaches: case analysis and modified lesson study. This combination allowed project participants to use the cases as a basis for inquiry into important aspects of mathematics teaching, independent of their own practice, and to use the modified lesson study to apply to their own practice the insights acquired from the case analysis. (For additional details, see Silver, Mills, Castro, & Ghousseini, 2006.)

The project also built on prior work in the QUASAR and COMET projects, particularly the Mathematical Tasks Framework (MTF) and the use of cogni-tively demanding tasks in the classroom (e.g., Stein et al., 1996). We selected nar-rative cases from *Implementing Standards-based Mathematics Instruction: A Casebook for Professional Development* (Stein et al., 2000) and other COMET Project materials (Smith, Silver, & Stein, 2005a, 2005b). These cases are closely tied to the MTF and illuminate many of the challenges faced by teachers working with cognitively challenging mathematics tasks in the middle grades. Addition-ally, they are deliberately constructed to stimulate reflection, analysis, and inquiry; provoke discussion regarding interactions among the teacher, students, and mathematics; and draw attention to the ways that these interactions affect students' opportunities to learn.

To engage the participants in some mathematical work and to set the stage for their reading, analysis, and discussion of the case, we usually started a session by asking them to solve a mathematical task drawn from the narrative case. A whole-group discussion followed, during which the participants presented and discussed different solutions to the mathematical task. The participants then read the narrative case and discussed it along framing questions and ideas intro-duced by the professional developers. The modified lesson study process fol-lowed, during which teachers, working in collaborative subgroups, selected and planned a target lesson using their curriculum materials. The teachers did this work with the aim of teaching the lesson, reflecting on their instructional moves in relation to evidence of students' thinking and understanding, and then dis-cussing their experience with colleagues. To support this process, we provided teachers with a lesson-planning tool, Thinking Through a Lesson Protocol (TTLP) (Smith & Bill, 2004), available at http://www.cometproject.com/alg/Assignment%202.pdf) that is closely connected to the MTF. This tool prompts teachers to specify their mathematical goals for the lesson, their expectations for students as they work on and complete the task, and the questions they plan to ask their students to provoke and support their thinking. Teachers generally began the lesson study portion of the session by discussing the enactment of a lesson that was jointly planned in a prior session. Then, they identified the next joint lesson and developed a plan for teaching it while attending to insights gained from the earlier case analysis portion of the session.

Data Sources and Analysis

The corpus of data used in this study consisted of transcriptions from the first year of the project of participants' interviews, videotaped professional development sessions, and participants' post-session reflections (see Silver, Ghousseini, Gosen, Charalambous, & Strawhun, 2005). The analysis of the data was completed in two phases. In the first phase, we conducted *open coding* (Strauss & Corbin, 1998), in which we identified all the issues, themes, and ideas suggested by the data. Then, given our interest in the phenomenon of curriculum implementation plateau, we scrutinized the themes identified in our initial open coding and developed categories relevant to the phenomenon of interest. For example, we were interested in themes related to *manifestations* of an implementation plateau in our participants' practice (e.g., instructional challenges). Another category included all the themes that suggested *sources and contributing factors* (e.g., dispositions toward using challenging tasks). A third category included the opportunities afforded to teachers to reconsider their role in using the curriculum materials. After identifying themes and organizing them into categories, we reviewed relevant data sources carefully to generate assertions and establish evidentiary warrants (Erickson, 1986). For each assertion, we searched different data sources for confirming and disconfirming evidence. Using this evidence, we revised our assertions as needed. Using narrative interpretive vignettes (Eisenhart, 2006), we documented evidentiary warrants for the final assertions.

Findings

We organize our presentation of findings around two major assertions that emerged from our analysis of the data. First, the curriculum implementation plateau appears to be associated with teachers having an underdeveloped understanding of their role as active agents in mediating the interaction of students and content through curriculum materials. Second, the curriculum implementation plateau appears to be associated with teachers having an underdeveloped repertoire of instructional strategies to use in effectively mediating the interaction of students and mathematics content through curriculum materials. In this section, we use evidence from our data sources to elaborate and support each of these assertions.

Teachers' Underdeveloped Understanding of Their Role as Active, Mediating Agents

At the first project session in May 2003, participants read a narrative case that depicts two teachers (Catherine and David) who approach the enactment of a lesson anchored by a cognitively demanding mathematics task in distinctly different ways.[1] To ensure her students' success, Catherine structured their problem-solving activity in ways that help them avoid struggling, by reducing the cognitive demand of the task to make it easier to solve. In contrast, David did not reduce the task demand, but he actively supported their engagement with the task, scaffolding their thinking rather than simplifying the task or telling them what to do. Thus, the lesson unfolds very differently in the two classrooms, with Catherine's students having fewer opportunities than David's students to engage in high-level thinking, reasoning, and communication. This case was selected for the first session because its analysis and discussion afford an opportunity for participants to consider the instructional challenge of supporting student thinking while maintaining students' high-level engagement with mathematics tasks.

Prior to reading the case, participants had an opportunity to solve the mathematics problem featured in the case, and to share and discuss their solution methods. The mathematics task embedded in this case requires finding the perimeters of "trains" formed by three adjacent hexagonal "cars," then four cars, then ten cars, and, finally, n cars. The participants used several different strategies to solve the problem, and they produced several different representations for the n-car solution. Near the end of the problem-solving portion of the session, they were asked how they thought their students would approach and solve this task. Several participants expressed concerns about the suitability of a task like this for middle school students, for example:

NINA: Dealing with patterns, in general, is a problem. Even when my students see a pattern, they don't trust themselves, and they don't trust the pattern. You may ask them about the fiftieth train and show them how to get it – they might try your way. But left on their own, they would still lay out the 50 pattern blocks and count them, because they don't trust the math.

NANCY: I am not sure that a sixth-grader's brain cells are there to absorb or to trust. I think they are still living in a very concrete world. Nicole [another participant] teaches eighth grade, and I teach seventh, and I think there are some of my kids in seventh grade who are maybe ready to trust it, but the majority aren't.

Looking across teachers' comments related to this issue in the May session, we note that they identified students' *abilities*, *readiness*, and *motivation* as major constraints for students' engagement with challenging tasks. Both comments given above suggest that students' ability and readiness are consequential for their engagement with complex mathematical tasks. Nina points to what she perceived as her students' limited capacity to engage in reasoning and generalization, preferring concrete rather than abstract modes of engagement with pattern generalization. Nancy's reference to the "concrete world" of her sixth-grade students resonates with Nina's comments and suggests a perceived developmental limitation related to tasks requiring generalization. To be sure, there are well-known developmental constraints related to abstraction and generalization, but these were not the only issues voiced by the teachers.

Concerns about low ability and poor motivation also arose in relation to the issue of multiple solution methods. Although there appeared to be general agreement among participants that it was helpful to see multiple solution methods for a problem, some participants expressed reservations about doing this with their students. In a comment about the lessons depicted in the narrative case, Roberta suggested that students needed to get comfortable first with "one method" before they encounter others:

ROBERTA: If it is the initial lesson in the subject, it is better not to present so many solutions and just stick with one. But I get the impression that David was maybe on the second or third generation of this lesson or presentation, and by that point I think you want to have as many different approaches as possible.

FACILITATOR: Why?

ROBERTA: I think sometimes there is this period of settling in – 24 hours thinking about that one method – and the next day [the students] come back … so now they have settled in, and maybe they think: "Oh, yeah, I have heard that!"

Implicit in Roberta's argument, and also evident in comments from other participants, is concern that students can be confused by the presentation of multiple solution strategies. Roberta appeared to perceive her students as unable to digest several solution strategies at once. Roberta's comment resonated with several other participants, who appeared to share her concern about the confusion that multiple solutions might create, especially for students who they perceived to be "low ability": "Sometimes, I am scared to put even two strategies up there because [students] are barely able to get one." And "I would be afraid to have someone explain this [non-conventional solution], I have kids struggling to understand the [conventional] stuff."

Regarding student motivation, some teachers spoke directly about the constraints it imposed on the work of sharing and discussing multiple solutions. As Kim suggests in the excerpt below, compared to her afternoon class, which she described as more challenging, her morning class was more suitable for sharing multiple solution strategies, because the students in this class were more active and motivated:

I think that you have to judge your students…. My morning kids could really do this. They are motivated, they are active, and they would really benefit from seeing all of these different ways. But then, I have an afternoon class that is made up of more special education students who struggle with math ... and everything is muddled in their brain.... If they saw seven approaches, they would walk out of here thinking, "What in the world did we do today?" In that situation, I would maybe just focus on one or two.

When Kim uttered this comment, she triggered a display of nodding heads from other participants in the room, suggesting that many other participants shared her opinion. Subsequently, and in support of Kim, another teacher claimed that David (the teacher in the narrative case) was able to use multiple solution strategies because his students appeared to be more confident and motivated. Nicole explained:

Doesn't it have to deal with confidence though?... In David's lesson they were more confident, and I think his approach would be more ideal in the second or third lesson. The kids were talking with each other. There were a couple of instances where he was not even doing the questioning. They were excited to ask the questions. The first thing I thought about was "Wow, they are really confident." I don't get enough of that in my room. I am usually the questioner.

We interpret these comments, and a number of similar ones at sessions early in the first year of the project, to mean that participants saw their use of the complex mathematics tasks that were made available in the CMP curriculum materials to be fundamentally constrained by their students' personal characteristics – ability level, developmental readiness and maturity, and degree of motivation and confidence. Although they acknowledged that the cognitively demanding tasks in the curriculum materials created opportunities for students to work on and with important mathematical ideas, they saw students' abilities and dispositions as shaping and limiting their interaction with the tasks.

There was little basis for argument that these student factors play a role in what happens in classroom lessons (see also Eisenmann & Even, Chapter 11 of this volume). Thus, the views of our participants were neither totally surprising nor completely incorrect. Nevertheless, what was strikingly absent from the portrait of classroom instruction painted by their comments was an active role for a teacher in shaping and orchestrating the interaction of students with tasks. There was an almost total absence of explicit attention to what role a teacher might play in mitigating perceived limitations in students.

Participants' comments suggested an underdeveloped conception of the teacher's role in facilitating and mediating the work of students with tasks from the curriculum materials. At times, it seemed that the curriculum materials alone were being perceived as the active agents shaping the learning opportunities for students. That is, in one class a task would work well, whereas in another it would not – because the students lacked ability or motivation, or because they were not ready for the challenge embedded in the task. Such comments reflect a view of curriculum tasks as active agents in the interaction between students and mathematical ideas – tasks succeed or they do not – but the comments did not portray a clear role for the teacher.

An underdeveloped conception of the teacher's role in facilitating and mediating the work of students with tasks from the curriculum materials was also evident in comments about students' engagement with complex tasks. For instance, in discussing the practice of engaging students in sharing multiple solution methods for a problem, one participant commented: "It depends on the class ... sometimes the kids have lots of ways, and at other times I present a topic and there is just Angela with her way, and no one else seems to have a way, so we just go with that." We interpret this comment to mean that the teacher felt that she could do little to influence student thinking and participation: if there was only one student who found a solution to a problem, the teacher had to work with just this one solution. The earlier comment from Nicole noting the difference between the confident students in David's class and the non-confident ones in her own class was also consistent with an underdeveloped conception of a teacher's role in catalyzing or influencing engagement, confidence, interest, or motivation.

To convey the underdeveloped conception that BIFOCAL participants appeared to have initially regarding the role of the teacher in using rich tasks from the curriculum materials as mediators of students' engagement with mathematical content, we could return to Figure 17.1b and insert a dashed line connecting the teacher vertex to the curriculum materials. This would denote an important contrast with the solid arrow that suggested the mediating role of the teacher with respect to students' engagement with curriculum materials to learn mathematics content.

It would be incorrect, however, to characterize participants as being passive in relation to tasks from the curriculum materials. In fact, participants acknowledged making decisions and taking action in response to what they perceived to be student characteristics that would limit the utility of a particular task. In some cases they simplified challenging aspects of tasks to make them more accessible to students, and in other cases they omitted a task entirely to avoid engaging (some or all of) their students with a task that they judged to be too challenging.

There are several plausible explanations for a tendency toward reducing (or avoiding) task complexity. For example, some BIFOCAL participants appeared to agree with Catherine, a teacher in the May 2003 narrative case, who initially thought that letting students struggle was an impediment to student learning. Several participants indicated that, because of the inherent challenges mentioned above, they were quite directive and explicit with students about how to handle tasks involving pattern generalization. The following comment by Roberta is illustrative:

> We start the year with sequences and I make it a point to tell them that if you have a sequence that is going up by a fixed amount then you know for sure that you are going to multiply the term number by that fixed amount.... That has done so much to make all of the sequence questions so much easier: letting them in on that little secret.

Thus, participants were not being passive in the face of conditions that might affect the ease with which students would solve problems. Rather, they sought to eliminate the challenge of the tasks, removing the need for students to determine a method by providing directions about how to generate the generalization.

Other comments from participants indicated that they sometimes availed themselves of another way to deal with the complexities inherent in engaging students with cognitively demanding tasks by removing them from a lesson for some or all students in a class. Roberta's claim that sixth-graders were not developmentally ready to solve problems calling for generalization suggests that such tasks should be assigned only to seventh- and eighth-graders. Another participant, Kim, suggested that the practice of sharing and discussing multiple solution methods should be reserved for those students who had *high ability and high motivation*; she worried that exposing other students to such activities could lead to confusion. Thus, we see that some participants initially portrayed their instruction in ways that suggested actively helping students work *around* the curriculum materials rather than working *with* them to learn mathematics content.

Referring to the MTF (see Figure 17.2), we argue that the limitations identified in participants' view of the role of the teacher are suggestive of an underdeveloped understanding of the teacher's role in supporting students' engagement with complex tasks (the third box), and in particular in selecting and setting up tasks for students (the first two boxes). At times, participants appeared to treat the tasks in the curriculum materials as self-enacting entities that had no clear mediating role for the teacher. At other times, when teachers anticipated that students might struggle with a complex task, the role of the teacher was seen as reducing or eliminating the struggle by revising or even omitting the task.

Although there may be other ways to interpret our participants' comments, our rendering is bolstered by notable shifts in discourse and stance as the project progressed over time. Participants less frequently depicted their roles as mere observers of interaction between students and tasks, and they made fewer references to fixed student characteristics as constraints on instructional possibilities. Rather, they developed a clearer conception of the teacher's role as crucial to orchestrating student engagement with tasks by attending to teaching strategies that proved to be powerful resources for them in supporting student's work with the complex tasks found in their curriculum materials.

Teachers' Underdeveloped Repertoire of Instructional Strategies as Active Mediating Agents

As teachers considered various aspects of mathematics teaching by reading narrative cases, collaboratively planning lessons, and reflecting on their own teaching, they became very interested in identifying and becoming proficient with specific ways to support and encourage students' thinking during the enactment of complex mathematics tasks. Toward that end, over the course of the first year, they co-constructed a "scaffolding strategies" list that organized and codified some of the ideas gleaned from reading, reflecting, and teaching. The list evolved over time as an accumulation of instructional moves and routines that teachers could initiate to support students' engagement with complex mathematical tasks. Excerpts from the list appear in part (a) of Table 17.1.

The TTLP lesson-planning tool, a portion of which is presented in part (b) of Table 17.1, provided a common structure that helped participants plan, analyze,

Table 17.1 (a) Excerpts from the Evolving List of Scaffolding Strategies; (b) Subset of the Questions in the Thinking Through a Lesson Protocol (TTLP)

(a) The Scaffolding Strategies List

February 2004
Strategies added to the list:
- Using manipulatives to help students develop concrete ideas
- Using student-work to clear-up misconceptions
- Deciding on the order of solutions:
  - Is it from simpler to more complex? Correct to incorrect or vice versa?
  - Which ones do we want to pose against one another?
  - Which ones might kids connect with first?
  - Which ones might get a mathematical idea on the table?
  - When do you get this misconception out on the table? (Putting the incorrect strategy out might help even the students with correct ones)
  - What is the role of "confusion"? How do we use it?

March 2004
Strategies added to the list:
- Reverse the order: students come up with question about the investigation
- Have students create concept-card files or make cards for them
- Allow students to use notes on the tests and quizzes
- Use posters/transparencies, etc to allow students to present their work to the whole class. Save and use with future classes if ideas are not brought up in later hours
- Sequence the order of which problems to present
- Use a poster with problem-solving strategies
- Ask the students to provide a description and/or explanation of their products (shapes)

(b) Thinking Through a Lesson Protocol (TTLP)

Part 1: Selecting and setting up a mathematical task
What are all the ways the task can be solved?
- Which of these methods do you think your students will use?
- What misconceptions might students have?
- What errors might students make?

Part 3: Sharing and discussing the task
How will you orchestrate the class discussion so that you accomplish your mathematical goals? Specifically:
- Which solution paths do you want to have shared during the class discussion? In what order will the solutions be presented? Why?
- In what ways will the order in which solutions are presented help develop students' understanding of the mathematical ideas that are the focus of your lesson?
- What specific questions will you ask so that students will:
  - make sense of the mathematical ideas that you want them to learn?
  - expand on, debate, and question the solutions being shared?
  - make connections between the different strategies that are presented?
  - look for patterns/begin to form generalizations?

and reflect on lessons. The TTLP prompted teachers to consider several critical components of the complex process of managing students' engagement with cognitively demanding tasks and for sharing multiple solutions: (a) anticipating students' solution approaches, (b) purposefully selecting responses for display, (c) deciding on the order of presentation, and (d) posing appropriate questions to challenge and support student thinking. These four specific teaching practices helped to frame teachers' discussions of cases and their collaborative lesson planning and debriefing in productive ways.

The TTLP framework provided structure and language to sharpen participants' analysis and understanding of challenges they faced in supporting student engagement with cognitively demanding tasks. Moreover, by focusing on these aspects of teaching, participants were able to develop new instructional routines to support these practices and more effectively engage students with complex mathematics tasks. In this section, we delineate these four teaching practices further and discuss how the project participants engaged with them.

ANTICIPATING POSSIBLE STUDENT RESPONSES

This teaching practice involves intentionally envisioning how students would be likely to approach a mathematical task within a lesson and recognizing, in advance, where students might encounter difficulties. BIFOCAL participants had many opportunities to observe, discuss, and rehearse this teaching practice during project sessions. For instance, the opening activity for each case involved solving a mathematical task and anticipating the ways that their students might try to solve it and the difficulties they might encounter. The case discussions offered opportunities to consider anticipated student responses in light of those depicted in the case. During the modified lesson study, the TTLP prompted participants to anticipate possible students' approaches to problems. During a lesson debriefing session, participants discussed the enacted lessons in relation to what was anticipated.

Some participants noted that the attention paid in BIFOCAL sessions to anticipating student responses was unusual, and sometimes difficult. Consider, for instance, this comment from one participant (Lily) in her end-of-year interview, in which she underscored the difficulty of this practice and the support teachers need in doing it:

> What I found hard was anticipating problems ahead of time that I might have when I teach a lesson.... Practicing a lesson here, ahead of time, you know, and see [sic] the different ways each one of our groups solved the problem was very helpful. It helps you see the different ways ... maybe one of us taught a lesson before and ... say "My kids have trouble here."... It's good to have these discussions. They are very helpful.

Nicole pointed to a slightly different but closely related challenge: "You can prepare questions beforehand, but you have to look at what the kids are doing, and [then] it changes." Nicole's comment suggests that the participants were not using the questions on the TTLP in a rote manner, nor were they viewing the four practices as a fixed linear sequence. Even if a teacher prepares thoroughly and anticipates well the responses of students, she needs to closely attend to students' contributions and ideas as they emerge during the enactment of a lesson, and deviate from the plan when warranted.

PURPOSEFUL SELECTION OF SOLUTIONS

This teaching practice involves choosing particular samples of work to display for consideration by the whole class. Initially, participants tended to think about such choices in terms of social normative goals, such as asking a student to display his work because he rarely made public contributions in class. In BIFOCAL, participants came to see the value of making selections in order to make certain mathematical ideas available for group discussion. They had many opportunities to observe, discuss, and rehearse this teaching practice during project sessions. To help participants develop an image of this strategy, we often modeled its use during the opening activity and explored it during case analysis and discussion. In addition, attention to this practice was prompted during the lesson planning and debriefing portions of sessions.

As participants became more attentive to the mathematical reasons for selecting and displaying student work, concerns arose about if or when to display errors. In discussions across the year, teachers had opportunities to voice their concerns and hesitations, and to develop or refine decision-making heuristics to guide this aspect of their practice. To illustrate this, consider an excerpt from the discussion of a case that depicted a teacher (Marie Hanson) who faced several challenges in trying to orchestrate her students' sharing of multiple solutions.[2] Marie's students generated a variety of solution strategies, including some incorrect ones, and she was uncertain about whether to display an incorrect solution method, though she ultimately decided to do so. Marie's dilemma stimulated our participants to reflect more deeply on this issue. Participants expressed differing views on Marie's decision to share an incorrect solution. Whereas some thought it was a good decision, others were concerned that doing so could aggravate students' confusion:

KENDRA: My question is: If you have a lot of kids doing it the wrong way, how do you get them to buy into these two [correct solutions]?... Sometimes [students] think, "I will just sit there and wait until [my answer] is shown," and they don't pay too much attention until you get to theirs. So, I don't know about throwing the wrong one out there and seeing how it goes.

NICOLE: I understand the worry about losing kids if you are putting the wrong answers up there and making it very confusing for them ... [but] you have to decide whether to "table the wrong answers" or share them – my decision is based on whether several kids have the same wrong answer. [If one student has] a wrong solution that is very different than everyone else's, I'm not going to have him go to the front of the room. But if it is a really a big group, I definitely start with the wrong answer.

In this exchange, we see that the conversation focuses on the selection of student solutions that contain errors. Kendra's comment pointed to a related challenge of creating a classroom culture in which students listen to and consider ideas different from their own, and suggested that selecting student solutions was not being treated as a simple matter divorced from other issues. Nicole attended directly to the issue of handling student work that contained errors, and she suggested a heuristic decision rule that she found useful. Given that *Standards*-based curriculum materials contain many complex problems that can be solved in diverse ways and that expose students' misconceptions and errors, it is important for a teacher to attend to this aspect of teaching practice and to be able to decide which samples of student work to display for public consideration in the classroom.

SEQUENCING STUDENTS' SOLUTIONS

This teaching practice involves deciding in what order to display student work. With reference to the key mathematical goals of a lesson, a teacher might decide to sequence student work to highlight certain relationships among solution methods, to lead naturally to a particular solution method or mathematical summary, or to optimize students' attention and engagement. As with other teaching practices, participants had opportunities during the BIFOCAL sessions to consider the issue of sequencing student solutions during case analyses and discussions, and during the lesson debriefings. On several occasions, participants also probed this aspect of the work of the facilitators, inquiring about how a facilitator decided which solutions to display and in what order.

Participants paid considerable attention to this teaching practice because it was something they had not previously considered. Many said that, prior to these experiences, they had not thought deeply about this issue in their planning and enactment of mathematics lessons. For example, when discussing the Marie Hanson case, one teacher (Natalie) remarked:

> One thing that I noticed, and that I don't know if I pay enough attention to, is that she [Marie] mentioned she wanted to expose her students,...
> [reads from the case]: "As the time to share solution strategies approached, I struggled with the decision as to which solution strategies to get out publicly and in what order." I guess I saw that as, "Do I or do I not pay attention as to what order I share solutions and does that make a big difference or not in the students' thinking?" So do I start with the most simplistic way and move up the ladder, or is it random? I guess in my classroom I don't consider that so much, but maybe I should.

Natalie's comment sparked a lively discussion about this aspect of teaching, and many participants took up this issue in a serious way in their work. Over the year, participants actively discussed possible rationales for sequencing solutions in a specific way (e.g., from simplest to most complicated, from common/frequent to unusual/rare strategies). Toward the end of the first year, in a lesson debriefing, one participant, Natalie, shared an instructional routine that she had developed to help her manage the public display of student solutions; the method involved placing "1" on solutions she deemed the simplest, "2" on those that were more complex, and "3" on the most complex solutions. She displayed student work using this method, and reported to the BIFOCAL group on her experience. In end-of-year interviews, participants frequently named Natalie's presentation and the associated discussions of this instructional issue, as important moments in the project.[3]

ASKING QUESTIONS TO SUPPORT AND CHALLENGE STUDENT THINKING

The questions teachers ask to support students' thinking during the sharing and discussion of multiple solutions are critical for drawing students' attention to important mathematical ideas targeted by the mathematical task. This aspect of teaching practice is at the core of the third box in the MTF, which, as we noted above was an area of uncertainty for the participants.

BIFOCAL participants had numerous opportunities – during case discussions and modified lesson planning portions of sessions – to consider the nature of questions that could support student engagement with complex mathematics tasks rather than subverting the cognitive demand. Consider, for instance, this excerpt from the discussion of a case in which the questions posed by the teacher may have reduced the cognitive demand of a mathematical task.[4] During this discussion, one teacher, Nicole, commented on the need to pose "appropriate" questions:

NICOLE: I noticed right off the bat that he [the teacher in the case] asked a lot of questions.... I think he did it because [a particular student's] understanding was so low. He was trying to get her up to where he thought she should be.... His question was far too specific and [the student] wasn't doing any higher-level thinking.... [The student] doesn't know but he walks her through what it should have been step by step – and I don't know if she has developed an understanding.... She gives all the right answers, but she wouldn't have gotten there without the questions.

FACILITATOR: So what would you do?

NICOLE: Honestly, in a case like this what I'd want to do is bring the other students in. I'd want them helping each other.... I would want to involve another student and another idea. How quickly? I don't know. But I know I would want the kids interacting more.

Nicole's suggestion that other students might be enlisted as allies was reasonable, though by not referring to discourse moves she would make. It also likely reflected her uncertainty at this time about what questions she could pose to address the situation that the teacher in the case faced.

Nicole and other participants paid considerable attention to this issue across the year, seeking examples and ways of posing questions to pique or sustain students' engagement with a task while preserving its cognitive complexity. At a subsequent session, when participants were discussing another case, Nicole talked about the importance of posing what she called "second-level questions," such as asking students to consider another way to solve a problem, or encouraging them to find a pattern. She suggested that such questions were useful to engage students in intellectually demanding work. This issue gave rise to the list of scaffolding strategies (see Table 17.1) that participants constructed and revised across several sessions.

Discussion

Earlier in this chapter we argued that an implementation plateau might be reached with *Standards*-based curriculum materials as a consequence of unresolved instructional issues. Using data from a professional development project involving teachers who were experienced users of the curriculum materials of the *Connected Mathematics Project*, we have added a bit more specificity to this argument. The curriculum implementation plateau appears to be associated with teachers having an underdeveloped: (a) conception of their role as active mediators of the interaction between students and content through the tasks found in the mathematics curriculum materials; and (b) repertoire of instructional strategies to use in shaping and facilitating students' learning of mathematics content through their engagement with the curriculum materials. As we have tried to illustrate in this chapter, these two features work in tandem to create the conditions that lead to a curriculum implementation plateau.

At the early stage of implementation, the curriculum materials offer a rich supply of new tasks, some of which can be used skillfully by teachers. Even if teachers have a narrow understanding of their role, implementation can proceed with success because the tasks in the curriculum materials can carry a considerable share of the instructional load. Some *Standards*-based curriculum materials provide teachers with a wide array of worthwhile tasks and supporting materials that can be used as resources for instruction regardless of teachers' visions and understandings of their roles. But after the initial surge of instructional innovation dissipates, as the curriculum materials become part of the new instructional routine, the contributions of the teacher become critical. It is at this point that an underdeveloped conception of role and limited repertoire of instructional strategies undermines further improvement, and a plateau is reached.

Our findings suggest that unresolved instructional issues can exist even for teachers who are in general agreement with *Standards*-based instructional precepts and who are eager users of *Standards*-based curriculum materials. BIFOCAL participants in the first year were viewed within their schools as accomplished teachers of mathematics; they were leaders among their colleagues. Moreover, they did not come to the project out of desperation, seeking help for instructional woes. In general, they were comfortable with themselves and their accomplishments, yet they also wished to continue refining their classroom practices.

Although our teachers began the project in a place where they attributed instructional challenges to factors such as time constraints, weak student motivation, and heterogeneity of student abilities, the experiences with narrative cases and collaborative lesson planning in BIFOCAL allowed them to: (a) develop a more elaborated and nuanced understanding of the teacher's role as mediator of students' interaction with curriculum materials and mathematical tasks; (b) deepen their understanding of some important aspects of teaching practice that are critical to success with *Standards*-based curriculum materials; and (c) enhance their repertoire of useful instructional strategies. A combination of individual reflection and group collaboration alongside activities, tools and frameworks that focus teachers' work on critical instructional issues seemed to allow our participants to move beyond the plateau. We base our judgment on the development in teachers' thinking about the instructional issues over the duration of the project sessions. Our close observation of teachers' discourse over the year points to progress in their ability to question certain instructional practices, including their own, and to analyze these instructional practices carefully using some of the tools provided by the project. In particular, the MTF provided the teachers with a language to capture a phenomenon of interest to them – when a lesson doesn't "go well" – and the TTLP provided structure and language to support their efforts to become more effective in their instructional practice.

This investigation has elaborated and illuminated aspects of the curriculum implementation plateau, but many questions remain and might be productively explored in future research. Is a plateau inevitable? Are there multiple plateaus? If the instruction-related issues unearthed in this study were made salient to teachers during preservice preparation, would they face the same difficulties? Suppose these issues were treated explicitly in the professional development offered when *Standards*-based curriculum materials are adopted? How do the issues unearthed in this study apply to curriculum materials that do not claim to be *Standards*-based? Interestingly, the participants in BIFOCAL thought that most of what they learned through the project would be useful no matter what curriculum materials they used. If so, then we hope that there are some useful ideas also embedded herein for teacher educators and professional developers.

Acknowledgments

This article is based upon work supported in part by the National Science Foundation under Grant Number 0119790 to the Center for Proficiency in Teaching Mathematics and in part by the Michigan State University Mathematics Education Endowment Fund for support of the BIFOCAL project. Any opinions, findings, and conclusions or recommendations expressed in this material are those of the authors and do not necessarily reflect the views of the NSF, the Center, or the university. We are grateful to Alison Castro and Gabriel Stylianides, whose input helped to shape the initial idea for this chapter. We also acknowledge the contributions of Dana Gosen, Kathy Morris, Beatriz Strawhun, Jenny Sealy, and Angela Hsu, who assisted with the planning of professional development sessions and the collection and/or analysis of data used herein. We are very grateful to the teachers who participated in the BIFOCAL project and shared with us their struggles as well as their accomplishments; their work on behalf of middle school students in Michigan is deeply appreciated. We want to note especially the contributions of Geraldine Devine, one of the participants in the first year of BIFOCAL and a colleague in later years, for sharing her insights into project experiences and the challenges of teaching with *Standards*-based curriculum materials. We also wish to acknowledge the positive influence on our thinking provided by the editors of this volume.

Notes

1. "Examining linear growth patterns: The case of Catherine Evans and David Young" (Smith et al., 2005a, pp. 10–27).
2. "Introducing ratios and proportions: The case of Marie Hanson" (Smith et al., 2005b, pp. 26–39).
3. See Silver et al. (2005) for more on this episode and its impact on participants.
4. "Connecting fractions, decimals & percents: The case of Randy Harris" (Smith et al., 2005b, pp. 10–22).

References

Banilower, E. R., Boyd, S. E., Pasley, J. D., & Weiss, I. R. (2006). *Lessons from a decade of mathematics and science reform: A capstone report for the Local Systemic Change through Teacher Enhancement Initiative*. Chapel Hill, NC: Horizon Research.

Begle, E. G. (1973). Lessons learned from SMSG. *Mathematics Teacher, 66*, 207–214.

Bell, M., Bell, J., Bretzlauf, J., Dillard, A., Hartfield, R., & Isaacs, A. (2001). *Everyday mathematics*. DeSoto, TX: Wright Group/McGraw-Hill.

Carroll, W. M., & Isaacs, A. (2003). Achievement of students using the University of Chicago School Mathematics Project's *Everyday Mathematics*. In L. Senk, & D. R. Thompson (Eds.), *Standards-based school mathematics curricula: What are they? What do students learn?* (pp. 79–108). Mahwah, NJ: Lawrence Erlbaum.

Clarke, D. M. (1997). The changing role of the mathematics teacher. *Journal for Research in Mathematics Education, 28*(3), 278–308.

Eisenhart, M. (2006). Representing qualitative data. In J. L. Green, G. Camilli, & P. B. Elmore (Eds.), *Handbook of complementary methods in education research* (pp. 567–581). Mahwah, NJ: Lawrence Erlbaum.

Erickson, J. (1986). Qualitative methods in research on teaching. In M. C. Wittrock (Ed.), *Handbook of research on teaching* (pp. 119–161). New York, NY: Macmillan.

Fullan, M. (2004). *System thinkers in action: Moving beyond the standards plateau*. London: Department of Education and Skills, Innovation Unit, in partnership with NCSL.

Hall, G. E., Loucks, S. F., Rutherford, W. L., & Newlove, B. W. (1975). Levels of use of innovation: A framework for analyzing innovation adoption. *Journal of Teacher Education, 26*(1), 52–56.

Henningsen, M., & Stein, M. K. (1997). Mathematical tasks and student cognition: Classroom-based factors that support and inhibit high-level mathematical thinking and reasoning. *Journal for Research in Mathematics Education, 29*, 514–549.

Hiebert, J., Stigler, J., Jacobs, J., Givvin, K., Garnier, H., Smith, M. et al. (2005). Mathematics teaching in the United States today (and tomorrow): Results from the TIMSS 1999 video study. *Educational Evaluation and Policy Analysis, 27*, 111–132.

Lampert, M. (2001). *Teaching problems and the problems of teaching*. New Haven, CT: Yale University Press.

Lappan, G., Fey, J. T., Fitzgerald, W. M., Friel, S. N., & Phillips, E. D. (1996). *Connected Mathematics Project*. Palo Alto, CA: Dale Seymour.

National Council of Teachers of Mathematics. (1989). *Curriculum and evaluation standards for school mathematics*. Reston, VA: Author.

National Council of Teachers of Mathematics (2000). *Principles and standards for school mathematics*. Reston, VA: Author.

Phillips, E., Lappan, G., & Grant, Y. (2000). *Implementing standards-based mathematics curricula:*

Preparing the community, the district, and teachers. East Lansing, MI: CMP, Mathematics Department, Michigan State University.

St John, M., Heenan, B., Houghton, N., & Tambe, P. (2001). *The NSF implementation and dissemination centers: An analytic framework.* Inverness, CA: Inverness.

Schoen, H. L., Cebulla, J. J., Finn, K. F., & Fi, C. (2003). Teacher variables that relate to student achievement when using a standards-based curriculum. *Journal for Research in Mathematics Education, 34*(3), 228–259.

Senk, S.L., & Thompson, D. R. (2003). *Standards-based school mathematics curricula: What are they? What do students learn?* Mahwah, NJ: Lawrence Erlbaum.

Silver, E. A., Ghousseini, H., Gosen, D., Charalambous, C., & Strawhun, B. T. F. (2005). Moving from rhetoric to praxis: Issues faced by teachers in having students consider multiple solutions for problems in the mathematics classroom. *Journal of Mathematical Behavior, 24,* 287–301.

Silver, E. A., Mills, V., Castro, A., & Ghousseini, H. (2006). Blending elements of lesson study with case analysis and discussion: A promising professional development synergy. In K. Lynch-Davis & R. L. Rider (Eds.), *The work of mathematics teacher educators: Continuing the conversation* (pp. 117–132). San Diego, CA: Association of Mathematics Teacher Educators.

Smith, M. S., & Bill, V. (2004, January). *Thinking through a lesson: Collaborative lesson planning as a means for improving the quality of teaching.* Presentation at the Annual Meeting of the Association of Mathematics Teacher Educators, San Diego, CA.

Smith, M. S., Silver, E. A., & Stein, M. K. (2005a). *Improving instruction in algebra: Using cases to transform mathematics teaching and learning,* Volume 2. New York, NY: Teachers College Press.

Smith, M. S., Silver, E. A., & Stein, M. K. (2005b). *Improving instruction in rational numbers and proportionality: Using cases to transform mathematics teaching and learning,* Volume 1. New York, NY: Teachers College Press.

Stein, M. K., & Lane, S. (1996). Instructional tasks and the development of student capacity to think and reason: An analysis of the relationship between teaching and learning in a reform mathematics project. *Educational Research and Evaluation, 2*(1), 50–80.

Stein, M. K., & Smith, M. S. (1998). Mathematical tasks as a framework for reflection: From research to practice. *Mathematics Teaching in the Middle School, 3*(4), 268–275.

Stein, M. K., Grover, B. W., & Henningsen, M. (1996). Building student capacity for mathematical thinking and reasoning: An analysis of mathematical tasks used in reform classrooms. *American Educational Research Journal, 33,* 455–488.

Stein, M. K., Remillard, J., & Smith, M. S. (2007). How curriculum influences student learning. In F. K. Lester (Ed.), *Second handbook of research on mathematics teaching and learning* (pp. 319–369). Charlotte, NC: Information Age.

Stein, M. K., Smith, M. S., Henningsen, M. A., & Silver, E. A. (2000). *Implementing standards-based mathematics instruction: A casebook for professional development.* New York, NY: Teachers College Press.

Strauss, A., & Corbin, J. (1998). *Basics of qualitative research.* Thousands Oaks, CA: Sage.

18

Part IV Commentary
Considering the Confounding Nature of Teachers' Use of Curriculum Materials

Thomas J. Cooney

Throughout the history of mathematics education there has been an emphasis on improving the teaching of mathematics. It seems fair to say that the typical mathematics classroom is teacher-dominated as teachers cover homework, explain new material, and assign homework. Certainly this theme has various nuances, but the general premise seems remarkably stable over the past 100 years. Perhaps we ought not to be surprised, given society's expectations of what constitutes appropriate schooling. Given the milieu that defines most classrooms and the necessity for teachers to deal with practical problems with limited resources, it is not surprising that reform, however defined, is difficult to achieve in other than limited circumstances. Some reform efforts have focused on curricular changes – for example, the "new math" of the 1960s. Others have focused on professional development programs in which teachers are encouraged to teach mathematics from a process orientation that honors the complexity of tasks and problem-solving behavior. The *Standards* (National Council of Teachers of Mathematics [NCTM], 2000), for example, emphasize the importance of process and students acquiring the ability to think quantitatively in real world settings.

The chapters in this part of the book share the common element of emphasizing process over the accumulation of information, and focus on teachers' use of *Standards*-based curriculum materials to achieve this end. In Chapter 16, Christou, Menon, and Philippou urge teachers to be listeners and not simply answer givers. Silver, Mills, Ghousseini, and Charalambous (Chapter 17) discuss the challenges of teaching that involve both mathematical and pedagogical considerations, and how teachers can move beyond the more immediate elements of instructional change. Similarly, Behm and Lloyd (Chapter 15) emphasize a kind of teaching that demands much more than delivering information. In each of these chapters, the authors explore issues related to how teachers interact with mathematics curriculum materials.

Given the many practical impediments teachers face in trying to teach in ways consistent with the *Standards* (NCTM, 2000), it should not be surprising that, whereas some teachers aim to implement curriculum materials as their author(s) intended, other teachers infuse their teaching with some elements of the intended curriculum but not in a fundamental way. This circumstance is true in almost every study of teacher change, whether the basis for reform is curriculum materials, professional development programs, or both. Behm and Lloyd's three teachers provide testimony to the variance in teacher implementation of curriculum materials. The fact that some teachers in the Silver et al. study reach a plateau of curriculum implementation and remain on that plateau is hardly news. The real question is what factors contribute to either facilitating or impeding the implementation of *Standards*-based curriculum materials. Although the three main chapters in this part of the book report isolated cases from studies with different goals and questions, the chapters jointly expose at least two important factors that I will examine below.

Managing a Classroom when Using *Standards*-Based Curriculum Materials

The essence of *Standards*-based instruction is to take advantage of critical moments – that is, moments that provide opportunities to capitalize on students' insights in order to promote a deeper understanding of mathematics. By definition, critical moments are aberrations to the norm. However, both teachers and students thrive on predictability. The notion of a didactical contract (see Brousseau, 1986) between teacher and students specifies that each operates within a certain agreed upon behavioral framework that provides a stable classroom environment. Implicitly defined didactical contracts are not, in themselves, impediments to change. Such contracts can certainly allow for and promote critical moments in which interesting mathematical phenomena outside a prescribed curriculum are explored. But, on the other hand, it is easy for didactical contracts to become pillars of predictability wherein critical moments become rarities rather than commonalities. In such cases, teaching mathematics is a matter of providing a literal translation of curriculum materials thus muting the potential richness of the curriculum program. A question worth considering is, "In a typical lesson, how many critical moments can a teacher reasonably handle?" This question strikes at the heart of teachers' use of *Standards*-based curriculum materials. The extent to which a curriculum program requires teachers to attend to student innovation – indeed, promote innovation – is the extent to which a certain tension exists between acknowledging that innovation and remaining within the framework of the didactical contract. Unfortunately, unpredictability is seldom perceived as a welcome addition to the workings of the classroom. This raises a question about a teacher's ability to implement *Standards*-based curriculum materials in which critical moments abound.

In Christou et al.'s study, novice teachers indicated considerable comfort with their new textbooks and their perceived ability to implement the curriculum program in an effective way. That is, beginning teachers in this study felt capable of meeting the demands of the new textbooks. The authors opined that their training generally accounted for this positive attitude. Yet, according to these same authors, beginning teachers expressed concern about the management factor and their ability to collaborate with parents, colleagues, and supervisors. Perhaps this concern accounts for their appreciation for the structure and the activities presented in the new textbooks. Still, beginning teachers were concerned about whether they had time to complete textbook activities given the considerable time required for organizing and implementing them. The authors suggest that the textbook's structured lessons appealed to teachers who shared this concern. In Chapter 15, Behm and Lloyd's Heather seemed to express a similar sentiment. Heather was not confident in her ability to teach mathematics, which probably contributed to her more literal use of the teaching guide. Her primary concern centered on time allocation, a managerial issue. She felt that implementation of the guide as it was intended would inhibit her ability to cover the material she was expected to cover. Consequently, she followed the guide in a rather scripted way, failing to represent the guide's process-oriented approach to teaching mathematics.

Without question, managerial issues are a primary concern to teachers, especially beginning teachers. The issue goes beyond time, and includes issues related to the insecurity associated with allowing instruction to venture into unchartered waters. In my many interviews with teachers, it was often the case that they used the language "step by step" to describe their method of teaching – a method they fully embraced. This atomization of teaching makes for certainty, a revered principle for many teachers, but generally excludes attention to critical moments.

This circumstance raises an important question regarding the use of curriculum materials embodied in scripted lessons. It may be that the scripts are better than most typical lessons; however, a scripted curriculum program is a rather pessimistic approach to changing teachers' instructional practices. Change should be grounded in the intelligence and creativity of teachers as they engage students, rather than follow a prescribed script. Perhaps the scripting of lessons can improve beginning teachers' ability to deal with their managerial concerns. But then it behooves teacher educators to convey the notion that a script is but a means to an end, and not an end in itself.

The Christou et al. study is encouraging in that it suggests that teacher education can prepare preservice teachers to have a positive disposition toward the vision of mathematics instruction described in the *Standards* (NCTM, 2000). This represents a counterpoint to Gellert's (2000) study of preservice elementary teachers who held the view that their primary task in teaching mathematics was to shield children from the kind of abstract and impersonal mathematical experiences that characterized their own experiences. If preservice teachers enter the profession with a positive attitude toward *Standards*-based curriculum materials, then an important question is the extent to which managerial concerns are significant impediments to innovative and effective use of curriculum materials. Teacher education programs need to address this concern, otherwise change efforts will likely be superficial or non-existent. I submit that Behm and Lloyd's Bridget is somewhat of an anomaly in that her adaptation of the curriculum guide was fundamental, running against the grain of other teachers and expectations at Walnut Street Elementary School. One can only surmise whether that kind of commitment could be sustained over several years were Bridget to remain at Walnut Street, or whether she would be "worn down" by the expectations of peers and parents. This concern deserves consideration especially because many teachers' mathematical experiences (unlike the teachers in the Christou et al. study) are contrary to the kind of mathematical experiences they are expected to provide their students (Frykholm, 1999).

The Issue of Multiplicity

One of the more intriguing questions was raised in Chapter 17, regarding the value of considering multiple solutions to mathematics problems. The question raised by one of Silver et al.'s teachers concerning the benefits of considering more than one solution strikes at the heart of instructional change in mathematics. Some teachers are undoubtedly intimidated by the prospect of exploring multiple solutions because of the pressure to cover a predetermined amount of content, a concern about possible management problems including time allocation, and the perception that it is only gifted students who profit from such an instructional approach. A common characteristic of all three chapters is their attention to transforming the teaching of mathematics into a thought-provoking and deep analysis of mathematical ideas – a circumstance that cries for multiplicity. Although this need not be the intent of every lesson, it should nevertheless have a prominent place in the teaching of mathematics; one that is observable on more than rare occasions.

The fact that some teachers, as suggested by Silver et al., were willing to embrace multiple solutions for the sake of affective concerns somewhat begs the question. Teachers rightfully take pride in promoting confidence in their students. But the question really is, "Confidence to do what?" Typically, when teachers talk about enhancing students' confidence, the reference point for that confidence is the production of correct answers. Skott's (2001) case of Christopher speaks directly to this point. As a preservice teacher, Christopher accepted many of the tenets of mathematics education reform, but when he had his own classroom other educational goals such as building student confidence overrode his beliefs about mathematics teaching, thus leading to a more teacher-directed instructional style. Skott summarized Christopher's approach to teaching in the following way: "The degree to which other aspects of Christopher's SMIs [School Mathematics Images] influence the classroom is contingent on their compatibility with the dominant organizational approach" (p. 26). I submit that Christopher's approach to reform is shared by many teachers.

From a reform perspective, multiplicity is fundamental. However, given the practicality of society's values, multiplicity is often subservient to efficiency. Of what value is conceptualizing different ways of finding the product $(3/4) \times (2/3)$ if the bottom line is whether a student can find the correct product regardless of process? Typically, academics are interested in *process* whereas society is interested in *product*. Consequently, the burden of the teacher educator is to depolarize the issue in such a way that the benefits of multiplicity not only embrace affective concerns (including students' confidence) but also increase students' capacity to deal with complexity. In some sense, this entails the teacher creating a different set of goals for student learning – goals that may be at odds with accepted norms for the community in which that teaching occurs. The case of

Behm and Lloyd's Bridget is an encouraging example of a teacher who was able to bring about change in an environment in which atomization prevailed.

The case of Nicole (Chapter 17) highlights the struggle teachers face in trying to decide how much guidance to provide students. The tension that Nicole experienced in trying to find a reasonable balance between maintaining a high level of cognitive demand and, at the same time, facilitating student success is central to teachers' efforts to enact *Standards*-based curriculum materials. The academic can take heart in the writing of scholars such as Dewey (1916), who thought of education as "the reconstruction or reorganization of experiences which add to the meaning of experience and which increases ability to direct the course of subsequent experiences" (p. 76). But teachers live in a practical world, one often torn between the importance of parents' pragmatism and that of realizing the canons of the profession as emphasized, for example, in the *Standards* (NCTM, 2000).

Silver et al. are to be commended for recognizing and trying to deal with the issue of multiplicity as they support teachers in their efforts to escape the plateau of simplicity. They rightly identify challenges to multiplicity such as management concerns (particularly time issues) and student readiness for multiplicity. I also applaud their emphasis on reflection and modeling as a way to enable teachers to move beyond the plateau. But the fact remains that teachers need to see multiplicity as the essence of teaching mathematics and not as an add-on to an already crowded agenda. Predictably, this is a tough sell. The good news is that the studies by Christou et al. and by Behm and Lloyd both suggest that preservice teacher education may provide a background for such instruction.

Unpacking the Confounding Nature of Teachers' Use of Curriculum Materials

When one thinks of reform via new curriculum materials, what often comes to mind is the "new math" era. Teachers were offered, either through projects or through commercially developed textbooks, an updated curriculum that emphasized reasoning and mathematical content that looked different from that in previous textbooks – but not too different. Although one might say that the "new math" failed, in fact the new math dominated the classroom for at least 20 years. What didn't change very much was the method of delivery. Instructional approaches remained teacher-centered. More recent studies (e.g., Wilson & Goldenberg, 1998) suggest a similar scenario: namely, teachers are easily persuaded to teach with new curriculum materials, but are reluctant to change their mode of instruction.

Forty years ago, the question of what it would take to enable teachers' enacted curriculum to match the intended curriculum was masked by the naiveté in expecting that teachers would deliver the curriculum as intended. No longer are we so naïve. Silver et al. meet this challenge frontally as they engage teachers in various kinds of reflective activities aimed at enhancing teachers' understanding of the mathematics (hence the mathematical challenge) and the means by which the curriculum materials can be enacted (hence the pedagogical challenge).

Although the authors mention the notion of disequilibrium almost in passing, this is a key concept for promoting change. It is through reflection that the inculcation of doubt arises in which alternative instructional methods can be discussed and debated. Without doubt and debate, there is little reason to change other than to accept unquestionably what an authority proposes – a form of indoctrination, if you will.

The use of scripts to influence change is a double-edged sword unless used very wisely. Teachers naturally gravitate to those things that enable them to make classroom life less hectic and more predictable. But such an outcome, almost by definition, is counter to a kind of teaching that honors the uncertainty associated with acknowledging students' ideas. Still, scripts can provide a start, a map of sorts, that can guide teachers as long as the map does not dictate the entire journey.

In Chapter 15, Behm and Lloyd propose some of the factors that may contribute to preservice teachers' ways of using *Standards*-based curriculum materials. Some of these factors are internal to the teachers (e.g., their confidence in teaching mathematics along with the degree to which they understand the mathematics), whereas other factors are external (e.g., the student-teaching placement). These factors, together with the results of the Christou et al. study, suggest that much can be done to enhance preservice teachers' understanding of and confidence in implementing a new curriculum program. The Silver et al. study demonstrates the strong need for teachers to (a) develop deeper understandings of their roles as mediators between students and curriculum materials, and (b) enhance their repertoires of pedagogical strategies to use in facilitating students' learning with *Standards*-based curriculum materials.

It seems reasonable to ask questions such as, "Whose reform is it?" and "Who wants it?" The short answer is generally not students or their parents, and often not teachers unless they participate in programs like that of Silver et al. So what leverage for reform exists? Perhaps the most fundamental reason that teachers are willing to engage in instructional change is not edicts from above but the recognition that it provides a context for recognizing how students can grow intellectually, and to take pride in that growth. Such an orientation allows teachers to transform their professional lives from something routine to something invigorating – namely, coming to understand students' thinking. Curriculum materials by themselves can provide a certain kind of excitement in that the teacher has something "new" to teach, but the real excitement comes from the teacher being engaged in the intellectual activity of trying to understand children's thought processes. The role of the teacher educator is to provide contexts in which teachers can see the possibility of having a different professional and intellectual life when implementing new curriculum materials.

A Concluding Thought

Consideration of teachers' use of *Standards*-based curriculum materials is a worthy arena in which to study the complexities of mathematics education. Ultimately, we strive for a teaching enterprise that honors reflection and analysis rather than the accumulation of information. Research can provide insights into how teachers at various levels of professional development can be supported in their efforts to use curriculum materials in mathematics instruction in meaningful ways. Building on the studies presented in Part IV, ongoing work in this area should aim to develop understandings of the knowledge and skills that teachers, at different points on the professional continuum, draw upon and develop as they use mathematics curriculum materials.

Friedman (2006) argues that as the world gets flatter, it is imperative that our students get smarter in terms of solving significant problems if our society is to maintain a strong economy. Teaching via a broadcast metaphor unravels the very intention of most *Standards*-based curriculum programs. Consequently, as argued previously, teachers must recognize the importance of multiplicity and students' flexibility in thinking about mathematics if we are to realize our goals in mathematics education and, indeed, in society. Fundamentally, this is a moral undertaking. Friere (1970) reminds us that pedagogy in which the "knower" transmits information to the "unknower" is a form of indoctrination often cloaked in a false sense of generosity. Although mathematics teachers would be loath to see themselves as indoctrinating students, there is nevertheless a great temptation, given the milieu of the classroom, to ask students to accept certain facts *sans* evidence – a form of indoctrination that underlies Friere's concern. As Taylor (1996) pointed out, "Epistemological reform of the traditional mathematics classroom is, therefore, synonymous with cultural reconstruction" (p. 168). We might be quick to argue that our goals in mathematics education are not nearly so dramatic. However, caution should prevail. The tensions experienced by Bridget (Chapter 15) and Nicole (Chapter 17) highlight a basic epistemological struggle about how education gets defined.

The authors of these chapters are primarily concerned with the nature of teachers' interactions with *Standards*-based curriculum materials. The evidence suggests that mathematics teacher educators are not passive conduits in enabling teachers to realize the potential of curriculum materials. This is good news. It is my contention that our goals are not simply about better mathematics or better test scores, or even enhancing the professional lives of teachers; rather, they are about embracing an interest in matters intellectual. It makes little sense for a teacher to proclaim that *Gone with the Wind* (Mitchell, 1936) is a classic unless the readers see the power of the author's ideas. Just as we ask teachers to teach mathematics from an evidential perspective, so should teacher educators address curriculum implementation from an evidential perspective. Teachers need to see the power in realizing curriculum innovation not only in terms of enhancing student learning but also in creating a more dynamic view of what it means to do mathematics. The question is not one of uncovering a sufficient condition for educational change, but rather one of exploring possible necessary conditions for innovation. The enterprise addressed in these three chapters provides a context for that exploration.

References

Brousseau, G. (1986). Fondements et méthodes de la didactique des mathématiques. *Recherches en Didactique des Mathématiques, 7*(2), 33–115.

Dewey, J. (1916). *Democracy and education.* New York, NY: Free Press.

Friedman, T. (2006). *The world is flat: A brief history of the twenty-first century.* New York, NY: Farrar, Straus and Giroux.

Friere, P. (1970). *Pedagogy of the oppressed.* New York, NY: Herder and Herder.

Frykholm, J. (1999). The impact of reform: Challenges for mathematics teacher preparation. *Journal of Mathematics Teacher Education, 2,* 79–105.

Gellert, U. (2000). Mathematics instruction in safe space: Prospective elementary teachers' views of mathematics education. *Journal of Mathematics Teacher Education, 3,* 251–270.

Mitchell, M. (1936). *Gone with the wind.* New York, NY. Macmillan.

National Council of Teachers of Mathematics. (2000). *Principles and standards for school mathematics.* Reston, VA: Author.

Skott, J. (2001). The emerging practices of a novice teacher: The roles of his school mathematics images. *Journal of Mathematics Teacher Education, 4,* 3–28.

Taylor, P. (1996). Mythmaking and mythbreaking in the mathematics classroom. *Educational Studies in Mathematics, 31*(1–2), 151–173.

Wilson, M., & Goldenberg, M. P. (1998). Some conceptions are difficult to change: One middle school mathematics teacher's struggle. *Journal of Mathematics Teacher Education, 1,* 269–293.

19

Part IV Commentary

Use of Curriculum Materials at Different Points on the
Professional Continuum

Eileen Phillips

As a practitioner respondent, I am viewing these chapters through my own eyes and experiences – the only way I can. I have been an elementary school teacher since 1971, and an elementary school administrator since 2000. During these years I have been seriously immersed in education: teaching all elementary grades (kindergarten to seventh grade); sponsoring more than 20 student teachers in my various schools and classrooms; working for higher degrees while continuing to teach full-time; working as a teacher-researcher and a co-researcher in my classroom; hosting various studies that others were exploring in my room; giving workshops; teaching occasionally at the university level in both face-to-face instruction and distance education; writing academic papers; presenting at conferences; and advising publishing companies.

In schools, we often find a mixture of each of the teaching and implementation cases depicted in these chapters – that is, we have new curriculum programs being adopted willingly and less willingly, resisted, subverted (whether consciously or not), and outright rejected. We run the gamut from skillful adoption to unskilled non-adoption; we have thoughtful, nuanced implementation, and that reminiscent of following a recipe. In schools, we have student teachers, novice teachers, experienced teachers, and expert teachers. We have teachers who are ready to change, ready to implement new programs or utilize new curriculum materials, and those who are seldom happy to move away from what is known and comfortable – and, of course, we encounter all motivational stances.

Curriculum change is a difficult arena for many teachers. I believe this is partly because teaching is such a human endeavor – we have people (teachers) working with other real, live, emotion-filled people (other teachers, students) who are growing and changing constantly. Because students and their needs are so variable, some teachers like the feeling of believing that, once mastered, the curriculum at least can remain constant, a fixed point in a turning world. Most teachers have learned to be eclectic, selecting only what they see the need to change and ignoring the rest. Many disregard the reasons offered for the new curriculum program and quickly pass through the stage of trying to understand the major differences between the old and the new. They become satisfied with outward change, not continuing the quest for their own sense-making. Some believe that change inheres only in *using* the new curriculum materials and need not involve a change in philosophy. And there are those who fully embrace the change and willingly work on needed transformations to align with new strategies and philosophies, as well as curriculum materials.

A common theme across the three main chapters in this part of the book is that of teacher concerns. Sufficient concern has been raised in me while reading these chapters to encourage reflection about what I find discomforting and disconcerting: the placement of student teachers and what they have to learn; curriculum material adoption without significant preparation of teachers for the changes that will be encountered; and ways to identify and support sustainable change in *more* teachers. I am also concerned when mathematics texts are viewed and talked about as *being* the curriculum, and when learning is viewed as occurring along a straightforward continuum. I will discuss each point briefly in the following sections.

The Context for Student Teaching

Becoming a teacher is a self-actualizing process that can continue throughout a teacher's career. It is also a non-linear process, and so envisioning it along a uniform continuum is difficult for me. Student teachers are learners – the very nature of being a student teacher means accepting that there will be mistakes made, choices will often need re-examining, there will be periods of rapid growth and times of struggle, and there will be occasions when one seems to be moving backward. A student teacher needs a safe and assisted context in which to learn, and deserves a sponsor teacher dedicated to supporting the initial stages of the process that we call "learning to teach." I believe that student teachers need lots of opportunities to view good practice and to discuss what makes good practice.

The student teachers introduced by Behm and Lloyd in Chapter 15 showed various levels of confidence with mathematics, and this is perfectly usual. The classrooms were early primary (kindergarten and first grade), so the mathematics content itself should not have been difficult for the student teachers; however, it can be expected that the strategies for teaching this content could be. I was concerned that the students did not seem to be optimally placed. For growth in awareness to occur, as it surely must in student teaching, ample discussion concerning what happened during a lesson needs to take place. Student teachers need to become increasingly clear about their own pedagogic intentions with respect to their students in mathematics, as well as those intentions imposed from the outside, through curriculum program specifications or guidelines and through curriculum materials (which are decidedly not the same thing, though the phrase "curriculum use" seemed to suggest that). They need to learn about time and timing of tasks and interventions, and about broadening and refining their repertoire of teacher possibilities.

Also, student teachers need the opportunity to see exemplary teaching. They need to know it is necessary and even desirable to struggle with mathematics, timing, management, and diverse student needs. They need to be aware of the complexity of planning lessons – and also of the necessity of seeing medium- and long-term goals and big ideas while working within constraints of time and timing; pondering choices about when to move on and when to persist, when to prod, prompt, and question; how to encourage more student voice; and how to ensure each student has a chance to contribute meaningfully.

I know that having a student teacher can also be excellent professional development for the sponsor teacher. By watching what works and what does not, by co-planning and making the range of choices more transparent, by considering whether intent and impact of a lesson align, and by discussing what I would normally at best only write a note to myself about, I grow alongside my student. And where do these "intents" come from? The intensity of noticing and questioning what is actually occurring increases my perception of why I do what I do.

Curriculum Change and Text Material Change: Adoption and Implementation

In my experience, successful curriculum change requires extensive familiarization and preparation prior to teaching (sometimes referred to as *front-end loading*), ongoing support, and many opportunities for in-depth discussion. In Chapter 16, some of the issues that result due to insufficient preparatory work are explored. Teachers need to understand the reasons for curriculum change, and know what will be expected of them and their students. In mathematics, current curriculum programs are moving our primary and middle school students beyond computation as an end in itself. There is, for instance, an increased emphasis on students knowing how to represent their thinking, understanding that there are various ways to reach a successful solution, and making decisions about how accurate an answer needs to be considering the context of the problem. In order for changes in the content of mathematics curriculum programs to be permanent, teachers need to change the way they view teaching mathematics. This teacher-change needs to be organic and cellular; it cannot be only cosmetic. Change that relies only on material change, such as exchanging one textbook for another or the addition of new manipulative tools, tends to be superficial. Often, in such cases, a classroom might *look* changed but does not *sound* changed.

Identifying and Sustaining Change in Teacher Practice

I found myself applauding the context for supporting change presented by Silver, Mills, Ghousseini and Charalambous in Chapter 17, because teachers and their administrators were actually given time during the school day, away from school, to explore their thinking. They were provided opportunities to identify and grapple with some really big issues – for example, when might multiple solution paths be clarifying and when might they be confusing? Could teachers be cheating their students when they try to simplify an idea? Might a teacher ever want to make the task easier for a particular student? How can students be encouraged to persevere with cognitively difficult problems? What entails a mathematically rich context? The sessions seemed to involve teachers exploring the pedagogic practices embedded within the text materials, as much as the tasks or explanations with which the teachers would have had a fair amount of experience. Time was when mathematics curriculum programs deliberately eschewed any discussion or proposals of specific pedagogies; that was seen as the domain of the teacher. Current text materials present a far more complex mix, as with the creation and expansion of the teacher guide. The discussions reported indicate how necessarily closely linked the two are.

As I read Chapter 17, I found myself wondering how such opportunities can be made available for more teachers – how can this study setting be moved into school sites so more teachers can participate? I also wondered whether teachers recognize when they have reached an implementation plateau. I thought about situations in which such comfort is not a "bad" thing, but rather a place that allows one to take more risks – hypothesizing that if a teacher is competent and comfortable with the curriculum, then more opportunities can be found to explore teaching practice and learning outcomes that were not expected. Reflecting on surprising outcomes often furthers personal professional growth. Ultimately, "good" teachers need ways to monitor their own growth and situations, and they require time during the day when they can question and discuss their own practice.

Perhaps instilling strategies for reflection into student teaching programs will result in a cohort of teachers who expect to be thoughtful practitioners and who welcome opportunities to observe and be observed. Other ways to achieve this supportive context include joining district-sponsored professional groups, attending interest group meetings at the school level, and, as discussed earlier, volunteering to sponsor student teachers.

The Role of Textbooks and Other Materials in the Process of Curriculum Program Change

In my experience, mathematics curriculum materials do not make a mathematics curriculum. Although textbooks and materials are customarily designed (or at least claim they are) to align with "the curriculum" (which in Canada is far from unitary) by providing tasks and strategies that support it, in themselves they are not the curriculum. Furthermore, in many cases a single textbook should not be the only resource used. Exceptions to this include instances when a new textbook is being assessed and those times when a teacher is unfamiliar with the concepts being presented. A mathematics textbook should not be used as a recipe book for teaching mathematics. When this happens, teachers are in danger of losing sight of the concepts and burying both themselves and their students in the details. The impact of such use (e.g., rushing through too superficially, not gaining trust in the concepts, not appreciating the process) often belies the intent (e.g., not to make mistakes, to follow expert advice, to give the students a comprehensive program) of such strict adherence. Textbooks published in recent years contain more tasks than can ever be done in depth by a student, and often rely on the teacher or the student to make choices about which tasks will be attempted. Over-reliance on a textbook can result in rich mathematical opportunities being missed. Teachers of mathematics need to be secure and confident in their own pedagogy to prevent missed opportunities that can arise when, for example, a student gives an incorrect answer but uses an outstanding strategy.

Again, it is necessary for teachers who are solid in their understanding of mathematical pedagogy to be the ones who have student teachers. Especially in primary and middle schools, where teachers' interests and expertise often are in the fields of language arts and social studies, it is important to see strength and confidence in the teaching of mathematics. Moreover, it is important that these confident teachers be encouraged to join professional groups that allow them to support and learn alongside other interested teachers.

Comfort with Discomfort

Many of the themes that run across these three chapters dealt with the ability to be comfortable with difficult tasks, cognitive dissonance, and ambiguity. Feeling comfortable with discomfort is one of the attitudes that students themselves require for successful mathematics learning. The ability to ponder a confusion, work through a frustration, and persevere through a problem (perhaps by leaving and subsequently returning to it) are all strategies for success in learning mathematics. They are also strategies for success in teaching mathematics. Teaching mathematics must be aligned with learning mathematics, and sensitivity to this alignment goes beyond what any set of mathematics materials can present. Somewhere and somehow in the course of becoming (and continuing to become) the best teacher one can be, discomfort needs to be regarded as encouraging, and questioning one's practice needs to become a routine part of being an engaged and aware teacher.

In Summary

These three chapters looked at the use of curriculum materials at different stages of curriculum program implementation and at different points on the professional continuum. In Chapter 15, we were introduced to three student teachers, each in different contexts and each with differing levels of confidence about teaching mathematics. We were led to consider the importance of match-making and fit between student teacher and sponsor teacher, as well as the classroom context, and knowledge about, and comfort with, teaching mathematics. We read how important high-quality curriculum materials are for student teachers, and we came to realize that the curriculum materials can form the backbone of some teachers' mathematics teaching.

In Chapter 16, we saw what can happen when the responsibility for implementation of new mathematics curriculum programs falls entirely on the shoulders of the teachers. We came to realize the stress that novice teachers feel when trying to adopt new curriculum programs with insufficient support at the same time as desperately trying to "fit into" their new profession, often while noticing that their more seasoned colleagues may not be implementing the new curriculum using all of the recommended curriculum materials. We saw how lack of time is a great stressor for both novice and experienced teachers, especially when initiating a new curriculum program.

In Chapter 17, Silver et al. presented a model for avoiding a situation that they termed a "curriculum implementation plateau." They explained this as a teacher's comfort level that might negatively impact a curriculum program. The authors worked with 12 experienced teachers, and were successful in supporting these teachers to delve more deeply into their personal understanding of the mathematics curriculum program and ways to use curriculum materials to support student learning. These authors pointed us toward considering the role of "struggle," and gave examples of teachers reflecting on times when things did not "go as expected."

These chapters took me to places of contemplation concerning professional experiences of teaching. I found myself looking through a small lens at three specific student teachers while they attempted to learn about teaching mathematics; at a large-scale study of beginning teachers' concerns while grappling with a new curriculum; at a group of experienced and capable teachers who found themselves at an implementation plateau using innovative mathematics materials that had become somewhat familiar and "normalized." The three chapters moved me back and forth, up and down, and in and out of focus about what is meant by curriculum, curriculum implementation, curriculum materials, instructional practice, and professional development. Also, I thought about why we change curriculum programs, how we change practice, what can get lost and what can get found in implementation, the timeline required for initial change, and how continued change can be supported and sustained. Additionally, I found myself wondering about the teacher–student–content–context relationships that are necessary for mathematics to be embraced and learned. Ultimately, I reflected on the nature of learning. As an educator, there is a perpetual need to deepen and sharpen my understanding of the learning process through the alignment of active professional reflection, discussion, and practice.

V

Teacher Learning Through and in Relation to the Use of Curriculum Materials

20

Negotiating the Literacy Demands of *Standards*-Based Curriculum Materials

A Site for Teachers' Learning

Helen M. Doerr and Kelly Chandler-Olcott

Midway through week two of summer work for the mathematics teachers at Belmont School, five teachers of grades six through eight have convened in their school library to reflect on the previous academic year, examine students' work, and engage in curriculum planning as part of a three-year study focused on mathematics and literacy. This summer, they have been collaborating mainly with Helen, the mathematics education professor who serves as the university researcher with their school, but Kelly, a literacy education professor who works primarily with another school in the project, joins the Belmont team today for a consultation. When she arrives, the teachers are working alone and in grade-level pairs to revise their writing plans – one- to two-page summaries for each Connected Mathematics Project book that list the writing tasks teachers have selected for students, given the key mathematical ideas explored in the investigations.

After 90 minutes of work time, the five teachers, two faculty members, and a graduate student assistant meet to discuss their progress. The teachers are pleased that their urban, often under-prepared students no longer resist writing so much, and Ashley shares that one of her eighth-graders pointed out in class recently that she knew Ashley wanted them to explain their answers in writing. But as Tracy, a sixth-grade teacher, points out, by the end of the year "The good writers are still good writers and the poor writers are still poor writers." To address this concern, Kelly suggests adding two columns to their writing plans, one explaining their rationale for selecting the task and the other explaining what differentiated instructional support they will provide so that all students can develop their writing over time. The teachers take up this idea, marking the beginnings of an important shift in their practices.

This vignette provides a glimpse of how a group of teachers collaborated with each other to make sense of the literacy demands of the *Standards*-based curriculum materials of the *Connected Mathematics Project* [CMP] (Lappan, Fey, Fitzgerald, Friel, & Phillips, 1998a). It also demonstrates the interdisciplinary nature of a study that brought faculty members and graduate students in literacy education together with their counterparts in mathematics education to work with mathematics teachers of grades six to ten. Finally, the vignette hints at a key theme of this chapter: a shift in the teachers' practice toward gradually releasing more responsibility for literacy learning to students over time.

One salient feature of *Standards*-based curriculum materials (such as those that were, like CMP, funded by the National Science Foundation in the 1990s) is the expectation that students will make mathematical sense of situations conveyed through stories, pictures, talk, charts, and diagrams. Further, when students engage in these sense-making activities, they are encouraged and expected to develop their mathematical thinking by communicating with peers and teachers. At the same time, teachers need to learn to facilitate the use of communicative practices that are significantly different from those involved in the use of commercially-developed textbook materials. The focus of our study is on the learning that occurred for a group of middle-grades teachers as they addressed the demands for mathematical writing when using *Standards*-based curriculum materials.

In the pages that follow, we discuss the role of communication in mathematics, particularly mathematical writing, and discuss the affordances and limitations of the NCTM *Standards* (2000) in this regard. Next, we describe our methods in conducting the study and provide more details about the setting and participants than can be found in the vignette. We share two key shifts that occurred in the teachers' perspectives and practices related to addressing the demands for mathematical writing offered by *Standards*-based curriculum materials, and we conclude with a discussion of the implications of these shifts.

Background and Theoretical Perspectives

Over the past 15 years, much research on the importance of mathematical communication for students' learning has been published. In 2001, Sfard argued that "communication should be viewed not as a mere aid to thinking, but as almost tantamount to the thinking itself" (p. 13). Other researchers drawing on sociocultural perspectives have argued that learning is constituted by participation in particular discursive practices (see Gee, 2002; Lerman, 2001). During this same timeframe, curriculum standards documents articulated a dual benefit of communication for students: "They communicate to learn mathematics and they learn to communicate mathematically" (NCTM, 2000, p. 60). This focus has been reflected in many *Standards*-based curriculum materials that offer students opportunities to learn mathematics by investigating situations that need to be interpreted and explained through text.

The Communication Standard

The NCTM's (2000) communication standard points to the value of rich conversations about worthwhile mathematical tasks for students' learning. The *Standards* suggest that "support for students is vital" (p. 60) as they learn to participate in these conversations, and that teachers need to build a community in which the exchange of ideas can freely occur – a potentially challenging task in the middle grades. The role of writing in the classroom is viewed as supporting the organization and consolidation of students' thinking. In the *Standards*, the middle grades are portrayed as a time of greater awareness of audience and purpose for written work, and as a time when students begin to shift from informal, ordinary language to more formal and conventional mathematical language. The *Standards* for the middle grades strongly emphasize the need for oral language to support this process. Two short recommendations suggest that teachers should encourage pupils to write reflective journals or write letters of explanations to younger pupils about recently learned concepts.

In addition to these affordances, however, we find three important limitations in the NCTM's recommendations. The first limitation is that the *Standards* document does not address the *development* of students' writing. The *Standards* offer little sense of how writing activities might fit together or how students' writing might develop across tasks and over time. Morgan (1998) pointed out that in mathematics practice, the development of writing is assumed to be "natural and spontaneous" (p. 39). The *Standards* appear to make this same assumption: "With experience, students will gain proficiency in organizing and recording their thinking" (p. 61) and "As students practice communication, they should express themselves increasingly clearly and coherently" (p. 62). There is little sense of what kinds of experiences students might need to gain proficiency with mathematical writing. There is only limited discussion of different genres of mathematical writing and how students might learn to attend to audience and purpose in each of those genres, and how these, in turn, might vary across mathematical tasks and grade level.

A second concern is the limited attention that is given to the writing difficulties that might be encountered by second-language learners, by students who struggle with academic literacy, or by students with special needs. These students are among those at greatest risk for not learning from experiences with these contextually complex materials (Schoenbach, Greenleaf, Cziko, & Hurwitz, 1999). Although the *Standards* recommend that students be encouraged to grapple with concepts by communicating them in their own words, the ability to do so varies among students with different experiences and language proficiencies. Students whose everyday language has the least congruence with traditional academic discourse will likely need considerable experience in authentic language contexts as well as considerable scaffolding from their teachers to achieve fluency with what Herbel-Eisenmann (2002) calls "official mathematics language."

A third difficulty with the *Standards* is related to the role of the teacher in relationship to written communication in the classroom. As Morgan (1998) has pointed out, in mathematics teaching, writing often "appears as a background activity that does not require specific attention" (p. 41). The teacher's role in orchestrating classroom conversations and establishing norms for argumentation has received considerably more attention in the research literature (Kieran, Forman, & Sfard, 2002; Lampert & Blunk, 1998; O'Connor, 2001; Pimm, 1987; Yackel & Cobb, 1996) than the teacher's role in supporting the development of students' written communication. Nonetheless, the teacher plays an important role in selecting writing tasks for students and in framing them in ways that attend to audience, purpose, and genre. The teacher also plays a role in responding to students' work, especially that of students who are struggling with written expression, in ways that support students in achieving greater clarity and coherence.

Mathematical Writing

Several researchers have investigated writing-to-learn approaches to mathematics instruction, especially in Australia, Great Britain, and the United States (e.g., Clarke, Waywood & Stephens, 1993; Durkin & Shire, 1991; Powell & Lopez, 1989; Pugalee, 2005; Waywood, 1994). Often the rationale for writing-to-learn is given in cognitive terms, citing the value of students reflecting on their mathematical work. Despite these rationales, in her work in South African classrooms Ntenza (2006) found that teachers infrequently used writing in their classrooms, which she attributed to a lack of resources and a need for professional development for the teachers on supporting learners in the production of mathematical writing. In addition to the cognitive value of reflecting on one's work in writing, others argue that such writing has value for the teacher in assessing students' understandings (Marks & Mousley, 1990; Miller, 1992). Generally, such arguments assume a transparent and unproblematic link between students' written expressions and their understanding of the topic, and between students' written expression and teachers' interpretations of that writing (Morgan & Watson, 2002). This suggests two aspects of teachers' learning that need to be addressed: support of the development of students' proficiency as mathematical writers, and increased sophistication on the part of the teacher in interpreting students' written expressions.

A Framework from Literacy Instruction

To address support for the development of students as mathematical writers, we drew on the framework of gradual release of responsibility put forward by Pearson and colleagues (Duke & Pearson, 2002; Fielding & Pearson, 1994; Kong & Pearson, 2003; Pearson & Gallagher, 1983). Originally framed to address students' increased proficiency as readers and more recently applied to writing (Fisher & Frey, 2003), we find this model useful because it directly addresses the relationship between teachers' and students' roles over time. In the gradual release model, responsibility for performing a task shifts from resting entirely with the teacher to being taken up by the students in their independent performance of a task. The model includes three stages. The initial stage is characterized by teaching approaches that include teacher modeling, explanation, and demonstration. The second stage is that of guided practice, in which the teacher gradually gives students more responsibility for performing tasks and provides scaffolds that support and guide the students' attempted performance. The final stage is that of independent practice and application to new situations. The gradual release of responsibility model provides a way for teachers to think about scaffolding instruction for increased student independence over time.

Methods

Our methodological approach is the multi-tiered teaching experiment (Lesh & Kelly, 1999), which allowed us to collect and interpret data at the researcher level, the teacher level, and the student level. This multi-level approach is intended to generate and refine principles, programmatic properties (such as interventions with teachers), and products (such as shareable tools and artifacts of practice) that are increasingly useful to both the researchers and the teachers. Central to our analytic approach is the notion that, as researchers, we examine the teachers' descriptions, interpretations, and analyses of artifacts of practice that are developed, examined, and refined during our collaborative work. At the student tier, the set of artifacts includes the writing that students generated in response to various text-based, mathematical tasks from the *Standards*-based curriculum materials, CMP (Lappan et al., 1998a). The artifacts located at the teacher tier consist of the literacy scaffolding approaches, including the writing plans we mentioned in the opening vignette, that the teachers and researchers developed collaboratively to support students in interpreting and responding to the tasks. The artifacts generated and analyzed at student and teacher tiers became the findings at the researcher tier that are reported here.

The research was carried out by a team of university-based researchers in mathematics education and literacy education, working in concert with mathematics teachers in a mid-sized urban district that had recently adopted *Standards*-based curriculum materials. The teachers were from one high school and its three feeder schools (two middle schools and a K-8 school). The results reported here are drawn from the work at the K-8 school. At the time of the study, that school had approximately 860 students and 45 teachers and support staff. The school population consisted of approximately 31 percent African-American, 21 percent Asian, 35 percent white, and 11 percent Latino students. About 20 percent of these students were English language learners, and 25 percent were identified as having special needs. About 88 percent of the students qualified for free or reduced lunch, suggesting a high degree of poverty.

The five teachers involved in the study from this site were volunteers and represented all but one of the middle-grade mathematics teachers in the school. Most of the teachers had used the CMP materials for one year. All five were female and white. The two sixth-grade teachers, Sara and Tracy, each had over 25 years of teaching experience. One of the teachers, Cassie, taught both seventh and eighth grades; another teacher, Arlene, taught seventh grade. Both Cassie and Arlene had over ten years of experience. The other eighth-grade teacher, Ashley, was in her first year of teaching as we began this project. Over three years, our work with the teachers consisted primarily of four ongoing activities: (a) summer workshops of a week or more, (b) quarterly project meetings with teams from other project schools, (c) bi-weekly team meetings, and (d) "lesson cycles" with individual teachers (described below).

The five teachers rarely shared planning times during the day and seldom taught the same lesson at the same time, even when teaching the same grade. Hence, a shared approach to jointly planning and observing common lessons was not feasible. However, the teachers did share a common focus on the need for their students to become better mathematical writers. This focus was driven, in part, by the high-stakes state testing that occurred at the end of the eighth grade, where students were asked to explain their reasoning or their solution strategies in writing. All the teachers in grades six through eight felt a shared responsibility for preparing students for this exam – something they frequently discussed during team meetings.

Their focus on writing was also driven by the CMP curriculum materials, which included many tasks requiring students to explain their reasoning or share solution strategies. The curriculum materials also included tasks that the teachers saw as higher-level thinking tasks, requiring elaborated descriptions and explanations. Finally, the focus on writing reflected the teachers' concerns about many of their students who were not reading or writing at grade level because they had special needs or were English language learners. This shared interest in student writing then became the focus of discussions at the bi-weekly team meeting and in the "lesson cycles." It drove the collection of student work to be analyzed and annotated. These samples of student work were the principal artifacts from the student tier that we examined in our work together.

Since our research question concerned changes in the teachers' practices, we used "lesson cycles" to work jointly on planning, implementing, and debriefing lessons for supporting literacy opportunities for students. The lesson cycles began halfway through the first year of the project and continued through the third year of the project. Each teacher participated in a lesson cycle approximately once every three weeks with a member of the research team. Each lesson cycle consisted of three elements: (a) a planning session that followed the overall CMP guidelines for the investigations and that focused on the question, "What are the literacy opportunities in this lesson?"; (b) the implementation of the lesson, which a researcher observed and documented with extensive field notes; and (c) a de-briefing session with the teacher to gain insight collaboratively into the teacher's thinking about the literacy opportunities of the lesson and to collect shareable artifacts from the lesson, such as instructional strategies used to support students' learning. The de-briefing sessions often centered on a discussion of the students' written work and how that might be used to inform subsequent lessons. The planning and debriefing sessions were audiotaped and later transcribed. Brief memos were written based on notes taken and the artifacts of the session.

At the end of the second year of the project, the teachers developed a set of writing plans (described more fully below) for each instructional unit at each grade level; these became artifacts at the teacher tier that were jointly examined by the researchers and teachers. Other data sources included field notes from the summer sessions and bi-weekly after-school team meetings; field notes and transcripts from the lesson cycles; and four interviews with each teacher, one conducted prior to the start of the project and one conducted at the end of each of the three school years. We also examined the artifacts that were produced by the teachers (e.g., lesson plans, student materials, and annotations of student work) as they worked with the research team in developing instructional approaches for supporting students' written communication. Our analyses of these artifacts of practice have been used to inform our continued work with the teachers, and are the primary basis of the findings reported here.

Mathematics and Literacy: New Perspectives and Practices

Over the three years of the project, two major shifts occurred in the teachers' perspectives and practices. First, these middle school teachers shifted from seeing the *Standards*-based mathematics curriculum materials as a barrier to their mathematics teaching to seeing that the materials provided new opportunities for students to learn mathematics. The second shift occurred as they saw that opportunities for writing needed to be addressed in systematic ways that supported the students' development as mathematical writers over time. We discuss each of these changes in turn.

The Shift from Barrier to Opportunity

Encountering the Barriers

Initially, the teachers reported that the curriculum materials presented significant challenges in the areas of readability and vocabulary, and they felt that the curriculum developers assumed a mastery of basic computational skills that many of their students lacked. Sara voiced others' concerns when she observed that "the materials are difficult to read. There is a lot of verbiage in places." All of the teachers agreed that they did not do enough writing with their students and, as Tracy observed, "It's the writing piece that follows [an investigation] that falls off and [the students] never get to." Ashley commented that many of the students "cannot write complete sentences or sentences without spelling errors ... and they need guidance." The teachers reported that students struggled to express and elaborate their ideas in writing when faced with the extended response questions typical of the curriculum materials.

In attempting to overcome these barriers, the teachers found that the curriculum materials provided little guidance for supporting students in generating appropriate written responses to the tasks in the texts. Cassie used the following writing prompt from the curriculum materials with her seventh-grade students: "Explain how you can find a scale factor between two similar figures. Use an example to explain your thinking." The teachers' guide of CMP's *Stretching and Shrinking* unit provided the sample student response shown in Figure 20.1.

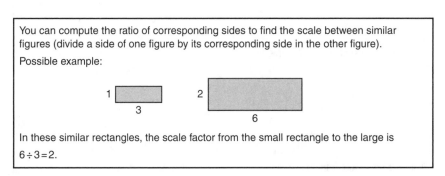

Figure 20.1 Sample student response from *Stretching and Shrinking* (Lappan et al., 2004b, p. 40).

The teachers' materials did not illustrate the range of responses that students might give to this writing prompt. There were no references to particular difficulties that students might encounter in creating a written response, nor were there any suggestions of strategies that teachers could use to help students improve their writing. In giving this prompt to her seventh-grade students, Cassie found many students responded in ways similar to the examples shown in Figure 20.2. Cassie observed with frustration that the sample response in the teachers' materials "looked nothing like what my students did," and that the teachers' materials offered her little by way of instructional strategies to support students in generating the types of responses that the CMP authors appeared to have envisioned.

When the teachers and researchers jointly examined the teachers' materials, we found the lack of elaboration around students' writing in sharp contrast to the detailed insights provided as to how students might approach the mathematics of the investigation. The development of the mathematical concepts in the curriculum materials was regarded by both teachers and researchers as rich, engaging, and coherently connected across investigations. The teachers' guides provided carefully thought-out strategies that the teachers could use to support the development of students' mathematical ideas, and suggested clear connections across investigations and units to other mathematical concepts. However,

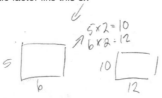

Anne's response

You can divied when you have a fraction. You divied the top into the bottom than you get what ever number the number on the figure is. Exampl

$$\frac{3}{2} = 8$$

Tung's response

You can find a scale factor like this ex

$5 \times 2 = 10$
$6 \times 2 = 12$

This is a scale factor that is similar

Figure 20.2 Early examples of student work in response to a writing prompt on similarity.

the support of the communicative practices associated with this mathematical development was left implicit and under-specified. To address this gap, the teachers and researchers began to talk about what good mathematical writing looked like, often in the context of student work, and then to develop what we referred to as "literacy scaffolding tools" that were built on our analyses of students' written work.

New Opportunities

At the beginning of the project, the teachers described their practices as including little or no writing, or, as Sara, an experienced sixth-grade teacher, expressed it, "ignor[ing] the reading and literacy part, and just deal[ing] with the math." Cassie described her practice in this way:

> Little or no writing was going on in my math class. The [suggested] reflections [in the student materials] looked pretty, but I didn't have time to do them. I just left them. If I did do writing, I took out a state assessment question, and I said, "Okay, kids, here's the question."

Cassie demonstrated to the students how she went about writing, but "there was no discussion at all about writing, what makes it good, what makes it acceptable, and what makes it mathematically correct." In terms of the gradual release of responsibility model, the teachers were assuming all the responsibility for the literacy aspects of the lesson. During the first year and a half of the project, the critical shift that occurred for the teachers was seeing the literacy elements of the curriculum as affording an opportunity for learning rather than as a perceived barrier to the mathematics. As Sara stated at the end of the first year, "We need to look at CMP, and the literacy element, as an opportunity." The teachers realized that they needed to devise strategies that would support student writing, rather than simply ignoring the literacy demands in order to focus attention on mathematical concepts and skills.

The first change in practice occurred as the teachers began to use "quick writes" (short, informal writing guided by an open-ended prompt) to drive their daily instructional practices. As we planned together in the lesson cycles, all five teachers started using quick writes to see what the students understood at the end of a lesson or series of lessons. The prompts almost always came from the CMP materials, either directly or with minor modification. Arlene, a seventh-grade teacher, used the following writing prompt: "When you add a positive and negative integer, you sometimes get a positive result; you sometimes get a negative result. Show that this is true" (modified from *Accentuate the Negative*, Lappan et al., 2004a, p. 33). In analyzing the students' work from this prompt, Arlene became increasingly aware of the need to provide instructional support for her English language learners, and of the need to continue working on the mathematical content before moving on to the next investigation.

This shift from viewing the literacy demands of the curriculum as a barrier to an opportunity for student learning was further supported as we began to examine more closely the characteristics of what the teachers called "good math writing" and to devise a richer set of shared instructional strategies. We considered this part of our collaborative work at the second tier of our multi-tiered teaching experiment, as we tried to make sense of the students' written work. During our second summer workshop, we began to ask "What does a good math writer look like?" and the teachers identified the characteristics of good math writing shown in Table 20.1.

As their classroom instruction shifted from writing as nearly non-existent to writing as a regular occurrence, the teachers continued to use quick writes. The primary purpose of this writing was to inform the daily instructional decision-making by the teachers. However, the teachers found they needed to convey to students the expectations for quality math writing that they had in mind, as shown in Table 20.1. Tracy, an experienced sixth-grade teacher, realized that students needed models of what constituted good written responses to questions. After a lesson in which her students wrote a persuasive letter as a class, the researcher asked her what she might do differently when teaching the same lesson again. She replied, "I'd probably do the letter ... I'll run [through] the letter [and] model it more, so they're clear on how to write a letter that includes mathematical details. And then I'd have them do it on their own." Tracy recognized that students needed to have models of good writing before they could be expected to write such responses independently.

One of the seventh-grade teachers, Arlene, began to use a heuristic called RAVE with her students; she had learned about this acronym at a professional development conference. The acronym stands for R (restate the question), A (answer the question), V (use math vocabulary), and E (explain your examples). She found that it seemed to convey to the students some of the most important qualities of good math writing. She also noted that it was easy for the students to remember: many of them were putting the letters RAVE on the top of their papers as a reminder to themselves. Over the year, as this was shared and discussed during school team meetings, teachers in the other grade levels began to make use of this heuristic.

Table 20.1 Teacher-Generated Description of Good Mathematics Writing

Characteristics of Good Math Writing	
• Contains examples/drawings	• Labels diagrams, examples, and numbers
• Uses math vocabulary	• Addresses all parts of the question
• Restates the question	• Addresses the key concepts
• Answers the question	• Is clear and legible
• Is edited	• Has complete sentences and appropriate grammar
• Responses are organized/sequential	
• Explains examples	
• Includes formulas where appropriate	

In addition to these relatively simple strategies of quick writes and RAVE, the teachers began to develop more sophisticated strategies to help students understand the nature of a quality written response and to improve their writing through revising and editing strategies. Both sixth-grade teachers began to model high-quality written responses during whole-class instruction, and to provide opportunities for students to edit and revise written work by (a) identifying what is needed or missing, (b) making sure that the question is answered, (c) clarifying the vocabulary, (d) labeling and explaining the examples, and (e) checking for accuracy. Sometimes this editing would be done with the whole class making suggestions of how to edit sample student work; other times, the students would engage in editing their own work, occasionally with peers. This instructional approach to the editing of student work began to yield improvements in the quality of students' written responses. For example, one of the sixth-grade teachers, Sara, was pleased at the quality of her students' responses to the prompt: "Use RAVE to answer the question. Explain how 3.0 is different from 0.3. Use a picture or diagram to support your answer" (motivated by and a variation of *Bits and Pieces I*, Lappan et al., 1998b, p. 52 #2). Sara identified one student's response (shown in Figure 20.3) as particularly exemplary because the student clearly maintained the size of the whole (an important mathematical concept in the lesson), and the mathematical language for describing parts as tenths in relationship to the whole was clear.

Cassie, one of the seventh-grade teachers, devised another strategy, which she called "writing over time." In the CMP unit *Stretching and Shrinking* (Lappan et al., 1998c), the central concept for students to understand is what makes two figures mathematically similar. The teacher asked her students to respond to the same writing prompt at the beginning, middle, and end of the unit: "How can

---

Yenni's response

3.0 is different from 0.3 because 3.0 means 3 wholes and 0.3 is three tenths. 3 wholes are bigger than 3 tenths. I converted the decimals to percents and confirmed my theory that 3.0 is bigger and different from 0.3

0.3 = 30%
3.0 = 300% ⟶ 300% is bigger.

300% is bigger and 0.3 is smaller. [To] test my theory or concept some more, I will draw a diagram.

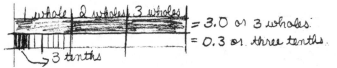

It is clear and obvious that they are different because 3 whole is bigger than 3/10 or .3.

It will take 2 wholes and seven tenths to get the .3 to 3.0. That is how I know that they are different.

Figure 20.3 An exemplary student response to a writing prompt.

you decide when two shapes are similar?" One student responded as shown in Figure 20.4.

Cassie felt that this writing "shows me that she's making growth" as the student moved from "one simple thought to a list" and finally to a paragraph that contained some of the key mathematical ideas, including the relationship between the magnitude of the scale factor and whether the resulting image figure was reduced or enlarged. She was pleased that the student had included a supporting example, and saw this as progress for this student. However, the incorrect example indicated to Cassie that this student's concept of similarity was not yet where it needed to be. Cassie shared this work with the other teachers at a team meeting, and later she recalled that her use of writing over time could be made more effective if she had "them [the students] look at their work and talk about what would make it better. So the second year, I did that and the writing did get better and more advanced." By the end of the second year, the teachers had developed a set of writing strategies (quick writes, RAVE, modeling, editing and revising, and writing over time) that were increasingly used in all of the project classrooms. The teachers reported that many of their students were increasingly able to express their mathematical ideas in writing, and that the students' written work provided them with useful feedback to guide daily instruction.

A pivotal event occurred in the middle of the second year during a lesson cycle with Ashley, then in her second year as an eighth-grade teacher, for the first

---

Alisha's response

Her first response:

the same shape makes them similer

Her second response:

1. same shape
2. same angle measure
3. same scale factor

Her third response at the end of the unit:

To decide whether two figures are similar they have to have same corresponding angle measure and they also have to have same scale factor and same shape.

To find a scale factor between two similar figures I think that you have to make into the fraction and if the figure is getting smaller the scale factor is less than one and if the figure is getting larger the scale factor is higher than one for example.

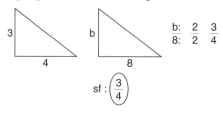

Figure 20.4 A student's response to the same writing prompt given three times during an instructional unit.

investigation in the *Kaleidoscopes, Hubcaps, and Mirrors* unit (Lappan et al., 1998d). After debriefing the lesson, Ashley wanted to meet to plan around all of the writing prompts for the unit. This set of writing prompts revealed some of Ashley's thinking about the essential mathematical ideas in the unit and her expectations for students' written expression of those ideas; however, much more importantly for the collective work of the teachers, the set of prompts became a shared tool that all of the teachers could use and revise. Not only did Ashley continue to create these unit-level writing plans for the rest of the year, but this approach was also taken up by veteran sixth-grade teachers, Tracy and Sara, as they developed a set of writing prompts for *Bits and Pieces I* (Lappan et al., 1998b). However, as Tracy expressed in an interview, "just doing the writing wasn't enough" to improve all students' performance. As we shared in the opening vignette, Tracy was troubled that her good writers were staying good writers, but the poor writers were staying poor. The teachers wanted to find a way to help all students improve as mathematical writers over the school year. This led to the second major shift that occurred in their work together, high-lighted in the vignette and marked by the development of the set of writing prompts into year-long writing plans.

The Shift from Opportunity to Development

The second result of this study was the shift that occurred as the teachers saw that opportunities for writing needed to be addressed systematically in ways that supported the students' *development* as mathematical writers within and across grade levels. The central question guiding the researchers and teachers now became "How can we support students in becoming *better* math writers?" The teachers responded to this question by creating grade-level writing plans. As noted above, initial drafts of these plans had emerged in the second year as the teachers and researchers began to plan for writing at the unit level. However, the major advance in the development of "writing plans" occurred during the second summer of the project, as described in the vignette that opens this chapter.

The teachers had identified the need for the plans both within and across grade levels. As Sara expressed it,

> We really need a planned progression. We really have to thoughtfully look at how we bring students from this level up to the next level. How do you get ... to a place where a student is ... an independent writer of math, really able to show understanding?... We really need a writing plan ... [that] look[s] at the longer term view of where [we] want children to go, September to June, sixth to eighth grade.

Tracy observed that CMP is "extremely consistent, however, it lacked a clear progression [for writing]." To plan for this progression and support increased student independence, the teachers drew on the model of gradual release of responsibility that had been discussed at our meetings. The teachers began work on the writing plans by creating an easy format that could be used by everyone and that would make visible and share both their rationales and their specific instructional approaches. Based on early drafts and Kelly's suggestions, the format eventually adopted by the team consisted of (a) a specific writing task, usually modified from the mathematical reflections in the CMP materials; (b) a rationale for choosing that specific task; and (c) a description of the instructional approach that would support improved writing through guided practice and the gradual release of responsibility. Table 20.2 includes a complete writing plan for *Bits and Pieces I* (Lappan et al., 1998b), a CMP book used in sixth grade. After developing their writing plans and sharing them across grade levels, the teachers began to use the plans during the third year of the project.

Taken together, the process of creating and using the plans influenced the teachers' practices in several ways. First, the writing plans supported the development of the teachers' mathematical understandings of the investigations. All the teachers felt enormous time pressure to cover existing curriculum materials, especially given the difficulties that they encountered with students lacking basic computational skills. Since the writing that the teachers were committing to do in their instruction would (of necessity) be part of limited instructional time, this forced the teachers to think through the mathematics of each investigation to identify the essential mathematical question that would be the focus of the writing. As Sara expressed herself:

> Writing the plans helped me think through the math of each investigation. What really did I think students should be able to understand and why? What should they be able to communicate to others about what they now know or understand?

The teachers' understanding of the essential mathematics of the lesson and the students' ability to communicate their understandings became linked in the process of developing a writing plan.

Second, the writing plans provided support for instructional decision-making on a daily basis. All the teachers used the writing plans as part of their regular instructional planning. Teachers commented that the plans "guide my instruction" and "guide my understanding of what I need to do to accomplish my goals for the students." For example, the writing plans made explicit the instructional strategies that the teachers would use with particular writing tasks in ways that the teacher's guide left unelaborated. Tracy commented on her recognition of "the need for being very clear [with students] on expectations of what quality writing is and being able to clearly communicate that to students." The RAVE rubric that Arlene had been using the previous year became part of the writing plans, and was used by all teachers as a way of sharing with students the expectations for high-quality written work.

Third, the teachers focused explicitly on how they might help students become better mathematical writers over time. The teachers had taken up the gradual release of responsibility model, and this was reflected in the design of the

Table 20.2 Writing Plan for *Bits and Pieces I* (CMP2 – 2005 Edition), Sixth Grade

Focus: explanation and justification of reasoning

Task	Rationale	Instructional Approaches
Investigation 1: p. 18 #2 (reflections) What do the numerator and denominator of a fraction tell you?	Critical concept Good question for essential vocabulary (numerator and denominator) and the use of OML	Focus on restate the question (the R in RAVE) Model completely teacher-led, teacher directed, whole group. Answer the question and show example
Investigation 2: (variation of p. 30 #3, old book) How do you know that 5/8 is bigger than a half?	Reinforce key concepts (comparing fractions) Develops the genre of explanation (a book level theme for writing)	Model the first question and work with a partner for the second question Done in class
How do you know that 6/8 is bigger than 2/3?	Interpretation of fraction benchmarks Students have to justify and explain their reasoning	Evaluate and follow up on next day Use RAVE rubric with a focus on A, answering the question
Investigation 3: (motivated by and a variation of p. 52 #2, old book) Explain how 3.0 is different from 0.3. Draw a picture or diagram to support your answer.	Explanation genre Will show if students are confused with the place value concept Use picture and diagram with writing Interpretation of decimals and a comparative question	Focus on the use of picture/diagram and referencing/labeling picture and using examples Do independently and then edit in small groups, focusing on E, using examples from RAVE rubric.
(variation of p. 66 #3, old book) Explain why 0.55 is smaller than 0.78. Explain why 0.57 is bigger than 0.559.	Need to interpret the questions correctly (same concept, three different questions) Need to justify their reasoning	
Investigation 4: (variation of p. 83 #3, old book) Change 30% to a decimal and to a fraction. Explain how you know that they are all the same value.	Multi-step task (two questions) Need to justify their reasoning Compares three things Easy enough for everyone to do independently Relates to the essential question/key concept	Independently Formal assessment

instructional approaches in the writing plans. Elements of the plan that were situated earlier in an instructional unit as well as earlier in the year called for more teacher direction and modeling. An example of this can be seen in the instructional approach described in the first entry of Table 20.2: "Model completely teacher-led, teacher directed, whole group [instruction]. Answer the question and show an example." The writing elements later in the plan called for work with partners and peer editing: "Model the first question and work with a partner for the second question" and "edit in small groups, focusing on E, using Examples from RAVE rubric." Finally, towards the end of units, the plan called for independent student work: "Discuss [the mathematical] table [from the lesson] with a partner. Independent written response [to the question]." This design of the writing plans made visible the instructional approaches that the teachers would use so that the students could develop strategies for increasing independent mathematical writing. As Sara said:

> I liked attempting to design specific types of writing to run through a series of writing pieces so that both teachers and students can build strategies to improve a particular type of writing, i.e., explain, describe an algorithm, justify a solution or process.

Along with a coherent plan for the development of students' written expression came a shift in the teachers' thinking about their active role in supporting this development. Cassie commented:

> I would also like to use my writing plan to help the kids become better writers. I would like to choose a piece or two and allow the students an opportunity to improve upon their writing by looking at and discussing good writing. This is new for me as a teacher of mathematics, but I think that it will be time well spent in the classroom.

Tracy said:

> I'm [now] thinking about what good writing is and how I think I can help students get there in different ways than I did before. It's not just going to magically happen.... They need lots of practice and more guidance than I've [given] in the past.

Student writing thus became more central to their classroom practice and the development of students as writers became integrated into their instructional decision-making.

The teachers wanted their students to be more competent and more independent in writing responses to the text-based problems of the curriculum materials and high-stakes state assessments. According to them, the challenge was in determining how to reduce the scaffolding support systematically over time so that students would be better, more independent writers at the end of the school year than they had been at the beginning. Moreover, the teachers needed to support such student independence in a setting in which many students are second-language learners, have special education needs, or have had very limited school-based experiences in communicating their mathematical thinking.

Discussion and Conclusions

We have attempted to capture changes in the teachers' perspectives on and practices surrounding the use of curriculum materials that place new demands on students for writing mathematically. Teachers reported that their students struggled with generating elaborated written responses to tasks; the readability and vocabulary were difficult for students. Initially, the teachers responded to these challenges as barriers. They routinely skipped the writing tasks in the curriculum materials. The teachers' guides carefully described the mathematical difficulties that students might have, and provided a rich set of mathematical tasks that would support the students' mathematical development. However, the teachers' guides lacked similar support for the related development of students' mathematical writing. The critical changes that occurred for the teachers were the shift from initially seeing the literacy demands as barriers to students' mathematical learning, later seeing the demands as affording opportunities, and finally identifying the need to support the development of students' abilities to communicate mathematically.

As in Roth McDuffie and Mather's study (see Chapter 21), the curriculum materials were both "a starting point and a continual referent" in the teachers' work. However, in our study the use of the materials extended beyond the work with a single investigation to encompass the investigations found in multiple units across a year-long instructional program. The nature of the adaptations and modifications teachers made had less to do with replacing and omitting activities as reported in Chapters 21 and 22 of this volume, and more to do with how the teachers used the "mathematical reflections" that accompanied each investigation. Initially, the teachers selected and modified those questions to give their students opportunities to write (an expectation of both the curriculum materials and the state assessments) and to drive their daily instructional decision-making.

As the teachers continued to gain what Drake and Sherin call the "familiarity with the materials that can only come with use" (Chapter 22), the teachers also gained curricular vision as they constructed a coherent vision for the development of students' mathematical writing that aligned with the mathematical development intended in the investigations. The reflection questions, in particular, supported the teachers in understanding the essential mathematical ideas of the investigations. As these questions were integrated into unit-level and year-long writing plans, the teachers maintained the coherence of the framework of the curriculum materials for the development of the mathematical content, while designing a parallel framework that supported the development of students' written communication. The decisions made in the design of the writing instruction were motivated by the teachers' understandings of the essential ideas in the curriculum materials, and by their new understandings of the active role that they needed to play in scaffolding the development of students' written communication.

This work appears to provide important evidence for a form of curricular knowledge that involves knowing the links between the development of communicative practices and the development of mathematical content. This development of communicative practices has been to large extent left implicit in both the curriculum materials and the *Standards* (NCTM, 2000). An implication of this study is the recognition that teachers need to facilitate students' interactions with both mathematical tasks and text (in this study, producing suitable written texts in response to the mathematical tasks). A further implication is the recognition that students' communicative practices develop over time as their mathematical learning develops. These developments are linked, but the communicative development does not just occur naturally. Rather, it needs the explicit attention of teachers in ways that shift the responsibility from them to the students with the goal of increasing independence for students as writers. Finally, we should not underestimate the power of a focus on literacy for mathematics teachers to learn in and from their own developing practices.

Acknowledgments

This material is based upon work supported by the National Science Foundation under Grant Number 0231807. Any opinions, findings, conclusions, or recommendations expressed in this material are those of the authors and do not necessarily reflect the views of the NSF.

References

Clarke, D., Waywood, A., & Stephens, M. (1993). Probing the structure of mathematical writing. *Educational Studies in Mathematics, 25*, 235–50.

Duke, N. K., & Pearson, P. D. (2002). Effective practices for developing reading comprehension. In A. Farstrup & J. Samuels (Eds.), *What research has to say about reading instruction* (3rd ed., pp. 205–242). Newark, DE: International Reading Association.

Durkin, K., & Shire, B. (Eds.) (1991). *Language in mathematical education: Research and practice.* Milton Keynes: Open University Press.

Fielding, L. G., & Pearson, P. D. (1994). Reading comprehension: What works. *Educational Leadership, 51*(5), 62–68.

Fisher, D., & Frey, N. (2003). Writing instruction for struggling adolescent readers: A gradual release model. *Journal of Adolescent and Adult Literacy, 46*(5), 396–405.

Gee, J. P. (2002). Literacies, identities, and discourses. In M. J. Schleppegrell & M. C. Colombi (Eds.), *Developing advanced literacy in first and second languages* (pp. 159–175). Mahwah, NJ: Lawrence Erlbaum.

Herbel-Eisenmann, B. (2002). Using student contributions and multiple representations to develop mathematical language. *Mathematics Teaching in the Middle School, 8*(2), 100–105.

Kieran, C., Forman, E., & Sfard, A. (Eds.). (2002). *Learning discourse: Discursive approaches to research in mathematics education.* Boston, MA: Kluwer Academic.

Kong, A., & Pearson, P. D. (2003). The road to participation: The construction of a literacy practice in a learning community of linguistically diverse learners. *Research in the Teaching of English, 38*(1), 85–124.

Lampert, M., & Blunk, M. (Eds.). (1998). *Talking mathematics in school: Studies of teaching and learning.* New York, NY: Cambridge University Press.

Lappan, G., Fey, J., Fitzgerald, W., Friel, S., & Phillips, E. (1998a). *Connected mathematics.* Menlo Park, CA: Dale Seymour.

Lappan, G., Fey, J., Fitzgerald, W., Friel, S., & Phillips, E. (1998b). *Bits and pieces I.* Menlo Park, CA: Dale Seymour.

Lappan, G., Fey, J., Fitzgerald, W., Friel, S., & Phillips, E. (1998c). *Stretching and shrinking.* Menlo Park, CA: Dale Seymour.

Lappan, G., Fey, J., Fitzgerald, W., Friel, S., & Phillips, E. (1998d). *Kaleidoscopes, hubcaps, and mirrors.* Menlo Park, CA: Dale Seymour.

Lappan, G., Fey, J., Fitzgerald, W., Friel, S., & Phillips, E. (2004a). *Accentuate the negative.* Menlo Park, CA: Dale Seymour.

Lappan, G., Fey, J., Fitzgerald, W., Friel, S., & Phillips, E. (2004b). *Stretching and shrinking: Teacher's guide.* Menlo Park, CA: Dale Seymour.

Lerman, S. (2001). Cultural, discursive psychology: A sociocultural approach to studying the teaching and learning of mathematics. *Educational Studies in Mathematics, 46,* 87–113.

Lesh, R., & Kelly, A. (1999). Multi-tiered teaching experiments. In A. Kelly & R. Lesh (Eds.), *Handbook of research in mathematics and science education* (pp. 197–230). Mahwah, NJ: Lawrence Erlbaum.

Marks, G., & Mousley, J. (1990). Mathematics education and genre: Dare we make the process writing mistake again? *Language and Education, 4*(2), 117–135.

Miller, L. D. (1992). Teacher benefits from using impromptu writing prompts in algebra classes. *Journal for Research in Mathematics Education, 23*(4), 329–40.

Morgan, C. (1998). *Writing mathematically: The discourse of investigation.* London: Falmer Press.

Morgan, C., & Watson, A. (2002). The interpretative nature of teachers' assessment of students' mathematics: Issues for equity. *Journal for Research in Mathematics Education, 33*(2), 78–110.

National Council of Teachers of Mathematics. (2000). *Principles and standards for school mathematics.* Reston, VA: Author.

Ntenza, S. P. (2006). Investigating forms of children's writing in grade 7 mathematics classrooms. *Educational Studies in Mathematics, 61,* 321–345.

O'Connor, M. C. (2001). "Can any fraction be turned into a decimal?" A case study of a mathematical group discussion. *Educational Studies in Mathematics, 46,* 143–185.

Pearson, P. D., & Gallagher, M. C. (1983). The instruction of reading comprehension. *Contemporary Educational Psychology, 8,* 317–344.

Pimm, D. (1987). *Speaking mathematically: Communication in mathematics classrooms.* London: Routledge and Kegan Paul.

Powell, A. B., & Lopez, J. A. (1989). Writing as a vehicle to learn mathematics: A case study. In P. Connolly & T. Vilardi (Eds.), *Writing to learn mathematics and science* (pp. 157–177). New York, NY: Teachers College Press.

Pugalee, D. K. (2005). *Writing to develop mathematical understanding.* Norwood, MA: Christopher-Gordon.

Schoenbach, R., Greenleaf, C., Cziko, C., & Hurwitz, L. (1999). *Reading for understanding: A guide to improving reading in middle and high school classrooms.* San Francisco, CA: Jossey-Bass and West-Ed.

Sfard, A. (2001). There is more to discourse than meets the ears: Looking at thinking as communicating to learn more about mathematical learning. *Educational Studies in Mathematics, 46,* 13–57.

Waywood, A. (1994). Informal writing-to-learn as a dimension of a student profile. *Educational Studies in Mathematics, 27,* 321–40.

Yackel, E., & Cobb, P. (1996). Sociomathematical norms, argumentation, and autonomy in mathematics. *Journal for Research in Mathematics Education, 27*(4), 458–77.

21
Middle School Mathematics Teachers' Use of Curricular Reasoning in a Collaborative Professional Development Project

Amy Roth McDuffie and Martha Mather

Imagine a teacher planning a lesson using the task shown in Figure 21.1 from the *Connected Mathematics Project* (CMP) (Lappan, Fey, Fitzgerald, Friel, & Phillips, 1998a), a curriculum development project funded by the National Science Foundation (NSF). How might teachers apply their knowledge of mathematics in planning and implementing the task? What questions and expectations would teachers have about students' knowledge and understandings? What instructional strategies might teachers consider? How do external standards and policies (e.g., district- or state-level learning expectations) influence the teacher's work with this lesson?

These questions focus on various aspects of teachers' *curricular reasoning* – a specific form of pedagogical reasoning that teachers employ while working with curriculum materials to plan, implement, and reflect on instruction. Curricular reasoning combines Shulman's (1986, 1987) and Grossman's (1990) earlier notions of curricular knowledge and pedagogical reasoning (each discussed further in the next section). Curricular knowledge and other forms of knowledge (e.g., content knowledge and pedagogical content knowledge) are often applied during curricular reasoning. However, the notion of curricular knowledge does not seem to go far enough in capturing how teachers work with curriculum materials.

When curricular knowledge was first discussed, mathematics textbooks in the United States typically maintained a different role from newer curriculum materials such as those developed in the 1990s as part of NSF-funded projects. Rather than textbooks acting as a primary source of authority and explaining mathematics to students through example problems and exercises (see, for example, Silver, Burdett, & Ginn, 1994), NSF-funded curriculum materials aimed to nurture students' mathematical reasoning in solving and evidencing solutions, organize materials around important mathematical concepts, develop knowledge from a problem-centered context, connect ideas, and develop communication and representation skills (Dossey, 2007). These materials were designed to meet visions for mathematics instruction set forth in the *Curriculum and Evaluation Standards* (National Council of Teachers of Mathematics [NCTM], 1989; Dossey, 2007) and are often called *Standards*-based curriculum

5.2 Using Mirrors to Find Heights

The shadow method is useful for estimating heights, but it only works outdoors and on a sunny day. In this problem, you will use a mirror to help estimate heights. The mirror method works both indoors and outdoors. All you need is a level spot near the object whose height you want to estimate.

The mirror method is illustrated below. Place a mirror on a level spot at a convenient distance from the object. Back up from the mirror until you can see the top of the object in the center of the mirror. The two triangles shown in the diagram are similar.

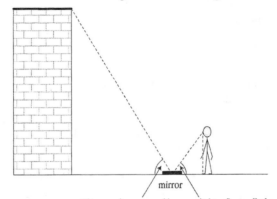

mirror

These angles are equal because light reflects off of a
mirror at the same angle at which it hits the mirror.

To find the object's height, you need to measure three distances and then apply what you know about similar triangles.

Think about this!

Examine the diagram of the mirror method. Can you explain why each angle of the large triangle is equal to the corresponding angle of the small triangle?

Investigation 5: Similar Triangles 61

Figure 21.1 Mirror problem (*Stretching and Shrinking,* Lappan et al., 1998b, p. 61).

materials. Change in curriculum materials, due to shifts in curricular goals and teaching recommended in the *Standards*, may also engender a change in how teachers engage in curricular reasoning. For example, to contrast *Standards*-based curriculum materials with past materials, we considered differences that might emerge in practice in regard to developing students' mathematics reasoning. In planning with *Standards*-based materials, teachers need to anticipate what prior knowledge, skills, and experiences students might use in reasoning about problems in the curriculum materials. With past curriculum materials, teachers may have focused on how to present clear examples from or similar to those in the textbook. While teaching with *Standards*-based materials, teachers need to use approaches to build from students' thinking, rather than focusing on showing students specific procedures. In assessing students, teachers need to look for valid and generalizable methods as contrasted with only checking for correct answers. This example indicates that teachers' work with *Standards*-based curriculum materials involves processes of reasoning with the curriculum program (curricular reasoning) that extends beyond only knowing the curriculum materials (curricular knowledge). With these potential differences in mind, we explored curricular reasoning as teachers worked with NSF-funded, *Standards*-based curriculum materials.

This chapter presents findings from a year-long study of two seventh-grade mathematics teachers' practices as they implemented CMP (Lappan et al., 1998a) and formed a professional development team (PDT) with a university mathematics educator (Roth McDuffie). CMP was developed with support from NSF to foster mathematical learning in the middle grades. Consistent with other NSF-funded materials, CMP was designed to reflect current research on mathematics instruction by emphasizing problem-solving, reasoning, communicating ideas, and making connections (Dossey, 2007). Each unit comprises a series of "investigations" for students to explore. The teacher's edition includes support for structuring lessons with a format of: "launching" the lesson with an engaging problem; "exploring" a problem (often students collaborate in small groups); and "summarizing" the lesson by students' sharing strategies used, important mathematical concepts and processes learned, and connections made. Instead of writing the materials in a scripted form for teachers to follow, the authors designed the materials as a resource with options for teachers' decision-making to meet students' needs. The materials include possible questions for teachers to pose; strategies and struggles students might share; mathematics content for teachers' learning; and essential concepts and processes on which to focus (Dossey, 2007). The professional development activities were situated in the teachers' practices in the sense that they included planning, implementing, and analyzing the teachers' CMP lessons. The study described in this chapter focused on the following research questions:

1. How do teachers use curricular reasoning in planning, implementing, and reflecting on CMP mathematics lessons?
2. How does collaborative, curriculum-based professional development support teachers' use of curricular reasoning with CMP?

In this chapter we first present our theoretical perspective by discussing foundations for curricular reasoning, as well as the methodological approaches we applied in the study. Next, we discuss findings for types of curricular reasoning activities that emerged as the PDT collaborated and how the collaboration supported these curricular reasoning activities. Finally, we examine implications for the complexities and necessity of teachers engaging in curricular reasoning.

Curricular Knowledge and Pedagogical Reasoning: Foundations for Curricular Reasoning

Recent research has focused on mathematics knowledge for teaching (see Ball, Lubienski, & Mewborn, 2001; Hill, Rowan, & Ball, 2005). Much of this research emerged from Shulman's (1986, 1987) and Grossman's (1990) seminal work on pedagogical content knowledge. In addition, a growing body of research has focused on how curriculum materials substantially influence the nature of teaching and learning (Boaler, 2002; Collopy, 2003; Lloyd, 1999; McCaffrey et al., 2001; Remillard, 2005; Stein, Smith, Henningsen, & Silver, 2000). With an interest in exploring the intersecting influences of teachers' mathematics knowledge and curriculum programs on teaching and learning, we returned to earlier work with a focus on curricular knowledge and pedagogical reasoning.

Building on Shulman's (1986, 1987) work, Grossman (1990) described curricular knowledge as a form of pedagogical content knowledge. Curricular knowledge "includes knowledge of curriculum materials available for teaching particular subject matter, as well as knowledge about both the horizontal and vertical curricula for a subject" (p. 8). Shulman (1986) argued that in using curricular knowledge, teachers draw on and evaluate whether resources present particular content and whether students demonstrate learning from the materials. Teachers consider alternate materials, analyzing strengths and limitations of various options.

Although curricular knowledge and other knowledge (e.g., content knowledge, other forms of pedagogical content knowledge, etc.) are important components of knowledge for teaching, Shulman (1987) recognized that the "usefulness of such knowledge lies in its value for judgment and action" (p. 14). Thus, he extended his discussion of knowledge to processes involved with using this knowledge. Shulman developed *A Model for Pedagogical Reasoning and Action* as a way to represent forms of teachers' thinking and activity that may occur during instruction. Shulman assumed that most teaching begins with teachers considering some form of "text" – a textbook or some other teaching material: "Given a text, educational purposes, and/or a set of ideas, pedagogical reasoning and action involve a cycle through the activities of *comprehension, transformation, instruction, evaluation,* and *reflection*" (p. 14). *Comprehension* refers to understanding the content of teaching, including how an idea relates to other ideas within the discipline and to other disciplines. Once comprehended, teachers transform ideas for students' learning. *Transformation* represents some combination of activities, including representing ideas for students, selecting teaching approaches, and tailoring adaptations to individual student needs.

Instruction occurs during the act of teaching, and involves facilitating discussion, management, interaction, explanation, and other observable aspects of teaching and learning. *Evaluation* includes assessing students' understandings and gaps in understanding, formal testing, and evaluating one's own instruction. *Reflection* is the process of looking back on teaching and learning and reconstructing the experience after teaching has ended, and reflection then leads to *new comprehension* as new understandings form from consolidating previous experiences.

We used Shulman's (1987) descriptions of these activities as a foundation for characterizing teachers' *curricular reasoning* in this study. We consider curricular reasoning as a more specific form of pedagogical reasoning in that it includes the activities described above, but curricular goals and materials remain a primary focus for activities throughout the reasoning process (compared to curriculum materials serving merely as a starting point, as Shulman discussed). Indeed, teachers are guided by curriculum goals and materials as they begin their work. However, teachers also use curriculum goals and materials to decide whether materials meet their students' learning needs, gain new mathematical understandings (for teachers' own learning), analyze how materials influence the process of learning over time (including how ideas are built through a series of tasks), and reflect on and revise materials from experiences with teaching and learning. In other words, for each of Shulman's activities, curriculum goals and materials could motivate or form the foundation of the work. Examining teachers' curricular reasoning helps to illustrate the complexities of the role and nature of working with curriculum goals and materials – a process fundamental to teaching for students' learning.

Research Methods

We applied Simon's (2000) conception of a *Teacher Development Experiment,* which calls for working with teachers and documenting the nature of our work and the teachers' practices *while* supporting their professional development. Roth McDuffie provided input and support as a participant in the PDT while researching the teachers' experiences using qualitative, interpretive approaches (e.g., Bogdan & Biklin, 1992; Strauss & Corbin, 1998).

Our Approach to Professional Development

The PDT (consisting of Roth McDuffie and two seventh-grade teachers) collaborated throughout teaching cycles, with each cycle including planning, implementing, and reflecting on instruction (Smith, 2001). In our work, we adapted two forms of professional development with the intent to situate the teachers' learning in the practice of their teaching: lesson study (Fernandez, 2005; Lewis, 2002) and video clubs (Sherin, 2000, 2004). For each cycle we met to plan a lesson (all team members, approximately three meetings, two hours each), enact the lesson while video-recording (one teacher and researcher, approximately three days, one-hour each day for each teacher), and analyze the video-taped lesson (all members, approximately two meetings, two hours each). Working throughout the school year (late August to early June), the PDT completed three cycles, and each cycle occurred over approximately three months. The primary difference between the PDT's approach and lesson study as described in the literature was that instead of the PDT observing the lesson in real time (and inviting guests to observe and participate in post-lesson discussions), Roth McDuffie videotaped the lesson for the PDT. Then, applying ideas from video clubs, the PDT analyzed the video, focusing on identified issues in the lesson.

Teacher Participants and Context

Throughout one school year, Roth McDuffie collaborated with two seventh-grade mathematics teachers (teachers' names are pseudonyms), Ms Dreana (ten years of teaching experience, first year implementing CMP) and Ms Gilmore (18 years of teaching experience, second year implementing CMP). In interviews conducted with the teachers prior to the study and Roth McDuffie's early interactions with the teachers, Dreana and Gilmore indicated that they believed students brought many ideas to mathematics learning, and a teacher's primary role was to provide opportunities for students to build understandings. They valued students who actively participated and persisted in solving problems. The teachers appreciated the vision for mathematics instruction set forth in the NCTM *Standards* (1989, 2000), and they supported their school district's adoption of CMP. Indeed, Dreana changed schools just prior to the study, primarily because she perceived that her former district was not endeavoring to meet the *Standards*. Gilmore served on her district's curriculum adoption committee, piloted CMP for a year, and advocated for its adoption. The teachers taught at the same middle school (sixth through eighth grades) with approximately 770 students, 12 percent ethnic minority and 27 percent free and reduced meals. They taught five of six class periods each day, with approximately 30 students in each class.

Data Collection and Analysis

Data were collected throughout each teaching cycle. Data sources consisted of field notes, audiotapes (with transcription) of planning and analysis meetings, video recordings (with transcription) of lesson enactments, email correspondences, curriculum materials, and student work. The teachers were interviewed at the beginning and end of the school year (using a modified version of Cognitively Guided Instruction's pedagogical beliefs protocol; see Peterson, Fennema, Carpenter, & Loef, 1989) to understand their beliefs as they began work with the professional development team. Initially, all data were analyzed by analytic induction (Bogdan & Biklen, 1992). Using open coding (Strauss & Corbin, 1998), patterns of similarities and differences were identified for the knowledge and reasoning teachers used during interactions and the role of the PDT in the cycles. From the initial analysis, we developed categories that included curriculum resources used (e.g., CMP materials, state learning expectations), curricular knowledge, pedagogical content knowledge, pedagogical reasoning, and curricular reasoning (coding reasoning for each phase in Shulman's (1987) model), and PDT interactions that influenced this reasoning. Finally, we focused on incidents in which curricular reasoning was evident and developed categories for the types of activities associated with curricular reasoning.

PDT Activities Involving Curricular Reasoning

We present findings for PDT activities from work with the *Stretching and Shrinking* unit (Lappan et al., 1998b). We selected this unit because it represented of the nature and types of curricular reasoning and PDT support that occurred throughout the PDT's teaching cycles. The teachers decided to focus the PDT's work on Section 5.2 of Investigation 5 (see Figure 21.1 and the discussion of this section at the beginning of the chapter). They believed that Section 5.2 provided opportunities for students to experience connections between mathematics concepts and the real world (a learning goal the teachers identified). However, neither teacher had taught this section. Investigation 5 comprises three sections (suggesting at least one class period for each section). Prior to Section 5.2, students had explored similar figures, worked with scale factor, and used similar triangles to find missing side-lengths. In Section 5.1, students used the "shadow method" for finding the height of a tall building. Students create two similar triangles: one formed by a building, its shadow, and the hypotenuse connecting these segments, and the second formed with a meter stick held perpendicular to the ground, its shadow, and corresponding hypotenuse. Using the similar triangles and the scale factor from one shadow to the other, students solved for the building's height.

We identified four primary instructional activities that engaged teachers' curricular reasoning: analyzing curriculum materials from learners' perspectives, doing tasks together as learners, mapping learning trajectories, and revising plans based on work with students during instruction. For each activity, we describe PDT interactions and discuss teachers' use of curricular reasoning. Following the discussion of the activities, we examine how the PDT supported teachers' use of curricular reasoning.

Analyzing Curriculum Materials from Learners' Perspectives

Dreana and Gilmore commented that with past curriculum materials, planning often consisted of reviewing material for the next day and then selecting a few key examples (either from the textbook or by creating problems similar to textbook examples) to clearly illustrate a concept or skill and with the goal of covering (making sure the teacher has presented) the lessons in the textbook. The teachers did not consider curriculum goals separately from the curriculum materials – the textbook served as both curriculum goals and curriculum materials. This approach aligns with common practices for most US teachers (Stigler & Hiebert, 1999). With a shift to emphasize students' understanding of concepts and building from students' prior knowledge and experiences (NCTM, 1989, 2000), not only do teachers need to consider how to present ideas, they also need to anticipate learners' perspectives, thinking, and approaches. These considerations are central to teaching for students' understanding, as contrasted with teaching to cover material in a textbook.

In an early planning meeting (September 26) the PDT examined Section 5.2 and anticipated difficulties students might have with the mirror problem. The teachers did not believe that their students had learned the terms *angle of incidence* and *angle of reflection*, or that these angles had equal measures. The mirror method depended on understanding this relationship. They perceived that the text "told" the students this information, yet their students needed more opportunities to understand and be convinced of the relationship between the angles before applying the mirror method for similar triangles. Gilmore shared her concerns in the following discussion:

GILMORE: I think it's going to be hard for the kids.
ROTH MCDUFFIE: ...Seeing the relationships [between the angles]?
GILMORE: [Yes]. ...This [pointing to Figure 21.1] ... It's putting a lot of ideas together.... If they start struggling and saying, "Wait a minute. How are these two [angles] connected?" ... For the students to just sit here and look at this [how the angle of incidence and reflection are related] and to go [outside] to figure this out.... I don't think they're going to get it.

In addition, from past experience, the teachers reflected that students struggled to understand exactly "what is an angle," and understanding *angle* was central to the unit. Dreana also mentioned that she found that students seemed to focus on measuring the rays forming an angle (rather than the opening formed by the rays). Roth McDuffie added that students might arbitrarily form a triangle across the angles rays and perceive that the length of the side connecting the rays determined the angle's measure. Indeed, researchers have found that these confusions are common for students (Mitchelmore, 1997; Tzur & Clark, 2006).

During the meetings on October 14 and 25, the teachers continued to develop plans for Section 5.2. Since the September meeting they had begun teaching the unit, and both teachers had observed that students' lacked prior knowledge for angles, as predicted earlier. Dreana reflected on an interaction she had had with a boy in class. The boy viewed angle measurement as a linear measure of the angle opening from perceived endpoints of the rays forming the angle, just as the PDT discussed in the September meeting. Dreana exclaimed, "He made a triangle out of it!" (October 25). When considering similar figures, the student was convinced that the angle of the larger similar figure was indeed larger than a corresponding angle in a smaller figure.

Dreana stated that the September discussion helped prepare her to understand, question, and assess her students' thinking. The teachers reflected on the importance of listening closely to students' struggles with problems. Dreana revealed that she often assumes her students understand when indeed confusions exist, as she continued to describe her experience with the above student: "Because he has been answering question after question in my class and leading discussion – So I'm thinking that he just ... wasn't thinking when he wrote [his answer].... I had no clue he didn't know what an angle was!" (October 25). The teachers agreed that they often do not recognize the underlying ideas that may be impeding students' learning, and they gained an increased appreciation for value of listening to students and adapting instruction accordingly.

The teachers identified that their state Grade Level Expectations (GLEs, the curriculum goals used) called for students to learn about angles in fifth grade. However, given that the teachers found that most of their students did not have this knowledge, the teachers were concerned because their students needed to demonstrate understanding of angles and angle measurement on the seventh-grade state-wide assessment. They did not see opportunities for their students to develop these ideas because the curriculum materials assumed that students had prior knowledge of angles. Thus, the PDT concluded that the curriculum materials needed to be adapted to address the students' needs for understanding angle and angles of incidence and reflection.

This example illustrates how the teachers analyzed their curriculum materials and goals to determine prior knowledge needed for students to engage in the materials, compared this analysis with their perceptions of their students' prior knowledge, assessed students' prior knowledge during instruction (using their analysis to guide assessment), and then determined that the teachers needed to adapt the materials. Throughout, the teachers worked with the curriculum materials and goals not just as a starting point but also to inform their reasoning as they examined and compared the task and the GLEs.

Doing the Task Together as Learners

To delve deeper into teaching and learning issues that might arise, the teachers not only analyzed the curriculum materials from learners' perspectives; Dreana and Gilmore also perceived that they needed to act out what students might do in solving the problem. The PDT engaged in the task as learners. This additional time spent acting out problem-solving proved to be important in revealing issues that the teachers had not anticipated in only analyzing the curriculum.

The value of doing the tasks was evidenced as the PDT reviewed the mirror problem (Figure 21.1). They acted out how students might solve the problem outside with real objects, discussing the measurements needed and the similar triangles formed. The teachers became confused as to where the similar triangles were in their physical model. In acting out the mirror problem, Gilmore shared her confusion as she said, "This is the mirror here, and so this and this angle are the same [not sure where to point]. I don't know ... I got lost" (October 25). After working together for several minutes and creating the similar triangles in the air (with string forming the sides of the triangles), the teachers resolved their confusion. The teachers realized that identifying the congruent angles was indeed difficult when looking at a physical model (rather than the representation on paper). They reflected that acting out the problem with the PDT helped them to identify this issue and then clarify their understandings. The teachers perceived that this confusion underscored the need to add a new activity (described below) to help students visualize and understand the relationship between angles of incidence and reflection.

Mapping Learning Trajectories

A third activity involved mapping learning trajectories to ensure that GLEs were met, prior knowledge assumed in GLEs aligned with their students' knowledge and skills, and implemented curriculum materials were coherent (i.e., continually building on prior knowledge and experiences). Given that these teachers were no longer teaching in a context in which covering a textbook implied that mathematics curriculum goals were met, the teachers discussed how tasks related to the state's GLEs, how students' understandings of important mathematics concepts and processes built over time, and whether the curriculum materials provided a coherent framework of tasks relative to the goals in the GLEs. After the PDT identified potential gaps in the learning trajectory for the mirror activity (as described in earlier sections), the PDT considered options to supplement Section 5.2. They shared ideas for adding a task in which students could learn about angles, measuring angles, and the relationship between angles of incidence and reflection. While brainstorming options, including shooting a ball on a pool table, Dreana introduced an idea to use a light box to shoot a beam of light into a mirror, creating angles of incidence and reflection (Figure 21.2). A light box works like a flashlight except that the beam of light is focused. The PDT then began to share ideas for a lesson using light boxes.

The teachers wanted their students to identify the angles of incidence and reflection and to be convinced that the angles had equal measures, rather than simply providing the information in Figure 21.1. They planned for students to create several angles of incidence and reflection with the light box and mirror. For each angle pair, the students needed to measure and record the angle measurements. The teachers decided that they would model how to use a protractor (or angle ruler) to measure the angles to adapt for students' lack of prior knowledge with measuring. The teachers anticipated that, after students had measured a few examples, they would see the pattern for angles of incidence and reflection having equal measures.

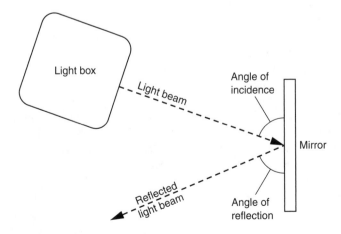

Figure 21.2 Light box and mirror activity.

Before ending the planning discussion, the teachers reviewed "Problem 5.2 Follow-Up" (Lappan et al., 1998b, p. 62), which asked students to make line plots of the estimates of the heights the students found with the mirror method and with the shadow method to determine which method seemed more consistent. The teachers questioned whether this activity was necessary. To aid in their decision, the teachers turned to a portion of the instructor's guide that provided ideas for planning and facilitating learning. Dreana and Gilmore read excerpts from the guide that indicated that the teacher should use the line plots to discuss issues with accuracy in measuring through both methods (p. 74f). The teachers decided that the line plot activity was not worthwhile because line plots were not part of their state's GLEs (they were taught in earlier grades), and they believed that students would have considerable inaccuracies through both methods such that comparing the methods would not reveal patterns that would contribute to the discussion. Instead, they planned to facilitate a summary discussion on sources of error that emerged for students.

At this point, the PDT's initial mapping of the learning trajectory included the following. First, the light-box activity was intended to provide opportunities for students to see angles formed, measure angles, and then observe that angles of incidence and reflection have equal measure. The teachers believed that this hands-on model was more accessible to the students than using the mirror method outside, and thus would provide a needed step to prepare students to apply the mirror method outside. Following the light-box activity, students would go outside to engage in Section 5.2 as it was written. Then, after heights were determined, the students would discuss sources of error, but the teachers planned to omit the more extended follow-up activity involving line plots. Supplementing the materials with the light-box activity and omitting the line-plot activity evidenced how the PDT reasoned about their curriculum materials relative to their students' learning and their State GLEs to navigate a learning trajectory.

Revising Plans Based on Work with Students during Instruction

The fourth activity involved looking back at planning and implementing the curriculum materials to assess efficacy of teaching and learning and to record ideas for revisions for future instruction. The interactions and reflections that occurred while implementing the light-box activity illustrate how the PDT generated revisions. Following Dreana's first day teaching the light-box activity, she informed Gilmore of the struggles she had in facilitating and supporting students' learning. Dreana reflected that although the PDT had identified the problem students were having with understanding angles, she perceived that the team had underestimated how widespread and deep this lack of understanding was. Dreana stated, "I'm thinking some kids still weren't getting [what they are supposed to be measuring with angles.... For example, one student I worked with] doesn't know what an angle is, that it's that opening. What can I do that would get him to get it?" (October 31, meeting following the lesson). Dreana realized in teaching the light-box activity that she needed to scaffold learning about angles even more than the PDT planned with the initial learning trajectory.

Dreana's analysis and reflections about students' limited understanding of angles led Gilmore, who was teaching the lesson the next day, to transform key aspects of the lesson's launch. Gilmore included a new representation for discussing angles and measuring angles, modifying the map of the learning trajectory to include more explicit instruction on angles. She decided to model angles using two colored paper plates. She cut a radius in each plate, and then slid the plates together at the radii to form a two-layered circle. After rotating the plates in opposite directions, an angle was formed by the contrasting colors. Gilmore found this idea in a university mathematics methods course textbook (Van de Walle, 2001), a book the PDT regularly used when seeking ideas for teaching and learning.

After spending 20 minutes discussing angle measurement and providing a variety of angles for students to measure, Gilmore introduced the light-box activity. Although her class ended with the students only having their angle measurements, Gilmore believed that they were ready to discuss the relationship between angles of incidence and reflection in their next class. Immediately following this lesson in a PDT meeting, Gilmore reflected on the lesson, noting that adding the plate-model discussion prepared the students for the light-box activity, and by the end of the class period, most students understood how to identify and measure angle of incidence and reflection. Dreana then decided to step back in her lesson and use the plate model also.

The next day, Dreana used the plate model and then brought her students back to the light-box activity. After completing the light-box activity, Dreana transitioned from the light box to the mirror method. Dreana illustrated the mirror method at the chalkboard with a picture resembling Figure 21.1, and discussed the similar triangles formed. Indeed, based on students' questions and comments it was evident to Dreana and Roth McDuffie (observing) that students initially struggled to see the angles formed in the picture. However, by the end of the discussion several students explained the model and almost all students indicated that they were ready to apply these ideas outside (observation, November 1). By learning from each other's instructional experiences and reflections, both teachers transformed the lesson and gained new understandings of the experiences students needed in order to learn from the curriculum materials.

Dreana stated that she appreciated the book's approach to posing open problems that require students to determine what is involved in solving problems, rather than following prescribed procedures. However, Dreana recognized that her role was important in preparing students to begin problems. Dreana gained a new perspective for how to use curriculum materials in that she recognized the need to anticipate and assess students' knowledge, and then make adaptations to the investigations when appropriate. In listening to Dreana, Gilmore indicated that she shared this perspective and also was realizing how important these processes are. Moreover, the teachers recognized that their assessment of students during the lessons indicated that students' understandings of mathematics concepts and processes were not immediately formed. The teachers reflected that they needed to facilitate discussions with multiple representations and experiences (e.g., light box and plate model) for students to make sense of the underlying mathematics before attempting the mirror problem (PDT meeting, November 5).

When the teachers' classes went outside to perform the mirror task (in groups of three to four), they collected relevant measurements to find the height of the school's flagpole (November 5 for Dreana's class and November 6 for Gilmore's class). Throughout the classes, the teachers continually needed to prompt students to consider where the angles and relevant sides were, where they saw similar triangles, and how to measure the relevant parts. The teachers referenced the light-box activity, and this prompt helped students to re-focus on the mirror approach and relevant angles formed. Reflecting on these events, the PDT found that the light-box activity became an important referent and step in the learning trajectory by helping students gain understandings about angles and the relationship between angles of incidence and reflection – concepts essential to performing the mirror investigation. Gilmore reflected,

> So my goal was to take the [light box] application of this [angle of incidence and reflection] … It was a hands-on group activity first before we went out [to find the height of tall objects] … There was no way they [students] could take [just the diagram from the book] … and go do it [the mirror activity] themselves.
>
> (November 24, PDT discussion)

They perceived that adaptations were needed for students to learn from the curriculum materials.

By the end of the class period, all groups had successfully collected measurements for similar triangles using the mirror method. As the teachers had anticipated in earlier planning meetings, the students found a wide range of calculated measures for the flagpole's height. The data set gathered did not lend itself to the line-plot activity (comparing the accuracy of the shadow and mirror methods) because both methods yielded substantial inaccuracies. Consequently, as planned, the teachers engaged students in a discussion about sources of error in applying the shadow method and the mirror method, but omitted the line-plot activity as an approach to compare methods. The teachers reflected that omitting the line-plot activity proved to be a good decision. Given that line plots were not in the state's seventh-grade learning expectations, by omitting this activity the teachers perceived that they saved time without missing important content. The teachers stated that they planned to use the adaptations they implemented again next year.

The Role of the PDT in Supporting Curricular Reasoning Activities

For each of the four activities described above, the PDT played an important role in supporting teachers as they engaged in curricular reasoning. The nature of the support for these activities is discussed below.

Support for Analyzing Curriculum Materials from Learners' Perspectives

The PDT's work supported teachers' curricular reasoning in anticipating how learners will interact with the problems as presented in the curriculum materials and in developing approaches to facilitate students' learning. Throughout conversations in which the teachers anticipated students' prior knowledge and skills needed (e.g., identifying learners' limited prior knowledge of angles, measuring angles, the relationship between angles of incidence and reflection, and translating the mirror method from the written materials to the real world) and then developed approaches to address students' needs (e.g., the plate model and the light-box activity), the PDT collectively generated ideas and extended curricular reasoning beyond any individual member's prior thinking about the lessons. It should be noted that each PDT member read the materials and wrote preliminary plans prior to the meetings. Throughout the above-described activities, we found that the curriculum materials initiated a problematic situation and the PDT supported the teachers in gaining understandings for how students might approach and struggle with the mathematics in the problem, and how to address students' needs.

Support for Doing the Task Together as Learners

Doing the task as learners was essential to curricular reasoning. While working on tasks, PDT discussions often focused on understanding the mathematics content of the curriculum materials. Indeed, on several occasions the teachers reflected that they were learning mathematics during PDT discussions. Consistent with research from Even, Robinson, and Carmeli (2004), acting out lessons and analyzing the curriculum materials provided opportunities for new insights to emerge. For instance, when the teachers acted out the mirror problem, the PDT helped translate Figure 21.1 to a real model with a mirror and a person. Neither teacher identified the relevant angles and relationships initially, but through PDT discussion they clarified understandings. This incident exemplified an issue that emerged throughout the year regarding content knowledge for teaching mathematics: the teachers often did not realize when they held inadequate or incorrect understandings of mathematics prior to collaborating with the PDT. The PDT's interactions increased the potential that the teachers identified confusions and developed stronger understandings for the mathematics content.

Support for Mapping Learning Trajectories and Revising Plans

For the last two activities, the nature of the support was similar: the PDT discussions supported the teachers in deciding whether and how to transform the curriculum materials. By collaborating to analyze and interpret GLEs relative to the curriculum materials and their students' learning, the teachers shared perspectives and gained confidence to enact changes. The teachers frequently expressed that they felt more confident in making changes after working with the PDT and arriving at decisions together, especially for lessons that they had not taught previously. For example, Dreana explained how she was anxious about using and adapting the curriculum materials, but by collaborating in the PDT she gained confidence for her teaching:

> I didn't know [some of the mathematical ideas] before this [PDT work]. I had never taught it, and it was a different concept for the kids. And because of our [work in the PDT], ... we talked about the content ... and talked about the kids. ... I walked out of [our meetings] very strongly feeling like we had a plan of action and I knew exactly how I was going to teach it.
>
> (May 31, discussion at the end of the year)

At the end of the year, the teachers also reflected on the importance of Roth McDuffie's participation in this process in that she served as an external resource with expertise in mathematics education, and this helped the teachers in feeling that decisions were sound. Working independently, each teacher was not sure that she would be willing to engage in the experimentation process or implement a plan different from the district's plan. Teachers' reflections indicated that the PDT fostered the teachers' use of curricular reasoning in supplementing the investigation with activities that would help students to learn from the curriculum materials (e.g., the plate model and the light-box activity) and omitting activities that did not meet their instructional goals or GLEs (e.g., the line-plot activity).

Conclusions and Implications

While working with an investigation of CMP's *Stretching and Shrinking* (Lappan et al., 1998b), the teachers engaged in four primary activities that used curricular reasoning: analyzing lessons from learners' perspectives, doing tasks as learners, mapping learning trajectories, and revising plans based on work with students during instruction. In addition, the PDT served as an important support of teachers' use of curricular reasoning as they engaged collaboratively in each of these activities.

Collaborating with the PDT in curricular reasoning empowered the teachers to work with the curriculum program as a coherent framework with approaches and strategies for teaching and learning, while also maintaining the view that the framework may need transforming based on students' needs and state learning expectations. Instead of merely following the curriculum materials, the teachers exhibited *curricular vision* as they engaged in curricular reasoning with the PDT. *Curricular vision* represents the idea that teachers understand where curriculum materials are relative to the mathematical ideas, and what students are learning (Darling-Hammond & Bransford, 2005; Drake & Sherin, Chapter 22 of this volume). Drake and Sherin found that as teachers gained more experience with *Standards*-based curriculum materials, they decreased efforts to create additional activities that did not match the curricular vision and to omit important activities. Instead, teachers increasingly used the big ideas of the curriculum program to guide their practices and to support interactions with students.

Consistent with Drake and Sherin's findings about teachers in their first year implementing a *Standards*-based curriculum program, the teachers in this study transformed the curriculum materials by adding activities (e.g., the light box and the plate model) and by omitting activities (e.g., the line plot). However, unlike the teachers in Drake and Sherin's study who added activities without regard to a curricular vision, Dreana's and Gilmore's decisions to add activities were motivated by interactions with students and their state's learning expectations to ensure that the students learned from Section 5.2 in their curriculum materials. Moreover, although they did not omit substantial portions, omitting the line plot was based on their analysis of the activity failing to account for the nature of the data the students collected and the lack of emphasis on line plots in their state learning expectations (i.e., they perceived that their students learning would not be enhanced by the activity). The iterative process by which the teachers shared ideas and experiences (gained through analysis and reflection) evidences how they refined their curricular reasoning and their curricular visions in the transformation process. The teachers commented that they were not accustomed to analyzing their materials relative to the learning expectations, and they benefited from the opportunity to conduct these analyses with the support of the PDT. The teachers' participation in the PDT may explain how these teachers were able engage in curricular reasoning to develop and focus on their curricular vision rather than clinging to prior practices and beliefs, as demonstrated by the teachers Drake and Sherin studied (see Chapter 22).

Perceiving and using curriculum materials as a resource (that may need adaptations for students' needs) rather than a script is not a typical US perspective. Teachers in the United States have a history of viewing curriculum as material to cover (Howson, Keitel, & Kilpatrick, 1981; Roth McDuffie & Mather, 2006; Stigler & Hiebert, 1999). This approach is not restricted to commercially developed curriculum programs. Lloyd (1999) found that high school teachers implementing *Standards*-based curriculum materials tended not to make changes in problems presented, despite their perceptions that features of problems caused struggles in teaching and learning. Given this history, we should not underestimate the challenges teachers face in transforming curriculum to meet students' needs.

Although mathematics education has made significant progress with the availability of *Standards*-based mathematics curriculum programs, teachers face increased demands in regard to knowledge and curricular reasoning to implement these programs. As we considered the four activities, we developed a model to capture the primary objects of and influences on curricular reasoning that emerged in the activities (see Figure 21.3). Because the curriculum materials were the starting point and a continual referent for all activities involving curricular reasoning, *Curriculum materials* appears at the top of Figure 21.3. For student-centered instruction, teachers need to anticipate what students might bring to the mathematics tasks and design instruction accordingly (represented by *Students' learning needs* in Figure 21.3). In addition, to effectively map learning trajectories and make adaptations to curriculum materials for students'

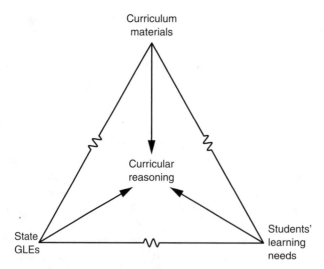

Figure 21.3 Influences on curricular reasoning.

learning, teachers increasingly are expected to interpret and align their materials with state learning expectations (represented by *State GLEs* in Figure 21.3). State learning expectations vary widely from one state to another (Reys et al., 2006), and it is unlikely that any nationally developed curriculum program will align completely with a state's GLEs or with the particular students' needs in a given teacher's class. Thus, the broken sides of the triangle indicate how these influential factors indeed could be out of alignment or represent differing goals and needs. In summary, teachers must use curricular reasoning to reconcile, develop, and implement a curricular vision based on their curriculum materials, their students' needs, and their state's learning expectations in creating a coherent learning experience. This work is in sharp contrast to and presents considerably more challenges than following a textbook with a lecture-style approach combined with individual seatwork (see Stigler & Hiebert, 1999). Yet the teachers' work in this study suggests that deliberately using curricular reasoning while engaging in activities such as those discussed above with a team of colleagues has the potential to support teachers in navigating among the influences shown in Figure 21.3.

Through this close analysis of one representative cycle of practice, we explored how teachers use curricular reasoning, and the role of colleagues in supporting this reasoning. In reflecting on the activities that involved curricular reasoning, we identified key influences on the curricular reasoning process. By examining the activities and identifying influences, we have made visible aspects of deliberately designed practice of teaching mathematics for students' learning that would otherwise have remained hidden.

References

Ball, D., Lubienski, S., & Mewborn, D. (2001). Research on teaching mathematics: The unsolved problem of teachers' mathematical knowledge. In V. Richardson (Ed.), *Handbook of research on teaching* (pp. 433–456). Washington, DC: American Educational Research Association.

Boaler, J. (2002). *Experiencing school mathematics: Traditional and reform approaches to teaching and their impact on student learning.* Mahwah, NJ: Erlbaum.

Bogdan, R., & Biklen, S. (1992). *Qualitative research for education: An introduction to theory and methods.* Boston, MA: Allyn and Bacon.

Collopy, R. (2003). Curriculum materials as a professional development tool: How a mathematics textbook affected two teachers' learning. *The Elementary School Journal, 103*(3), 287–312.

Darling-Hammond, L., & Bransford, J. (Eds.). (2005). *Preparing teachers for a changing world: What teachers should learn and be able to do.* San Francisco, CA: John Wiley.

Dossey, J. (2007). Looking back, looking ahead. In C. Hirsch (Ed.), *Perspectives on the design and development of school mathematics curricula* (pp. 185–199). Reston, VA: National Council of Teacher of Mathematics.

Even, R., Robinson, N., & Carmeli, M. (2004). The work of providers of professional development for teachers of mathematics: Two case studies of experienced practitioners. *International Journal of Science and Mathematics Education, 1,* 227–249.

Fernandez, C. (2005). Lesson study: A means for elementary teachers to develop the knowledge of mathematics needed for reform-minded teaching? *Mathematical Thinking and Learning, 7* (4), 265–289.

Grossman, P. (1990). *The making of a teacher: Teacher knowledge and teacher education.* New York, NY: Teachers College Press.

Hill, H., Rowan, B., & Ball, D. (2005). Effects of teachers' mathematical knowledge for teaching on student achievement. *American Educational Research Journal, 42* (2), 371–407.

Howson, G., Keitel, C., & Kilpatrick, J. (1981). *Curriculum development in mathematics.* New York, NY: Cambridge University Press.

Lappan, G., Fey, J., Fitzgerald, W., Friel, S., & Phillips, E. (1998a). *Connected mathematics.* Menlo Park, CA: Dale Seymour.

Lappan, G., Fey, J., Fitzgerald, W., Friel, S., & Phillips, E. (1998b). *Connected mathematics: Stretching and shrinking, similarity.* Menlo Park, CA: Dale Seymour.

Lewis, C. (2002). *Lesson study: A handbook of teacher-led instructional change.* Philadelphia, PA: Research for Better Schools.

Lloyd, G. M. (1999). Two teachers' conceptions of a reform-oriented curriculum: Implications for mathematics teacher development. *Journal of Mathematics Teacher Education, 2*(3), 227–252.

McCaffrey, D., Hamilton, L., Stetcher, B., Klein, S., Bugliari, D., & Robyn, A. (2001). Interactions among instructional practices, curriculum, and student achievement: The case of *Standards*-based high school mathematics. *Journal for Research in Mathematics Education, 32*(5), 493–517.

Mitchelmore, M. (1997). Children's informal knowledge of physical angle situations. *Learning and Instruction, 7,* 1–19.

National Council of Teachers of Mathematics. (1989). *Curriculum and evaluation standards for school mathematics.* Reston, VA: Author.

National Council of Teachers of Mathematics. (2000). *Principles and standards for school mathematics.* Reston, VA: Author.

Peterson, P., Fennema, E., Carpenter, T., & Loef, M. (1989). Teachers' pedagogical content beliefs in mathematics. *Cognition and Instruction, 6*(1), 1–40.

Remillard, J. T. (2005). Examining key concepts in research on teachers' use of mathematics curricula. *Review of Educational Research, 75*(2), 211–246.

Reys, B., Dingman, S., Olson, T., Sutter, A., Teuscher, D., Chval, K. et al. (2006). *The intended mathematics curriculum as represented in state-level curriculum standards: Consensus or confusion?* Center for the Study of Mathematics Curriculum. Retrieved April 26, 2006, from http://www.mathcurriculumcenter.org.

Roth McDuffie, A., & Mather, M. (2006). Reification of instructional materials as part of the process of developing problem-based practices in mathematics education. *Teachers and Teaching: Theory and Practice, 12*(4), 435–459.

Sherin, M. (2000). Viewing teaching on videotape. *Educational Leadership, 57*(8), 36–38.

Sherin, M. (2004). Teacher learning in the context of a video club. *Teaching and Teacher Education, 20*(2), 163–183.

Shulman, L. (1986). Those who understand: Knowledge growth in teaching. *Educational Researcher, 15*(2), 4–14.

Shulman, L. (1987). Knowledge and teaching: Foundations of a new reform. *Harvard Educational Review, 57*(1), 1–22.

Silver, Burdett, & Ginn. (1994). *Mathematics: Exploring your world.* Morristown, NJ: Author.

Simon, M. (2000). Research on the development of mathematics teachers: The teacher development experiment. In A. Kelly & R. Lesh (Eds.), *Handbook of research design in mathematics and science education* (pp. 335–360). Mahwah, NJ: Erbaum.

Smith, M. (2001). *Practice-based professional development for teachers of mathematics.* Reston, VA: National Council of Teachers of Mathematics.

Stein, M., Smith, M., Henningsen, M., & Silver, E. (2000). *Implementing standards-based mathematics instruction: A casebook for professional development.* New York, NY: Teachers College Press.

Stigler, J., & Hiebert, J. (1999). *The teaching gap.* New York, NY: Free Press.

Strauss, A., & Corbin, J. (1998). *The basics of qualitative research: Grounded theory procedures and techniques.* Newbury Park, CA: Sage.

Tzur, R., & Clark, M. (2006). Riding the mathematical merry-go-round to foster conceptual understanding of angle. *Teaching Children Mathematics, 12*(8), 388–393.

Van de Walle, J. (2001). *Elementary and middle school mathematics: Teaching developmentally.* Boston, MA: Allyn and Bacon.

22

Developing Curriculum Vision and Trust

Changes in Teachers' Curriculum Strategies

Corey Drake and Miriam Gamoran Sherin

The only question would be how to transition [students] to a math sentence. I was reading in [the] book how they used the [drawings] to transition them into a math sentence but I just like the idea of the stories transitioning them into a math sentence.

(Fall, Year 1)

I am beginning to not go page by page. I look at my standards, say what needs to be covered and look for it in here. What do I feel is beneficial for the kids? More of using it as a resource even though there is a lot of it I am using. [Using it] as more to get the standard, instead of just letting the book guide me.

(Winter, Year 2)

I trust the book now. I know it has a natural flow between what's [here in today's lesson] and what's [coming later on] ... I understand the connections more ... There is a reason they are using these two numbers. In that sense I am still following the book.

(Spring, Year 2)

These excerpts come from interviews with Beth, a first- and second-grade teacher in a large urban school, about her experiences piloting a set of *Standards*-based mathematics curriculum materials. As Beth gained experience with the curriculum program, her interactions with the curriculum materials changed. In her initial months using the materials, Beth was concerned with making transitions from one activity to the next and from one day to the next. She read the teacher's guide very closely for specific ideas about how to make these transitions. She was often frustrated that she did not find the information she was looking for and felt she had to create these transitions for herself and her students. Later, she moved away from this search for detailed information and began using the curriculum materials as more of a "resource." From the middle quotation alone, one might suspect that Beth was moving away from using the curriculum materials altogether or that she was beginning to use them in a piece-meal or incoherent way. However, as the third quotation suggests (and as was confirmed by our observations of her teaching), Beth was instead moving towards a more connected and trusting use of the materials, confident in the decisions "they" [the curriculum developers] had made in creating a set of materials in which there was a "natural flow" for students across the year.

As researchers interested in understanding how teachers learn from and about curriculum materials, we wanted a method and a framework for systematically characterizing these changes in Beth's curriculum interactions and exploring whether other teachers who used the curriculum materials for more than one year experienced similar changes. Understanding how and what teachers learn over time is crucial to leveraging the potential of these materials as a mechanism for fostering teacher learning and large-scale changes in mathematics teaching practices (Ball & Cohen, 1996). For curriculum materials to be effective vehicles for teacher learning, we need to understand how teachers *use* new curriculum materials and how teachers' use of new materials *changes* as teachers gain experience with those materials. We need to answer the question posed by Shulman in 1986: "How do teachers take a piece of text and transform their understanding of it into instruction that their students can comprehend?" (p. 8).

In this chapter, we first introduce *curriculum vision* and *curriculum trust* as constructs from the research literature that capture key aspects of changes observed in Beth's interactions with the curriculum materials. We then describe our development and use of teachers' *curriculum strategies* as a framework for characterizing the ways that teachers interact with curriculum materials. Then, in the final sections of the chapter, we use the curriculum strategy framework to argue that the changes observed over two years in the ways that Beth and two other veteran urban teachers used *Standards*-based curriculum materials constitute evidence of the teachers' development of curriculum vision and curriculum trust.

The use of new curriculum materials requires both change and learning on the part of teachers. We know from experience and prior research (e.g., Remillard & Bryans, 2004; Richardson, 1990) that learning to use new materials, particularly *Standards*-based materials, often involves multiple facets of teachers' practices and understandings. We also know that curriculum materials can provide information and scaffolding to help teachers learn about, among other things, student thinking, the design of activities, and mathematical content (Ball & Cohen, 1996; Davis & Krajcik, 2005; Remillard, 1999, 2000). In this chapter, we focus on the development of teachers' curriculum strategies in order to better understand changes in teachers' uses of *Standards*-based curriculum materials. By *curriculum strategies*, we mean the consistent patterns in the ways that teachers read, evaluate, and adapt curriculum materials before, during, and after instruction. The curriculum strategies framework allows us not only to describe shifts in teachers' practices and in the teacher–curriculum relationship, but also to examine what teachers learn over time about what it means to "use" curriculum materials.

Research Context

Participating Teachers

The three teachers described in this chapter were part of a larger study of K-3 teachers piloting *Children's Math Worlds* (Fuson, 2000), a *Standards*-based mathematics curriculum program. In the larger study, more than 20 teachers were followed during the first year they implemented *Children's Math Worlds*. The three teachers who are the focus of this chapter were studied for an additional year, allowing us to detail changes in their practices from Year 1 to Year 2. These teachers were a voluntary sample, both in their original decisions to participate in the pilot project and in their decisions to continue for a second year. At the beginning of the study, Beth was in her seventh year of teaching, Fran had 17 years of teaching experience, and Kate had 19 years of teaching experience. It is important to emphasize that all three of these teachers were veteran urban teachers – a group that is often considered to be resistant to change (Guskey, 1989).

Data Collection

Each of the teachers was observed teaching mathematics between 15 and 30 times over the course of the two school years. These observations included several "cluster" visits in which a researcher observed instruction for two or three consecutive days, allowing us to understand in greater detail the ways in which teachers used the results of one day's activities to inform the next day's use of curriculum materials and instruction. Most of the observations were videotaped and transcribed. Each observation was followed by a post-observation interview that lasted between 15 and 30 minutes and was audiotaped and transcribed.

Children's Math Worlds

The curriculum program that served as the context for this study was *Children's Math Worlds* (CMW) (Fuson, 2000), an elementary-level mathematics program developed at Northwestern University. CMW was explicitly designed to blend aspects of both traditional pedagogy (including teacher demonstration, fact memorization, and worksheets) and reform-oriented instructional methods (including the development of math talk, the use of drawings, and building on children's thinking) in order to build an "equity pedagogy" (Fuson et al., 2000) in urban classrooms. The curriculum materials were intended to promote student understanding of mathematics through the use of meaningful verbal, situational, and visual representations, and the promotion of classroom discourse around problem-solving and children's multiple solution methods (Hufferd-Ackles, 1999). The focus of the curriculum program was on using children's drawings and strategies to help them develop efficient and generalizable solution methods for a variety of mathematical problems. A complementary focus was on the development of "math talk" (Hufferd-Ackles, Fuson, & Sherin, 2004), or high levels of questioning and explaining among teacher and students, within the mathematics classroom.

Curriculum Vision and Curriculum Trust

Based on our observations and interviews with the three teachers over two years, as well as our initial analyses of the data, we sensed that there were fundamental changes between Year 1 and Year 2 in the ways the teachers approached their interactions with the curriculum materials. Turning to the literature, we identified the constructs of curriculum vision and curriculum trust as potentially useful lenses for understanding these changes. In the sections that follow, we first provide our definitions, based on the literature, of the two constructs. We then present our analyses of the three teachers' curriculum strategies to illustrate how they had begun to develop curriculum vision and trust during their first two years using CMW.

Defining Curriculum Vision

One concept that teachers might learn from and about using a set of curriculum materials over time is a "vision" of the particular kinds of learning and teaching practices described[1] in the curriculum materials. In CMW, for instance, these kinds of practices include focusing on problem-solving, multiple representations, and "math talk." Although we agree that, as prior research suggests, teachers can learn about both content and pedagogy through their use of curriculum materials (e.g., Davis & Krajcik, 2005), we propose that using a set of curriculum materials for at least one year can also help teachers develop a curriculum-based vision of mathematics teaching and learning. Remillard and Bryans (2004) described this as the "mathematical *vision* within the materials" (p. 352).

Other researchers have also recently invoked the term "vision" in their descriptions of teachers' practices and, in particular, in their descriptions of teacher learning and the development of teacher expertise. Darling-Hammond et al. (2005) identified "curricular vision" in their description of the knowledge, understandings, and skills that successful teachers need:

> Well-prepared teachers have developed a sense of "where they are going" and how they and their students are going to get there. They are able to create a coherent curriculum that is also responsive to the needs of students and to construct a classroom community in which the "hidden curriculum" fosters respectful relationships and equitable learning.
>
> (p. 177)

Similarly, Zumwalt (1989) argued that teacher educators and researchers need to develop a "curricular vision of teaching" in which teachers are viewed as professionals who make curricular decisions and thus need significant curricular knowledge. Hammerness (2001) described the ways in which teachers gain an "up-close vision" of instruction. Finally, Sherin (2001) introduced the concept of "professional vision," and suggested, "The idea is that, as we become part of a professional discipline, we are trained to look at and see a certain set of phenomena in a particular way" (p. 75). Here we are arguing that a key phenomenon of interest to teachers is the use of curriculum materials and that, therefore, the development of curriculum vision is an important aspect of teacher expertise.

We conjectured that, through the enactment over time of *Standards*-based curriculum materials, the teachers in our study developed a vision of where the curriculum program was going mathematically and, in so doing, gained an "up-close vision" of the kinds of learning and teaching practices described in the curriculum materials. In other words, we are claiming that teachers might develop "curriculum vision" as they gain both experience and expertise with a particular set of curriculum materials. As described below, we looked to teachers' changing curriculum strategies for evidence of their development of this kind of curriculum vision. Before presenting this analysis, we first introduce our second construct of interest – curriculum trust.

Defining Curriculum Trust

By curriculum trust, we refer to a set of teacher beliefs and practices that reflect an understanding that the curriculum materials, as written, provide a developmental mathematics trajectory that will support students in achieving the mathematical goals defined by the curriculum vision. Implicit in this definition is the constraint that, in most cases, the existence of curriculum vision is a necessary, but not sufficient, prerequisite for the development of curriculum trust. In other words, teachers must first develop their ideas about where the curriculum program is going mathematically (curriculum vision) before deciding whether the curriculum materials will help them reach that mathematical goal (curriculum trust).[2] At the same time, curriculum vision and curriculum trust seem to be mutually reinforcing constructs in that increasing curriculum trust can support the development of increased curriculum vision and vice versa. To be clear, we are not claiming that curriculum trust is synonymous with curriculum fidelity. In fact, the research examples we draw on suggest that curriculum trust can involve making significant adaptations to the materials, based on the needs of students, that support and enhance the written materials while remaining within the curriculum "envelope" (Ben-Peretz, 1990) and maintaining the goals and trajectory of the curriculum materials.

Here, we provide an example from prior research on curriculum materials use to help illustrate what we do and do not mean by curriculum trust. In their work with teachers implementing the *Investigations* curriculum program, Remillard and Bryans (2004) described one teacher, Zoe Kitcher, who seemed to develop increasing trust in the curriculum materials as she continued to use them for more than one year. In her second year of using the curriculum materials, Kitcher felt she had "a clearer sense of how things fit together and a clearer sense of why we're doing what we're doing. So even though I still have some questions, I trust that somehow, it's in there and it's being addressed somewhere" (p. 368). Several aspects of this comment are important for our understanding of curriculum trust. First, trust is an aspect of the teacher–curriculum relationship that develops *over time*. Although some teachers might be predisposed to trust the curriculum program, the kind of trust that Zoe Kitcher describes requires a familiarity with the materials that can only come with use. Second, curriculum trust is not only about what is in the curriculum materials, but also about *why* it is in there. This is again dependent on the existence of curriculum vision. Kitcher describes herself as having developed both curriculum vision ("a clearer sense of how things fit together") and curriculum trust ("a clearer sense of why we're doing what we're doing" and "I trust that somehow, it's in there and it's being addressed"). Finally, curriculum trust is not an absence of questions, nor is it a relinquishing of teachers' authority, but instead it is a belief that answers to questions, and instructional guidance, can be found within, rather than outside of, the curriculum materials.

It is important to note here that these ideas about curriculum vision and trust, though seemingly robust within the literature related to teachers' use of curriculum materials, are based on small numbers of teachers using fairly exclusive sets of curriculum materials. It is an open empirical question as to how these constructs develop with different sets of curriculum materials, as well as whether and how different sets of curriculum materials provide different levels or kinds of support for the development of curriculum trust and vision.

Identifying Teachers' Curriculum Strategies

Based on our observations of the teachers' mathematics instruction and interviews with the teachers, we identified Year 1 and Year 2 curriculum strategies for each teacher by examining the data for evidence concerning how teachers interacted with and used the curriculum materials at various stages in the instructional process. Specifically, we represented the teachers' curriculum strategy with a 3×3 matrix that describes teachers' engagement in three interpretive activities (reading, evaluating, and adapting curriculum materials) before, during, and after enacted lessons. These three activities have been identified by prior research as important contexts for understanding the relationship between teachers and curriculum materials (e.g., Ben-Peretz, 1990; Collopy, 2003; Lloyd, 1999; Remillard, 1999, 2000).

Characterizing an individual teacher's curriculum strategy was a three-stage process. In the first phase, a researcher reviewed all post-observation interviews for comments that the teacher made about how he or she prepared for instruction, any questions the teacher raised about the curriculum materials, changes the teacher made in the lesson when it was implemented, and changes that might be made in the future if this lesson were re-taught. The observational data were then reviewed in order to compare the written lesson with the enacted lesson. Specifically, the researcher identified changes that had been made in the written lesson and confirmed or disconfirmed changes that the teacher had described in the interviews. The researcher also drew on the interview data to identify whether these changes had been made before, during, or after instruction.

In the second phase of analysis, this information was organized into a table that described existing evidence from each observation that the teacher had (or had not) read, evaluated, and adapted the curriculum materials, and whether this had taken place before, during, or after instruction. Such tables allowed us to explore the extent to which a teacher interacted with the curriculum materials in a consistent manner – that is, whether the activities in which the teacher engaged before, during, and after instruction changed from lesson to lesson or were consistent over time. Based on this information, the researcher developed the teacher's curriculum strategy matrix as a way to capture those consistencies detected in the table. Next, the researcher compared the information for each lesson in the table with the matrix. In this way, the number of observed lessons that were consistent with the identified curriculum strategy was determined. Both confirming and disconfirming examples were noted. Finally, a subset of data from each of the three teachers was reviewed by two additional researchers in order to check the reliability of the coding.

Using this approach, we identified a stable approach in the ways in which each teacher used the curriculum materials across each school year. In particular, the curriculum strategy identified for each of the first year teachers applied in at least 77 percent of the observations conducted. For the second year data, there was a similar level of consistency in the curriculum strategies identified for Kate and Fran, whereas Beth shifted back and forth between two curriculum strategies.

In the sections that follow, we present the Year 1 and Year 2 curriculum strategy matrices for each of the three teachers, followed by a discussion of the findings that were common across the three teachers. In particular, we highlight patterns in the teachers' changing curriculum strategies that suggest that the teachers were developing both curriculum vision and curriculum trust.

Teachers' Year 1 and Year 2 Curriculum Strategies

Beth's Curriculum Strategies

Table 22.1 presents the Year 1 and Year 2 curriculum strategy matrix for Beth. Several important aspects of Beth's use of the curriculum materials are made visible through the curriculum strategy matrix. First, in Year 1, as can be seen in the "Adapt" column, Beth consistently adapted the curriculum materials both before and during instruction. Furthermore, these adaptations generally involved *creating* new activities, explanations, or terminology to supplement those provided in the curriculum materials. This tendency is different from that of many other teachers, also using the curriculum program for the first time, who chose to either omit portions of the materials or replace them with familiar substitutes (Sherin & Drake, 2008).

Looking at Beth's Year 1 approach to evaluating and adapting the curriculum materials, both before and after instruction, it seems that she focused on transitions and connections between activities and between lessons. She often looked at the series of activities that comprised a lesson, evaluated whether or not there were sufficient transitions between the activities, and, if not, created activities that she believed would provide the necessary transition for her students. This focus on transitions is apparent in Beth's comments throughout the year that mention "steps," "bits and pieces," and "transitions":

Table 22.1 Beth's Year 1 and Year 2 Curriculum Strategy Matrix (Italicized activities occurred for approximately half of observed lessons)

	Read	Evaluate	Adapt
Before Instruction	Examines general outline of activities in lesson; examines broadly how mathematical ideas in lesson are communicated (Year 1 and Year 2)	Considers own understanding of conceptual connections among activities in lesson (Year 1) *Considers conceptual importance of activity; considers how she would do the activity if she were a student (Year 2)*	Creates transitional activities (Year 1) *Replaces materials (Year 2)*
During Instruction	Examines how book explains particular concepts and activities (Year 2)	Considers students' understanding of mathematics in lesson (Year 1 and Year 2)	Creates new explanations and new terminology (Year 1) Creates pedagogy and new terminology (Year 2)
After Instruction		Considers whether students need more review; considers whether she successfully managed activities in lesson (Year 1) *Considers how activity could be improved for next year (Year 2)*	*Replaces activities and pedagogy (Year 2)*

How I was going to get from story to math story and what would be the next logical step. I didn't want to overwhelm them.

(October 6, 1998)

I'm going for an overall understanding of all the bits and pieces that they've got. And I don't have a clue how to do that for them.

(January 28, 1999)

I was going to do just the dimes and pennies, but then I was reading how first they were going to do it with the pennies and show the dimes. I was thinking, "Well, that is true, maybe it would give them a transition."

(May 26, 1999)

In Year 2, Beth's curriculum strategy changed in several ways. In particular, the emphasis on adaptation and the focus on transitions that were so apparent in the Year 1 strategy are substantially less apparent in Beth's Year 2 curriculum materials use. As the matrix indicates, Beth evaluated and adapted before and after instruction in only about half of the observed lessons during Year 2. The adaptations she made in Year 2 were more likely to be replacements of a curriculum element with something she thought might work better for her students than creations of additional activities to supplement or "fill in" things that she felt were missing from the curriculum materials (her Year 1 strategy). At the same time, her Year 2 readings and adaptations were focused more on pedagogy and conceptual explanations than in Year 1. Specifically, in Year 2 Beth sought pedagogical methods and techniques that would allow her to facilitate students' conceptual understanding and development of multiple problem-solving and computational strategies. When asked to describe the "big ideas" of the curriculum program in Year 2, Beth responded with the following, indicating her focus on student thinking and interactions with students:

The focus is different, you have to change your paradigm for what math is. Instead of it being a system you teach kids to get answers, it's more an exploratory interaction to finding different ways to get to the answers and what the problem really is asking you ... The focus is on the process not so much the answer. It is a higher level of thinking, so get ready for challenges and teaching kids to challenge. It's a more interactive math curriculum.

(March 24, 2000)

Finally, Beth's Year 2 evaluations were typically made in planning for using the curriculum materials next year, rather than planning for using the materials the next day, as in Year 1.

In summary, Beth's curriculum strategy changed between Year 1 and Year 2, not only in the timing of some of the processes (i.e., before, during, or after instruction) but also in the meaning of the processes. In Year 1, Beth consistently evaluated and adapted the curriculum materials before, during, and after instruction, and many of these evaluations and adaptations were focused on identifying and creating connections and transitions within and across lessons. In Year 2, Beth's adaptations centered on student thinking and facilitating discussion of multiple strategies and representations for solving problems. Recall that this shift is also evident in the quotations from Beth at the beginning of the chapter. In the Fall of Year 1, Beth was very concerned with the transitions and scaffolds (between circles and number sentences) described in the curriculum materials compared with the transition (between math stories and number sentences) she wanted her students to make. In the winter of Year 2, she described a shift in her use of the curriculum materials: from being guided by the curriculum materials to being guided by her students' thinking and using the curriculum materials as a "resource." Finally, by the spring of Year 2, she had developed a "trust" in the "flow" and "connections" of the curriculum materials. These shifts in Beth's relationship and interactions with the curriculum materials are important because they indicate significant changes in Beth's use of the curriculum materials as a tool for guiding or informing her practices both before and during instruction. The curriculum strategy matrix both revealed and described these critical changes in Beth's practices.

Kate's Curriculum Strategies

We also found that Kate's and Fran's curriculum strategies changed between Year 1 and Year 2. For Kate, as for Beth, the change was in both the timing and the meaning of the processes. In her first year using the curriculum materials (Table 22.2), Kate evaluated and adapted the curriculum materials both before and during instruction. Furthermore, many of her evaluations and adaptations emphasized "control" of the classroom, both behaviorally and intellectually. Evidence for this tendency is found in her evaluations being focused on "maintaining control" and "following directions," and in the fact that her evaluations and adaptations centered on ways to group students for lessons. Notice also that, according to her curriculum strategy matrix, in Year 1 Kate looked primarily for details when reading the materials, focusing on the specific concepts and terminology she would need to teach the lesson.

Looking at Kate's Year 2 use of curriculum materials, it is clear that, similar to Beth, Kate changed both the timing and the focus of her use of curriculum materials. First, Kate no longer evaluated or adapted the curriculum materials *during* instruction. Instead, her evaluations and adaptations were primarily done before instruction. Second, the issues around which Kate evaluated and adapted the curriculum materials during Year 2 were substantially different than they had been in Year 1. In the Year 2 matrix, there is much less emphasis on detail, control, and grouping, and much more attention to the big conceptual ideas and to her Year 1 students' experiences with the curriculum program.

Thus, although the specific changes were different, the shifts in Beth's and Kate's curriculum strategies from Year 1 to Year 2 of using the materials were similar in that both involved fundamental changes in both the order and the foci of their curricular processes. In practice, this meant that both Kate and Beth

Table 22.2 Kate's Year 1 and Year 2 Curriculum Strategy Matrix

	Read	*Evaluate*	*Adapt*
Before Instruction	Examines specific concepts introduced in lesson; Examines terms introduced and specifically how they are used in lesson (Year 1) Examines objectives of lesson (Year 2)	Considers whether recommended ways of grouping students will work for her students (Year 1) Considers last year's implementation of same lesson (Year 2)	Replaces group work with individual work and whole-class discussion (Year 1) Replaces questions Combines concepts (Year 2)
During Instruction		Considers whether she is maintaining control of class; Considers whether students are following directions (Year 1)	Changes the way that students are grouped for selected activities (Year 1)
After Instruction			

approached the curriculum materials less from a reactive perspective (how to change the curriculum materials) and more from a proactive perspective (how to use the curriculum materials in ways that would work for the long-term development of students' mathematical thinking). Although our focus in this study was not on students' experiences with the curriculum materials, it seems likely that this shift in teachers' perspective led to a more coherent, or connected, mathematics experience for the students as well.

Fran's Curriculum Strategies

The case of the third teacher, Fran, is somewhat different from the other two teachers. Specifically, as illustrated in Table 22.3, the changes in her strategy between Year 1 and Year 2 were only in the content, or meaning, of the processes, and not in the timing of the processes. In both Year 1 and Year 2, Fran read, evaluated, and adapted the curriculum materials before instruction, and then continued to read, evaluate, and adapt during instruction.

Despite the consistency in the timing of the processes across the two years of Fran's use of curriculum materials, there were two significant changes in the ways she engaged in these processes. First, between Year 1 and Year 2, Fran shifted the focus of her evaluations *during* instruction from an appraisal of her own teaching and explanations to an assessment of her students' understanding. Second, Fran's adaptations during Year 2 were primarily substitutions or modifications of curricular activities, whereas in Year 1 she often omitted activities from the curriculum materials, particularly during instruction.

Table 22.3 Fran's Year 1 and Year 2 Curriculum Strategy Matrix

	Read	*Evaluate*	*Adapt*
Before Instruction	Examines general outline of activities in lesson (Year 1 and Year 2)	Considers whether students will understand mathematics in lesson (Year 1 and Year 2)	Replaces activities (Year 1 and Year 2)
During Instruction	Examines precise wording of examples used in lesson (Year 1 and Year 2)	Considers whether she is explaining mathematical ideas correctly (Year 1)	Unintentionally omits or replaces activities (Year 1)
		Considers whether students are understanding mathematics being presented (Year 2)	Replaces or modifies activities (Year 2)
After Instruction			

Patterns of Change: Developing Curriculum Vision and Trust

Having established that each of the three teachers' curriculum strategies changed substantially between Year 1 and Year 2, we now examine patterns in these changes across the three teachers. In particular, we ask what the shifts in these teachers' curriculum strategies tell us about the development of teachers' curriculum vision and curriculum trust, and about what teachers might learn about and through their use of curriculum materials.

Changing Curriculum Strategies: Similarities Across the Three Teachers

Although the details of change differed among the three teachers, the changes in all three teachers' curriculum strategies reflected some important shifts in teachers' interactions with the curriculum materials. In other work (Sherin & Drake, 2008) we examined the first-year curriculum strategies of ten elementary teachers (including Beth, Kate, and Fran), and identified three categorization schemes for distinguishing among and identifying patterns across teachers' strategies: reading for broad overviews or details; evaluating in terms of students, teachers, or others; and adapting as creating, replacing, or omitting. The curriculum strategy matrices for Beth, Kate, and Fran indicate that there were significant changes in all three of these categories. These changes are illustrated in Table 22.4.

In Year 1, all three teachers were intent on understanding the *details* of the curriculum materials and determining what they might *add* to or *omit* from the curriculum materials in order to support their ongoing practices or prior beliefs about students' needs.[3] In Year 2, teachers' curriculum strategies indicate that

Table 22.4 Summary of Changes in Teachers' Curriculum Strategies

	Year 1	Year 2
READ	Focus on details	Focus on broad overviews
EVALUATE	Focus on teacher understanding before instruction and student understanding during instruction	Focus on student understanding before *and* during instruction (able to anticipate student understanding based on prior year's experience with curriculum).
ADAPT	Focus on creating or omitting	Focus on replacing

they were more likely to consider the broad overviews provided in the curriculum materials to guide their practices, and adaptations tended to be *replacements* (rather than additions or omissions) that met the needs of particular students while still maintaining the conceptual and pedagogical goals of the curriculum program. In other words, in Year 2, teachers were more likely to make changes based on their increased understanding of the long-term mathematical goals of the curriculum program and what it would take for their students to achieve those goals, rather than consistently adding or omitting sections of the curriculum materials out of fear that their students would not "get it."

At the same time, because of their experience in Year 1 with the curriculum materials, all three teachers were able in Year 2 to make evaluations focused on *student understanding* both before and during instruction. Specifically, before instruction, teachers were less concerned with their own understanding of the materials (having already experienced them once before) and were, at the same time, better able to anticipate student reactions to the materials (having already used the materials with students).

Developing Curriculum Vision

Curriculum vision is, in essence, an understanding of the mathematical and pedagogical goals of the curriculum materials – an understanding of what the curriculum materials are intended to help students accomplish and how the various pieces (activities, lessons, materials, etc.) fit together to accomplish these goals. As discussed above, curriculum trust and curriculum vision are closely linked and mutually reinforcing, and thus each of the curriculum strategy shifts likely reflects the development of curriculum vision *and* curriculum trust. Nonetheless, for the purposes of analytic clarity, we suggest that changes in the ways in which teachers read and evaluated the curriculum materials provide evidence of increased curriculum vision, while changes in teachers' adaptations reflect greater curriculum trust.

In Year 2, teachers' curriculum strategies indicate that they were more aware of and more knowledgeable about the mathematical and pedagogical "big ideas" of the curriculum materials. This development of teachers' curriculum vision is reflected in the ways teachers read and evaluated the curriculum materials. In terms of reading, we argue that the move from reading for details to reading for a broad overview suggests that teachers (particularly Kate) recognized that (a) there was a long-term mathematical vision contained within the curriculum materials and that they could better understand this vision by reading each day for the broad overview of lessons, and (b) it was important to understand how each day's lesson fit within their curriculum vision. In fact, as teachers moved from Year 1 to Year 2, it became more important to understand how a particular lesson fit within the long-term goals of the curriculum materials than to know in detail how particular topics were explained or introduced. Of course, this shift in priorities when reading was facilitated by the teachers' prior experiences with the curriculum materials, through which they had already gained substantial knowledge about the details of individual lessons.

At the same time, the three teachers' shift in evaluative focus from teacher to students reflects important progress in their development of a curriculum vision – a shift in focus from what is being taught to what is being learned. We claim that these changes in teachers' curriculum strategies suggest that the teachers were beginning to develop a vision of the kind of instruction described in the *Standards* (National Council of Teachers of Mathematics, 2000) through their use of the *Standards*-based curriculum materials. Ultimately, curriculum vision is about long-term mathematical goals for *students*, not teachers, and this shift in evaluative focus is an important aspect of the development of curriculum vision.

Developing Curriculum Trust

As discussed above, our examination of the three teachers' curriculum strategy matrices over the two years revealed a third shift in their relationship to the curriculum materials – a shift in teachers' approaches to adapting curriculum materials. This shift in adaptation provides evidence of teachers' increasing curriculum trust – trust that the curriculum materials, as written, would help them to achieve the mathematical and pedagogical goals of the curriculum program (the curriculum vision), with appropriate adaptations for their particular students and contexts.

Evidence of this developing curriculum trust can be seen in the decreasing role of adaptation in Beth's and Kate's curriculum strategies, and in the elimination of "omit" from Fran's curriculum strategy. One way of understanding this change from Year 1 to Year 2 is that all three teachers moved from approaching the curriculum program as something that needed to be *changed* to viewing it as something that could be *used*. Although this use still involved some degree of change and adaptation, as we would expect with the use of any curriculum materials, the changes became less tinkering and more coherent as teachers "bought in" to the underlying structure and trajectory of the curriculum program and worked *with* the activities in the curriculum materials as opposed to bringing in significant materials from outside the curriculum program. Davis and Krajcik (2005), drawing on Brown and Edelson (2003), described these kinds of adaptations as "productive changes" (p. 9) to curriculum materials.

Implications for Professional Development and Curriculum Design

In this chapter, we have presented three related stories of teacher learning. As illustrated by their curriculum strategies, Beth, Kate, and Fran initially used the CMW curriculum program in quite different ways. Yet by the second year of implementing this curriculum program, all three teachers had developed greater curriculum vision and trust. They came to focus more closely on how the curriculum program supported their students' learning and on how they, as teachers, could effectively adapt the activities described in the curriculum materials for their students. Although we cannot make claims about the generalizability of these results, we believe they are, nevertheless, quite important for several reasons.

First, we have presented evidence of teacher learning from using curriculum materials that extends beyond most current claims of teacher learning about mathematical content and pedagogy from using *Standards*-based materials. Instead, here we find that an important arena for teacher learning is learning about the curriculum itself. This includes developing an appreciation for the central goals of a curriculum, as well as how the curriculum hopes to achieve those goals. In addition, we have shown that as teachers use new materials over time they may in fact learn new ways to interact with curriculum materials. This is particularly noteworthy given that in their first year of using CMW, Beth, Kate, and Fran each had a consistent approach to using the materials. Prior research has repeatedly documented the stability of teachers' practices over time. In contrast, here we found that in their second year of implementing CMW these three teachers developed curriculum strategies that differed significantly from the first year.

Second, the results of this study have implications for the design of curriculum materials. A number of researchers (Ball & Cohen, 1996; David & Krajcik, 2005; Remillard & Bryans, 2004) express the need for educative curriculum materials – that is, curriculum materials that support teacher learning in addition to student learning. This study provides insights into the kind of learning that must be addressed by such materials. For example, the teachers initially looked for detailed information about lessons and activities, but they also needed information about the broad goals of the curriculum program and about how various components in a unit were related both conceptually and in terms of specific activities. Exploring ways to provide such information within the context of daily lesson plans (where teachers focus most of their attention) is an important challenge for designers of curriculum materials.

Third, in terms of professional development, it may be useful to discuss with teachers the notions of curriculum vision and curriculum trust. Teachers who understand that one of their objectives is to understand the long-term goals of a new curriculum program may find ways to focus both on the details of activities as well as on the broad purposes of a lesson. Similarly, teachers who become aware of their initial lack of curriculum trust may find, over time, that they do in fact have insights about why the curriculum program presents information in a particular form. Furthermore, helping teachers to become aware of the ways in which they tend to use curriculum materials may open up for them the possibilities of trying alternate approaches to reading, evaluating, and adapting curriculum materials.

In sum, examining changes in teachers' practices through the framework of curriculum strategies provides a valuable lens for researchers investigating teacher learning and development in the context of implementation of *Standards*-based curriculum materials. In addition, understanding how and why teachers use curriculum materials in particular ways can help us both to design effective materials and to develop appropriate supports for teachers as they use such materials in their classrooms.

Acknowledgment

This work was supported in part by the James S. McDonnell Foundation. Thanks to Gwen Lloyd and Janine Remillard for their helpful comments on multiple versions of this chapter.

Notes

1. These descriptions might be more or less explicit, depending on developers' stances towards offering a design rationale to teachers (Davis & Krajcik, 2005; Stein & Kim, Chapter 3 of this volume).
2. There are instances in the literature of teachers developing curriculum trust and then, through this trust, developing curriculum vision. For example, the "thorough piloters" described by Remillard and Bryans (2004) decided to try the curriculum materials as written and see what happened mathematically. These teachers exhibited curriculum trust before knowing in detail what the curriculum vision would be.
3. This focus on details in Year 1 was evidenced in different ways for the three teachers. For example, although Beth read the curriculum materials for broad overviews, she considered the materials at a detailed level – as indicated by her focus on *creating* transitions and explanations as well as new vocabulary for her students.

References

Ball, D. L., & Cohen, D. K. (1996). Reform by the book: What is – or might be – the role of curriculum materials in teacher learning and instructional reform? *Educational Researcher, 25*(9), 6–8, 14.

Ben-Peretz, M. (1990). *The teacher-curriculum encounter: Freeing teachers from the tyranny of texts.* Albany, NY: SUNY Press.

Brown, M., & Edelson, D.C. (2003). *Teaching as design: Can we better understand the ways in which teachers use materials so we can better design materials to support their changes in practice?* Evanston, IL: Center for Learning Technologies in Urban Schools.

Collopy, R. (2003). Curriculum materials as a professional development tool: How a mathematics textbook affected two teachers' learning. *Elementary School Journal, 103*, 287–311.

Darling-Hammond, L., Banks, J., Zumwalt, K., Gomez, L., Sherin, M.G., Griesdorn, J. et al. (2005). Educational goals and purposes: Developing a curricular vision for teaching. In L. Darling-Hammond & J. Bransford (Eds.), *Preparing teachers for a changing world: What teachers should learn and be able to do* (pp. 169–200). San Francisco, CA: Jossey-Bass.

Davis, E., & Krajcik, J. (2005). Designing educative curriculum materials to promote teacher learning. *Educational Researcher, 34*(3), 3–14.

Fuson, K. C. (2000). *Children's math worlds.* Unpublished manuscript: Northwestern University, Evanston, IL.

Fuson, K. C., De La Cruz, Y., Lo Cicero, A. M., Smith, S. T., Hudson, K., Ron, P. et al. (2000). Blending the best of the 20th century to achieve a mathematics equity pedagogy in the 21st century.

In M. Burke (Ed.), *Learning mathematics for a new century, 2000 Yearbook of the NCTM* (pp. 197–212). Reston, VA: National Council of Teachers of Mathematics.

Guskey, T. R. (1989). Attitude and perceptual change in teachers. *International Journal of Educational Research, 13,* 439–453.

Hammerness, K. (2001). Teachers' visions: The role of personal ideals in school reform. *Journal of Educational Change, 2*(2), 143–163.

Hufferd-Ackles, K. (1999). *Learning by all in a math-talk learning community.* Unpublished doctoral dissertation, Northwestern University, Evanston, IL.

Hufferd-Ackles, K., Fuson, K., & Sherin, M. G. (2004). Describing levels and components of a math-talk community. *Journal for Research in Mathematics Education, 35*(2), 81–116.

Lloyd, G. M. (1999). Two teachers' conceptions of a reform-oriented curriculum: Implications for mathematics teacher development. *Journal of Mathematics Teacher Education, 2*(3), 227–252.

National Council of Teachers of Mathematics (2000). *Principles and standards for school mathematics.* Reston, VA: Author.

Remillard, J. T. (1999). Curriculum materials in mathematics education reform: A framework for examining teachers' curriculum development. *Curriculum Inquiry, 29*(3), 315–341.

Remillard, J. T. (2000). Can curriculum materials support teachers' learning? Two fourth-grade teachers' use of a new mathematics text. *Elementary School Journal, 100*(4), 331–350.

Remillard, J. T. & Bryans, M. (2004). Teachers' orientations toward mathematics curriculum materials: Implications for teacher learning. *Journal for Research in Mathematics Education, 35*(5), 352–388.

Richardson, V. (1990). Significant and worthwhile change in teaching practice. *Educational Researcher, 19*(7), 10–18.

Sherin, M. G. (2001). Developing a professional vision of classroom events. In T. Wood, B. S. Nelson, & J. Warfield (Eds.), *Beyond classical pedagogy: Teaching elementary school mathematics* (pp. 75–93). Mahwah, NJ: Lawrence Erlbaum.

Sherin, M. G. & Drake, C. (2008). Curriculum strategy framework: Investigating patterns in teachers' use of a reform-based elementary mathematics curriculum. *Journal of Curriculum Studies,* in press.

Shulman, L. S. (1986). Those who understand: Knowledge growth in teaching. *Educational Researcher, 15*(2), 4–14.

Zumwalt, K. (1989). The need for a curricular vision. In M. C. Reynolds (Ed.), *Knowledge base for the beginning teacher* (pp. 173–184). New York, NY: Pergamon Press.

23

Part V Commentary
Development of Teaching Through Research into Teachers' Use of Mathematics Curriculum Materials and Relationships Between Teachers and Curriculum

Barbara Jaworski

In this part of the book there are three chapters addressing the theme of *Teacher Learning Through and In Relation to Use of Curriculum Materials*. My response to these chapters is in three sections: first, a short account of my perspective of the research setting in which these chapters are located; then a summary of each of the chapters, with suggestions about its contribution to knowledge in the field; and finally, a discussion of compelling themes suggested through my reading of the chapters leading to questions and theoretical issues to be prioritized in future research.

The Settings of These Studies

The setting of each of these studies includes a number of objects, processes, and activities:

1. A curriculum as defined by policymakers (e.g., at national or state level)
2. A written set of curriculum materials – primarily a published book series
3. Teachers' activity in preparing for teaching, drawing on each of the above as well as their own knowledge and experience of teaching
4. Teachers' activity in the classroom with students, using and adapting the preparation in (3), (potentially) informed by (1) and (2)
5. Students' activity and learning outcomes in relation to (4).

Here we can see a transition from the *intended* curriculum (1), through the *interpreted* curriculum (2–3) to the *enacted* curriculum (4–5) (Howson & Wilson, 1986).[1] The focus in these chapters is on the activity of the teachers who work between the intended curriculum and the pupils toward whose learning the curriculum is directed using specially designed *curriculum materials*. The chapters, and hence the research they report, focus on the activity of teachers as they interact with curriculum materials, prepare for interaction in the classroom, and translate their planning into classroom activity.

The setting, in each case, involves classrooms in which teachers and pupils interact within an educational system with sociohistorical precedents, deeply embedded socially and culturally. Schools are configured within a society that has strongly rooted perspectives on education and expectations of its outcomes. Educators, curriculum developers, and researchers bring expert knowledge, professional awareness, and social responsibility, involving principled professional practices, sound academic rationales, and sensitive public awareness, to work analytically between rooted perspectives and expected outcomes. An intended curriculum is a result of deliberation on these complexly related areas with their own academic and professional discourse; it is imbued with deep levels of expertise and professional judgment, also with their own particular discourse. Although its words relate to school systems, classroom activity, and human relations, the intended curriculum is nevertheless far distant in its conception and discourse from the humans who inter-relate in school settings and the societal networks in which schools are located.

Curriculum materials are a recognition of such distance. The professionals who write the materials interpret the intended curriculum to provide a bridge between its academic conceptualization and the sociocultural settings in which teaching and learning activity is located. The writing of the materials introduces new dimensions, so that their interpretation of the intended curriculum becomes or offers a new layer of academic expertise and professional judgment, a new discourse. It is here that the ordinary classroom teacher enters the scene. I say "ordinary" to distinguish from those teachers who have been a part of the deliberations either on the intended curriculum or the curriculum materials (as described in several of the chapters in Part III). Such teachers, I would claim, have had the opportunity to become legitimate participants in the academic and professional discourses that pertain to writing curricula or curriculum materials, and therefore come to their classrooms as members of wider academic communities than the ordinary teacher. The ordinary teacher is not (yet) a participant in these discourses.

As I see it, part of the task of the curriculum materials is to socialize ordinary teachers into a professional discourse represented by the curriculum materials with the associated possibility of making sense of the intended curriculum. The bridging of which I spoke above is one of seeking to bring together two related but independent discourses – that of academics and professionals conceptualizing teaching, learning, and mathematics in intellectual terms, and that of teachers (who are also professionals) working in the social settings of schools and society, participating in local norms of practice, dealing with youth culture, and embodying local political, economic, and societal values. One of the issues here concerns the extent to which the curriculum materials can relate sympathetically (or empathetically?) with these settings in which teachers are active.

In their preparation, experienced, ordinary teachers are aware of kinds of activity that they see to be possible in their classrooms, both in terms of what they themselves can engender and with what their students will be prepared to engage without disruption. Their task is to create activity in which their students will engage that can have the educational outcomes they seek in relation to curricular and societal expectations. The classroom activity that can be observed reflects a complexity of academic and social factors in which the curriculum might be a distant organ, and in which the curriculum materials play a possible variety of roles, from their use by teachers in preparation, to their use by students in classroom tasks. Measurable outcomes from such activity, such as those reflected through standardized tests, can show only marginally how this complexity influences students' academic learning.

The Research Arena and the Three Studies

The research arena in each case is that of classrooms in which teachers and pupils work together, with the introduction of a new curriculum and associated curriculum materials and the professional interactions between academic educator-researchers and teachers. In each case the curriculum materials are based on the *Standards* (National Council of Teachers of Mathematics [NCTM], 1989). In Drake and Sherin's study (Chapter 22), the curriculum materials are *Children's Math Worlds* [CMW] and participating teachers came from schools at K-3 level. In the studies of Roth McDuffie and Mather (Chapter 21) and of Doerr and Chandler-Olcott (Chapter 20), the curriculum materials are from the *Connected Mathematics Project* (CMP) with middle schools involving, respectively, seventh-grade students and students of ages 11–13.

In all three cases, researchers studied the ways teachers interacted with and made use of the curriculum materials in their work with pupils. There are many focuses that research can take in addressing this arena, and we see each of the three chapters taking its own particular focus.

In Chapter 22, Drake and Sherin examine Shulman's (1986) question "how do teachers take a piece of text and transform their understanding of it into instruction that their students can comprehend?" (p. 8).

They studied teachers' use of curriculum materials whose focus was on using children's drawings and strategies to help them develop efficient and generalizable solution methods for mathematical problems, also on development of "math talk." Their research sought and traced teachers' strategies in responding to their curriculum and in their use of curriculum materials. Drake and Sherin conjectured that these strategies change from year to year as teachers learn about and experiment with a new curriculum program. They asked also what teachers learn over time about what it means to "use" a curriculum program. They found that each of the three teachers' curriculum strategies changed substantially between Year 1 and Year 2 of their research. Whereas in Year 1 teachers' involvement with the curriculum materials might be characterized as familiarization with an adaptation of the materials to support their ongoing practices, perhaps developing a new discourse for classroom activity, in Year 2 the teachers showed a more aware use of the curriculum materials with ability to meet the needs of particular students while maintaining the conceptual and pedagogical goals of the curriculum – here establishing the new discourse.

This research contributes to knowledge in at least three ways: first, in the matrix approach to mapping and comparing teachers' strategies; second, in the recognition and mapping, over time, of teachers' deepening familiarity with the curriculum materials and associated curriculum goals, and awareness of how their own classroom activity can develop through the use of curriculum materials; and third, in the particularity of the accounts that show the nature of teachers' developing awarenesses and characterize the developmental process. We see the process for only three particular teachers, but we gain insights into issues germane to a broader range of settings.

In Chapter 21, Roth McDuffie and Mather present findings from a year-long study of two seventh-grade mathematics teachers' practices as they implemented the CMP curriculum materials and formed a professional development team with a university mathematics educator (Roth McDuffie). Their research studied the influence of curriculum-focused professional development on teachers' development of curricular knowledge and pedagogical reasoning for teaching mathematics. Research findings suggested that the team's work with the curriculum materials facilitated teachers' curricular knowledge development by supporting new comprehensions for the curriculum, including mathematics content and instructional approaches as well as a deeper awareness of students' needs.

Here, contribution to knowledge seems to be particularly strong in relating the lesson study methodology and use of video clubs to a development of curricular knowledge and application to practice. The research uses analytical constructs related to curricular knowledge and its development by the teachers in the study to provide insights into ways in which the lesson study sequences afforded opportunity for teachers and researcher to achieve "new comprehension" in realizing curriculum goals through the actual developmental practices of curriculum interpretation and curriculum materials use. Such "new comprehensions" might be expressed in terms of speaking the new discourse. Teachers' insights included a deeper awareness of their students' capacities to make sense of methods offered by the curriculum materials. The research also affords insights to the role of an educator-researcher working alongside teachers in such a developmental process.

In Chapter 20, Doerr and Chandler-Olcott ask the question, how do teachers' practices change so as to support the development of students' mathematical writings? They observe that *Standards*-based curriculum materials provide students and teachers with significant opportunities to mathematize situations that need to be interpreted through talk, texts, stories, pictures, charts, and diagrams. Their research was located in a school with high numbers of students with language difficulties and low socioeconomic status.

This chapter contributes to knowledge explicitly in linking a focus on students' writing, as demanded by the kinds of tasks proposed in the curriculum materials, to a developmental approach to use of the curriculum materials. There are interesting similarities in findings between this chapter and the two others. The first concerns shifts in teachers' perceptions of the value of the tasks proposed in the curriculum materials as they became familiar over time with opportunities they afforded. This chapter talks of "the shift from initially seeing the literacy demands as barriers to students' mathematical learning, later seeing the demands as affording opportunities, and finally identifying the need to support the development of students' abilities to communicate mathematically." This shift, although specifically related to literacy, might be seen also in the terms expressed by Drake and Sherin as a "shift in evaluative focus from teacher to students … from what is being taught to what is being learned" (Chapter 22). A second similarity, this time with Chapter 21, was the explicit use of the cyclic process of lesson planning, observation, and reflection in collaboration with an educator-researcher. This seems to me a highly significant factor in the research reported in these two chapters, and one that I take further below.

Compelling Themes with Questions and Theoretical Issues to be Prioritized in Future Research

Many themes could be explored but I choose to focus on three, reflected in the following questions:

1. In what ways does the social setting of the classrooms studied (social groups, expectations, traditions, problematics) feature in the research, and what issues arise?
2. In what ways is the research itself a factor in what is studied?
3. What assumptions are made in curriculum documents and curriculum materials, and how are these influential on teachers' use of the curriculum materials?

Social Settings of the Classrooms Studied

The above account has emphasized issues and tensions for teachers in relating the academically expressed curriculum, materials and goals to the (perceived) realities of their own social setting. In each of the chapters, we see teachers' activity acting as a bridge between the written materials and the enactive setting with the gradual establishing of a new discourse. Doerr and Chandler-Olcott (Chapter 20) indicate that their study was carried out in a school in a mid-sized urban district with a diverse school population including 20 percent of students who are English language learners, 25 percent who have special needs, and 88 percent who qualify for free school meals (indicative of high poverty). This setting includes students who struggle with academic literacy and are at the greatest risk of not learning from experiences with contextually complex materials. The researchers chose to root their study in sociocultural theory of discourse communities with a focus on written communication in the classroom. They perceived a limited vision in curriculum documents (the *Standards*, NCTM, 2000) that emphasize oral communication (academic discourse) but say little about developing the reading and writing of mathematical texts (enactive discourse). Teachers working with the curriculum materials had to learn to foster and interpret students' mathematical writing, and the research looked particularly at ways in which this posed problems for teachers and how these problems were faced over time. It seems clear from the chapter that the sociocultural setting provided a centrally significant discourse for the research that was undertaken in this study.

Roth McDuffie and Mather (Chapter 21) indicate that the school in which their research took place had 12 percent ethnic minority students and 27 percent with free school meals. Drake and Sherin (Chapter 22) report that they worked with "veteran urban teachers," and that the curriculum with which they worked "was explicitly designed to blend aspects of both traditional pedagogy … and reform-oriented instructional methods in order to build an 'equity pedagogy' … in urban classrooms." It is not clear how these socially-related factors influenced the research that is reported, and we might ask what assumptions underpin the decision, explicit or tacit, not to comment further on them. Roth McDuffie and Mather suggest that teachers in their study had to transform the curriculum relative to their state's learning expectations and their students' understandings and approaches in order to enable students to achieve curriculum goals. Teachers, unaccustomed to analyzing the materials relative to students' needs and state learning expectations, commented that they benefited from the opportunity afforded by the project. It seems likely that a more detailed study of such findings in relation to the particular social settings would be illuminative. This, of course, would be going beyond the bounds of the particular studies.

We might see details of study in terms of the zoom of the analytical lens (Lerman, 1998). Different zooms of the lens offer different units of analysis. In Roth McDuffie and Mather's study, the unit of analysis was the interaction between teachers and materials through opportunity provided by the video setting. In Drake and Sherin's research, the unit of analysis was teachers' strategies and their categorization – very different. In both cases, in relation to the five-point narrative above, the research reported affords insights particularly into points (3) and (4) as related to (1) and (2), but little insight into (5). Yet we need to know more about the enacted curriculum and how it relates to particular students and socially-related learning issues. Doerr and Chandler-Olcott, referring to teachers' desire that their students should become more competent and independent in writing responses to text-based problems in the curriculum materials, write, "Teachers needed to support such student independence in a setting where many students are second language learners, have special education needs, or have had very limited school-based experiences in communicating their mathematical thinking." It seems that future research might valuably zoom in on the complex factors and relationships of particular social settings to allow us to gain insight into the ways in which teachers' transformation of curriculum materials relates to social and political factors and leads to an "equity pedagogy" (Apple, 2000; Lerman, 2000).

The Research Itself as a Factor in What is Studied: Roles and Relationships in the Research Teams

All three projects had developmental goals with respect to teachers' use of curriculum materials and outcomes for classroom teaching and learning. Over one, two, or three years, these projects involved university researchers working with or studying the activity of teachers as the teachers developed their use of the particular curriculum materials. According to the reports, the roles of the university researchers were different in each project. Drake and Sherin gathered data from the activity of teachers and analysed it using the curriculum strategy matrix. Roth McDuffie formed a lesson-study team with the two teachers to enact, together, a research cycle (plan → act → observe → reflect → feedback). Doerr and Chandler-Olcott and their research team held regular meetings with teachers and worked one-on-one with teachers in the lesson cycles, observing classroom activity. Although not explicitly reported in all the chapters, it seems clear that relationships between teachers and the research team played an important role in the developmental processes described.

Wagner (1997) offers a three-point typology of relationships between researchers and practitioners (in these cases, the teachers), namely, data extraction agreements, clinical partnerships, and co-learning agreements. In *data extraction*, teachers are largely subjects or informants in the research. In *clinical partnership*, teachers are participants, with a stake and involvement in the research, but the university researchers design and conduct the study. In *co-learning agreements*, teachers and university researchers both contribute to the design and conduct of the research. In this mode, teachers also become researchers. These three modes might be seen as defining a spectrum of relationships from research in which researchers study the practices of teachers from an *outsider* position, with little involvement in teachers' thinking or activity, to research in which teachers and researchers work together, as *insiders*, to design and study teaching and learning (Jaworski, 2003). From the three chapters, it seems as if the research of Drake and Sherin fits into this spectrum between data extraction and clinical partnership, that of Doerr and Candler-Olcott fits around clinical partnership, and that of Roth McDuffie and Mather between clinical partnership and co-learning agreement. These are rough designations, but they allow further discussion of relationships between research and development in the three projects. I would claim that, to differing degrees, the research project and outsider-researchers played an important developmental role with some degree of influence on the developmental outcomes observed. Although such influence might be seen as a problematic factor in research rigor, it is also centrally important to the research activity these chapters report. We therefore need some kind of rationalization for this apparent tension.

One rationalization is to remove the tension, to acknowledge that all participants in the research process are learning from the research – the educator-researchers as well as the teachers. A shift of focus is needed from outsider-researchers looking into how teachers engage with and interpret the curriculum toward both groups together looking into what it means to interpret this curriculum in the sociocultural arenas in which they interact. Thus teachers are drawn into the research process as researchers and the research itself is acknowledged as a developmental process. Together these researchers look critically at curriculum materials and at their constructed activity within the research setting. I continue these ideas as part of my third theme below.

Interpreting Curriculum and Curriculum Materials for the Enacted Curriculum

Curriculum materials are not independent of the sociocultural settings in which teaching and learning take place. It should not be a case of teachers adapting their social setting to the materials, but rather of the materials' designers flexibly taking cognizance of the social factors that surround learning and teaching. As researchers into the interpretation of curriculum programs, we should be asking what assumptions curriculum materials' designers are making about the sociocultural setting in which they will be used. Cooper and Dunne (2000), for example, point out that mathematical tasks that include pseudo real-world contexts disadvantage students of lower socioeconomic status, although the assumption of the text writer is that providing the context will aid students in tackling the mathematics. The opposite was found to be true – students' attention was engaged in questions about the context, rather than seeing the context only as a route to the mathematics. To what extent are writers of materials aware of such factors? What other factors are there that research has not yet revealed? Teachers may be aware implicitly or explicitly of such factors, but have no power to translate this knowing into curriculum action.

More research is needed into ways in which curriculum materials interpret the intended curriculum, also into ways in which researchers address the intended curriculum as part of their research. Researchers need to look critically at ways in which the curriculum materials interpret the intended curriculum and the assumptions they make about those who use the materials. Co-learning agreements (Wagner, 1997) between educators and teachers, both acting as researchers, bring complementary forms of knowledge to such research. Educators are able to design activity that enables teachers to make explicit their informal knowledge, so that together they can explore more critically what informal knowing suggests. Such co-learning is empowering for both groups, and central to a developmental process that promotes new knowledge and generates new practice (Jaworski, 2003, 2006).

Note

1. Various terms are used for these three stages of curriculum. Howson and Wilson (1986) speak of the *intended*, the *implemented*, and the *attained* curriculum, respectively.

References

Apple, M. (2000). Mathematics reform through conservative modernization? Standards, markets, and inequality in education. In J. Boaler (Ed.), *Multiple perspectives on mathematics learning and teaching* (pp. 243–260). London: Ablex.

Cooper, B., & Dunne, M. (2000). *Assessing children's mathematical knowledge: Social class, sex and problem solving.* Buckingham: Open University Press.

Howson, G., & Wilson, B. R. (1986). *School mathematics in the 1990s.* Cambridge: Cambridge University Press.

Jaworski, B. (2003). Research practice into/influencing mathematics teaching and learning development: Towards a theoretical framework based on co-learning partnerships. *Educational Studies in Mathematics, 54*(2–3), 249–282.

Jaworski, B. (2006). Theory and practice in mathematics teaching development: critical inquiry as a mode of learning in teaching. *Journal of Mathematics Teacher Education. 9*(2), 187–211.

Lerman, S. (1998). A moment in the zoom of a lens: Towards a discursive psychology of mathematics teaching and learning. In A. Olivier & K. Newstead (Eds.), *Proceedings of the 22nd Annual Meeting of the International Group for the Psychology of Mathematics Education* (Vol 1., pp. 66–84). Stellenbosch, South Africa: University of Stellenbosch.

Lerman, S. (2000). The social turn in mathematics education research. In J. Boaler (Ed.), *Multiple perspectives on mathematics learning and teaching* (pp. 19–44). London: Ablex.

National Council of Teachers of Mathematics. (1989). *Curriculum and evaluation standards for school mathematics*. Reston, VA: Author.

National Council of Teachers of Mathematics. (2000). *Principles and standards for school mathematics*. Reston, VA: Author.

Shulman, L. (1986). Those who understand: Knowledge growth in teaching. *Educational Researcher, 15*(2), 4–14.

Wagner, J. (1997). The unavoidable intervention of educational research: A framework for reconsidering research-practitioner cooperation. *Educational Researcher, 26*(7), 13–22.

24

Part V Commentary
What Does it Take to Learn From and Through Curriculum Materials?

Linda Ruiz Davenport

Strengthening mathematics teaching and learning is not just about getting strong *Standards*-based curriculum materials into classrooms. There are important questions having to do with how teachers might be prepared to use these curriculum materials thoughtfully and well as a tool to support student learning. As the Senior Program Director of Elementary Mathematics in a large urban district, an important focus of my work is ensuring that schools have the support they need so *all* students are learning the important mathematics expected by our state frameworks.

Like many districts, we offer a range of professional development institutes, seminars, and workshops designed to support teachers' use of curriculum materials by acquainting them with the materials themselves, deepening their knowledge of the mathematics content addressed in the materials and helping them consider how student thinking associated with that mathematics content develops, and considering implications for their instruction. These professional development offerings are typically available after school, on Saturdays, and during the summer. Although these professional development offerings are important and make a difference, professional development alone simply cannot provide what is often needed as teachers move through their curriculum materials day by day.

Helping teachers learn from and through their curriculum materials on an ongoing basis during the context of the school day becomes an essential undertaking if we are to strengthen mathematics teaching and learning in schools. The chapters in *Teacher Learning Through and In Relation to Use of Curriculum Materials* provide us with some useful images of what this can look like in practice. They also raise some important questions about how we can support teacher learning from and through curriculum materials on a large scale. As I read these chapters, I found myself thinking about lessons to be learned about how, at a district level, we might do a better job of supporting teachers and schools in this endeavor.

Images of Teachers Learning Through and From Curriculum Materials by Focusing on What We Want Students to Learn

The five middle school teachers we see in Chapter 20, by Doerr and Chandler-Olcott, are all participating in a professional development study group that focuses on the literacy demands of their *Standards*-based curriculum materials. Over a three-year period that included institutes during the summer and "learning cycles" during the school year, they collaborated with a mathematics educator and a literacy educator and each other to develop writing plans to better prepare students for the writing tasks in their curriculum materials and on their state assessments. It was useful to learn what developing these writing plans entailed, particularly since these teachers were working at different grade levels and were not using the same curriculum materials at the same time.

One thing I found striking about the development of these writing plans was the extent to which it involved focusing on the important mathematics content of the curriculum materials and considering what students needed to be able to articulate about that mathematics content in order to show their understanding. This meant examining each curriculum unit for the important mathematical ideas, articulating a rationale for why each of these ideas were important, and developing writing prompts that might be used to address these mathematical ideas in the context of their instruction. This also involved debating what might be expected in a strong student response, analyzing particular samples of student responses with an eye to what these samples suggested about student understanding, and considering any implications for their ongoing instruction. What productive opportunities for these teachers to get strongly grounded in the mathematical goals of a set of curriculum materials! How much they seemed to be able to talk and learn even across grade-level settings!

After reading this chapter, I found myself thinking about opportunities for teacher learning through their involvement in the development of assessment tasks more generally. I could imagine teachers coming together on an ongoing basis to consider what assessment tasks they might pose, why and how those tasks captured the important mathematics of their curriculum materials, what they would want to see in a strong student response using selected samples of student work to help them think about this question, and implications for their instruction if student responses were not all they might have hoped. Although this is somewhat easier to imagine among a group of teachers from the same grade level, using the same curriculum materials at more or less the same time, it seems that there is also much that teachers can learn by collaborating across grade levels to consider mathematical learning goals more broadly. Like the development of writing plans, the development of assessment tasks more generally might provide a useful lens for learning through and from curriculum materials.

Images of Teachers Learning From Curriculum Materials by Planning and Debriefing Lessons Together

In Chapter 21, by Roth McDuffie and Mather, we see two seventh-grade teachers working closely with a mathematics educator and each other in a professional development team to plan, enact, and reflect on lessons from their *Standards*-based curriculum materials. The chapter provides us with vivid images of how this team worked together to plan and adapt a particular lesson, scheduled to be taught over several days, on finding the heights of triangles using angles of incidence and reflection. The chapter also provides us with images of what the enacted lesson looked like in each classroom, including how what happened in one classroom informed how the lesson unfolded in the other classroom as a consequence of even more planning and adaptation.

I was struck by how one important feature of the team's planning included doing the mathematics of the lesson together, outside and with real objects, just as would be expected for students. Although the teachers encountered confusions of their own as they worked through the content of the lesson, unsure of where the similar triangles were in the physical models they were using, they were able to resolve their confusions as they worked together in their team. The teachers proceeded to develop adaptations of the lesson using their own experiences with the content while also taking into account what they were learning about their students' understanding of the mathematics addressed in the curriculum unit prior to this lesson (where confusions were likely to arise) and what they believed it would take for students to understand these ideas.

My thoughts after reading this chapter centered on the complexity of what it means to use curriculum materials in thoughtful ways to support student learning. The authors highlight the importance of teachers doing the mathematics of the lesson together, analyzing the lesson from the students' perspectives, and thinking about how the understanding of the mathematics develops over time through the unfolding of prior lessons. These are not simple tasks and, fortunately for these two teachers, they had the collaborative support of their professional development team. But what would it take to apply this same level of effort to other equally complex lessons? What about the teachers at their grade levels working with these same curriculum materials that were *not* part of the professional development team? How might the learning opportunities afforded by this collaboration become more broadly available?

Teachers Learning from Curriculum Materials: Making Sense of What Curriculum Materials Offer

In Chapter 22, Drake and Sherin describe how three primary teachers interpret and enact mathematics lessons using *Standards*-based curriculum materials during their first two years of use. Beth initially had concerns with connections and transitions between activities in the curriculum materials, and created new activities she believed would ease these transitions and "fill in" what she believed to be missing. Kate focused on following directions and maintaining control, often replacing group work with individual work and whole-group discussions. Fran attended to her own teaching and the quality of her own mathematical explanations as she omitted or replaced activities from the curriculum materials. While all three teachers were involved in a pilot of newly published *Standards*-based curriculum materials and were periodically observed, videotaped, and interviewed, it is not clear to what extent these teachers received classroom support or professional development as part of the pilot project.

What struck me about this chapter was how differently each teacher seemed to engage with the curriculum materials, and how freely they seemed to make adaptations to lessons, supplement lessons with additional activities, or omit lessons altogether during their first year with these materials. How much of the integrity and cohesiveness of the curriculum materials did they sacrifice during this first year of use? What informed the choices they then made during Year 2 after not having used the curriculum materials fully during Year 1? We know some teachers working with *Standards*-based curriculum materials take advantage of the opportunity to struggle with mathematics and confront student thinking in ways that are unfamiliar, whereas others do not (Remillard & Bryans, 2004). We also know that some teachers working with *Standards*-based curriculum materials can reduce the cognitive demand of those materials depending upon their knowledge base of mathematics, their knowledge of student thinking, and their goals for students (Henningsen & Stein, 1997). Unless teachers approach their curriculum materials as learners, they may not be well positioned to take advantage of the learning opportunities that are afforded by using *Standards*-based curriculum materials (Russell et al., 1995). The teachers described in this chapter were engaged in curriculum strategies that helped them make sense of their curriculum materials and over time develop a trust in their curriculum materials, but how confident are we that teachers were moving in the direction of using these curriculum materials in thoughtful ways to support students' mathematical thinking?

After reading this chapter, I found myself thinking about the students in the classrooms of teachers who are beginning to work with *Standards*-based curriculum materials. What are *their* opportunities to learn, as teachers themselves are learning to work with new curriculum materials? My image of a classroom in which a teacher is using *Standards*-based curriculum materials includes problems being discussed and posed at the start of class; students working in small groups to engage with the mathematics embedded in those problems while the teacher circulates to listen, asks questions about their thinking, and poses any additional questions for their consideration based on where they are in their thinking; and the class ending with a strategic discussion and analysis of the ideas that came up while students were working. Admittedly, this may be an oversimplification and might not hold true for every lesson with every set of *Standards*-based curriculum materials. But this structure, combined with purposeful planning and facilitation by the teacher using strong curriculum materials, seems to provide students with needed opportunities to make sense of important mathematics. What are the implications if a teacher chooses to sacrifice small-group work for individual seatwork and whole-class instruction? Or chooses to substitute an activity that is less demanding cognitively for one that is more demanding? Or skips an activity because it feels unfamiliar or unimportant? The quality of teacher engagement with curriculum materials feels as important as the fact that teachers are developing strategies that help them make sense of these materials.

How Might Districts Support Teachers Learning from and through Curriculum Materials?

These chapters provide vivid images and discussions of teachers learning from and through *Standards*-based curriculum materials. We see teachers working hard with colleagues and mathematics education partners to examine the mathematics in these curriculum materials, explore student thinking related to that mathematics, and consider implications for their practice. We learn about teachers engaging in curriculum strategies that, over time, result in their developing a trust in their curriculum materials. What stands out in all three chapters is the complexity of what teachers need to figure out as they work with their curriculum materials on a day-by-day basis as a tool to support student learning. What might school districts do to ensure that as many teachers as possible are engaging in these kinds of opportunities to learn from and through curriculum materials?

These chapters strongly suggest the importance of teachers coming together on a regular basis to examine, discuss, and reason with their curriculum materials. Districts can support this effort by making sure that teachers have time to come together for this purpose on a regular basis during the school day – for instance, during a grade-level team planning meeting once a week or every other week. This requires setting school schedules that bring teachers at a single grade-level together for shared planning periods. This also means setting agendas for these meetings so teachers are clear on the particular goals for each, and bring copies of their curriculum materials, samples of student work, or anything else that might be required for the planned discussion and analysis. This also means setting norms and expectations about what it means to participate in these meetings, including arriving on time fully prepared, staying for the duration, and being actively engaged as a learner with colleagues. In our district, we have found it useful to have building administrators involved in these meetings as learners as well, working with teachers to understand the complexity of what it means to use and learn from curriculum materials in order to strengthen one's practice.

These chapters also strongly suggest the importance of informed partners who are able to take teachers more deeply into the mathematics of the curriculum materials, help teachers examine their beliefs about what students understand or do not yet understand, and explore with teachers the assumptions about teaching and learning that shape their practice. Might it be possible to cultivate teacher leaders who could take on roles similar to those of these educators? In districts, we are accustomed to cultivating teacher leaders who can help us offer seminars, institutes, and workshops. Similarly, we should be able to cultivate teacher leaders who can work in the settings described in these chapters to support their colleagues learning from and through *Standards*-based curriculum materials. This feels like an important additional goal for the development of teacher leadership in districts.

Many districts regularly organize and offer professional development designed to support teachers as they begin to use *Standards*-based curriculum materials. These offerings often are designed to deepen the mathematics content knowledge of teachers, help them learn more about how student thinking develops, and help them consider implications for practice using these curriculum materials. These chapters suggest that such offerings may not offer all that is needed. It appears that teachers also need ongoing opportunities to work with their curriculum materials in thoughtful ways, lesson by lesson, with colleagues and informed partners, if they are truly to be able to use their curriculum materials in powerful ways to support student learning. This takes time and resources. The more we know about what this process of learning through and from *Standards*-based curriculum materials, the better prepared we can be to address this important need.

References

Henningsen, M., & Stein, M. K. (1997). Mathematical tasks and student cognition: Classroom-based factors that support and inhibit high-level mathematical thinking and reasoning. *Journal for Research in Mathematics Education, 28*(5), 524–549.

Remillard, J. T., & Bryans, M. B. (2004). Teachers' orientations toward mathematics curriculum materials: Implications for teacher learning. *Journal for Research in Mathematics Education, 35*(5), 352–388.

Russell, S. J., Schifter, D., Bastable, V., Yaffee, L., Lester, J. B., & Cohen, S. (1995). Learning mathematics while teaching. In B. S. Nelson (Ed.), *Inquiry and the development of teaching: Issues in the transformation of mathematics teaching* (pp. 9–16). Newton, MA: Center for the Development of Teaching, Education Development Center.

Author Biographies

Stephanie L. Behm is a doctoral student in mathematics education at Virginia Tech and a middle school mathematics teacher at a charter school in North Carolina. During her doctoral program, she participated in two NSF-funded teacher education projects focused on preservice teachers' experiences with *Standards*-based curriculum materials. She is interested in student teachers' and beginning teachers' ways of using curriculum materials and textbooks for mathematics instruction.

Erik Bowen teaches high school mathematics at the University School of Nashville. Erik received his BS from Weber State University with a double major in psychology and mathematics. He continued his studies at Vanderbilt University, where he received his master's degree in mathematics education. Erik's focus of study was on teachers' learning situated in institutional context.

Matthew W. Brown, Director of Inquirium LLC, is a former teacher who is involved in research and design to support teaching and learning. His work centers on providing students with inquiry and information tools to support critical thinking and educators with tools to adapt and integrate such resources to everyday educational settings. Matt has helped design innovative learning environments for the Museum of Science and Industry, the Adler Planetarium and Astronomy Museum, the Chicago Zoological Society, the Illinois Holocaust Museum and Education Center, University of Chicago, Northwestern University, University of Illinois at Chicago, Intel Education, and Adobe Systems. He received his doctorate in the Learning Sciences from Northwestern University.

Nesrin Cengiz, Assistant Professor in the Department of Mathematics and Statistics at University of Michigan-Dearborn, received her doctorate in mathematics education at Western Michigan University. During the development of this chapter, she worked as a doctoral fellow for the Center for the Study of Mathematics Curriculum. Her research interests include exploring ways in which teachers create opportunities for extending student thinking during whole-group discussions, the relationship between teachers' knowledge/beliefs and their instructional actions, how the support provided in curriculum materials impacts instruction, and the ways in which elementary school students represent and justify their mathematical thinking.

Kelly Chandler-Olcott is Associate Professor and Director of English Education in the Reading and Language Arts Center at Syracuse University. A former high school English and social studies teacher, she now teaches courses in English methods, content literacy (including a course taken by all preservice students seeking secondary mathematics certification), and writing for professional publication. Her research interests include adolescents' technology-mediated reading and writing, teacher inquiry, and inclusive approaches to literacy instruction across school subjects. She is concluding a multi-year research project with several colleagues on intersections between mathematics and literacy in urban settings.

Charalambos Y. Charalambous, a graduate student at the University of Michigan, is a member of the Beyond Implementation: Focus on Challenge and Learning (BIFOCAL) project. A former elementary school teacher, he is interested in exploring how different factors such as teacher knowledge and their use of curriculum materials contribute to the quality of mathematics instruction and student learning.

Óscar Chávez is Assistant Professor in the Department of Learning, Teaching, and Curriculum at the University of Missouri, where he received his doctorate in mathematics education in 2003. His research interests include teachers' use of curriculum materials and its impact on student achievement. Currently he is co-PI on Comparing Options in Secondary Mathematics: Investigating Curricula (COSMIC), a longitudinal NSF-funded study.

Constantinos Christou is Professor of Mathematics Education at the University of Cyprus and the chairperson of the Department of Education. He is a board member of the European Society for Research in Mathematics Education. He serves on the editorial boards of the *Mediterranean Journal of Mathematics Education* and *The Montana Mathematics Enthusiast*. He was the National Representative of Cyprus in the TIMSS 2003 study, chairs the committee for the Cyprus National Standards in Mathematics, participates in the working group for the incorporation of information technology in primary school mathematics, and serves as scientific advisor to the committee for Cyprus primary school mathematics textbooks. His research focuses on the cognitive development of mathematical concepts, including mathematical modeling in problem-solving, student spatial reasoning, the reasoning of students in mathematical tasks, and the effects of integrating technology in the teaching of mathematics on the cognitive development of students.

Kathryn B. Chval is Assistant Professor at the University of Missouri. Previously, she worked at the National Science Foundation and the University of Illinois at Chicago. Dr Chval's research interests are related to critical issues that impact the teaching and learning of mathematics including effective models and support structures for the teacher professional continuum, effective elementary teaching of underserved populations, especially Latinos and other English language learners, and curriculum standards and policies.

Irma Colón (El Barrio-Hunter College PDS Partnership) is the mathematics coach at PS 112 in El Barrio. She has facilitated inquiry groups at her school since the onset of teacher research, and conducts professional-development workshops in the local district and citywide. She has presented PDS-related work at the 2005 NCTM Eastern Regional Meeting in Hartford and the 2006 Association of Mathematics Teacher Educators Annual Conference in Tampa.

Thomas J. Cooney, Professor Emeritus of Mathematics Education, University of Georgia, is the founding editor of the *Journal of Mathematics Teacher Education* and has authored numerous books and articles on mathematics teacher education. He was a member of the writing team for NCTM's *Curriculum and Evaluation Standards for School Mathematics* (1989) and *Professional Standards for Teachers* (1991). He has chaired the Editorial Board of the *Journal for Research in Mathematics Education*, served as co-chair of SIG/RME, and was a member of the United States Commission on Mathematics Instruction. He has been a frequent speaker at national and international meetings, particularly on research on teachers' beliefs.

Raquel Corujo (El Barrio-Hunter College PDS Partnership) is retired from first-grade teaching at PS 112 in East Harlem. While at PS 112, she was a mentor teacher and member of the PDS Advisory Committee. Her degrees are in early childhood education and bilingual education.

Carol Crumbaugh is Associate Professor of Teacher Education at Western Michigan University. Her research interests include teachers' use of *Standards*-based mathematics curriculum materials and student discourse during mathematics discussions. She has worked extensively in the professional development of teachers who implement *Investigations in Number, Data, and Space.*

Linda Ruiz Davenport has been the Senior Program Director of Elementary Mathematics for the Boston Public Schools since 2000 where she oversees an effort to strengthen mathematics teaching and learning at the elementary level. Prior to that time, she co-directed several projects at Education Development Center including the Developing Mathematical Ideas Network, was an Assistant Professor of Mathematics Education at Portland State University, and taught middle school and high school mathematics. She has a BA in Liberal Arts from the University of Texas and a MEd and PhD in Educational Curriculum and Instruction, with a focus on mathematics education and bilingual education, from the University of Washington.

Helen M. Doerr, dual Professor in the Teaching and Leadership Program in the School of Education and in the Department of Mathematics in the College of Arts and Sciences at Syracuse University, specializes in secondary mathematics education, with particular interests in teacher learning, mathematical communication, and mathematical modeling. Her most recent research has examined secondary teachers' practices and perspectives on the inter-related development of mathematics and literacy in urban settings. She has been a co-PI on many NSF-funded research projects and has authored numerous papers and book chapters. She currently teaches undergraduate mathematics and is a former teacher of mathematics at the middle and high school levels.

Corey Drake is Assistant Professor of Mathematics Education at Iowa State University. Her research focuses on teacher learning from and about curriculum materials, family and community engagement in mathematics and science education, and the relationship between teachers and policy. Her work has been published in *American Education Research Journal, Curriculum Inquiry*, and the *Journal of Mathematics Teacher Education*.

Tammy Eisenmann is a post-doctoral researcher in the School of Education, the Hebrew University of Jerusalem, Israel. Her main research interests include the way teachers use curriculum materials and technological tools in their instruction, and the connections between enacted curriculum and context (i.e., school, students, etc.) in which it is enacted. Her PhD research was done at the Weizmann Institute of Science, Israel. She holds a BSc in Mathematics and Philosophy and a MSc in Mathematics Education, both earned at the Hebrew University of Jerusalem. She has five years of experience teaching high school mathematics.

Ruhama Even, Associate Professor at the Weizmann Institute of Science, received her doctorate from Michigan State University. Her main research interests include teachers and professional development providers' knowledge and learning, and practices of mathematics teaching and curriculum enactment. She is head of the mathematics group in the Department of Science Teaching and the MANOR project. She has been a member of the International Committee of the International Group for the Psychology of Mathematics Education (PME) and is a co-chair of the International Commission on Mathematical Instruction (ICMI) Study on the Professional Education and Development of Teachers of Mathematics.

Elaine Funches (El Barrio-Hunter College PDS Partnership) is a paraprofessional at PS 112. She has been at the school for 17 years. Elaine has an associate's degree in liberal arts. She has been a member of the PDS Advisory Committee from the beginning of the PDS Partnership and has presented at the 2006 Professional Development Schools National Conference in Orlando. Before becoming a paraprofessional, Elaine was a day-care provider.

Priscilla Gelinas (El Barrio-Hunter College PDS Partnership) is a first-grade teacher in New York City. She holds degrees from Hunter College in early childhood/elementary education and special education. While at PS 112, she taught first grade in a Collaborative Team Teaching classroom and was involved in professional presentations on PDS work.

Hala Ghousseini is a post-doctoral fellow at the University of Michigan. She currently works with the Michigan Mathematics and Science Teacher Learning Collaborative and the Learning Teaching in, from, and for Practice (LTP) Project. During her time as a doctoral student at the University of Michigan, she worked on the BIFOCAL project since its inception and taught in the teacher education program. Her current research interests focus on the initial preparation and ongoing professional development of teachers of mathematics.

Theresa J. Grant is Professor in the Department of Mathematics at Western Michigan University. She is interested in the knowledge teachers need in order to base mathematics instruction on student thinking, and the processes by which they come to know and utilize this information. Her work in this area has three main components: designing professional development for practicing teachers and courses for prospective teachers; studying the impact of these experiences; and researching the impact of implementing *Standards*-based curriculum materials on teachers' efforts to focus on student thinking.

Eric W. Hart is Adjunct Associate Professor of Mathematics at Maharishi University of Management and an independent consultant in curriculum, instruction, and professional development in mathematics education. He is currently a senior curriculum developer for the Core-Plus Mathematics Project, co-director of a Math and Science Partnership grant, and a principal consultant for the Iowa Department of Education. He has been director of the NCTM *Illuminations* project and co-director of several NSF teacher enhancement projects for high school mathematics teachers.

Beth A. Herbel-Eisenmann, an Assistant Professor of Teacher Education, was at Iowa State University during the development of this book and is now at Michigan State University. As PI of an NSF-funded CAREER project, she works with a group of secondary mathematics teachers who are using action research to align their discourse practices with their professed beliefs. As a former junior high mathematics teacher, she is committed to working *with* mathematics teachers in order to understand teacher–student classroom experiences through the lens of discourse literature. She serves on the SIG/RME Board and is a research associate for the Center for the Study of Mathematics Curriculum.

Barbara Jaworski is Professor of Mathematics Education at Loughborough University in the UK. Her specialist research area is the development of mathematics teaching through inquiry communities of teachers and educators. Her recent research in this field in Norway resulted in a book

Learning Communities in Mathematics (Jaworski et al., Caspar, 2007) that charts two developmental research projects and links theory and practice in mathematics learning and teaching development.

Gooyeon Kim, Assistant Professor of Mathematics Education at the University of Missouri-St Louis, received her doctorate from the University of Georgia and did postdoctoral work in the Learning Research and Development Center at the University of Pittsburgh. Her research interests include mathematics teaching and learning of teachers and mathematics curriculum materials.

Ok-Kyeong Kim, Associate Professor in the Department of Mathematics at Western Michigan University, received her PhD from the University of Missouri-Columbia in 2002. She has taught mathematics and mathematics methods courses for preservice elementary teachers and worked with classroom teachers through classroom-based research and teacher professional development projects. Her current research interests include teacher knowledge and curriculum material use, and using prediction as an instructional practice in the mathematics classroom.

Kate Kline, Associate Professor at Western Michigan University, was co-PI of two NSF-funded professional development grants, one of which involved over 350 elementary school teachers using the *Investigations in Number, Data, and Space* curriculum. She is currently a member of the Center for the Study of Mathematics Curriculum and works with teachers using *Investigations* at one of the CSMC's partner school districts. Her primary research interests involve studying the enactment of curriculum materials that focus on developing reasoning and understanding.

Matthew R. Larson, K-12 Curriculum Specialist for Mathematics for the Lincoln Public Schools in Lincoln, Nebraska, holds a doctorate in Administration, Curriculum, and Instruction from the University of Nebraska-Lincoln. He has taught mathematics at the elementary through the college level and has served as an adjunct professor at the University of Nebraska-Lincoln, where he has taught in both the Mathematics Department and the College of Education. He has served on a number of committees for the National Council of Teachers of Mathematics and is a co-author of mathematics programs published by Houghton Mifflin.

Gwendolyn M. Lloyd, Professor in the Department of Mathematics at Virginia Tech, received her doctorate in mathematics education from the University of Michigan in 1996. Her work focuses on the role of mathematics curriculum materials in teachers' professional development. She chairs the Editorial Panel of the *Journal for Research in Mathematics Education*, serves on the SIG/RME Board, and is a research associate of the Center for the Study of Mathematics Curriculum.

Kay McClain directs the Materials Research and Development at the Center for Research in Education in Science, Mathematics, Engineering and Technology at Arizona State University where she is overseeing the development of video-based resources for teacher development. Her research has focused on the proactive role of the teacher in classrooms where mathematics is taught with understanding. Her current research interests build on this earlier work to include ways of supporting teacher change. Her extensive work in classroom-based research grounds her current efforts to understand teaching, including the use of innovative instructional materials.

Patricia Maiorano (El Barrio-Hunter College PDS Partnership) has been a general education teacher at PS 112 for seven years. Five of those years have been spent in a Collaborative Team Teaching setting. Patricia completed her undergraduate degree at Hunter College, majoring in English language arts and early childhood education, and holds a master's degree in literacy, also from Hunter. Her goal is to become a reading specialist in the early grades.

Robin Marcus is a doctoral candidate in Curriculum and Instruction, specializing in mathematics education, at the University of Maryland, the mathematics instructional support teacher at the Baltimore Freedom Academy, and a member of the development team for the second edition of *Core-Plus Mathematics*.

Martha Mather is a first-year middle school teacher and a recent graduate of the Master in Teaching program at Washington State University Tri-Cities. While a graduate student, she was a research assistant for Roth McDuffie and developed an interest in middle school mathematics curriculum programs and small-group mathematics instruction. A licensed professional engineer, Mather completed a bachelor's and Master of Science degree in civil engineering from Penn State University.

Maria Eliophotou Menon received her PhD from the Institute of Education, University of London in 1995. She is now an Assistant Professor of Educational Administration and Policy in the Department of Education, University of Cyprus. Her research interests include job satisfaction in education; concerns and decision-making processes in relation to education and career choice; and the influence of economic factors on the demand for higher education. She has published papers in several journals including *Higher Education, Economics of Education Review, Higher Education Policy, Education Economics*, and *Educational Research*.

Valerie Mills is Supervisor and Mathematics Education Consultant for Oakland Schools, a Michigan intermediate agency serving 28 districts. She is a former high school teacher, mathematics coordinator, and director of curriculum. She is co-director of Beyond Implementation: Focus on Challenge and Learning (BIFOCAL), director of the Mathematics

Education Resource Center (MERC) serving 15 urban schools, and co-author of the *Lenses on Learning: Secondary* project. Mills was a teacher author on the Core-Plus Mathematics Project, past president of the Michigan Council of Teachers of Mathematics, and past chair of NCTM's Academy Services Committee.

Fadwa M. Nacel (El Barrio-Hunter College PDS Partnership) is a bilingual-transitional second-grade teacher at PS 112. She is a liberal-arts graduate of the State University of New York at Stony Brook and has an MS degree from the Bank Street College of Education. Fadwa's interests include techniques in ESL instruction and identifying children's strengths as a springboard for teaching.

Christine Passarelli (El Barrio-Hunter College PDS Partnership) is a kinder-garten ESL teacher at PS 22 in Staten Island. She has a BA in early child-hood/elementary education and an M.A. in TESOL, both from Hunter College. Christine has been teaching for four years and enjoys being with her students.

George Philippou is a retired Professor of Mathematics Education at the University of Cyprus. He joined the Department of Education of the newly established University in 1992, where he continues to teach courses in mathematics education. He has also taught graduate courses at the University of Athens, Greece. His research interests include affective variables and history of mathematics.

Eileen Phillips is Principal of Maple Grove Elementary School in Vancouver, British Columbia. Maple Grove is a kindergarten to grade 7 school, and enrolls a traditional as well as a Montessori stream. Eileen started teaching in 1971 and has an MA from the University of British Columbia. In her MA thesis, *This Too is Math: Making Sense With a Preschooler*, she explored her young daughter's mathematizing in the home over three years. She also has a PhD from the Open University in the UK. Her dissertation, *Classroom Explorations of Mathematical Writing with Nine- and Ten-Year-Olds*, examined the mathematical and paramathematical writing of her students over several years.

David Pimm is Professor of Mathematics Education at the University of Alberta, a position he took up in 2000. Prior to this appointment, he was a professor in the Department of Teacher Education at Michigan State University for a couple of years, but most of his working life he spent in the Department of Mathematics at the Open University in the UK, producing distance education materials for inservice teacher education. His particular research interest has been in exploring interrelationships between language and mathematics, both in the classroom setting and within mathematics itself. He has also researched aspects of new teacher induction and mathematical esthetics.

Janine T. Remillard is Associate Professor at the University of Pennsylvania, specializing in mathematics education. Her research interests include teachers' use of and learning from mathematics curriculum materials and mathematics teaching and learning in urban schools and communities. She is a co-PI of MetroMath: The Center for Mathematics in America's Cities, an NSF-funded Center for Learning and Teaching and a research associate with the Center for the Study of Mathematics Curriculum.

Barbara J. Reys, Lois Knowles Distinguished Professor of Mathematics Education, is program coordinator for Mathematics Education at the University of Missouri. Her current research focuses on the role and influence of curriculum standards and textbooks in teaching and learning mathematics. She co-directs the Center for the Study of Mathematics Curriculum, an NSF-sponsored Center for Learning and Teaching.

Beth Ritsema, a faculty member at Western Michigan University, is the Professional Development Coordinator for the Core-Plus Mathematics Project and a contributing author for *Core-Plus Mathematics*. She was co-PI for Renewing Mathematics Teaching through Curriculum, an NSF-funded Local Systemic Change project. She has taught mathematics in grades 7–12, and at the college level.

Bill Rosenthal is the former director of the El Barrio-Hunter College Professional Development School Partnership and is currently a visiting instructor of secondary education at the University of South Florida. All of his academic degrees are in mathematics, which he taught at the college level for a decade before changing careers to teacher education. His current professional interests are school–university collaborations, feminist critiques of mathematics, and middle school mathematics curriculum resources and teaching.

Amy Roth McDuffie is Associate Professor of Mathematics Education in the Department of Teaching and Learning at Washington State University Tri-Cities. She previously taught at the middle and high school levels. Roth McDuffie's teaching and research focuses on preservice and inservice teacher education and development in mathematics. Her research interests are aimed at improving teaching and learning through practice-based approaches to on-going professional learning.

Marty J. Schnepp, a mathematics teacher at the high school level for 20 years, earned his Masters degree in Teaching and Curriculum from Michigan State University in 1998. He has worked as a consultant on the Bridging Research and Practice Project at MSU (2000–2001), Math of Change Project (1996–2000), and SimCalc Project (1996–2000) at TERC. He teaches at Holt High School in Holt, Michigan.

Harold L. Schoen, Professor Emeritus of Mathematics and Education, University of Iowa, has been co-director of the Core-Plus Mathematics Project since

1992. Professor Schoen was a member of the Curriculum Working Group for Grades 9–12 of the NCTM's (1989) *Curriculum and Evaluation Standards* and chair of the 1989 Task Force on Implementing the Standards. He co-edited *Teaching Mathematics Through Problem Solving Grades 6–12*, a 2003 professional resource that elucidated the pedagogical approach intended for secondary school by the NCTM *Standards* documents. He is past co-chair of SIG/RME.

Laura Sebel (El Barrio-Hunter College PDS Partnership) was a Collaborative Classroom special education teacher in Manhattan for five years. She received her BS in elementary education from Adelphi University and master's degree in special education from Hunter College. Laura has held leadership positions in the El Barrio-Hunter PDS partnership, been a representative to the Collaborative Communities of Practice Lab Site Leaders, and conducted presentations at Hunter College and the AERA Annual Meeting.

Miriam Gamoran Sherin is Associate Professor of Learning Sciences in the School of Education and Social Policy at Northwestern University. Her interests include mathematics teaching and learning, teacher cognition, and the use of video for teacher learning. Sherin's articles have appeared in *Cognition and Instruction, Teaching and Teacher Education*, and the *Journal of Mathematics Teacher Education*.

Renée Sillart (El Barrio-Hunter College PDS Partnership) is a longtime second-grade teacher at PS 112 in Manhattan. She is a specialist in Collaborative Team Teaching, was an original member of the PDS Advisory Committee, and presented with her colleagues at the 2005 AERA Annual Meeting in Montréal.

Edward A. Silver is the William A. Brownell Collegiate Professor of Mathematics Education at the University of Michigan. He is co-PI of the NSF-funded Center for Proficiency in Teaching Mathematics, under the auspices of which he is co-director of the BIFOCAL project, and he is co-director of the mathematics portion of the Michigan Mathematics and Science Teacher Leadership Collaborative. Silver was editor of the *Journal for Research in Mathematics Education* from 2000–2004; he received the Award for Outstanding Contributions of Educational Research to Practice from AERA in 2004 and the Iris Carl Memorial Leadership and Equity Award from *TODOS* in 2007. His scholarly interests include mathematical thinking, especially mathematical problem solving and problem posing; the design and analysis of intellectually engaging and equitable mathematics instruction; innovative methods of assessing and reporting mathematics achievement; and effective models for enhancing the knowledge and proficiency of teachers of mathematics.

Esther Robles Soto (El Barrio-Hunter College PDS Partnership) is a prekindergarten and kindergarten teacher at PS 112. She has served on the El Barrio-Hunter PDS Advisory Committee, been a leader in curriculum implementation and adaptation, and made professional presentations at the annual conferences of the Association of Teachers of Mathematics of New York City and the National Association of Professional Development Schools.

Mary Kay Stein holds a joint appointment at the University of Pittsburgh as Professor in the School of Education and Senior Scientist at the Learning Research and Development Center. Her early research focused on classroom-based teaching and learning with the aim of understanding the nature of effective instructional practices in mathematics. In the early 1990s, Dr Stein's research interests expanded to include the school and district contexts of teacher learning and professional development. She is the founding director of the Learning Policy Center at the University of Pittsburgh.

James Tarr, Associate Professor in the Department of Learning, Teaching, and Curriculum at the University of Missouri, received his doctorate in mathematics education from Illinois State University. His research focuses on the development of statistical and probabilistic reasoning as well as the impact of curriculum materials on student achievement and the classroom learning environment. He has authored numerous articles and book chapters for NCTM publications, including *Results of the 2003 National Assessment of Educational Progress* and the *Navigations* series. Most recently, he is co-PI on Comparing Options in Secondary Mathematics: Investigating Curricula (COSMIC), a longitudinal NSF-funded study.

Jenny Tuten is the current director of the El Barrio-Hunter College Professional Development School Partnership. In her first career, she taught grades 3–12 in classrooms in New York City, Hoboken, New Jersey, and London, England. She is now an Assistant Professor in the literacy program at the Hunter College School of Education. Her professional interests include literacy education, assessment, and parent-school collaborations.

Jana Visnovska, a doctoral candidate in mathematics education at Vanderbilt University, collaborated as a research assistant on the longitudinal studies, Supporting and Sustaining the Learning of Professional Teaching Communities in the Institutional Setting of the School and School District (2002–2005) and Designing Schools and Districts for Instructional Improvement In Mathematics (2006–2007). Her research interests include design of instructional sequences in mathematics that support students' as well as teachers' learning.

Rebecca Walker, Associate Professor of Mathematics at Grand Valley State University, has been working with the Core-Plus Mathematics Project since 1995. During the work on the second edition, her main responsibility has been developing the review portion of the curriculum program and all curriculum material embedded assessments. In addition to her curriculum material development work, she teaches elementary and secondary mathematics education courses. She also taught high school for seven years in California and New Jersey.

Gloria Whatts (El Barrio-Hunter College PDS Partnership) is a paraprofessional at PS 112. She has been at the school for 18 years. She specializes in knowing the school's children and parents, and she takes pleasure and pride in seeing the children develop into young adults.

Qing Zhao is currently a doctoral candidate in mathematics education at Vanderbilt University. Her research interests include supporting mathematics teachers' learning as it is situated in the institutional context, using design research as a methodology to support learning, and supporting students' learning of mathematics by designing coherent instructional sequences.

Steven W. Ziebarth is Associate Professor of Mathematics Education in the Department of Mathematics at Western Michigan University. His research interests focus on secondary school mathematics, student assessment, and evaluation. He has been lead evaluator on several projects including the NCTM Project to Implement the Standard in Discrete Mathematics, the Iowa Local Systemic Change Initiative, and the NSF-funded Core-Plus Mathematics Project and Second Edition Revision. As a member of the leadership team for the Center for the Study of Mathematics Curriculum, his recent projects include the development of doctoral-level curriculum courses and, in collaboration with Horizon Research, Inc., the development of an on-line curriculum evaluation tools database and of instruments for the study of enacted curriculum in school districts.

Index